Library of
Davidson College

Advanced Pascal Programming Techniques

Paul A. Sand

Osborne/McGraw-Hill
Berkeley, California

Published by
Osborne/McGraw-Hill
2600 Tenth Street
Berkeley, California 94710
U.S.A.

For information on translations and book distributors outside of the U.S.A., please write to Osborne/McGraw-Hill at the above address.

Apple is a registered trademark of Apple Computer, Inc.
CalcStar is a trademark of MicroPro International Corp.
Multiplan is a trademark of Microsoft Corporation.
Othello is a registered trademark of Gabriel Industries, Inc.
SuperCalc is a registered trademark of Sorcim.
UCSD Pascal is a registered trademark of the Regents of the University of California.
VisiCalc is a registered trademark of VisiCorp.

Advanced Pascal Programming Techniques

Copyright © 1984 by McGraw-Hill. All rights reserved. Printed in the United States of America. Except as permitted under the copyright Act of 1976, no part of this publication may be reproduced or distributed in any form or by any means, or stored in a data base or retrieval system, without the prior written permission of the publisher, with the exception that the program listings may be entered, stored, and executed in a computer system, but they may not be reproduced for publication.

1234567890 DODO 89876543

ISBN 0-88134-105-3

Judy Ziajka, Acquisitions Editor
Paul Hoffman, Technical Editor
Ted Gartner, Copy Editor
Jan Benes, Text Design
Yashi Okita, Cover Design

Contents

Introduction		v
ONE	What is a Good Program?	1
TWO	CRT Techniques	10
THREE	Interactive Input	30
FOUR	Crunching Numbers: A General-Purpose Calculator	69
FIVE	Text File Tools	105
SIX	Games and Strategy	151
SEVEN	Simulation and Animation	202
EIGHT	The Plane Truth: An Electronic Worksheet	246
Appendix A	Portability Problems and Solutions	342
Index		367

Introduction

This book is written for amateur and professional programmers who wish to enhance their knowledge of the Pascal programming language and its use in solving programming problems. The book's primary emphasis is on presenting complete and usable programs, while topics like language features, algorithms, and data structures are presented as they arise in building those programs. As a prerequisite, the reader should have already completed an introductory course or text in Pascal programming and be able to read Pascal program listings and write simple Pascal programs.

Why should the reader be interested in an "advanced" book on Pascal? Typical introductory Pascal texts contain many small programs, each designed to show how a particular language element is used. The tasks the programs perform are often of limited interest and usually trivial. In addition, small programs, while ideal for teaching the correct use of language features, do not adequately demonstrate how to use those features to construct larger programs. As a result, the student who diligently struggles through one of the introductory Pascal texts often has the tools necessary to write a Pascal program, but very little idea of how to use those tools to design a real program.

Every program in this book is "real"; each is designed to do something useful or at least interesting. Although both these qualities are somewhat subjective, we hope many readers will actually want to run these programs on their own computers. There are no programs in this book that "test whether an input string is a palindrome" or "print out the first hundred Fibonacci numbers," although as previously noted such programs have their place.

As a consequence, most programs in this book are longer than the average introductory text's programs. Composing longer programs allows us to demonstrate some of the methods used in splitting up a large task into a number of smaller tasks, each one accomplished with a relatively small and understandable program module.

Interested readers should feel free to modify these programs, adapt them to their own particular circumstances, add or delete program features, improve their efficiency or flexibility, and so on. Indeed, the programs in this book are designed to be relatively easy to modify. Some improvements will be suggested in the text, and readers are also encouraged to invent and implement their own improvements.

Finally, we hope this book will serve as a programmer's bag of tricks. The programs developed here make repeated use of a few dozen modules which solve common programming problems. When readers run across such problems in writing their own programs, there is a good chance they may be able to use one of these routines instead of "reinventing the wheel."

Book Overview

A good portion of this book is concerned with the design decisions that go into writing a program: Why do we choose one program organization over another? What is a good algorithm to accomplish a certain task? How do we decide which is the best method to represent real-world quantities and abstract data structures in the computer's memory? Chapter One discusses a number of goals to aim for when making such design decisions.

Another major theme of this book is the design of general-purpose "tool" routines that are useful in many different programs. Although we develop such tool routines in writing most of the book's programs, several early chapters concentrate on tool development. Chapter Two develops CRT screen output routines used in all subsequent chapters; their use is demonstrated in **theseus**, a program that creates and solves simple mazes on the CRT screen.

Chapter Three presents routines used for interactive user input of different types of data from the keyboard and for converting data from one type to another. The demonstration program in this chapter is **gaslog**, a program that accepts data on an automobile's gasoline consumption and optionally prints a report based on the data. Chapter Five is another tool-building chapter concerned with designing flexible and efficient routines for reading and writing text files. These tools are used in **print**, a utility program for printing text files in a paginated format.

The remaining chapters each build one or two interesting and useful programs: Chapter Four presents **calc**, which accepts arithmetical formulas from the user and outputs their values. The program designed in Chapter Six is **reversi**, a game of skill played against the computer. Two versions of **reversi** are presented: one that can be used on a normal text screen, another that makes use of the graphics capabilities of the Apple II.

Chapter Seven is an introduction to computer simulation, a powerful tool for understanding real-world systems. The programs presented in Chapter Seven are **bouncer**, which models the behavior of bouncing balls in a box, and **isaac**, which simulates how planetary bodies move under the influence of gravity. Chapter Eight is devoted to designing **pascalc**, a flexible and powerful "electronic worksheet" program similar to those available commercially.

The Pascal Language

Pascal was developed in the late 1960s by Niklaus Wirth. His aims were to produce a language suitable for teaching programming concepts clearly and systematically, and to make the language usable on a large number of computers. His success is obvious; Pascal's popularity has increased rapidly since its introduction, and versions of the language are available on many computers ranging from small and inexpensive personal computers to large mainframe systems.

What are the reasons for Pascal's popularity? The primary reason is that Pascal makes the job of writing, reading, and modifying programs easier than do many other programming languages.

- Pascal has structured control statements (**while**, **repeat**, **for**, **case**, and **if-then-else**) that allow the programmer to write clear and concise code with the flow of control proceeding from top to bottom. The control flow in programs written in languages without these control statements often resemble tangled webs of **if** tests and **goto** statements, which are far less easy to understand.

- Pascal permits the programmer to break up a large program into smaller independent procedures and functions, each one performing a certain task. Each module can have its own private variables that are only used when that module is executed. Each module has well-defined input and output parameters used for communicating with its calling routine. This modularization greatly aids those who attempt to read the program by minimizing the amount of code they have to understand all at once.

- Pascal allows programmers to define their own data types and data structures in addition to those already built into the language. The judicious use of this feature makes a program more compact and easier to understand.

- Pascal permits the use of long identifiers for variables, procedures, and functions. (Standard Pascal guarantees that the first eight characters are significant in distinguishing between identifiers.) This allows the programmer to use names with mnemonic significance, which is another aid in understanding a program.

- Pascal provides recursive procedures and functions, that is, procedures and functions that can call themselves. This feature can be misused, but in many cases it is a much clearer and more straightforward way to program than the equivalent non-recursive code.

Although Pascal is a very good language, it is not a perfect one. No widely available computer language is perfect. Pascal's file-handling capabilities have been criticized as inadequate and poorly designed. Another telling flaw of Pascal is that the size of an array is part of its type, making it difficult to write general-purpose modules to process arrays of arbitrary length. (The new ISO standard for Pascal remedies this problem, but versions of Pascal reflecting this new standard are not widely available at the time of this writing.) In addition, Pascal specifies that variables local to a given routine are "forgotten" on exit from the routine; this means a variable that is to keep its value between calls to a routine must be declared *globally* to the routine, making it accessible to a larger part of the program than necessary. These are a few deficiencies in Pascal; others will arise later on.

For better or worse, however, programmers must use *some* available language for their programs. Pascal remains an excellent choice for program development, as its widespread popularity attests.

A Note on Portability

A portable program is one that can be run with little or no modification on a large number of computer systems. The advantages of portability are well known, and we'll have more to say about them later. It is generally recognized that unfortunately Pascal has not been defined in such a way as to make it easy for the programmer to write portable programs.

There are a number of barriers to portability. One set of barriers consists of restrictions on the built-in data types: the maximum integer value allowed, the precision and magnitude of real numbers, the maximum number of elements allowed in a set, and so forth. All versions of Pascal have such restrictions. Insofar as these restrictions differ between versions of the language, portability problems can arise; for example, a program written for one computer may assume eight digits of precision in the **real** data type. When run on a second computer with more or less precision, the program might fail miserably.

A second, more serious barrier is caused by language implementors. When implementing Pascal on a particular computer or operating system, implementors may add attractive features to the standard language to make the programmer's job easier (in their opinion, of course). They may also leave out certain features of the standard language because the features are too difficult to implement. They may even cause standard language features to behave in a non-standard way. Thus, for a program to be transportable between two different versions of Pascal, it must only use language features common to both versions. Such a restriction can cause severe portability problems, especially if the differences between the two versions of Pascal are great.

A third barrier to portability is caused by programmers. Often they stray from writing portable code because of the capabilities or restrictions of the computer system for which they are programming. For example, they may code portions of programs in their computers' assembly language, or they may use their knowledge of the way variables are represented in their computers' memories. They may write code to drive a special feature of a printer, a terminal, and so on.

Given these barriers, what can programmers do to avoid portability problems and ensure that their programs run with little or no change on a large number of different computers? To achieve maximum program portability, the programmer should implement the following techniques:

1. Ignore all non-standard language extensions and stick to the standard version of the language.
2. Avoid features of the standard language not present in some implementations.
3. Make only the most rudimentary assumptions about the computer system on which the programs are to be run.
4. Make only "lowest common denominator" assumptions on such language parameters as the precision of real numbers, the maximum number of elements allowed in a set, the contents and ordering of the underlying character set, and so on.

This is attractive; indeed, many introductory texts take this approach to appeal to the widest possible audience. However, for most programming, this ideal of maximum portability is impractical. Most programmers find it necessary (or at least desirable) to make use of the non-standard extensions in their versions of Pascal. Such language enhancements usually fulfill a real need. We have previously mentioned some of the bad aspects of Standard Pascal; many extensions were introduced to solve or alleviate these problems. If pro grammers refuse to use such extensions, they often wind up having to reinvent them in a portable way. Such circumlocutions waste both the programmer's time and the computer's memory; they are also usually much less efficient than the original extensions.

Similarly, real constraints of execution time, memory usage, and program esthetics often require programmers to make their programs non-portable.

Apple Pascal vs. Standard Pascal

All the programs in this book were written on an Apple II computer system using Apple Pascal version 1.1. Whenever the term "Apple Pascal" is used in this book, it is referring specifically to version 1.1 on the Apple II. All programs will run unchanged on an Apple II Plus or an Apple IIe. Most of the programs will run on a minimal Apple Pascal system with one disk drive and the Apple's normal 40-column screen. The major exception is that an 80-column card is recommended for **pascalc**. A printer is required to fully use programs such as **print** and **pascalc** that generate printed output.

What are users of other versions of Pascal to do? Let's consider the case of UCSD Pascal. In the family tree of Pascal implementations, Apple Pascal is a direct descendent of, and therefore "closest" to, UCSD Pascal version II.1. Users of UCSD version II.1 (and earlier versions) will be able to run these programs with minimal or no changes, at most having to "program around" the cases where we have used routines that take advantage of the Apple's special hardware features. The same caveats apply to users of UCSD Pascal version IV.0 and later, although they may be able to use new features added to their versions to improve the programs' performance. In the remainder of the book, references to "UCSD Pascal" should be taken to refer to *all* versions of UCSD Pascal unless otherwise stated.

Apple Pascal for the Apple III is also quite similar to that for the Apple II. Most of these programs will run without modification and may be changed to take advantage of whatever improved features Apple III Pascal offers.

Users of other versions of Pascal may have to make more extensive modifications to these programs, although detailed instructions on the exact translations needed are well beyond the scope of this book. Those modifications will depend on the special features of the other Pascal; if the Pascal in question has features equivalent or similar to those of Apple Pascal, the translation will be much easier. As a practical matter, many Pascal implementations have similar if not identical extensions to Standard Pascal.

Here is a list of the major differences between Apple Pascal and Standard Pascal:

STRINGS Apple and UCSD Pascal offer a built-in *string* data type in addition to the built-in data types of Standard Pascal. A string is a sequence of an arbitrary number of characters up to a certain maximum length. This maximum length is usually 80 characters, but it can be as many as 255 characters. A string is stored in memory as an array of bytes with one character per byte; the first byte in the array (numbered zero) contains the current length of the string.

In addition, several built-in functions are available for string manipulation. Strings are also available in many other versions of Pascal, although the precise details of the implementation may differ.

LONG INTEGERS   Apple and UCSD Pascal provide a *long integer* data type in addition to the normal integer data type defined in Standard Pascal. While Apple Pascal integers are limited to the range −32767 to 32767, long integers may have as many as 36 digits. For example, the declaration

```
<type>
   longint = integer[10];
```

says that variables of the type **longint** may be any integral value between −9999999999 and 9999999999. Long integers are used when a program demands higher precision than that available from the standard data types. Many versions of Pascal offer some sort of extended-precision data type.

INPUT AND OUTPUT   Apple and UCSD Pascal greatly extend Standard Pascal in the areas of input and output. Built-in routines are provided to open disk files for reading or writing. There is a method provided to catch I/O errors (for example, a hardware malfunction or an attempt to read from a non-existent file). Programs may access files randomly, that is, read or write individual data records anywhere within the file without reading or writing intervening records. There are low-level I/O routines that allow direct access to peripheral devices. Other versions of Pascal will usually offer similar routines to accomplish such functions.

DYNAMIC VARIABLES   Apple Pascal does not provide the function **dispose**, which is present in Standard Pascal. Instead it provides the **mark** and **release** built-in procedures, which require somewhat different memory-management methods. Apple and UCSD Pascal both offer a **memavail** function, which returns the amount of memory available for dynamic variables.

GRAPHICS   Apple Pascal offers routines to make use of the Apple's graphics capabilities.

SEPARATE COMPILATION   Apple and UCSD Pascal allow commonly used groups of subroutines to be compiled together as *units*. These units may then be used in other programs without recompilation.

SEGMENT PROCEDURES   Apple and UCSD Pascal permit some procedures in a program to be declared as *segment* procedures. A segment procedure does not have to be in memory when the program is run; when the procedure is called, it is read into memory from the disk. When the procedure is finished, it is "forgotten," allowing the memory it took to be used by other parts of the program. Such a feature allows more efficient use of memory, which is often at a premium in smaller computers.

MISCELLANEOUS   Apple and UCSD Pascal provide the following routines to make the programmer's job easier:

> **moveleft** and **moveright** procedures that allow an arbitrary number of bytes to be copied from one part of memory to another.
>
> **fillchar** a procedure provided to "fill" an array of characters (or an arbitrary region of memory) with a given value.
>
> **sizeof** a function returning the size in bytes of a variable or type.
>
> **exit** a procedure that provides for an orderly exit from a program module or the program itself.
>
> **gotoxy** a procedure that sends the cursor on the user's CRT screen to a specified position.

Apple Pascal also provides a number of additional routines. Among the most useful are

> **keypress** a Boolean function that returns **TRUE** if one of the computer's keys has been pressed, and **FALSE** otherwise.
>
> **random** a function that returns a pseudo-random integer between 0 and 32767.
>
> **randomize** a procedure to initialize the pseudo-random number generator.

The reader can easily see that using these features in a Pascal program can make it difficult or impossible to run a program under a version of Pascal lacking those features. We do not ignore this problem; to make our programs as good as possible, we do sacrifice a certain amount of portability. However, we will try to *minimize* the portability problem by observing the following rules:

- Hardware-dependent code will be largely isolated in a (relatively) small number of program modules. For example, only two procedures are used to control the Apple's CRT screen (one of these, **gotoxy**, is a built-in function in Apple and UCSD Pascal); to move programs to another computer or terminal, the programmer only needs to change this code.

- Non-standard features of Apple Pascal will not be used when a portable solution is as good. (For example, we will not use the non-portable **exit** routine to escape from a procedure unless the result is a corresponding increase in the clarity or efficiency of the code.) When non-standard features are used they will be noted.

- Routines coded in the Apple's 6502 assembly language will also be presented in Pascal, allowing easier translation to another processor.

Appendix A offers detailed suggestions for solving some of the portability problems that cannot be fixed by minor adjustments to the book's code.

Recommended Reading

The original, full description of Pascal is given in the book *Pascal User Manual and Report* by K. Jensen and N. Wirth (Springer-Verlag, 1978). This book is also a good, brief introduction to Pascal for those already familiar with a computer language, but it leaves some formal details about the language unspecified. The new ISO Standard Pascal was designed to clear up these ambiguities. A good, readable description of ISO Standard Pascal is *Standard Pascal User Reference Manual* by D. Cooper (W. W. Norton, 1983). When we refer to "Standard Pascal" we will be referring to either the original Jensen and Wirth description or to the ISO Standard. In nearly all cases, there is no difference between the two. In cases where there *is* a difference, we will explicitly say which interpretation we are using.

There are many good introductory Pascal texts; one of the best is *Programming in Pascal* by P. Grogono (Addison-Wesley, 1978). Another is *Introduction to Pascal* by J. Welsh and J. Elder (Prentice-Hall International, 1979).

There are at this writing only a few books that go beyond an introductory level about Pascal. Two excellent choices are *Algorithms + Data Structures = Programs* by N. Wirth (Prentice-Hall, 1976) and *Software Tools in Pascal* by B. Kernighan and P. J. Plauger (Addison-Wesley, 1981).

ONE

What Is a Good Program?

What is a good program? The question is not as easy as it looks; there is no objective measure of the "goodness" of a program. The question goes beyond the narrow confines of programming and extends into the fields of economics, psychology, and even philosophy. So we can't even pretend to give the final answer to the question here. But let's try to examine the question briefly.

When we talk about good and bad programs, we refer, of course, to the programs' quality, rather than the actual use to which they are put. The words "good" and "bad" are slightly misleading here: we are stealing words from the vocabulary of morality and applying them to objects to which morality doesn't apply. Computers and computer programs are entirely amoral, of course; they are simply tools. But just as a hammer can be used to build a hospital or to smash a skull, computers may be used for good or evil.

This book isn't a tract on moral philosophy. Beyond noting that even "good" programs can be used for evil ends, we will stick to a strictly utilitarian definition: a program's goodness is how well it accomplishes its tasks and not the virtue of the tasks themselves.

We can look at a program's quality from two natural and well-defined viewpoints: that of the programmer and that of the user. The user is concerned with the *external* appearance of the program: its performance, ease of use, error-handling capabilities, and so on. The programmer, on the other hand, is also concerned with the *internal* appearance of the program: its clarity, portability, and modularity. Of these two viewpoints, the user's is by far more important—after all, the only point in writing a program is that it be used. Sometimes a program's author and its user are the same person, but more often the programmer is writing a program to be used by someone else. Whether that someone else is an easily identified individual or ten thousand personal computer owners, the conclusion is the same: a good program is written with the user in mind. A program that will not be used is, literally, a waste of time to write.

Users' Criteria

Obviously, a good program must "work," that is, do what it was designed to do with no errors (or, more realistically, a manageable number of errors). Yet there are multitudes of programs that "work" just fine but have been abandoned by their users as unusable, or were *never* used because they didn't fulfill the user's needs. Thus, we need additional "goodness criteria" in addition to a program's workability.

The following criteria overlap to some degree:

USEFULNESS Should the program be written in the first place? Or would the programmer's time be more productively spent on other tasks? Will the program fill a perceived need or desire of the prospective users? These questions may seem obvious, yet many programs have been written to solve problems that don't exist except in the minds of their programmers. (This phenomenon has been ubiquitous in the personal computer field.) Conversely, some programs have found wide acceptance for solving problems not envisioned by even the programs' designers.

Usefulness is often measured in objective terms. For example, a doctor's billing program may save $1489.34 per month over the previous manual system because of timelier payments and more accurate late-payment information. Or a word processing program may cut a document's preparation time by 53%. Similarly, a bad computer program might be seen to *increase* costs.

A program's usefulness may also be partially or entirely measured in subjective terms; this is certainly true of programs designed to play games or otherwise entertain the user.

EASE OF USE The computer is a tool that should eliminate drudgery. So why do so many programs require their users to perform time-consuming and error-prone tasks that the computer is perfectly able to do? Why are the most commonly used features of some programs harder to use than features that are seldom used? Why is software documentation often so badly written?

In most cases, the reason programs are hard to use is laziness on the part of the programmer. It's even understandable in a way: once a program works, the rest is window dressing. (Or so some programmers think.)

The first exposure users have to any given program is when they first attempt to use it. This is when the user's attitude toward the program is set. Learning is usually a hard and even painful experience; learning how to use a program is no exception. A program should be extremely kind to the first-time user.

The user should neither be expected nor required to learn the entire program at once. This is especially true of large, complex software with a lot of useful commands and features. The user should be able to use the program without first reading through a thick document. The program may be menu-driven: a list of possible options described in understandable language is presented to the user at relevant points, and the user chooses one of the options by pressing one or two keys. The program's user manual may present tutorial lessons that the novice can follow step by step. Or the program may be self-explanatory so that even first-time users can use it without consulting a manual. Finally, some programs contain instructions within themselves: a special "help" command causes the program to display instructions on how to use the program or a particular feature of it.

There are a few programs that are relatively easy to learn but become rather cumbersome to use after a while. The hand-holding that the program once did for the novice becomes boring and even frustrating to the experienced user. Designing a program that is pleasant for both beginners and experienced users alike is a very challenging task. Some programs have "expert" and "novice" modes, tailoring their requests and responses to the expertise of the user.

Another important feature that makes a program easier to use is *consistency*. This may be as simple as ensuring that the user need not keep dozens of different "rules" in mind as the program is run. For example, the user should always be able to answer yes-or-no questions or enter numeric information in the same way throughout a program. Error messages should always appear in the same place in the same manner. It's also a good idea to maintain consistent procedures by which the user controls the flow of a program; for example, a program may consistently use the <ESCAPE> key as a signal to stop the current process and return to the previous major section of the program. Or a program may provide help to a confused user whenever the <?> key is pressed.

EFFICIENCY Consider two programs that are identical in every way except that Program A runs 20% faster than Program B. Which one will people prefer to use? Or consider two mailing-list programs, one of which stores twice as many names as the other in the same amount of space, but are otherwise similar. Again, which one would *you* want to use?

People use computers because computers make tasks easier and less time-consuming. This fact leads directly to the issue of efficiency: all other things being equal, users will prefer a more efficient program because it allows them either to accomplish more in the same time, or to do the same tasks in less time.

Efficiency is often overrated by programmers who squeeze every last unnecessary microsecond out of their code and carve every extra byte from their program's storage requirements. This results in program code that is unreadable and convoluted at best. (At worst, the program fails to work at all.) The best course is to treat efficiency as a desirable quality that should be neither neglected nor overemphasized.

FLEXIBILITY Programs that do one thing well are relatively common. Somewhat more rare are programs that may be easily used for a variety of purposes. Even more rare are programs that work in a natural and efficient way with other programs.

A flexible program is one that can be used in a number of different applications. One example is a text editor that is suitable for entering both program text and normal prose. Another example is a general data storage and retrieval program that can be used to store many different kinds of information, as opposed to a program that could only be used to store a mailing list.

Another approach to flexibility is seen in programs that can be tailored to a user's own needs, desires, or idiosyncrasies. Such programs allow the user to specify the way in which the program asks questions, accepts data, formats output, and so on. A flexible program might also be designed to take advantage of any special hardware available on the system on which it is run.

Flexibility is sometimes confused with an abundance of program features. But unless features work together in a cooperative and sensible way, the resulting program will be a disorganized shambles that will be very difficult to learn and use. A truly flexible program is adaptable to diverse circumstances in simple and straightforward ways.

RELIABILITY For a multitude of reasons, programs that work under normal circumstances often fail mysteriously at unexpected times. (And, by Murphy's Law, programs will fail at the worst possible time.) An unreliable program is obviously frustrating to users, especially when the cause of the program's failure is unknown. Unreliability is often discovered only long after the program was considered to be finished, and this lapse of time can add to the difficulty of finding the offending bug.

The most common cause of unreliability is the failure of the program to check input data. Sometimes this failure is obvious; for example, a program may ask the user to respond to a question with a "Y" (for "Yes") or an "N" (for "No") and then fail to verify that the user entered one or the other response. A numerical calculation program may only work correctly if the numbers it is fed fall within a certain range, yet it doesn't check to see that the numbers are actually within that range. The program may crash or (perhaps worse) give incorrect answers. Although no program can stop a user from entering data that is wrong but otherwise reasonable, it makes sense to install safeguards against innocent and detectable user input errors.

Reliability problems result from a poorly planned design. Making a program crash-proof is a matter of constantly checking for numerous unexpected conditions: division by zero, attempting to read from a nonexistent file, overflows and underflows, and so on. Some unexpected conditions are easy to detect (such as division by zero); others may be difficult or impossible to detect (such as serious hardware malfunctions).

Of course, merely detecting an unexpected condition is only part of the problem. The programmer must then decide what the program should do in response to the condition, which is often even more difficult. We will see examples of error detection and response later.

SUITABILITY The criteria mentioned here will be satisfied in different ways for different users. Efficiency will be less important to a user who will start a program running on Friday afternoon and come back for the results on Monday morning. Ease-of-use criteria for a debugging utility used by experienced programmers will likely be very different from those for a word processing program used by secretaries. Still different will be the criteria for a program for third-grade schoolchildren. Therefore, programmers should know the prospective audience of their programs.

Of course, software may be aimed either at a narrowly defined group or a broad spectrum of users. Each approach has its pitfalls: software designed for a small group of people may be so specialized that it is unusable by anyone outside the group. The other side of the coin is that programs aimed at too many different types of users often end up satisfying none of them very well.

Programmers' Criteria

We have seen that programmers should be concerned that their programs will satisfy their users. Programmers also have concerns that users may neither know nor care about: issues of program clarity, modularity, portability, and the like.

If programmers wrote perfect programs without fail, they wouldn't have to worry about these criteria. But programs usually need to be debugged. They are often moved to different computers or different software environments on the same computer. Or users may decide that they need additional features in the program or demand that a feature be taken out. Any of these situations may require revisions in the program.

For these reasons, any non-trivial program should be designed with the idea that it will later be reread, debugged, and upgraded. Most important to a program's upgradability is that its design be *open-ended*: adding or changing features should not require major rewriting of all parts of the program.

Another way to decrease the number of problems in program modification, especially on large multi-programmer projects, is careful documentation of the original program and subsequent changes. (Who made the change, when, and why?)

In addition to these design considerations, it is important that a program be as easy to comprehend as possible. Even if the person modifying the code is the original programmer, it is very easy to forget the coding details and tricks originally used. If the program is unnecessarily complex or sloppy, it just makes the modification more difficult and error-prone.

The following criteria, like the users' criteria, overlap to a certain extent:

READABILITY A program can be made more understandable through simple formatting of the program code. Indentation may be used to reflect the control structure of a program. Blank lines may be inserted in the source text to separate distinct parts of a program. Blanks can be inserted within program statements to avoid a cramped and unclear appearance. Since Pascal places nearly no restrictions on the format of a Pascal source program, programmers are free to adopt their own formatting rules.

We will use a consistent formatting convention in this book. There is no point in being dogmatic about such conventions, however; readers should feel free to develop and use their own rules. The important thing is that formatting rules should be consistently followed. This gives a program a uniform appearance that may help to reveal coding flaws or logical mistakes.

PORTABILITY A portable program is one that can be run in another computing environment without major modifications. The fewer modifications that must be made, the more portable the program. Usually, portability refers to how easily a program may be moved to another computer. It can also refer to how well a program survives a modification of a computer's operating system or a change in a computer's hardware.

Portability is important for programmers who want their programs to be used: the more computers on which a program can be run, the wider the possible audience for the program. Portability has even greater consequences when one considers the rapidly increasing quality and decreasing cost of computer hardware. Today's popular computers will undoubtedly be obsolete in a few years. A portable program will have a better chance of running on computers of the future as well as those popular today.

CLARITY Clarity is closely related to readability. Instead of referring to the physical formatting of the program text, however, it refers to how well the program text communicates the underlying ideas of the program. Briefly, the program should clearly indicate what the programmer is trying to accomplish. In this regard, good programming is very similar to good writing.

A primary method of making a program clearer is the use of meaningful identifiers. If a given variable is supposed to contain the root of an equation, its name probably should not be **x0**; **root** would be much better. A procedure to insert a node into a binary tree would probably be more obvious if its name were **insertnode** rather than **doit**. Identifiers in a program should be assigned so that the possibility of confusing them with each other is minimized; do not, for example, use two identifiers named **finddel** and **finddle**. One popular suggestion is to use different parts of speech for different identifier classes: verbs for procedures, adjectives for Boolean functions, and nouns for other functions.

Another major aid to clarity is the judicious use of comments in the program's source code. Comments are valuable logical signposts, summarizing the action of a code segment, indicating under what conditions a branch in the program's control flow is taken, or (occasionally) pointing out a tricky spot in the program's logic. Comments are especially important in larger programming projects in which many programmers read and modify one another's code over a long period of time. One never knows when the only programmer who truly understands a crucial program segment will be unavailable.

Pascal programmers are fortunate because the language encourages the use of structured programming, recursion, pointer variables, and the definition of new data types. If used wisely, all these can be used to improve a program's clarity.

Clarity is often confused with wordiness, but exactly the opposite is true. *Conciseness* is one of the most important virtues of clear code. Do not think a program is clearer simply because every fifth line is a comment—it's more likely *less* clear because the comments obscure the program's logic. (If the program's logic is so unclear as to require massive commenting, surely the code itself should be improved before comments are added.)

Neither do meaningful identifiers have to be long; a lot of long identifiers can be tiring to wade through. Long identifiers may also create pesky program bugs. Since many Pascals only guarantee that identifiers are unique if they differ in the first eight characters, two or more identifiers may unintentionally come to represent the same variable. With luck this will cause a compiler error; otherwise it probably will cause baffling program behavior.

MODULARITY Breaking up a program into a number of relatively small and easy-to-understand modules can be the single most important contribution to a program's quality. (Note that we use the term "module" to refer to either a

Pascal procedure or function.) But how does simply splitting a program into pieces benefit the programmer?

A well-designed module accomplishes one precisely defined task (no more, and certainly no less). It communicates with its calling routine over a simple communication path, usually affecting only a small number of variables. Modules like these minimize the amount of code the programmer has to understand all at once. They can be studied and changed without examining or rewriting the remainder of the program, which is a great aid in debugging and modifying a program. And once the module is debugged and understood, it may be treated as a "given" while the rest of the program is examined.

Modularity may also result in decreased programming time for accompanying programs. General-purpose modules can often be used in a number of programs, thus reducing the need for "reinventing the wheel." The key is to keep modules as flexible as possible so they will be usable in a variety of situations, not just the one for which they are first written.

Programming Languages

Programming languages (or, more precisely, language implementations) are programs too; they may be judged by the users' criteria previously outlined. In these cases, the *programmer* is the user. For example, does the language handle simple bookkeeping tasks itself, or does it require the programmer to keep track of a multitude of details? Does it give useful and helpful error messages when the programmer slips up? If the language is implemented as a compiler, how fast are programs compiled? What are the limits on the size of a program? Does the language allow programmers to use the hardware features available on the host computer system and the capabilities of the operating system? Are there things the language "can't do" that the computer can? (You can probably add more questions to this list with a little thought.)

Most important, a good language should make it as easy as possible to write good programs. A programmer should not be forced to spend hours "programming around" an artificial restriction placed on the language. There should be no efficiency penalty placed on commented, readable code and mnemonic identifiers. The language should encourage modular, portable code.

In the real world, there is no "perfect" programming language, let alone a perfect language implementation. And it's possible no such language will ever come about for the simple reason that no single language will be suitable in all programming situations: the researcher in artificial intelligence, the seven-year-old programming student, the computer hobbyist, the engineer, and the economist all have vastly different requirements and desires.

In the following chapters, we will see that Pascal is usually an excellent choice for the programs we have chosen to write; it encourages well-structured and understandable programming. However, both the Pascal language and the Apple Pascal implementation have a few drawbacks, some more serious than others. When we run across them later, we will see that instead of *using* Pascal to do what we want, programming can rapidly become a matter of *tricking* Pascal into doing what we want. Instead of avoiding such situations, we'll treat them as facts of life for the programmer, which is a more realistic and useful approach.

Recommended Reading

The book *The Elements of Programming Style* by Brian Kernighan and P. J. Plauger (McGraw-Hill, 1978) should be on every programmer's shelf. The authors expain the basics of good programming style in a fascinating manner with plenty of good and bad examples. The book *When People Use Computers* by Marilyn Mehlmann (Prentice-Hall, 1981) discusses methods for making programs easier for people to use.

The book *Computer Power and Human Reason* by Joseph Weizenbaum (W. H. Freeman, 1976) is a readable and interesting discussion on the proper use of computer technology.

TWO

CRT Techniques

As we have seen, the most important criterion for the quality of a program is the way in which it interacts with the user. For most users, this communication is usually accomplished through a video display (the CRT). Although the term "CRT," or *Cathode Ray Tube*, only refers to the tube itself, we will use it as a synonym for the computer's video display system.

Effective use of the CRT's screen can make a program much easier to use and give the program a professional look. Fortunately, taking advantage of a CRT's features can be relatively easy for the Pascal programmer.

Not too long ago, using a CRT as a tool to communicate with an interactive computer was a relatively expensive luxury. Most users were restricted to "batch" environments where interaction with the computer was reduced to a minimum. Even the early interactive computers like timesharing mainframe machines and minicomputers "talked" to their users largely through printing terminals.

Today's video displays are faster, quieter, and less expensive than printing terminals, and the decreased cost of computer hardware has made interactive computers more common than non-interactive ones. As a result, you would be hard-pressed to find a personal computer sold with a printing terminal as its primary output device. Most have some sort of video display: personal computers may have a built-in CRT, a video interface to be connected to a TV set or video monitor, or a serial interface attached to a stand-alone CRT terminal. Most newer non-personal computers also talk to their users through video displays.

The development of the low-cost CRT has made possible a new type of computer software that, for lack of a better term, we'll call *screen-oriented* software. Screen-oriented programs differ from other programs in that they require a video display to work to their full potential or to work at all. Typically, they take advantage of the CRT's ability to place data at any point on the screen quickly and quietly. They may also take advantage of screen highlighting, alternate character sets, and even sound, depending on the CRT's capabilities. In contrast, non-screen-oriented software is designed so it may be used with either video displays or printing terminals.

Screen-oriented programs tend to be verbose—they give the user information on the status of the program, extensive prompting messages, and other data. All this feedback should help the user make more effective use of the program. On the other hand, non-screen-oriented software understandably tends to limit output to the minimum necessary to run the program. After all, no one wants to wait for (and listen to) a printing terminal grinding out line after line of possibly irrelevant information. Such non-screen-oriented programs have also been called "low bandwidth" programs because of the limited feedback given the user. The bottom line is that screen-oriented programs usually allow the user to conveniently accomplish things that are less practical with a non-screen-oriented program.

All popular CRTs can be sent commands by a program that will cause them to erase all or part of their screens, place the cursor at a specified spot on the screen, or move the cursor in a given direction. In addition to these basic functions, more advanced capabilities are often present, like the ability to "scroll" the data up and down (or sometimes left and right) on the screen or to make independent windows in the screen. A CRT may have the option of displaying blinking or inverse-video characters, or even alternate character sets (like boldface or italics). Finally, many CRTs offer various combinations of graphics capability, all the way from simple graphics character sets to sophisticated full-color line and figure-drawing functions.

Any two brands of CRTs may differ in the functions they provide. Even if they perform identical functions, they often will require different commands to accomplish these functions. As a result, one disadvantage of screen-oriented software is its lack of portability. There is an ANSI (American National Standards Institute) standard for accessing some CRT special functions, but it is not the only method used. Thus, a program that runs nicely on one computer and CRT combination may not work at all on another. Giving a certain command to CRT A may cause it to clear its screen, but giving the same command to CRT B may cause it to display gibberish. A screen-oriented program must either be distributed in a different version for every possible CRT or modified by a CRT-dependent installation procedure before it is used.

Using a CRT's Special Features

Let's look at one possible approach to writing a screen-oriented program in Pascal. First, we'll choose a few of the most common CRT functions to implement. Then we'll define a normal Pascal scalar type called **crtcommand**, a simple list of the functions we may ask our video display to carry out.

```
<type>
   crtcommand = (HOME, CLEAR, ERASEOL, ERASEOS, UP, DOWN, LEFT, RIGHT, BEEP);
```

The word <type> is used here to indicate that **crtcommand** is defined in the **type** declaration section of a Pascal program. A list of the CRT commands and what they do is shown in Table 2-1.

Our next step is to write a Pascal procedure called **crt** that executes these CRT commands. For example, the program statement **crt(UP)** will cause the CRT's cursor to move up one line. The commands are easy to implement on all major CRT terminals; indeed, most terminals have many more special functions than the basic ones given here. Of course, we still have a portability problem: **crt** will be different for each different CRT. But in most cases, writing a **crt** procedure for a specific terminal will be a straightforward

Table 2-1. CRT Commands

Command	Result
HOME	Send cursor to upper left-hand corner of screen
CLEAR	Clear CRT screen, home cursor
ERASEOL	Erase screen from current cursor position to the end of the line
ERASEOS	Erase screen from current cursor position to the end of the screen
UP	Move cursor up one line
DOWN	Move cursor down one line
LEFT	Move cursor left one space
RIGHT	Move cursor right one space
BEEP	Beep the terminal's (or computer's) speaker

task. The main stumbling block could be finding and deciphering the required information in the appropriate terminal or operating system manuals. Here is a version of **crt** usable in Apple Pascal:

```
procedure crt(cc: crtcommand);
{ Do CRT command, Apple Pascal version }
begin { crt }
   case cc of
      HOME:
         write(chr(25));
      CLEAR:
         write(chr(12));
      ERASEOL:
         write(chr(29));
      ERASEOS:
         write(chr(11));
      UP:
         write(chr(31));
      DOWN:
         write(chr(10));
      LEFT:
         write(chr( 8));
      RIGHT:
         write(chr(28));
      BEEP:
         write(chr( 7))
   end
end;
```

The **crt** procedure uses a case statement to perform the necessary action for each command. For the Apple II, this action in all cases only requires sending out a single character: a <LF> (linefeed, ASCII 10) for **crt(DOWN)**, a <GS> (group separator, ASCII 29) for **crt(ERASEOL)**, and so on. The case statement organization is very flexible and clear; if more complicated actions are necessary for any CRT function other than simple character output, the necessary code is simply inserted after the corresponding case label.

In designing **crt**, we have made a hidden, and possibly non-portable, assumption about the built-in procedure **write**. We have assumed that **write** *immediately* sends a character to the CRT. A different implementation of **write** might instead send output text to wait in an "output buffer" and be sent when the buffer is full or when an entire line of text is accumulated. Although Standard Pascal does not specify buffered output, it does not prohibit it either. If your Pascal buffers output text, you must replace the calls to **write** in **crt** (and subsequent routines) with calls to a routine that does immediate character output. This could be a call to the computer's operating system or **write** followed by a buffer flush.

The other procedure we need to write screen-oriented programs is one that will send the CRT cursor to a given point on the screen. Such a procedure is built into Apple and UCSD Pascal—it is called **gotoxy**. The procedure call **gotoxy(x, y)** will send the cursor to column x and row y of the CRT screen, where the upper-left corner of the screen is considered to be column 0, row 0. Column numbers increase to the right and row numbers increase going down the screen. On an 80-column by 24-row screen, the lower-right position is column 79 and row 23, since we are counting from zero.

The **gotoxy** procedure is used throughout this book because it performs a vital function for screen-oriented programs. It is rather easy to add **gotoxy** to a version of Pascal that doesn't offer it as a built-in procedure. Here is a sample version of **gotoxy**.

```
procedure gotoxy(col, row: integer);
  { Send cursor to given position, Z-19 version }
begin { gotoxy }
   write(chr(27), 'E', chr(32 + row), chr(32 + col))
end;
```

The listing assumes, as an example, that the CRT used is a Zenith Z-19 terminal. Modification for other CRTs is a matter of finding the necessary data in the CRT's hardware manual.

All the CRT dependencies in **gotoxy** are isolated in the single **write** statement. In the case shown, the Z-19 requires four characters to be sent to the CRT to position the cursor: an <ESC> (escape, ASCII 27), an <E> (ASCII 69), and two ASCII characters obtained by adding 32 to both the column and row numbers.

Once the two modules **crt** and **gotoxy** have been written and debugged, the remainder of our programs may be written to call those routines whenever we want to invoke some CRT function. This ensures that all the CRT dependencies of the software are limited to only two modules. Portability problems are minimized; moving a program to another computer or terminal requires changing only those two routines.

Now is a good time to consider the issue of parameter checking. Note that the version of **gotoxy** presented here assumes that it is being passed valid parameters: values of **col** and **row** that correspond to a real screen position. Also note that we have not considered what happens in various extreme situations in **crt**. What happens, for example, if the CRT cursor is on the last screen row and the program executes a **crt(DOWN)** command? Depending on the hardware, the entire screen could scroll up one line, or the cursor could "wrap around" to the first screen row. Or *nothing* might happen.

The point of this discussion is that neither **crt** nor **gotoxy**, as presented here, assumes responsibility for what happens if they are called in inappropriate situations or with strange parameters. This is neither good nor bad programming practice in itself; it is simply a *design decision* to make the routines calling **crt** and **gotoxy** responsible for such cases. (You may want to consider how **crt** and **gotoxy** would change if we had made the decision differently. If, as in Apple and UCSD Pascal, **gotoxy** is available as a built-in procedure, find out what it does when handed bad parameters.)

The **crt** and **gotoxy** modules act as building blocks to accomplish more complicated tasks. For example, the following statements will clear the CRT screen and display the string <Hello, there!> at row 10, column 5:

```
crt(CLEAR);
gotoxy(5, 10);
write('Hello, there!');
```

One major advantage of this method of executing CRT functions is that it is very easy to support advanced CRT features beyond the simple ones just listed. Suppose that a terminal is able to display inverse (black on white) characters under software control. Two more commands could be added to the **crtcommand** type declaration:

```
<type>
   crtcommand = (HOME, CLEAR, ..., BEEP, INVON, INVOFF);
```

Then the **crt** procedure is modified (again, the Zenith Z-19 terminal is used as an example):

```
procedure crt(cc:  crtcommand);
  ...
  case cc of
     HOME:
  ...

     INVON:
        write(chr(27), 'p');
     INVOFF:
        write(chr(27), 'q')
  ...

end;
```

At this point, the call **crt(INVON)** will turn on inverse characters, and **crt(INVOFF)** will turn them off again.

One possible criticism of **crt** is its inefficiency. It might be argued that the control characters **crt** sends out could be kept in an array instead of wired into the **case** statement. The array would be initialized when the program starts. Then **crt** could simply look up the appropriate character sequence and output it. You may want to try this approach and compare its speed with the version here.

Still another method of implementing **crt** and **gotoxy** would be to place CRT-dependent information into a data file that would be read by an initialization routine in each program. This would have the advantage that the program itself would be portable; only the data file would have to be changed to adapt it to another hardware situation. A variant of this technique is used by the Apple and UCSD Pascal operating systems. In these systems the CRT and other hardware-dependent information is kept in a file called **SYSTEM. MISCINFO**, which is read into memory when the system is booted; system programs then access this data to accomplish hardware-dependent tasks such as screen-clearing. (What are the advantages and disadvantages of this method?)

theseus

Let's use the tools we have developed so far to write a program. As an example, we'll design a program called **theseus** that will create and solve simple mazes directly on the CRT screen. (**theseus** is named after a hero in Greek mythology who, after successfully finding his way through a vast labyrinth, slew a deadly monster, the Minotaur.) This choice may seem frivolous to some, but other, more practical programs will be presented in later chapters.

Here is the main routine of **theseus**:

```
program theseus;
{ Create and solve mazes on CRT }

uses applestuff; { for "random" and "randomize" }

const
    MAZECOLS = 38;        { Maximum maze column number }
    MAZEROWS = 22;        { Maximum maze row number }
    MAXCRTCOL = 39;       { Maximum CRT column number }
    MAXCRTROW = 23;       { Maximum CRT row number }
    XINDENT = 0;          { Number of columns to indent maze }
    YINDENT = 0;          { Number of rows to indent maze }

type
    mazesquare = (WALL, PATH);
    mazearray = array [0..MAZEROWS, 0..MAZECOLS] of mazesquare;
    crtcommand = (HOME, CLEAR, ERASEOL, ERASEOS, UP, DOWN, LEFT, RIGHT, BEEP);
    direction = UP..RIGHT;
```

```
var
   maze: mazearray;
   won: boolean;
   ch: char;
{-------------------------------}
{ Modules to be included here:  }
{          crt                  }
{          dispsquare           }
{          createmaze           }
{          solvemaze            }
{-------------------------------}
begin { theseus }
   randomize;
   repeat
      crt(CLEAR);
      createmaze(maze);
      gotoxy(0, MAXCRTROW);
      write('Press <C> to continue:');
      read(ch);
      won := solvemaze(maze);
      gotoxy(0, MAXCRTROW);
      write('Press <C> to continue, <Q> to quit:');
      read(ch)
   until ch in ['Q', 'q'];
   crt(CLEAR)
end.
```

Figure 2-1 shows a maze created and solved by **theseus**.

Since this is our first program, we'll study it carefully. The first line, **program theseus;**, simply serves to name the program; other versions of Pascal may require a list of files used in the program: **program theseus(input, output);**.

The next line, **uses applestuff;**, notifies the compiler that a separately compiled unit is to be used. This is a feature of Apple and UCSD Pascal that allows commonly used routines to be grouped together and used in a number of programs without recompilation. The **applestuff** unit is furnished as part of the Apple Pascal system. **theseus** only uses two routines from the **applestuff** unit: **random** (which returns a pseudo-random integer between 0 and 32767) and **randomize** (which causes different pseudo-random sequences to be generated). If a version of Pascal does not offer built-in routines similar to **random** and **randomize**, they must be added by the programmer. See Appendix Λ for one possible method.

The mazes created by **theseus** are rectangular arrays of squares stored in the array **maze**; each square can be a **WALL** or a **PATH**. To solve a maze, the computer must find a continuous sequence of **PATH** squares from one point on the boundary of the maze to another. The size of the maze array is controlled by the two constant declarations for **MAZECOLS** and **MAZE-ROWS**; they are set so the maze is just large enough to fill an Apple's 40-

column by 24-line screen. (For use on an 80-column CRT, **MAZECOLS** could be increased to 78.)

The constants **MAXCRTCOL** and **MAXCRTROW** are used to hold the size of the CRT screen. **MAXCRTCOL** is the number of character positions per CRT line minus 1—remember, we are counting from zero. Similarly,

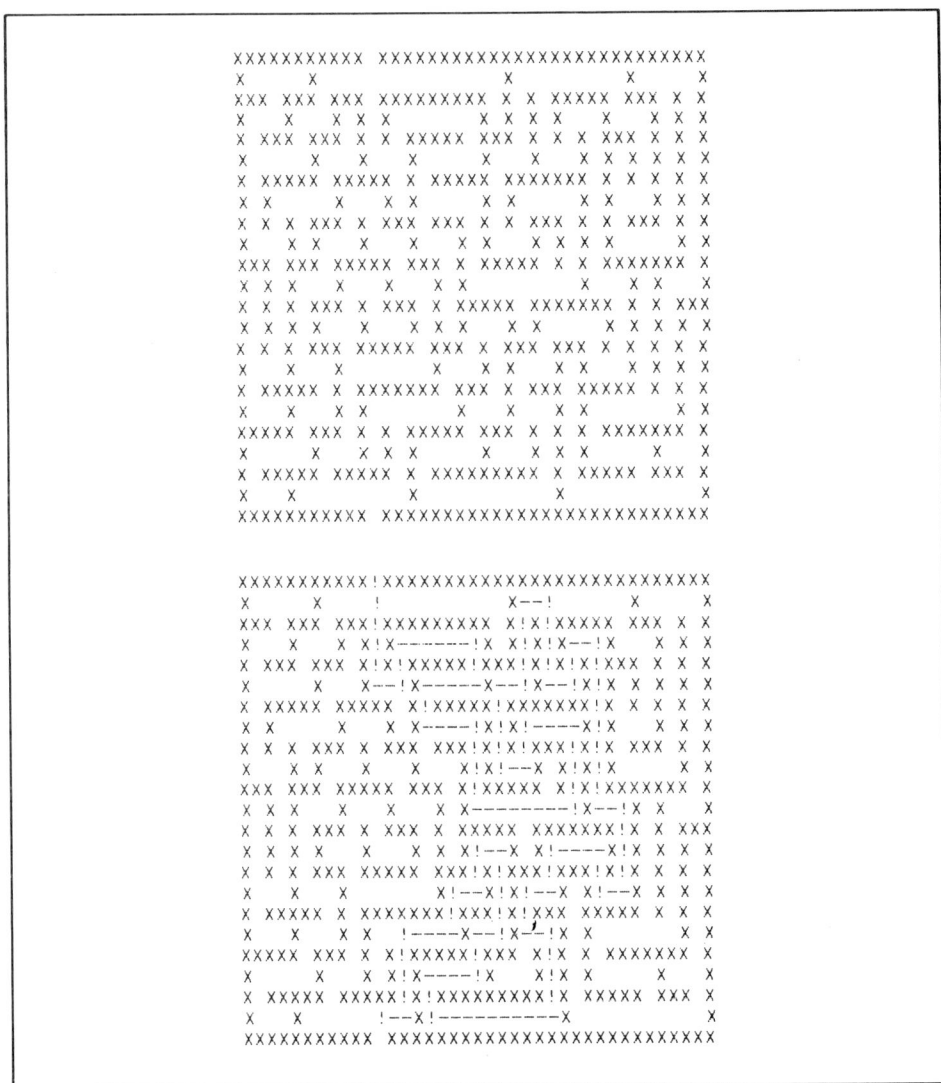

Figure 2-1. Sample maze and its solution

MAXCRTROW is the number of CRT lines minus 1. The values shown are appropriate for the Apple's 40-column by 24-line display; a program for use on 80-column by 24-line displays would set **MAXCRTCOL** to 79.

The constants **XINDENT** and **YINDENT** control where the maze is placed on the screen. The upper left-hand corner of the maze will appear in column **XINDENT** and row **YINDENT**.

The type declaration of **direction** indicates that it is a subrange of the **crtcommand** type containing the four directions **UP**, **DOWN**, **LEFT**, and **RIGHT**. This is more convenient than declaring a new scalar type for **direction**.

The box comment

```
{------------------------------}
{ Modules to be included here: }
{          crt                 }
{          dispsquare          }
{          createmaze          }
{          solvemaze           }
{------------------------------}
```

serves to indicate the placement and ordering of the named procedures and functions within the final program source text. In the source text, the box comment would be replaced by the source text for the modules listed in the order shown. The modules may themselves contain nested modules; this will be indicated by box comments within those modules. We do not list any modules that are provided by Apple Pascal, such as **gotoxy** and **random**, however. Such built-in routines are also assumed to be "global," that is, accessible to all parts of the program.

The box comment will be the standard method in this book for indicating what parts of a program go where. It is a simple alternative to either presenting an entire program's source code all at once or relying on a non-portable "include" mechanism offered by the Pascal compiler or a utility program. The actual method you use to insert the named modules at the specified positions should be as convenient and automatic as possible, depending on the details of your text editor, Pascal compiler, and operating system.

Now consider the actual code. **theseus** first calls the **createmaze** routine, which constructs the maze on the screen. The program will then display the message **Press <C> to continue:** at the bottom of the screen. After the user presses the <C> key, **theseus** calls **solvemaze**, which (as might be expected) solves the maze.

The **solvemaze** routine returns a Boolean value indicating whether the maze was actually solved or not. In our case, the mazes generated by

createmaze always have a solution, so the value returned by **solvemaze** will always be **TRUE**. Why, then, did we write **solvemaze** to return a value? Simply because the program may someday be changed to include mazes that *do not* have solutions. Our design minimizes the amount of rewriting that might have to be done in that case.

After the maze is solved the program will prompt: **Press <C> to continue, <Q> to quit:**. Pressing the <Q> key will stop the program; pressing the <C> key will cause a new maze to be created and solved.

It should be noted that the user's pressing of a key is the weak link of the program. The program does not check for invalid input; for example, if the user presses the <RETURN> key in response to the **Press <C> to continue:** prompt, the created maze will scroll up one line, thus spoiling the solution. This situation may be remedied once we build some interactive input tools. This will be done in the next chapter.

Creating the Maze

Our next step is to design **createmaze**, the routine that builds the maze. To make things more interesting for the user, we show the creation process on the CRT screen. This is easily done by displaying the **maze** array on the screen. If an element of the array is a **WALL**, we put an <X> at the corresponding position on the screen. If the element is a **PATH**, we put a blank there.

Our initial strategy for **createmaze** is first to set up an initial maze that is "solid rock," that is, made up of all **WALL** squares. The maze will then be "excavated" by setting the appropriate elements of the maze to **PATH**. First, pick a random point within the maze and a random direction and start digging a path, making random zigs, zags, and multi-way branches to keep things interesting. Keep digging until no more paths can be excavated without breaking out of the maze boundaries or onto a previously excavated path. Finally, dig "entrance" and "exit" paths on the boundaries of the maze.

We could proceed from this informal description to write the Pascal code for **createmaze**. But sometimes it is useful to write down the procedure in a combination of informal English and formal Pascal called *pseudo-code*. This is a valuable technique to use as an intermediate step when designing complex routines, because it allows programmers to organize their thoughts. A good deal of logic development and debugging can be done in the pseudo-code stage before a single line of Pascal code is written.

There are no "rules" for pseudo-code; it is simply an organizational technique. A pseudo-code version of **createmaze** reflecting a description of what we have just done might look like this:

```
begin
    set maze squares initially to WALLs
    pick random point within maze
    set it to a PATH
    pick a random (legal) direction
    build maze path from that random point in random direction
    put entrance & exit on maze boundary
end
```

From pseudo-code, we can usually write the routine in Pascal. This process involves translating each pseudo-code step into a small number of Pascal statements, which involve calls to routines to be designed later, usually by adding details not considered in pseudo-code. Here is the Pascal version of **createmaze**:

```
procedure createmaze(var maze: mazearray);
{ Create a maze }
var
    row, col: integer;
    dir: direction;
{----------------------------}
{ Modules to be included here: }
{            setsquare         }
{            rnd               }
{            randdir           }
{            legalpath         }
{            buildpath         }
{----------------------------}
begin { createmaze }
    for row := 0 to MAZEROWS do
        for col := 0 to MAZECOLS do
            setsquare(row, col, WALL);
    row := 2 * rnd(0, MAZEROWS div 2 - 1) + 1;
    col := 2 * rnd(0, MAZECOLS div 2 - 1) + 1;
    setsquare(row, col, PATH);
    repeat
        dir := randdir
    until legalpath(row, col, dir);
    buildpath(row, col, dir);
    col := 2 * rnd(0, MAZECOLS div 2 - 1) + 1;
    setsquare(0, col, PATH);
    col := 2 * rnd(0, MAZECOLS div 2 - 1) + 1;
    setsquare(MAZEROWS, col, PATH)
end;
```

The **createmaze** routine follows our rough description pretty closely. But we have added the details that the initial random point picked within the maze must be at an *odd* column and row number (why?) and that entrance and exit points are chosen on the top and bottom of the maze. (Actually, any two distinct points on the maze boundaries could be chosen.)

Most of the actual work is done in routines called by **createmaze**, however; they are **setsquare**, **rnd**, **randdir**, **legalpath**, and **buildpath**. The most elementary one is **setsquare**, which sets a given maze element to be a **PATH** or a **WALL**:

```
procedure setsquare(row, col: integer; val: mazesquare);
{ Set maze square to given value }
begin { setsquare }
   maze[row, col] := val;
   case val of
      PATH:
         dispsquare(' ', row, col);
      WALL:
         dispsquare('X', row, col)
   end
end;
```

In addition to assigning the square's value, **setsquare** calls **dispsquare**, which displays the specified square on the screen. If the square is a **WALL**, an **X** is displayed; a **PATH** is displayed as a blank. Since all maze assignment is done via **setsquare**, this arrangement is sufficient to ensure that the maze-creating process is displayed on the screen as it is carried out. Here is **dispsquare**:

```
procedure dispsquare(ch: char; row, col: integer);
{ Display specified character in maze square }
begin { dispsquare }
   gotoxy(col + XINDENT, row + YINDENT);
   write(ch)
end;
```

The **createmaze** procedure also calls the **rnd** function, which finds "random" positions within the maze. The **rnd** function returns a random integer within a specified range:

```
function rnd(low, high: integer): integer;
{ Return random number between low and high }
begin { rnd }
   rnd := low + random mod (high - low + 1)
end;
```

rnd returns a random integer between the values **low** and **high**, inclusive. (In Apple Pascal **random** returns random integers between 0 and 32767.) We write **rnd** as a general-purpose routine that we can use any time we require a random integer between two limits; this allows **rnd** to be used in a number of places in **theseus** and in future programs as well. Purists may object that the calculation shown in **rnd** will not always give a uniform distribution of numbers (why not?), but it is totally adequate for our purposes.

createmaze also calls **randdir**, which returns a random value of type **direction**; **randdir** translates a random integer returned from **rnd** into one of the following four directions:

```
function randdir: direction;
{ Return random direction }
begin { randdir }
   case rnd(1, 4) of
      1:
         randdir := UP;
      2:
         randdir := DOWN;
      3:
         randdir := LEFT;
      4:
         randdir := RIGHT
   end
end;
```

To discover whether it is "legal" to extend a path from a given point in a given direction, **createmaze** calls **legalpath**:

```
function legalpath(row, col: integer; dir: direction): boolean;
{ Return whether a legal path can be built }
var
   legal: boolean;
begin { legalpath }
   legal := FALSE;
   case dir of
      UP:
         if row > 2 then
            legal := (maze[row - 2, col] = WALL);
      DOWN:
         if row < MAZEROWS - 2 then
            legal := (maze[row + 2, col] = WALL);
      LEFT:
         if col > 2 then
            legal := (maze[row, col - 2] = WALL);
      RIGHT:
         if col < MAZECOLS - 2 then
            legal := (maze[row, col + 2] = WALL)
   end;
   legalpath := legal
end;
```

As previously mentioned, a path is illegal if it breaks through the maze boundaries to the outside; it is also considered illegal if it breaks through a wall to a previously constructed path. **legalpath** checks for these two conditions and returns the value **TRUE** if the path is legal; otherwise it returns a value of **FALSE**.

The final routine called by **createmaze** is **buildpath**, which actually digs all the paths in the maze. Roughly speaking, **buildpath** first extends the maze path from the specified point in the specified direction. Then it attempts to construct new paths by branching out from the new path head. This is accomplished through the magic of recursion—**buildpath** simply calls itself to make the new paths.

Again, let's try to express this in pseudo-code:

```
begin
   extend path from specified point in specified direction
   for each possible direction from new path head
      check whether a path is legal
      if it is, extend the path in that direction
   end-for
end
```

In addition, we want the new directions to be checked for legality in a *random order;* this ensures against non-randomness in the maze itself. Here is **buildpath** in Pascal:

```
procedure buildpath(row, col: integer; dir: direction);
{ Extend path in given direction }

var
   unused: set of direction;

begin { buildpath }
   case dir of
      UP: begin
         setsquare(row - 1, col, PATH);
         setsquare(row - 2, col, PATH);
         row := row - 2
      end;
      DOWN: begin
         setsquare(row + 1, col, PATH);
         setsquare(row + 2, col, PATH);
         row := row + 2
      end;
      LEFT: begin
         setsquare(row, col - 1, PATH);
         setsquare(row, col - 2, PATH);
         col := col - 2
      end;
      RIGHT: begin
         setsquare(row, col + 1, PATH);
         setsquare(row, col + 2, PATH);
         col := col + 2
      end
   end;
   unused := [UP..RIGHT];
   repeat
      dir := randdir;
```

```
         if dir in unused then begin
            unused := unused - [dir];
            if legalpath(row, col, dir) then
               buildpath(row, col, dir)
         end
      until unused = []
end;
```

As **buildpath** attempts to build new paths in each of the four possible directions in a random order, the set variable **unused** holds the directions not yet tried. As each direction is tested, it is removed from the set. When the set is empty, we know we have tried all possible directions.

This is all there is to creating the maze. This algorithm ensures the maze is "filled" with paths and that there is only one path between any two points in the maze (there are no "loops" in the maze). Of course, changing the algorithm could also change these maze properties.

Solving the Maze

The method used for solving the maze is similar in philosophy to that used for creating it. The requirement for a procedure to solve the maze can be described simply: it must look for a continuous sequence of **PATH** squares from one point on the boundary of the maze to another.

Here is the **solvemaze** routine:

```
function solvemaze(var maze: mazearray): boolean;
{ Attempt to solve maze, return TRUE if solved, else FALSE }

var
   solved: boolean;
   row, col: integer;
   tried: array [0..MAZEROWS, 0..MAZECOLS] of boolean;
{------------------------------}
{ Module to be inserted here:  }
{          try                 }
{------------------------------}
begin { solvemaze }
   for row := 0 to MAZEROWS do
      for col := 0 to MAZECOLS do
         tried[row, col] := FALSE;
   solved := FALSE;
   col := 0;
   row := 1;
   while not solved and (row < MAZEROWS) do begin
      solved := try(row, col, RIGHT);
      row := row + 1
   end;
   col := MAZECOLS;
   row := 1;
   while not solved and (row < MAZEROWS) do begin
      solved := try(row, col, LEFT);
```

```
         row := row + 1
    end;
    row := 0;
    col := 1;
    while not solved and (col < MAZECOLS) do begin
        solved := try(row, col, DOWN);
        col := col + 1
    end;
    row := MAZEROWS;
    col := 1;
    while not solved and (col < MAZECOLS) do begin
        solved := try(row, col, UP);
        col := col + 1
    end;
    solvemaze := solved
end;
```

The first thing **solvemaze** does is initialize the elements of the Boolean array **tried** to **FALSE**. This array acts as a maze map; as each cell of the maze is visited by the solution-searching procedure, the corresponding element of **tried** is set to **TRUE**.

solvemaze then searches the boundary of the maze, trying to find an entrance. It first checks the left edge, and then the right, top, and bottom boundary. (For all mazes built by **createmaze**, the entrance at the top of the maze will be found.) The Boolean variable **solved** is used as a flag to signal whether a maze solution has been found. If the maze has no solution, **solvemaze** returns the value **FALSE**; otherwise it returns **TRUE**.

The Boolean function **try** checks whether there is a path to the boundary from a given point in a given direction; for example, the call

```
try(row, col, UP)
```

returns **TRUE** if there exists a path upward from the **row**th row and **col**th column to the maze boundary; otherwise it returns a value of **FALSE**. As in **buildpath**, **try** uses recursion to help with the search.

A pseudo-code version of **try** might look like the following:

```
begin
   if the specified square is a WALL
      no solution from this point
   else
      set tried flag for this square to TRUE
      consider neighboring square in specified direction
      if neighboring square is a WALL or has previously been examined
         no solution (at least not in specified direction)
      else
         display move to neighboring square on CRT
         if neighboring square is on boundary
            we've found a solution!
         else
            look for solution from neighboring point in each direction
            if no solution found
```

```
                    erase previously displayed move
             end-else
        end-else
     end-else
end
```

The key point in the pseudo-code is "look for solution from neighboring point in each direction"; that is where the recursion comes in. In Pascal, the **try** function becomes

```
function try(row, col: integer; dir: direction): boolean;
{ Attempt maze solution from point in given direction }

var
    ok: boolean;

{------------------------------}
{ Modules to be inserted here: }
{          showmove            }
{          erasemove           }
{------------------------------}
begin { try }
    ok := (maze[row, col] = PATH);
    if ok then begin
       tried[row, col] := TRUE;
       case dir of
          UP:
             row := row - 1;
          DOWN:
             row := row + 1;
          LEFT:
             col := col - 1;
          RIGHT:
             col := col + 1
       end;
       ok := (maze[row, col] = PATH) and not tried[row, col];
       if ok then begin
          showmove(row, col, dir);
          ok := (row <= 0) or (row >= MAZEROWS) or
                (col <= 0) or (col >= MAZECOLS);
          if not ok then
             ok := try(row, col, LEFT);
          if not ok then
             ok := try(row, col, DOWN);
          if not ok then
             ok := try(row, col, RIGHT);
          if not ok then
             ok := try(row, col, UP);
          if not ok then { no solution from this point }
             erasemove(row, col)
       end
    end;
    try := ok
end;
```

The progress of the solution is displayed on the CRT. As the neighboring square is tested, **try** calls **showmove**, which draws the attempted move on the screen:

```
procedure showmove(row, col: integer; dir: direction);
{ Show move on CRT }

begin { showmove }
   case dir of
      UP, DOWN:
         dispsquare('!', row, col);
      RIGHT, LEFT:
         dispsquare('-', row, col)
   end
end;
```

If there is no solution from the adjacent point, **try** calls **erasemove**, which erases the path from the screen:

```
procedure erasemove(row, col: integer);
{ Erase move on CRT }

begin { erasemove }
   dispsquare(' ', row, col)
end;
```

The net effect of repeated calls to **showmove** and **erasemove** is to leave the correct path on the screen as the solution is found.

theseus is fun to watch as it creates and solves mazes on the CRT screen. The CRT tools presented here are extremely useful in more serious programs.

Suggestions

There is no program that cannot benefit from criticism, and **theseus** is no exception. You might want to use the criteria in Chapter One as a starting point for your comments.

theseus seems to be non-portable to the extent that it is usable only in interactive CRT-based computing environments. How could it be modified to work in other situations?

If you have a printer, modify **theseus** to print out the last maze or its solution. Instead of text characters, use whatever graphics capabilities your system possesses to display the creation and solution of the mazes.

You might want to experiment with different algorithms for creating and solving the mazes. You could do this with an eye toward improving efficiency or simply to explore different situations. What would non-recursive routines for either algorithm look like, and how would they compare to the recursive versions for efficiency and clarity?

theseus both creates and solves its mazes, which might get boring after a while. You could write a new program that will allow the user to solve the maze. To make it more challenging, display only the section of the maze the user would see if he or she were actually in the maze. Sticking with the mythological theme, put a Minotaur in the maze to catch and eat the user. Experiment with different Minotaur strategies.

Recommended Reading

A slightly different and more limited version of **crt** is offered in the demonstration software supplied by Apple Computer with Apple Pascal. The basic technique is widely used and appears in a number of public-domain Pascal programs.

The algorithm used by **theseus** for solving the mazes is adapted from one given in Chapter 4 of *The Elements of Programming Style* by B. Kernighan and P. J. Plauger (McGraw-Hill, 1978).

THREE

Interactive Input

Have you ever crashed a program by making a simple typing mistake? Or have you ever been mystified as to the kind of response a program wanted you to make? Has a program ever told you that you were making an input error but failed to disclose the nature of the error or how to correct it? If any of this has happened to you, you have been victimized by a "lazy" interactive input routine. Such lazy routines are the weak spots of far too many programs; they make programs difficult and frustrating to use and can cause valuable data to be lost or hours of work to be wasted.

Good interactive input routines make a program more reliable and much easier to use. The most important rule to follow when writing code that accepts data from the user is simply *check all input*. To put it more strongly, assume the users of your program will make dreadful blunders in entering information, because by Murphy's Law, they are certain to do so.

Although it is impossible to detect all errors, careful input checking will catch the most common ones. The best strategy is to detect input errors as soon as possible and make it as easy as possible for the user to correct the mistake. In addition, sensible design should make it difficult for the user to make a mistake in the first place.

Our goal in this chapter is to develop and demonstrate a set of "user-friendly" interactive input tools. Like the **crt** procedure in Chapter Two, the procedures developed in this chapter are used in all of the programs in the remainder of this book.

Standard Pascal Text Input

Standard Pascal provides the built-in routines **read** and **readln** for text input. But **read** and **readln** were initially designed (as defined in Jensen and Wirth) for use in batch environments: reading data from punched cards, disk files, magnetic tape, and so on. When **read** and **readln** are used for interactive input, some of the following difficulties may occur:

- Standard Jensen and Wirth Pascal requires that the first input character be "pre-fetched" before execution of a program begins; that is, the user must type the first character before it is asked for. This is a result of Pascal's general requirements that (a) **reset** on a file initializes the file's buffer variable with the first component of the file and (b) the predefined file **input** is *implicitly* reset at the beginning of a program.

- **read** and **readln** do not return direct information about end-of-file and end-of-line situations; instead, the functions **eof** and **eoln** are used to detect such occurrences. Although **eof** and **eoln** functions are valuable when reading characters from a file, they are less important in keyboard input and may even needlessly complicate matters. (It's an arguable point at best whether it is even sensible to talk about an end-of-file condition from the keyboard. After all, a keyboard—unlike a disk file—can generate an unlimited number of characters; it has no "beginning" or "end.")

- Pascal specifies no method of error recovery from **read** and **readln**, and it offers no way for erroneous input characters to be "erased." User input errors can cause the program to crash or behave strangely.

As a result of these conditions, **read** and **readln** are not suitable for any but the most rudimentary interactive input. A measure of this unsuitability is shown by the number of schemes invented to make Pascal "work" in interactive systems. For example, UCSD and Apple Pascal define a new text file type called **interactive**, which does not pre-fetch the first input character, while the ISO Standard specifies that the implicit reset of **input** (or any text file) need not occur until the first occurrence of **read** or **readln** (or access to the buffer variable **input**^).

Keyboard Input

Instead of trying to make **read** and **readln** work in a sensible manner, we will *isolate* keyboard-reading in one module called **getkey** and make sure **getkey** works sensibly. The most logical approach is to design **getkey** to provide the simplest "primitive" function: to return a character corresponding to whatever key the user types. There is no special handling of the end-of-file or end-of-line characters; **getkey** simply returns those characters to the calling routine if the user types them.

It is also important to note that **getkey** does *not* "echo" the input character; that is, **getkey** only gets the character, without also printing it on the screen. This allows **getkey** to be easily used for accepting non-printing "control" characters (where echoed characters might be erroneously interpreted as CRT commands) and password input (where for secrecy's sake the characters typed by the user should not appear on the screen).

In addition to this simple function, **getkey** provides two additional useful features: first, it requires the input character to be one of a set of *valid* characters supplied by the calling routine. This is our most basic (and most effective) error prevention; if the character is not valid, the key is ignored and the speaker beeps.

The second feature is a *software shift lock:* **getkey** optionally converts input lowercase alphabetic characters to uppercase ones. This feature is useful in those cases where a program requires an uppercase-only answer, or where allowing both upper- and lowercase letters would needlessly complicate the program's logic. Here is the complete listing:

```
function getkey(var ch: char; valid: charset; shiftlock: boolean): char;
{ Get valid key typed at keyboard, no echo }

var
   ok: boolean;

begin { getkey }
   repeat
      read(keyboard, ch);
      if eoln(keyboard) then
         ch := chr(13);
      if shiftlock and (ch in ['a'..'z']) then
         ch := chr(ord(ch) - 32);
      ok := ch in valid;
      if not ok then
         crt(BEEP)
   until ok;
   getkey := ch
end;
```

getkey employs an unorthodox but often useful technique: the input character is returned to the calling routine both as the function result and the **var** parameter **ch**. This allows the calling routine to test the value of the typed character immediately and save it for future use. We will use this technique in several future routines.

The input parameter **valid** indicates to **getkey** which input characters are legal. **getkey** assumes that the type **charset** has previously been declared:

```
<type>
   charset = set of char;
```

This gives rise to a portability question: How many elements may be contained in a set? In order for a **set of char** to be legal, a set must be able to contain as many elements as there are different characters. In Apple Pascal one may have a set with as many as 512 elements. Since Apple Pascal's underlying character set defines 256 different characters, there is no problem. UCSD Pascal can also handle a **set of char**. Other versions of Pascal may have more stringent set restrictions. (See Appendix A for more discussion.)

getkey's software shift lock is turned on or off by the Boolean input parameter **shiftlock**. The code segment

```
if shiftlock and (ch in ['a'..'z']) then
   ch := chr(ord(ch) - 32);
```

converts lowercase letters to uppercase if **shiftlock** is **TRUE**. The number 32 is the "difference" between upper- and lower cases in the ASCII character set; here, and throughout this book, we assume that the computer's underlying character set is ASCII.

To accomplish non-echoed input, **getkey** uses a special feature of Apple Pascal, which is also present in UCSD Pascal. The statement

```
read(keyboard, ch)
```

gets a character from the keyboard without displaying it on the screen; if the <RETURN> key is pressed, the function **eoln(keyboard)** returns **TRUE**.

getkey may be modified for different hardware situations. For example, if a keyboard does not generate the <~> (tilde) character, **getkey** could be changed to recognize a typed two-character sequence, say <ESC><6>, as the tilde. (To input an <ESC> character, the user could type in *two* <ESC>s.) Obviously, this approach could be used to allow the user to input any ASCII character not present on the keyboard. Another possibility is to modify **getkey** to handle a keyboard's "special function" keys, allowing a single keystroke to represent a sequence of characters of your own choosing.

The interested reader may want to return to the previous chapter and modify **theseus** to use **getkey** rather than **read**.

String Input

Now that we have a "primitive" routine to accept single characters from the keyboard, our next step is to design a routine that accepts a sequence of characters, or a *string*. The string is a built-in data type provided by UCSD

Pascal and Apple Pascal. Most versions of Pascal have a string-like data type that allows the programmer to define a variable to hold a sequence of characters of an arbitrary length. Our string-processing routines may be easily modified to run under these implementations. If your version of Pascal does not have a built-in string data type, you will have to implement your own. See Appendix A for one possible method.

Our string-input routine is **getstring**, which is a screen-oriented routine that accepts input information at any point on the CRT screen. This routine applies uniform and easily remembered rules for entering data and correcting mistakes. As an example, assume a program uses **getstring** to input a person's name. The initial display on the CRT may look like this:

```
Subject's Name?:▒_____
```

The underline characters indicate the maximum number of characters that may be entered; if the user attempts to type characters beyond this limit, the additional characters are ignored and the terminal's or computer's speaker beeps. The CRT cursor initially sits on the first underline. As the user types in characters, they replace the underlines, as follows:

```
Subject's Name?:Thomos Je▒_____
```

Typing errors are corrected by pressing either the <**BACKSPACE**> (ASCII 8) or <**DELETE**> (ASCII 127) key. Each <**BACKSPACE**> or <**DELETE**> erases the last character typed, replacing it with an underline. Attempting to erase more characters than were typed is an error; no action is taken and the terminal's speaker beeps. Pressing <**BACKSPACE**> five times in the previous example results in

```
Subject's Name?:Thom▒_____
```

An additional editing command is <**CONTROL-X**> (ASCII 24). Typing it erases the *entire* line entered so far. This method is easier than typing a large number of backspaces. After an error is corrected, typing continues as before:

```
Subject's Name?:Thomas Jefferson▒___
```

The entry is finished by pressing the <**RETURN**> (ASCII 13) key.

Data entry rules should be in agreement with the ones most familiar to the user; the ones given here are compatible with those used by the Apple Pascal operating system. The user should not have to remember different data entry guidelines in different situations.

getstring is flexible enough to use as a basis for *all* user input where more than one character is required. All types of information may be initially entered as strings through **getstring** and then converted to the desired type. As a bonus, this decision implies that the rules outlined here will apply every time the user enters data, ensuring again that the user does not have to memorize different methods for entering different kinds of information.

getstring uses **getkey** to obtain individual input characters. This allows each input character to be checked for validity; only "legal" characters can be successfully typed in. For example, if the program wants the user to input an integer, **getstring** may be instructed to accept only digits and the <+> and <−> characters and reject other characters. Since **getstring** uses **getkey**, **getkey**'s software shift lock may be used by routines calling **getstring**.

getstring may be told by its calling routine to specify a *default answer* (also often referred to as a *default*). A default answer is the answer supplied by the program if the user simply presses the <**RETURN**> key instead of typing an entry. Judicious use of defaults can greatly reduce the time needed to enter data. **getstring** displays the default answer at the entry position. For example:

```
Loan Principal   ($):$92.87___
```

In this case, "192.87" is the default. If the user presses <**RETURN**> at this point, the program will act *just as if* the user had actually typed in the default answer, 192.87. (Notice that the default may overwrite some or all of the underlines used to show the entry field.) If the user begins to type in another answer instead, the default answer will disappear and the underlines will be shown. If the user subsequently erases all the characters typed in so far, the default will reappear.

Interactive user input is usually preceded by a prompt from the program indicating that the program expects the user to enter some data. The prompt should be informative, indicating what kind of response is expected. For example, the prompt **Do you want to continue?(Y/N):** indicates that the user is to enter a <Y> (meaning "Yes") or an <N> (meaning "No"). Or the prompt **Enter today's date (mm/dd/yy):** might be used to show that the date should be typed in the indicated format, such as 12/25/84.

There are two common methods for getting information from the user: one is the "question and answer" method, where the program displays a prompt (asks the question) and the user then supplies the desired information (answers the question). The second is the "fill in the form" method, applicable when the user must enter a large amount of related data. In this second method, all the prompts are displayed on the CRT and the user types in information in response to each prompt. This method is analogous to filling in a printed form.

getstring does not supply a prompt to the user; it does not ask the question, it only accepts the answer. Prompts must be provided from some other part of the program. Thus, **getstring** may be used in both "fill in the form" and "question and answer" modes.

The pseudo-code for **getstring** might look like the following:

```
begin
   set input string to null
   display underlines to show input field width
   display default, if any
   while input key isn't a <RETURN>
      if input key is a <BACKSPACE> or <DELETE>
         delete last character from input string
         erase last character on screen
      else if input key is a <control-X>
         erase entire line
         set input string to null
      else if input key is a valid character
         display it on screen
         add it to input string
      else
         signal user error
   end-while
   if input string is null
      set input string = default answer
   erase leftover underlines
end
```

From this point, writing the actual **getstring** routine is straightforward; the only modifications to the pseudo-code involve checking for various illegal situations (entering too many characters, attempting to erase more characters than were entered, and so on) and erasing or redisplaying the default answer as required.

Here is the complete **getstring** listing:

```
procedure getstring(var inpstr: string; maxlen, col, row: integer;
                    default:string; valid:charset; shiftlock:boolean);
{ Get an input string from the user }

const
   BS = 8;              { ASCII backspace }
   CAN = 24;            { ASCII cancel }
   CR = 13;             { ASCII carriage return }
   DEL = 127;           { ASCII delete }
   FLDCHR = '_';        { Input field marker }

var
   ch: char;
   okset: charset;
   i: integer;
```

```
begin { getstring }
   inpstr := '';
   okset := valid + [chr(BS), chr(CR), chr(CAN), chr(DEL)];
   gotoxy(col, row);
   for i := 1 to maxlen do
      write(FLDCHR);
   if length(default) > 0 then
      posstr(default, col, row);
   gotoxy(col, row);
   while getkey(ch, okset, shiftlock) <> chr(CR) do begin
      if (ch in [chr(BS), chr(DEL)]) and (length(inpstr) > 0) then begin
         crt(LEFT);
         write(FLDCHR);
         crt(LEFT);
         chopchar(inpstr);
         if (length(inpstr) = 0) and (length(default) > 0) then begin
            write(default);
            gotoxy(col, row)
         end
      end
      else if (ch = chr(CAN)) and (length(inpstr) > 0) then begin
         gotoxy(col, row);
         for i := 1 to length(inpstr) do
            write(FLDCHR);
         gotoxy(col, row);
         inpstr := '';
         if length(default) > 0 then begin
            write(default);
            gotoxy(col, row)
         end
      end
      else if (ch in valid) and (length(inpstr) < maxlen) then begin
         if (length(inpstr) = 0) and (length(default) > 0) then begin
            for i := 1 to length(default) do
               write(FLDCHR);
            gotoxy(col, row)
         end;
         addchar(inpstr, ch, MAXSTR);
         write(ch)
      end
      else { Illegal character typed }
         crt(BEEP)
   end;
   if length(inpstr) = 0 then begin
      inpstr := default;
      gotoxy(col + length(inpstr), row)
   end;
   for i := length(inpstr) + 1 to maxlen do
      write(' ')
end;
```

The input parameters to **getstring** are:

maxlen   The maximum length of the input string.

col   The CRT column where input is expected.

row   The CRT row where input is expected.

default   The default answer, if desired. If a default answer is not desired this parameter should be set to the null string.

valid   The set of valid characters allowed in the string.

shiftlock   A Boolean value. This value is **TRUE** if lowercase input characters are to be converted to uppercase, and **FALSE** otherwise.

The input string is returned in the variable **inpstr**.

A more sophisticated version of **getstring** might (1) allow more versatile editing, permitting the insertion or deletion of characters at any point in the input string without erasing correct characters, (2) allow entry of very long strings that would extend beyond the right edge of the CRT screen, (3) provide a method to enter non-printing characters reliably, or (4) provide a "help key" that a confused user could press to get more detailed directions on what the program expected. (You can probably think of more items to add to this list.) The challenge lies not in the actual programming effort involved in adding such features; instead, the difficult part is adding them in such a way that the user finds the features easy to remember and use.

getstring uses one Apple Pascal built-in function that is not part of Standard Pascal: **length** accepts a string variable or constant as an argument and returns (as expected) the number of characters in the string.

String Manipulation Routines

In addition to **crt** and **getkey**, **getstring** calls three routines that are useful in their own right. First, the procedure **posstr** places a string at a given position on the CRT:

```
procedure posstr(s: string; col, row: integer);
{ Put positioned string on CRT }

begin { posstr }
   gotoxy(col, row);
   write(s)
end;
```

The **addchar** procedure adds a character to the end of a string:

```
procedure addchar(var s: string; ch: char; max: integer);
{ Add character to end of string }

begin { addchar }
   if length(s) < max then begin
      {$r-}
      s[0] := succ(s[0]);
      {$r+}
      s[length(s)] := ch
   end
end;
```

This routine is not very portable. It makes use of the fact that strings are arrays of characters in Apple and UCSD Pascal. The element **s[i]** is the *i*th character in the string, and the *numeric value* of **s[0]** is the string's length. **s[0]** cannot be accessed directly without turning off "range checking"; that is what the line {r−} does. After **s[0]** is accessed, range checking is turned back on with {r+}. {r+} and {r+} are *compiler directives*, and as such they are specific to the Apple and UCSD compilers although other Pascals have similar directives.

addchar first makes sure there is enough room in the string to add the character by comparing the string's length to **max**, a value supplied from the calling routine to **addchar**. In most cases, **max** is set to **MAXSTR**, a global constant. **MAXSTR** is defined to be the maximum number of characters allowed in a string — in our case, the value of **MAXSTR** is 80. If there is room to add the character, **s[0]** is increased by 1; this is the same as increasing the string's length by 1. Then the new last character of the string is set to the desired value.

In other versions of Pascal, the **addchar** procedure will probably be somewhat different, depending on the particular way strings are implemented. It may also be available as a built-in procedure.

The third string-manipulation routine is **chopchar**, which deletes a character from the end of a string:

```
procedure chopchar(var s: string);
{ Delete character from end of string }
begin { chopchar }
    if length(s) > 0 then
        {$r-}
        s[0] := pred(s[0])
        {$r+}
end;
```

This routine simply checks that there is at least one character in the string and then decreases the number of characters in the string by 1. Like **addchar**, this version of **chopchar** is only applicable to Apple and UCSD Pascal, although it should be relatively easy to duplicate in other versions.

gaslog

To develop our interactive input tools further, we will write a simple application program called **gaslog** that maintains gasoline usage data for an automobile. This program stores the information for a relatively large number of gas purchases on disk and prints a report based on the data when requested. The data file is made up of a sequence of *records*, one record for each time the tank is filled. Each record contains the following information:

- The date of the gasoline purchase
- The brand of fuel purchased
- The odometer reading at the time of purchase
- The cost of fuel per gallon
- The number of gallons purchased
- The total amount of money spent.

We chose a record data structure to store our gas purchase data because it is a natural choice in Pascal. The language makes it easy to group related data elements into a record and subsequently to treat the record as a unit, reading and writing it to disk, passing it as an argument to procedures, and so on.

The user may use **gaslog** to add records to the file (entering the data from recent gas purchases) or to print a report showing the car's gas consumption, or both.

A good place to begin in our design is to describe what the program will look like to the user.

When **gaslog** is run, the title **Gasoline Usage Log** is displayed at the top of the CRT screen, and the message **Initializing data file...** is displayed below it. If the data file is not present, it is created; this is indicated by the message **Creating data file...** on the screen.

In any case, after the data file is readied, **gaslog** displays its data entry form, shown in Figure 3-1. Near the bottom of the screen, **gaslog** asks the question **Add more records?(Y/N):**. This question is answered with either a <Y> (if the user wants to add data to the file) or an <N> (if the user does *not* want to add more records to the file).

If the user wants to add more data to the file, the program requests the data for a gas purchase. Each data item is requested next to the appropriate prompt on the CRT. This is the "fill in the form" method of entering data mentioned earlier. Here are guidelines for entering each piece of information:

Date Only digits and the </> (slash) character are allowed. The default answer is the date from the previous record. The date should be entered in the form **mm/dd/yy**; the month must be in the range 1 to 12, the day in the range 1 to 31, and the year in the range 0 to 99. If the program detects an "illegal" date, it displays the message **Please enter date in the form mm/dd/yy**; the user is then given another opportunity to enter a legal date.

```
                    Gasoline Usage Log
                  39 Records Used Out of 200

    Record Number:
      Date:
      Brand:
      Odometer Reading:
      Price (cents/gallon):
      Amount (gallons):
      Total Cost:


                   Add more records?(Y/N): __
```

Figure 3-1. **gaslog** data entry form

gaslog assumes gasoline usage data will be entered in chronological order, so it "complains" if the user enters a date that is out of order. If the date entered is prior to the date entered in the previous record, the program displays the following warning:

```
WARNING - Before last record's date
    Press <RETURN> to continue
```

This is simply a warning to the user, however; after <**RETURN**> is pressed, the program prompts for the next data item. In general, unless information entered by the user is obviously wrong, it is best for the program to adopt a "user knows best" attitude.

One special rule applies to entering calendar dates: to speed data entry, if the user only enters the month and day parts of the date, the year from the default date is used. For example, if the default date is **10/13/84** and the user only enters **10/26**, the program interprets this as **10/26/84**.

Brand   The data entry is limited to ten characters; all printable characters are accepted and the input is not converted to uppercase. The default answer is the previous record's brand.

Odometer Reading   In entering numeric data like this, only digits and the <.>, <+>, and <−> characters are accepted. If the user enters a number less than 0 or greater than 999999.9, the program displays

```
Please enter a number between
        0.0 and 999999.9
```

and the program again requests the mileage. If the mileage entered is less than or equal to the previous record's mileage, the program alerts the user:

```
WARNING - mileage <= prior mileage
    Press <RETURN> to continue
```

Again, this is just a warning; after the user presses <RETURN>, the program asks for the next item.

Price (cents/gallon)   This is a numeric data entry and the rules discussed for the odometer reading apply here as well. The cost is entered in cents per gallon; for example, if the cost is $1.258, this would be entered as **125.8**. The default answer is the previous record's fuel price. The program does not allow entry of a price less than 0.1 cents per gallon or greater than $3.00 per gallon.

Amount (gallons)   Legal amounts are between 0.01 and 99.99 gallons. No default answer is provided.

Total Cost   Legal values are between $0.01 and $300.00. The default answer is estimated from the fuel price and the amount purchased. For example, if the gas is priced at 123.6 cents per gallon and 12.3 gallons are purchased, the default is $15.20 (1.236 times 12.3, truncated to two decimal places).

If the amount the user enters differs from the estimated total cost by more than 2%, a warning is given.

After all six items have been entered, the program asks: **Any changes? (Y/N):**. If the user answers <Y> to this question, the program goes back through the form, requesting each data item to be re-entered. This process is speeded up by setting the default answers to the user's *previous* answers. This means the user may just press <RETURN> to skip over an item that need not be changed; only incorrect answers actually require new data to be entered. (The only exception is the default for the total cost; this is still calculated from the fuel price and gallons pumped.)

After the changes have been made, the program again asks **Any changes? (Y/N):**. This cycle is repeated until the data is correct to the user's satisfaction.

After all changes have been made, the program asks **OK to add record? (Y/N):**. If the current record is entirely wrong or was entered by mistake, the user may answer <N> at this point and the record will not be added to the data file. Otherwise, the user should reply <Y>.

Then the program asks **Add more records?(Y/N):**. If the user answers <Y>, the program requests a new record.

After the user is finished adding records (or the file becomes full) the program asks **Print gas usage report?(Y/N):**. If a gasoline usage report is desired, the user answers <Y>. The program requests the user to enter the current date to print at the top of each page of the report, and then it prints the report. A sample report is shown in Figure 3-2.

The control flow of **gaslog** is controlled by the user's answers to yes-or-no questions. This method is easy for the user to understand and also easy to program. More complicated programs often require a more complicated control flow; for example, if we wanted the user to be able to delete or modify records in **gaslog**'s data file, we would have to provide a method to access these options, and the simple yes-or-no organization would have to be eliminated.

One final design note. Most messages to the user (questions, instructions, warnings, error indications, and so on) are displayed on the bottom two lines of the CRT screen. **gaslog** (and the following programs) will not use those bottom two lines for "normal" program display. We have also followed the convention that an audible signal (provided via a call to **crt(BEEP)**) indicates some occurrence that requires the user's attention, such as typing an illegal character in **getkey** or attempting to type more characters than allowed in **getstring**.

This is another example of sensible user-oriented design. Generally speaking, user errors (as opposed to program errors) and other matters that demand the

		Gasoline Usage Report				09/15/82 Page 1
Date	Brand	Odometer Reading	Fuel Cost (cents/gal)	Amount (gals)	Total Cost	MPG
08/02/82	Mobil	45062.1	132.9	9.50	12.60	----
08/05/82	Mobil	45310.9	130.8	9.70	12.70	25.6
08/10/82	Old Colony	45602.1	129.9	9.90	12.90	29.4
08/15/82	Exxon	45888.2	132.9	8.50	11.30	33.7
08/18/82	Mobil	46201.6	127.5	9.80	12.50	32.0
08/25/82	Mobil	46449.2	127.5	8.90	11.35	27.8
09/02/82	BP	46751.4	124.9	9.80	12.25	30.8
09/05/82	Lido	47002.5	123.6	8.40	10.40	29.9
09/12/82	Amoco	47298.4	126.9	7.90	10.00	37.5
09/15/82	Getty	47560.6	129.9	8.60	11.20	30.5

Figure 3-2. Sample gas usage report

user perform some action should be handled as consistently as possible. As we discussed in Chapter One, consistency is an important component of a program's ease of use.

Now that we know what the program should look like to the user, we can begin to write it. The pseudo-code for the main routine of **gaslog** looks like this:

```
begin
   initialize data file (create it if necessary)
   display number of records in file
   display capacity of file
   display data entry form
   repeat
      if there's room in the file for more records
         ask user if there are more records to add
      if there are more records to add and there's room in the file
         get gas purchase data from user
         ask if it's OK to add record to file
         if it's OK
            write record to file
            display new number of records
   until file is full or there are no more records to add
   if the user wants a gas report
      print a gas report
   close data file
end
```

This outline translates into Pascal in the following way:

```
{$s+}
program gaslog;
{ Maintain gasoline usage records }

const
   BRANDSIZE = 10;       { Maximum length of gasoline brand }
   FIXSIZE = 12;         { Maximum digits in fixed number }
   MAXCRTCOL = 79;       { Maximum CRT column number }
   MAXCRTROW = 23;       { Maximum CRT row number }
   MAXRECS = 200;        { Maximum records in data file }
   MAXSTR = 80;          { Maximum length of string }
type
   crtcommand = (HOME, CLEAR, ERASEOL, ERASEOS, UP, DOWN, LEFT, RIGHT, BEEP);
   charset = set of char;
   date = packed record
      month: 0..12;
      day: 0..31;
      year: 0..100
   end;
   fixed = integer[FIXSIZE];
   gasrec = record
      fdate: date;
      brand: string[BRANDSIZE];
      mileage, fuelcost, gallons, totcost: fixed
   end;
   gasfile = file of gasrec;

var
   gf: gasfile;
   margin, nrecs: integer;
```

```
      lastrec, newrec: gasrec;
      s1, s2: string;
      filefull, more: boolean;

   {-----------------------------}
   { Modules to be included here: }
   {        crt                   }
   {        posstr                }
   {        getkey                }
   {        addchar               }
   {        chopchar              }
   {        getstring             }
   {        eraseline             }
   {        center                }
   {        getboolean            }
   {        ask                   }
   {        gchar                 }
   {        gnbchar               }
   {        stof                  }
   {        ftos                  }
   {        getfixed              }
   {        dtos                  }
   {        getdate               }
   {        wait                  }
   {        remark                }
   {        readgasrec            }
   {        writegasrec           }
   {        initgasfile           }
   {        dispgasform           }
   {        getgasrec             }
   {        gasreport             }
   {-----------------------------}
begin { gaslog }
   margin := (MAXCRTCOL - 25) div 2;
   crt(CLEAR);
   center('Gasoline Usage Log', 0);
   initgasfile(gf, nrecs, lastrec);
   ftos(MAXRECS, 0, 0, s2);
   s2 := concat(' records used out of ', s2);
   ftos(nrecs, 0, 0, s1);
   center(concat(s1, s2), 2);
   dispgasform;
   more := TRUE;
   repeat
      filefull := (nrecs >= MAXRECS);
      if not filefull then begin
         more := ask('Add more records?(Y/N):', MAXCRTROW - 1, TRUE, TRUE);
         eraseline(MAXCRTROW - 1)
      end;
      if more and not filefull then begin
         getgasrec(newrec, lastrec, nrecs);
         if ask('OK to add record?(Y/N):', MAXCRTROW - 1, TRUE, TRUE) then begin
            nrecs := nrecs + 1;
            writegasrec(gf, nrecs, newrec);
            ftos(nrecs, 0, 0, s1);
            center(concat(s1, s2), 2);
            lastrec := newrec
         end
      end
   until filefull or not more;
   if ask('Print gas usage report?(Y/N):', MAXCRTROW - 1, TRUE, FALSE) then
      gasreport(gf, nrecs);
   close(gf);
   crt(CLEAR)
end.
```

gaslog is a large enough program to require that the Apple Pascal compiler be put into "swapping" mode. This is accomplished by the first line of the program, {$s+}. Without this directive, the compiler runs out of memory during compilation and halts. Rather than going into detail on the inner workings of the Pascal compiler, we will simply note that swapping mode makes more efficient use of memory at the expense of slower compilation. Other Pascal versions may or may not provide this feature.

Data Structures

gaslog also requires the invention of two data types we have not discussed as yet. The first one is **date**, used for storing calendar dates. **date** is defined as

```
<type>
   date = packed record
      month: 0..12;
      day: 0..31;
      year: 0..100
   end;
```

This says that a variable of type **date** is made up of three integer subranges, one each for the month, day, and year. Specifying the record to be **packed** instructs the Pascal compiler to minimize the storage requirements for the data type. This results, at least in Apple Pascal, in a very compact representation for dates, only requiring two bytes. It is also compatible with the method the Apple Pascal operating system uses to store dates.

The second data type is **fixed** and it is defined this way:

```
<type>
   fixed = integer[FIXSIZE];
```

where the constant **FIXSIZE** has been earlier defined as

```
<const>
   FIXSIZE = 12;
```

This definition makes use of a non-standard data type provided by Apple and UCSD Pascal, the long integer. In Apple Pascal, the standard integer data type can represent integers in the range -32767 to $+32767$. Long integers, on the other hand, can represent a much larger range of numbers; for example, the declaration

```
<var>
   count: integer[8];
```

says the variable **count** can hold integers of not more than eight digits. Thus, **count** can range from −99999999 to 99999999. Our definition says that our **fixed** variables can hold integers between −999999999999 and 999999999999, or just 1 short of a trillion. The limit on the length that can be declared for a long integer is 36 digits.

Now that we know what the **fixed** data type is, we may ask ourselves what it is good for. In **gaslog**, we are going to use **fixed** variables to represent numeric values. *Monetary values* are represented as integral numbers of pennies; for example, the amount $123.87 is represented by the integer 12387. *Fuel amounts* are represented as integral numbers of hundredths of gallons; for example, 10.50 gallons would be translated into the integer 1050. The *vehicle mileage* is represented by an integral number of tenths of miles; for example, 46123.5 miles becomes the integer 461235. Finally, the *cost of fuel* is represented as an integral number of tenths of cents per gallon; for example, if you pay $1.258 per gallon for gas, this becomes the integer 1258.

This method is often called "fixed-point representation." Thus, we call the data type **fixed**. When using fixed-point representation, we store a number that is understood to have a decimal point at some fixed position within it. The program (or, more accurately, the programmer) must keep track of where the decimal is located. The integer 1289 might represent an amount of fuel, in which case it is actually 12.89 gallons. If it represents the fuel price per gallon, it becomes $1.289 per gallon. Care must be taken when using these numbers in arithmetic calculations; for example, decimal points must "line up" when adding or subtracting.

The **fixed** data type is primarily useful for those applications where data must be manipulated with controlled precision. This allows us to represent billions of dollars without losing track of individual pennies. Although such accuracy is probably not required for an application like **gaslog**, remember that we are building tools that can be used in other applications. And it is nice to know that **gaslog** has more precision than we need.

Many versions of Pascal provide some sort of extended-precision integer data type. If your version of Pascal does not have one, you may be able to add one yourself. See Appendix A for some hints.

Given these definitions, the data file definition becomes straightforward:

```
<type>
   gasrec = record
      fdate: date;
      brand: string[BRANDSIZE];
      mileage, fuelcost, gallons, totcost: fixed
   end;
   gasfile = file of gasrec;
```

The definition of **gasrec** serves to gather together all the items that apply to a single purchase into a single record type. And the disk file in which the data is to be stored is just a sequence of these records, one after another.

String Concatenation

One routine used by **gaslog** is furnished by Apple and UCSD Pascal and is not part of Standard Pascal: **concat**, which concatenates (links together) two or more strings into one string. For example, the code

```
s1 := 'one, ';
s2 := 'two, ';
s3 := 'three.';
s  := concat(s1, s2, s3);
write(s);
```

displays the string **one, two, three**.

concat accepts an arbitrary number of string arguments and returns a string as the function result. Note that neither one of these features can be accomplished by a module written by a programmer. Standard Pascal demands that a procedure or function have a fixed number of arguments and that a function return a scalar result. Appendix A gives hints on constructing a string concatenation routine for Pascal versions that do not furnish one.

Boolean Input

The user controls the flow of **gaslog** primarily by answering yes-or-no questions: **Add more records?**, **Print gas usage report?**, and so on. Such questions are so common in nearly all applications that it is worthwhile to write a general-purpose routine to handle them. In our case, yes-or-no questions are handled by the Boolean function **ask**, a simple routine that asks a question and returns the value **TRUE** if the user answers yes, or **FALSE** if the user answers no:

```
function ask(prompt: string; row: integer; defbool,defaulted: boolean): boolean;
{ Ask user yes-or-no question }
begin { ask }
   center(prompt, row);
   ask := getboolean((MAXCRTCOL+length(prompt)+1) div 2,row,defbool,defaulted)
end;
```

The input parameters to **ask** are

prompt The question to be asked.
row The line on which the question is to be asked.
defbool The default answer, **TRUE** for yes, **FALSE** for no.
defaulted **TRUE** if a default answer is to be allowed, otherwise **FALSE**. If **FALSE**, **defbool** is ignored.

The procedure **center** is used to display a string in the middle of the CRT screen on a specified line:

```
procedure center(s: string; row: integer);
{ Center line on CRT }
begin { center }
   eraseline(row);
   posstr(s, (MAXCRTCOL - length(s) + 1) div 2, row)
end;
```

We want to ensure that the string displayed by **center** appears on the line all by itself, so the line is erased first, using the procedure **eraseline**:

```
procedure eraseline(row: integer);
{ Erase line on CRT }
begin { eraseline }
   gotoxy(0, row);
   crt(ERASEOL)
end;
```

That takes care of "asking" the yes-or-no question, that is, displaying the prompt. Accepting the user's response is accomplished by **getboolean**. This routine accepts the user's answer at a specified point on the CRT screen with a specified default answer:

```
function getboolean(col, row: integer; defbool, defaulted: boolean): boolean;
{ Get yes-or-no from user }

var
   defstr, inpstr: string;
   ok, booboo: boolean;
begin { getboolean }
   if not defaulted then
      defstr := ''
   else if defbool then
      defstr := 'Y'
   else
      defstr := 'N';
```

```
      booboo := FALSE;
      repeat
         getstring(inpstr, 1, col, row, defstr, ['Y', 'N'], TRUE);
         ok := (length(inpstr) = 1);
         if not ok then begin
            booboo := TRUE;
            crt(BEEP);
            center('Please enter "Y" or "N"', MAXCRTROW)
         end
      until ok;
      if booboo then
         eraseline(MAXCRTROW);
      getboolean := (inpstr = 'Y')
   end;
```

The reader should be able to deduce from these routines what the "rules" are for answering yes-or-no questions.

Fixed-point Numeric Input

getboolean is just one example of a routine that calls **getstring** to input a specific data type as a string and then does the necessary conversion to the desired data type. Here is an informal method expressed in pseudo-code we will follow to accept different types of data from the user:

```
begin
   set up parameters to getstring:
      maximum length
      valid characters
      convert default to a string
   repeat
      get input string from user (using getstring)
      convert it from a string to desired data type
      check it for validity
      if it's valid
         convert it to standard form and display it (if desired)
      else
         signal user error, offer advice
   until valid input
end
```

This is a general and not very detailed strategy. In specific cases some of these steps may be relatively complex; others may be trivial or even unnecessary. As an example, we will develop a routine that accepts a **fixed** number from the user. Following the pseudo-code just given, the Pascal routine becomes

```
procedure getfixed(var f: fixed; col, row: integer; min, max, deffix: fixed;
                                 ndigs: integer; defaulted: boolean);
{ Get fixed number from user }
```

```
var
   minstr, maxstr, defstr, s: string;
   maxlen, i: integer;
   booboo, good: boolean;
begin { getfixed }
   ftos(min, 0, ndigs, minstr);
   ftos(max, 0, ndigs, maxstr);
   if length(minstr) > length(maxstr) then
      maxlen := length(minstr)
   else
      maxlen := length(maxstr);
   if defaulted then
      ftos(deffix, 0, ndigs, defstr)
   else
      defstr := '';
   booboo := FALSE;
   repeat
      getstring(s, maxlen, col, row, defstr, ['0'..'9','+','-','.'], FALSE);
      good := (length(s) > 0);
      if good then begin
         i := 1;
         good := stof(s, i, ndigs, f)
      end;
      if good then
         good := (f >= min) and (f <= max);
      if good then begin
         ftos(f, maxlen, ndigs, s);
         posstr(s, col, row)
      end
      else begin
         booboo := TRUE;
         crt(BEEP);
         center('Please enter a number between', MAXCRTROW - 1);
         center(concat(minstr, ' and ', maxstr), MAXCRTROW)
      end
   until good;
   if booboo then begin
      gotoxy(0, MAXCRTROW - 1);
      crt(ERASEOS)
   end
end;
```

The input parameters to **getfixed** are

col, row The position on the CRT where the number is to be accepted.

min The minimum number that will be accepted from the user.

max The maximum number that will be accepted from the user.

deffix The default answer.

ndigs The number of decimal places in the answer.

defaulted **TRUE** if the default answer feature is desired, otherwise **FALSE**. If **FALSE**, **deffix** is ignored.

The number the user inputs is returned in the parameter **f**. This number is scaled according to the parameter **ndigs** to convert it to the **fixed** data type. For example, if **ndigs** is 3 and the user enters the string "3.142", **getfixed** would return the number 3142. If **ndigs** is 2, the number returned would be 314.

getfixed makes use of two routines we have not yet seen: the first, **ftos** (pronounced "f-to-s"), converts a fixed number to a string. **ftos** accepts two input parameters, **width** and **ndigs**, which control the formatting of the number as it is converted to a string. **ndigs** digits appear after the decimal point, and the string is padded on the left with blanks, if necessary, to lengthen it to **width** characters. The algorithm used is complex enough to warrant an outline in pseudo-code:

```
begin
   if number is negative
      set f to -f
      remember that f was negative
   set string to null
   set number of digits converted to 0
   repeat
      get units digit of f
      add digit character to string
      set f to (f div 10)
      increase number of digits converted by one
      if number of digits converted = ndigs
         add decimal point to string
   until (f = 0) and (digits converted > ndigs)
   if f was negative
      add minus sign to end of string
   while length(s) < width
      add space to end of s
   reverse string
end
```

The only slightly tricky part of **ftos** is that it builds the string in reverse order and then transposes it before it is returned to the calling routine.

```
procedure ftos(f: fixed; width, ndigs: integer; var s: string);
{ Convert fixed to string }

var
   negnum: boolean;
   f1: fixed;
   i, j, nc: integer;
   ch: char;

begin { ftos }
   negnum := (f < 0);
   if negnum then
      f := -f;
   s := '';
   nc := 0;
   repeat
      f1 := f div 10;
      addchar(s, chr(trunc(f - 10 * f1) + 48), MAXSTR);
      f := f1;
      nc := nc + 1;
      if nc = ndigs then
         addchar(s, '.', MAXSTR)
```

```
        until (f = 0) and (nc > ndigs);
        if negnum then
            addchar(s, '-', MAXSTR);
        while length(s) < width do
            addchar(s, ' ', MAXSTR);
        i := 1;
        j := length(s);
        while i < j do begin
            ch := s[i];
            s[i] := s[j];
            s[j] := ch;
            i := i + 1;
            j := j - 1
        end
end;
```

The function **trunc** accepts a long integer as an argument and returns a normal integer. This is in addition to its customary use in Standard Pascal, where it accepts a real argument and returns an integer. In either case, an overflow error results if the value of its argument exceeds **MAXINT**.

Another special feature of Apple and UCSD Pascal is that if a regular integer appears where the program would expect a long integer, it is automatically converted to a long integer. This allows us to use **ftos** to convert integers to strings as well. An example is seen in the main routine of **gaslog**.

The second routine used by **getfixed** is **stof** (pronounced "s-to-f"), which converts a string to a fixed number. The call

```
ok := stof(s, i, ndigs, f);
```

scans the string **s** beginning at the **i**th character and returns the number seen as the fixed number **f**. The number is assumed to have a maximum of **ndigs** digits after the decimal point. The scanning continues until either the end of the string is reached or a character that cannot be part of the number is seen. In any case, the variable **i** returns the point in the string where conversion stopped.

stof returns a Boolean value as its function result, signaling whether the number found in the string was successfully translated into a **fixed** variable: **TRUE** if the number was successfully translated, **FALSE** if the number contained in the string was too large to be accommodated in a number of **FIXSIZE** digits.

stof keeps track of the number of *significant* digits it has seen at any point in the conversion in the variable **nsig**. We do not want to accidentally go over our limit of **FIXSIZE** digits in a **fixed** variable. But it is clear that only significant digits matter; the number 00000000.000042 has 14 digits but only two of them are significant. If more than **FIXSIZE** significant digits are seen in the input string, the additional digits are skipped over.

The number of digits seen after the decimal point is kept in the variable **nafter**; if more than **ndigs** digits are seen after the decimal point, they too are skipped over but otherwise ignored. If *fewer* than **ndigs** digits are seen after the decimal point, the output **fixed** number is scaled by the appropriate power of ten.

Here is the **stof** routine:

```
function stof(var s: string; var i: integer; ndigs: integer; var f: fixed):
                                                                  boolean;
{ Convert string to fixed }
var
    negnum: boolean;
    nsig, nafter: integer;
    c: char;
begin { stof }
    f := 0;
    nsig := 0;
    nafter := 0;
    negnum := FALSE;
    if gnbchar(s, i, c) in ['+', '-'] then begin
        negnum := (c = '-');
        i := i + 1
    end;
    while gnbchar(s, i, c) = '0' do
        i := i + 1;
    while gnbchar(s, i, c) in ['0'..'9'] do begin
        if nsig < FIXSIZE then
            f := 10 * f + ord(c) - 48;
        i := i + 1;
        nsig := nsig + 1
    end;
    if c = '.' then begin
        i := i + 1;
        if nsig = 0 then
            while gnbchar(s, i, c) = '0' do begin
                nafter := nafter + 1;
                i := i + 1
            end;
        while gnbchar(s, i, c) in ['0'..'9'] do begin
            if (nsig < FIXSIZE) and (nafter < ndigs) then
                f := 10 * f + ord(c) - 48;
            i := i + 1;
            nsig := nsig + 1;
            nafter := nafter + 1
        end
    end;
    if (nafter < ndigs) and (f <> 0) then
        while (nsig < FIXSIZE) and (nafter < ndigs) do begin
            f := 10 * f;
            nsig := nsig + 1;
            nafter := nafter + 1
        end;
    if negnum then
        f := -f;
    stof := (nsig - nafter) <= (FIXSIZE - ndigs)
end;
```

stof allows the possibility of imbedded blanks in a number; at every place the routine retrieves the "next character" from the string, it actually scans the string for the *next non-blank* character. The interested reader might reflect on the advantages and disadvantages of this design decision, considering not only **stof**'s use in this application, but also its possible use in other situations.

Note that **stof** *truncates* the number seen to **ndigs** places after the decimal point. How difficult would it be to modify **stof** to round the result instead of truncating, and what are the advantages and disadvantages?

Accessing String Characters

The function **gnbchar** used in **stof** scans a string for a non-blank character:

```
function gnbchar(var s: string; var i: integer; var c: char): char;
{ Get next non-blank character from string }
begin
   while gchar(s, i, c) = ' ' do
      i := i + 1;
   gnbchar := c
end;
```

Scanning begins at the **i**th character of the string; if the **i**th character is a blank, the next character is scanned. Scanning ends when either the character seen is non-blank or the end of the string is encountered. The non-blank character seen (or <NUL>, ASCII 0, if the end of the string is seen) is returned both as the function result and the **var** parameter **c**. The **var** parameter **i** returns the position of the first non-blank character.

Individual characters are extracted from a string with the **gchar** routine:

```
function gchar(var s: string; i: integer; var c: char): char;
{ Get character from string }
begin { gchar }
   if (i < 1) or (i > length(s)) then
      c := chr(0)
   else
      c := s[i];
   gchar := c
end;
```

gchar returns the **i**th character of the string **s** both as the function result and the **var** parameter **c**. If **i** is outside the current limits of the string, the routine returns the <NUL> character.

Date Input

Our next step is to write **getdate**, which accepts a typed date from the user:

```
procedure getdate(var inpdate: date; col, row: integer; defdate: date;
                                                       defaulted:boolean);
{ Get date from user }

var
    defstr, inpstr: string;
    booboo, good: boolean;
{-------------------------------}
{ Modules to be included here: }
{           stod                }
{-------------------------------}
begin { getdate }
   booboo := FALSE;
   if defaulted then
      dtos(defdate, defstr)
   else
      defstr := '';
   repeat
      getstring(inpstr, 8, col, row, defstr, ['0'..'9', '/'], FALSE);
      stod(inpstr, inpdate);
      with inpdate do begin
         if (year = 100) and defaulted then
            year := defdate.year;
         good := (month in [1..12]) and (day in [1..31]) and (year in [0..99])
      end;
      if good then begin
         dtos(inpdate, inpstr);
         posstr(inpstr, col, row)
      end
      else begin
         booboo := TRUE;
         crt(BEEP);
         center('Please enter a date in the form mm/dd/yy', MAXCRTROW)
      end
   until good;
   if booboo then
      eraseline(MAXCRTROW)
end;
```

Again, this routine follows our general outline for input of a specific type. **getdate** uses the **stod** ("s-to-d") procedure to convert a string to a date:

```
procedure stod(var s: string; var d: date);
{ Convert string to date }

var
   i: integer;
   f: fixed;
   c: char;
```

```
begin { stod }
   with d do begin
      month := 0;
      day := 0;
      year := 100;
      i := 1;
      if stof(s, i, 0, f) then
         if (f >= 1) and (f <= 12) then
            month := trunc(f);
      if gnbchar(s, i, c) = '/' then
         i := i + 1;
      if stof(s, i, 0, f) then
         if (f >= 1) and (f <= 31) then
            day := trunc(f);
      if gnbchar(s, i, c) = '/' then begin
         i := i + 1;
         if stof(s, i, 0, f) then
            if (f >= 0) and (f <= 99) then
               year := trunc(f)
      end
   end
end;
```

stod uses the previously written string-to-fixed conversion routine plus the **trunc** function to convert each part of the date string to an integer.

Finally, the **dtos** routine converts a variable of the type **date** to a string. It is relatively short and simple:

```
procedure dtos(d: date; var s: string);
{ Convert date to string }
begin { dtos }
   s := '00/00/00';
   with d do begin
      year := year mod 100;
      s[1] := chr(month div 10 + 48);
      s[2] := chr(month mod 10 + 48);
      s[4] := chr(day div 10 + 48);
      s[5] := chr(day mod 10 + 48);
      s[7] := chr(year div 10 + 48);
      s[8] := chr(year mod 10 + 48)
   end
end;
```

There are a few things worth noting about our date-input routines. First, if you prefer a different format for typing in and displaying dates (for example, 15-Sep-84 instead of 9/15/84), all you need do is change these three routines to reflect your desires. Second, the error checking performed by **stod** catches many "illegal" dates but not all of them. The date "23/45/67" is sensed as illegal, for example, but the nonexistent date "4/31/51" is not caught. How much more complicated would **stod** have to be in order to do more rigorous error checking?

Data File Initialization

Now that we have built input routines for numbers and dates, we can return to writing **gaslog**. Our first routine is **initgasfile**, which either opens the existing gas data file or creates a new gas data file.

Obviously, the first time **gaslog** is run there will be no data file present; it must be created. We could follow either one of two strategies: (1) create an empty file or (2) create a file with the maximum number of records and mark them, somehow, as "empty" records. In the first case, new records would be appended to the end of the file and the file would get "bigger," that is, take up more space on the disk. In the second case, new records would replace empty records and the file would remain the same size.

Although we do not want to get too technical about how data is stored on a disk, Apple and UCSD Pascal require a disk file to occupy contiguous disk blocks. This means that if, for example, File A immediately precedes File B with no unoccupied blocks between them, File A cannot get any bigger, even if there is unused space in other sections of the disk. This strongly suggests that we follow the second strategy. That way we will not have to worry about accidentally placing a file immediately following our data file and thus prevent it from getting bigger.

In cases where the host operating system allows files to occupy noncontiguous blocks, we do not have this worry. Yet it may still be worthwhile to follow the fixed-size file strategy in these cases, especially if disk capacity is limited. If the disk contains many other files, it is possible that a record added to the gas data file could exceed the capacity of the entire disk.

One situation in which the growing-file method is indicated is a timesharing system where the user pays for the amount of disk storage used. In this case, it is wasteful to maintain a lot of empty records in the data file.

For the **gaslog** program we use the fixed-size file method. When the file is initially created, we write **MAXRECS** empty records in it. (**MAXRECS** is a previously defined constant; we have taken it to be 200.) An empty record is considered to be one where the year of the date is 100. This is an "illegal" value that cannot be entered by the user, thanks to the error checking in **stod** and **getdate**.

If the gas data file exists, **initgasfile** uses a binary search to find the first empty record in the file. Records are added to the file starting at this point. The routine also reads the last record entered, if it exists; this is used for some default values in entering the next record.

```
procedure initgasfile(var gf:gasfile; var nrecs: integer; var lastrec: gasrec);
{ Initialize gas file, create if necessary }
const
    GASFILE = 'GASLOG.DATA';        { Name of data file }
var
    grec: gasrec;
    lorec, hirec, i: integer;
{---------------------------}
{ Module to be included here: }
{        findfile             }
{---------------------------}
begin { initgasfile }
    center('Initializing data file...', MAXCRTROW);
    if findfile(GASFILE) then begin
        reset(gf, GASFILE);
        lorec := 0;
        hirec := MAXRECS + 1;
        while hirec - lorec > 1 do begin
            i := (hirec + lorec) div 2;
            readgasrec(gf, i, grec);
            if grec.fdate.year = 100 then
                hirec := i
            else
                lorec := i
        end;
        if lorec > 0 then
            readgasrec(gf, lorec, lastrec);
        nrecs := lorec
    end
    else begin
        center('Creating data file...', MAXCRTROW);
        with grec do begin
            with fdate do begin
                month := 0;
                day := 0;
                year := 100
            end;
            brand := '';
            mileage := 0;
            fuelcost := 0;
            gallons := 0;
            totcost := 0
        end;
        rewrite(gf, GASFILE);
        for i := 1 to MAXRECS do
            writegasrec(gf, i, grec);
        close(gf, LOCK);
        reset(gf, GASFILE);
        nrecs := 0;
        lastrec := grec
    end;
    eraseline(MAXCRTROW)
end;
```

This version of **initgasfile** suffers from two drawbacks. First, it assumes there is room on the disk to accommodate the data file as it is created. If there is no room, a fatal error results. One possible improvement would be to turn off I/O error checking while building the file and then report the error to the user if it occurs.

A second drawback is the lack of flexibility in the location of the data file; the program as currently written assumes the data file is on the "default disk," that is, no particular disk is specified. The user might like to be able to tell the program on which disk the data file is to reside.

initgasfile uses the routine **findfile** to determine whether the data file exists; **findfile** returns **TRUE** if the file is present on disk, otherwise **FALSE**.

```
function findfile(name: string): boolean;
{ Look for file, return TRUE if found, else FALSE }
var
   found: boolean;
   f: file;
begin { findfile }
   {$i-}
   reset(f, name);
   found := (ioresult = 0);
   {$i+}
   if found then
      close(f);
   findfile := found
end;
```

findfile is, of course, non-portable; Standard Pascal has no mechanism for accessing a file by name or for determining whether the file exists. In Apple and UCSD Pascal, the function **reset(f, name)** attempts to open the file specified by the string **name** and permits it to be accessed by the file variable **f**. If the file is not present, the attempt to reset it is considered to be an I/O error and would normally terminate the program. However, the directive {$i−} allows the program to continue on I/O errors; instead the error is signaled by the function **ioresult**, which returns a non-zero value. The directive {$i+} turns normal I/O error checking back on.

The declaration

```
<var>
   f: file;
```

is also non-portable. Apple and UCSD Pascal allow this "untyped" file declaration to allow direct manipulation of the blocks of a file. In this case, it allows us to write **findfile** in a general way: it works whether the file in question is a text file, a data file, or even a program file.

The function **readgasrec** reads a specific record from the file:

```
procedure readgasrec(var gf: gasfile; recno: integer; var grec: gasrec);
{ Read gas record from file }

begin { readgasrec }
  seek(gf, recno - 1);
  get(gf);
  grec := gf^
end;
```

As in Standard Pascal, after a call to **get**, the file buffer variable **gf**^ contains the desired record.

The opposite procedure is **writegasrec**, which writes a record to the file:

```
procedure writegasrec(var gf: gasfile; recno: integer; var grec: gasrec);
{ Write gas record to file }

begin { writegasrec }
  seek(gf, recno - 1);
  gf^ := grec;
  put(gf)
end;
```

This time the file buffer variable **gf**^ must be assigned the record to be written before the call to the Standard Pascal routine **put**.

Both these procedures make use of **seek**, a routine provided by Apple and UCSD Pascal that positions the file pointer so that the next **get** or **put** reads from or writes to the specified record. (Records are numbered starting from 0, hence the expression **recno** − **1** in both procedures.) Versions of Pascal that are able to do random access on disk files will have some way to duplicate the action of **seek**.

Data Entry

The routine **dispgasform** displays our data entry form on the screen:

```
procedure dispgasform;
{ Display gas log entry form }

begin { dispgasform }
  posstr('Record Number:', margin - 2, 5);
  posstr('Date:', margin, 7);
  posstr('Brand:', margin, 9);
  posstr('Odometer Reading:', margin, 11);
  posstr('Price (cents/gallon):', margin, 13);
  posstr('Amount (gallons):', margin, 15);
  posstr('Total Cost:', margin, 17)
end;
```

The variable **margin** was defined in the main routine of **gaslog** in order to keep the form reasonably centered on both 40- and 80-column screens. **margin** should really be a constant, but since it is arrived at by a calculation, it has to be a variable.

We also spread out the individual data entry items vertically by writing them only on every other line. On CRTs with fewer than 24 lines there may not be room for this cosmetic luxury; the routines **dispgasform** and **getgasrec** will have to be slightly modified in these cases.

The data that goes in the gas file record is obtained from the user in the routine **getgasrec**:

```
procedure getgasrec(var newrec, lastrec: gasrec; nrecs: integer);
{ Get new gas record from user }

const
    THRESH = 0.02;          { Maximum relative difference between estimated
                              and entered cost }

var
    estcost: fixed;
    change: boolean;

{----------------------------}
{ Modules to be included here: }
{       datecomp             }
{       ftor                 }
{----------------------------}

begin { getgasrec }
    gotoxy(margin + 13, 5);
    write(nrecs + 1);
    newrec := lastrec;
    change := FALSE;
    repeat
        with newrec do begin
            getdate(fdate, margin + 5, 7, fdate, TRUE);
            if (datecomp(fdate, lastrec.fdate) < 0) and (nrecs > 0) then
                remark('WARNING - before last record''s date');
            {$v-}
            getstring(brand, BRANDSIZE, margin + 6, 9, brand, [' '..'~'], FALSE);
            {$v+}
            getfixed(mileage, margin + 17, 11, 0, 9999999, mileage, 1, TRUE);
            if mileage <= lastrec.mileage then
                remark('WARNING - mileage is <= prior mileage');
            getfixed(fuelcost, margin + 21, 13, 1, 3000, fuelcost, 1, TRUE);
            getfixed(gallons, margin + 17, 15, 1, 9999, gallons, 2, change);
            estcost := fuelcost * gallons div 1000;
            getfixed(totcost, margin + 11, 17, 1, 30000, estcost, 2, TRUE);
            if abs(ftor(totcost) - ftor(estcost))/ftor(totcost) > THRESH then
                remark ('WARNING - cost disagrees with estimate')
        end;
        change := ask('Any changes?(Y/N):', MAXCRTROW - 1, FALSE, TRUE);
        eraseline(MAXCRTROW - 1)
    until not change
end;
```

This routine is largely straightforward, making use of our previously described input tools. The only tricky part is turning off string-length type checking with the {$v−} directive; this is a special feature of Apple Pascal. The gasoline brand is limited by our declaration to ten characters, but **getstring** can theoretically return an 80-character result. The compiler recognizes that this could cause problems, so it normally flags situations like this as errors. But this error check can be bypassed with the {$v−} option. It is safe to do this because we make sure that the brand does not have more than ten characters with our own stringent error checking in **getstring**.

getgasrec uses two routines to help in error checking. The first is **datecomp**, which compares two dates. It returns the values −1, 0, or +1, depending on whether the first date is less than, equal to, or greater than the second, respectively:

```
function datecomp(d1, d2: date): integer;
{ Compare two dates, return -1,0,1 if d1 is <,=,> d2 }
begin { datecomp }
   if d1.year < d2.year then
      datecomp := -1
   else if d1.year > d2.year then
      datecomp := 1
   else if d1.month < d2.month then
      datecomp := -1
   else if d1.month > d2.month then
      datecomp := 1
   else if d1.day < d2.day then
      datecomp := -1
   else if d1.day > d2.day then
      datecomp := 1
   else
      datecomp := 0
end;
```

The second routine is **ftor**, which converts a **fixed** variable to a real number.

```
function ftor(f: fixed): real;
{ Convert fixed to real }
var
   new: fixed;
begin { ftor }
   if f < 0 then
      ftor := -ftor(-f)
   else if f <= MAXINT then
      ftor := trunc(f)
   else begin
      new := f div MAXINT;
      ftor := trunc(f - new * MAXINT) + MAXINT * ftor(new)
   end
end;
```

When **getgasrec** detects a possible mistake, it reports it with the **remark** procedure:

```
procedure remark(rem: string);
{ Put a message on the screen }

begin { remark }
   crt(BEEP);
   center(rem, MAXCRTROW - 1);
   wait;
   eraseline(MAXCRTROW - 1)
end;
```

We use **remark** whenever the user's attention has to be drawn to a warning message or instruction. It uses the **wait** procedure, which simply displays the message **Press <RETURN> to continue** and waits for the user to press the <RETURN> key:

```
procedure wait;
{ Wait until the user hits the return key }

var
   ch: char;

begin { wait }
   crt(BEEP);
   center('Press <RETURN> to continue', MAXCRTROW);
   ch := getkey(ch, [chr(13)], FALSE);
   eraseline(MAXCRTROW)
end;
```

Report Generation

The only part of the program left to write is report generation. The report is printed by the procedure **gasreport**:

```
procedure gasreport(var gf: gasfile; nrecs: integer);
{ Gas usage report }

const
   HDRSIZE = 132;         { Maximum length of report header }
   LPP = 66;              { Lines per printed page }
type
   header = string[HDRSIZE];
var
   pageno, lineno, rmarg, lmarg, i: integer;
   p: text;
   title, s: string;
   today: date;
   hdr1, hdr2: header;
   grec: gasrec;
   mpg: fixed;
```

```
{------------------------------}
{ Modules to be included here: }
{        initprinter           }
{        checkhead             }
{        checkfoot             }
{------------------------------}
begin { gasreport }
   crt(CLEAR);
   title := 'Gasoline Usage Report';
   center(title, 0);
   posstr('Today''s Date?:', margin, 12);
   getdate(today, margin + 14, 12, today, FALSE);
   pageno := 1;
   lineno := 1;
   initprinter(p);
   hdr1 :=
   '                          Odometer   Fuel Cost   Amount   Total';
   hdr2 :=
   '  Date       Brand        Reading   (cents/gal)  (gals)    Cost       MPG';
   lmarg := 5;
   rmarg := 75;
   for i := 1 to nrecs do begin
      checkhead(p, title, '', '', hdr1, hdr2, lmarg, rmarg, today, pageno,
                                                                lineno, 1);
      readgasrec(gf, i, grec);
      with grec do begin
         dtos(fdate, s);
         write(p, ' ': lmarg, s, ' ': 2, brand, ' ': 12 - length(brand));
         ftos(mileage, 8, 1, s);
         write(p, s);
         ftos(fuelcost, 10, 1, s);
         write(p, s);
         ftos(gallons, 11, 2, s);
         write(p, s);
         ftos(totcost, 8, 2, s);
         write(p, s);
         if (i = 1) or (gallons <= 0) or (mileage <= lastrec.mileage) then
            writeln(p, ' ': 4, '----')
         else begin
            mpg:=(((1000*(mileage-lastrec.mileage)) div gallons) + 5) div 10;
            ftos(mpg, 8, 1, s);
            writeln(p, s)
         end
      end;
      lineno := lineno + 1;
      lastrec := grec;
      checkfoot(p, '', lmarg, rmarg, pageno, lineno, LPP - 4)
   end;
   checkfoot(p, '', lmarg, rmarg, pageno, lineno, 2);
   close(p)
end;
```

Note that the miles-per-gallon calculation is carried out by subtracting the previous record's mileage from the current record's mileage and dividing by the gallons purchased. This, of course, is only accurate if the tank is filled to the same level each time.

The procedure **initprinter** initializes the printer to accept data from the program. The user is asked to "check" the printer before it is initialized, that is, make sure it is ready to print the report.

```
procedure initprinter(var p:  text);
{ Initialize printer }
begin { initprinter }
   remark('Please check printer');
   rewrite(p, 'PRINTER:')
end;
```

Like many of our I/O routines, **initprinter** is non-portable because Standard Pascal offers no method to specify the printer (or any named file) as an output text file. This version works in Apple and UCSD Pascal; users of other versions will have to write a version of **initprinter** that somehow attaches the text file **p** to their computer's printer.

A more sophisticated version of **initprinter** might give the user the option of displaying the report on the CRT or writing it to a disk file in addition to or instead of printing it. We will write a better version of **initprinter** later.

The report page formatting in **gaslog** is general enough to be used in other programs. Both left and right margins are adjustable for different printer widths. Three "title" lines are centered at the top of each page; any or all titles may be absent. The report date and page number, justified on the right margin, are also printed at the top of the page. Two lines are set aside for "column headers," the labels for the columns of report data. There is also provision for a "footer" line at the bottom of each page.

Before each line is printed, **gasreport** calls **checkhead**, which prints the titles and header lines if the current line number is less than or equal to a program-specified value:

```
procedure checkhead(var p:text; ttl1, ttl2, ttl3:string; hdr1, hdr2:header;
                    lmarg, rmarg: integer; today: date;
                    var pageno, lineno: integer; checklin: integer);
{ Check for header }
var
   s: string;
   i, nb: integer;
begin { checkhead }
   if lineno <= checklin then begin
      writeln(p);
      dtos(today, s);
      nb := lmarg + (rmarg - lmarg - length(ttl1)) div 2;
      writeln(p, ' ': nb, ttl1, ' ': rmarg - nb - length(ttl1) - 8, s);
      nb := lmarg + (rmarg - lmarg - length(ttl2)) div 2;
      writeln(p, ' ': nb, ttl2, ' ': rmarg - nb - length(ttl2) - 8, 'Page ',
                                                                   pageno);
      nb := lmarg + (rmarg - lmarg - length(ttl3)) div 2;
      writeln(p, ' ': nb, ttl3);
      writeln(p);
      writeln(p, ' ': lmarg, hdr1);
      writeln(p, ' ': lmarg, hdr2);
      write(p, ' ': lmarg);
```

```
            for i := lmarg to rmarg do
                write(p, '-');
            writeln(p);
            lineno := lineno + 8
        end
end;
```

The procedure **checkfoot** does the bottom-of-page formatting; it is called after each report line is printed, and also at the end of the program:

```
procedure checkfoot(var p: text; footer: string; lmarg, rmarg: integer;
                               var pageno, lineno: integer; checklin: integer);
{ Check for footer }
begin { checkfoot }
    if lineno >= checklin then begin
        while lineno < LPP - 3 do begin
            writeln(p);
            lineno := lineno + 1
        end;
        writeln(p, ' ': lmarg + (rmarg-lmarg-length(footer)) div 2, footer);
        lineno := lineno + 1;
        while lineno <= LPP do begin
            writeln(p);
            lineno := lineno + 1
        end;
        lineno := 1;
        pageno := pageno + 1
    end
end;
```

Those are all the routines needed for **gaslog**. We have seen a lot of Pascal code, but the result is worth it. We have written a working program that does something useful, and we have also built a number of tools that will be used in later programs.

Suggestions

There are many possible ways to improve **gaslog**; some improvements are very easy to achieve with the tools we have already built. Some will be somewhat more difficult.

The most obvious step is to increase the amount of information printed in the report. A number of statistics can be deduced from the information contained in the data file: cost per mile, miles per tankful, miles per day, and so on. It would also be useful to calculate "moving averages" to smooth out the normal variations in the data. As a little more challenging exercise, you might be interested in calculating the average MPG resulting from the use of different brands of gasoline; the tricky part is to be able to accumulate data from a possibly large number of different brands.

Once all this information can be calculated, you may want an option to allow the user to choose the data to be printed in the report.

Another possibility would allow the user more flexibility in entering data. You may want to permit the modification or deletion of previously entered records containing erroneous information, or you may want to remove the restriction that the user enter the data in chronological order by adding an option to sort the data file by, say, odometer reading.

Recommended Reading

The idea of **gaslog** was suggested by one of the exercises in *Etudes for Programmers* by C. Wetherell (Prentice-Hall, 1978), a collection of programming problems and projects ranging from simple to very advanced. This was one of the simpler ones.

FOUR

Crunching Numbers: A General-Purpose Calculator

In this chapter we will build **calc**, a program that accepts arithmetic statements from the user and calculates their values. We begin our design with a description of how the program works.

When **calc** is started, the screen clears except for the program's name in a box at the top of the screen and a string of underline characters near the bottom. As before, the underline characters indicate a data entry field in which **calc** expects the user to type in some information.

calc works on input strings, which we will call *statements*. The simplest kind of statement is an arithmetic expression, for example:

```
2 + 3
```

After the user presses the <**RETURN**> key to terminate the input, **calc** responds by displaying the result immediately following the statement. (Note: **calc**'s responses are underlined.) For example:

```
2 + 3 = 5.00
```

After displaying the result, **calc** scrolls the screen up one line and asks for another statement. Scrolling allows the most recent calculated results to remain on the screen.

calc can perform addition, subtraction, multiplication, and division. For example:

```
2 + 7 = 9.00
2 - 7 = -5.00
2 * 7 = 14.00
2 / 7 = 0.29
```

These basic operations can be combined into a single statement, as in the following:

```
5.3 + 13.4 * 1.2 - 19.6/5.8 = 18.00
```

The operators have an order of precedence common to most algebraic programming languages: multiplications and divisions are performed first, followed by additions and subtractions. This order may be changed with parentheses; operations contained within parentheses are performed first, for example:

```
1 + 2 * 3 + 4 = 11.00
(1 + 2) * (3 + 4) = 21.00
```

Statements can be arbitrarily complex, as in the following:

```
3 + 1/(7 + 1/(15 + 1/(1 + 1/293))) = 3.14
```

In addition to simply performing calculations, **calc** optionally stores the result of a calculation in a *variable* for use in further computations. For example:

```
APPLE = 5/6 = 0.83
ORANGE = 1/2 = 0.50
APPLE + ORANGE = 1.33
(APPLE - ORANGE)/(APPLE + ORANGE) = 0.25
```

Here we have defined two variables with the names **APPLE** and **ORANGE**. Variable names, or *identifiers*, may be one to eight characters long. (Actually, more than eight characters may be used, but **calc** ignores any extra characters.) The first character of the identifier must be a letter; the rest of the characters may be letters or digits.

The user may define more than one variable in a statement. For example:

```
PI = (NUMER = 355)/(DENOM = 113) = 3.14
```

This defines three variables, **PI**, **NUMER**, and **DENOM**.

The user may change the format of the displayed numbers by imbedding a *formatting directive* in a statement, as in the following:

```
[F6] 10/7 = 1.428571
[S3] 1.928 * 6.792 = 1.309e1
```

The formatting directive is contained between brackets. The user may place it anywhere in the statement, not only at the beginning. The directive consists of a letter and a number. The letter is either <**F**> (for *fixed-point* format) or <**S**> (for *scientific* format). The numeric part sets the number of digits after the decimal point. For example:

```
[F0]  A = 5/3 = 2
[F1]  A = 1.7
[F2]  A = 1.67
[F3]  A = 1.667
...
[F13] A = 1.6666666666667
```

The legal range of the number of digits after the decimal point is 0 to 13; numbers in **calc** have 14 digits of precision. If the number is either too small to be displayed with accuracy or too large to be displayed compactly with fixed-point format, **calc** displays the result in scientific format with 13 digits after the decimal.

Once the user issues a formatting directive, it remains in effect until another one is entered. The initial format is **F2**. If either the alphabetic or numeric part is missing from the formatting directive, the corresponding attribute remains unchanged. For example:

```
[F6]A = 8/29 - 10/37 = 0.005592
[3]  A = 0.006
[S]  A = 5.592e-3
```

The user may put more than one formatting directive in a statement, although there is not much point in doing so. Each directive is processed left-to-right and the final result is formatted according to the last directive seen.

To exit from **calc**, the user presses the <**RETURN**> key when prompted for the next statement. The program asks **Exit?(Y/N):**. Answering **Y** exits to the operating system, and answering **N** resumes the program.

Error Recovery

calc detects only two possible syntax errors in an entered statement. First, it "complains" if it does not see a right parenthesis in the correct place to balance a previous left parenthesis. (The term "correct place" is vague; we will discuss where **calc** expects to see a right parenthesis shortly.) Second, it also "complains" if reference is made to an undefined identifier. These are not fatal errors in themselves; in the case of a missing parenthesis, **calc** pretends there is a parenthesis in the expected place. If reference is made to an undefined variable, **calc** assumes the variable has a value of 0. In both cases, **calc** reports the error to the user and continues to evaluate the statement.

There are three fatal errors: *overflow* (an attempt to calculate a number that is too large), *underflow* (an attempt to calculate a number that is too small), and division by 0. The errors are only fatal to the current calculation; they do not cause the program to crash. Instead, they simply cause the calculation to end and the error to be reported to the user.

Other than these situations, **calc** tries to make sense out of an input statement, even if the statement contains essentially random combinations of symbols and numbers. **calc** scans the input until it can proceed no farther and then displays whatever numeric result it has. This is a common-sense design; instead of needlessly restricting the syntax of legal statements, we do our best to guess what the user really means to do. With sensible design, we will usually be right. And in the worst case, **calc** only returns a nonsense answer; it does not collapse.

Data Structures

Numeric values in **calc** are *not* represented by Pascal's built-in real data type. Instead, we use a program-defined "extended real" data type called **xreal**.

For **calc**'s purposes, the real data type has two disadvantages that make it desirable to use our own data type instead. First, reals have implementation-defined limits on both their range and precision. These limits may or may not be acceptable for any given application. In **calc**, we define these limits in the program itself; *we* are in control rather than the language implementors. If we need more or less precision or more or less range, we simply change the program.

Second, it is difficult to handle underflow and overflow errors when using the built-in reals. Some versions of Pascal offer a non-standard mechanism to catch such errors; Apple Pascal, however, does not. And it is *very* difficult to predict whether a given calculation will result in overflow or underflow before the calculation is actually done. Such a prediction involves detailed knowledge of the way reals are represented in memory and the way arithmetic is done on them.

Our first step in designing the **xreal** type is to define the precision and range of numbers we want it to represent. We choose that **xreal**s are to have 14 digits of precision, the smallest positive **xreal** is 1.0e−65, and the largest positive **xreal** is 9.9999999999999e62. These choices are somewhat arbitrary; in general, we want to define a "useful" range and precision suitable for most real-world calculations. We would also like to design **xreal**s that can be stored efficiently in memory and accessed quickly. (We do not claim to have done that here, however.)

A variable of the type **xreal** is made up of two numbers: (1) a *fraction* part, which is a long integer capable of holding as many digits of precision as we desire, and (2) an *exponent* part, which is an ordinary integer that expresses the "power of ten" of the number. The two numbers combine to represent the actual number. This is the customary method used to represent floating-point reals in memory, although the details of any specific implementation will undoubtedly differ from those given here.

In Pascal, we can express this structure easily with

```
<type>
   xreal = record
      frac: fixed;
      expo: MINEXP..MAXEXP
   end;
```

where **MINEXP** and **MAXEXP** are the minimum and maximum values of the exponent part, respectively. The type **fixed** is defined as in Chapter Three:

```
<type>
   fixed = integer[FIXSIZE];
```

where **FIXSIZE** is defined to be the number of digits of precision (14) we want in our calculations:

```
<const>
   FIXSIZE = 14;
```

Note that the value of **FIXSIZE** here differs from that used in Chapter Three.

Converting a number into an **xreal** involves splitting it up into **frac** and **expo** parts. To see how this is accomplished, we will look at an example with the value of π as a sample number:

```
pi = 3.14159265358979323846264338327950288...
```

The first step is to express the number in scientific notation in the form

```
<fpart>e<epart>
```

with <fpart> and <epart> adjusted so that

```
0.1 <= <fpart> < 1.0
```

We also assume that <fpart> is rounded to exactly **FIXSIZE** digits, the assumed precision of the number. In the case of π, this becomes

```
pi = .31415926535898e1
```

The **frac** part of the **xreal** number is obtained by dropping the decimal point from <fpart>, resulting in a 14-digit integer:

```
pi.frac = 31415926535898
```

Finally, the **expo** part of the **xreal** number is obtained by adding a constant **EXCESS** to <epart>. In our case, **EXCESS** is chosen to be 64:

```
pi.expo = <epart> + EXCESS = 65
```

The value of **EXCESS**, although arbitrary, is often chosen so that the **expo** part of the **xreal** variable will always be non-negative, which usually reduces the amount of storage required. Our choice of **EXCESS** is based on our choice of the smallest and largest positive **xreal**s. To see how this works, note that, as previously stated, the minimum positive **xreal** is

```
minx = 1.0e-65
```

Let's convert this to an **xreal**. Following our procedure, we first shift the decimal point in **minx**:

```
minx = .10000000000000e-64
```

so that the **frac** part becomes

```
minx.frac = 10000000000000
```

and **expo** is calculated by adding **EXCESS** to the power of 10:

```
minx.expo = -64 + EXCESS = 0
```

This implies that, given our choice of **EXCESS**, the minimum exponent (**MINEXP**) is 0, as desired. We can figure out the value of **MAXEXP**, the maximum exponent, by making a similar calculation on the maximum **xreal**:

```
maxx = 9.9999999999999e62 = .99999999999999e63

maxx.frac = 99999999999999

maxx.expo = 63 + EXCESS = 127
```

Of course the **xreal** data type can also represent an equally large range of negative values. A negative value of **frac** indicates a negative number.

Legal **xreal** variables are always *normalized;* their **frac** values are assumed to have a full precision of **FIXSIZE** significant digits. The only exception is 0, which is represented by a **frac** value of 0 and an **expo** value of **MINEXP**.

Variable Storage

Anyone using **calc** may define an arbitrary number of variables. Within the rules mentioned earlier in the chapter, the variables may have any names the user desires. We want **calc** to be able to retrieve the value of a previously defined variable, assign a value to a variable and store it under the variable's name, and replace the old value of a variable with a new one. Furthermore, we want all these operations to be relatively fast, even when there are a large number of variables in use.

A number of storage and retrieval methods could be used to represent variables in memory. Our choice is the *binary tree*. Many computer science texts describe binary trees; the reader unfamiliar with their use should consult one of the books in the bibliography at the end of this chapter.

Each node of the binary tree contains the name of the variable, its **xreal** value, and "left" and "right" pointers to the two subtrees below the node. This data structure is easy to build in Pascal; the following declarations serve to define the contents of a node:

```
<type>
   node = record
      name: identifier;
      value: xreal;
      left, right: nodeptr
   end;
```

where the type **nodeptr** has previously been declared as a pointer to a **node**:

```
<type>
   nodeptr = ^node;
```

and the **identifier** type has been defined as a string with a maximum length of 8:

```
<const>
   IDSIZE = 8;
<type>
   identifier = string[IDSIZE];
```

In addition to these major data structures, **calc** uses three more data types of lesser importance, **register**, **xresult**, and **format**.

- We define the **register** data type to be a long integer that can hold up to 30 digits.

    ```
    <const>
       REGSIZE = 30;
    <type>
       register = integer[REGSIZE];
    ```

    In **calc**, we use variables of the type **register** to hold intermediate results of our calculations. If we increase or decrease the precision of the **xreal** data type, we must also increase or decrease the length of the **register** data type. The arithmetic routines we develop later in this chapter require that **register** variables be capable of holding 2 * **FIXSIZE** + 2 digits.

    Since the maximum length of a long integer in Pascal is 36 digits, **FIXSIZE** has an upper limit of 17 digits (because 2 * 17 + 2 = 36). For applications requiring more precision, you may either modify the algorithms given here to use a smaller register size (see the recommended reading at the end of the chapter) or invent your own "long integer" data type with a less stringent length restriction (see Appendix A).

- We use variables of the **xresult** data type to represent the status of the calculation:

    ```
    <type>
       xresult = (OK, OVERFLOW, UNDERFLOW, ZERODIVIDE);
    ```

Most often the status will be **OK**, but whenever the program detects overflow, underflow, or division by 0, the status is set to the appropriate value.

- Finally, we hold **calc**'s current formatting mode in a variable of the type **format**:

```
<type>
   format = (FIXEDPOINT, SCIENTIFIC);
```

If the format is **FIXEDPOINT** the program displays results in fixed-point format. If it is **SCIENTIFIC**, results are displayed in scientific notation. The current number of digits to be displayed after the decimal point is held in the global integer variable **ndigs**.

calc — The Main Routine

Based on the previous description of the way **calc** works, we can describe the program's main routine in the following pseudo-code:

```
begin
   initialize
   repeat
      while the user's input statement is non-null
         extract formatting directive(s), if any
         evaluate statement
         if no fatal errors
            display result
         else
            display error message
         scroll CRT
      end-while
      ask if user is done
   until user is done
end
```

The pseudo-code and our data structures translate into Pascal in the following way:

```
{$s+}
program calc;
{ Calculator Emulator }
const
   MAXCRTCOL = 79;        { maximum CRT column }
   MAXCRTROW = 23;        { maximum CRT row }
   MAXSTR = 80;           { maximum string length }
   EXCESS = 64;           { xreal exponent excess }
```

```
        MINEXP = 0;              { minimum xreal exponent }
        MAXEXP = 127;            { maximum xreal exponent }
        FIXSIZE = 14;            { maximum digits in fixed number }
        REGSIZE = 30;            { max digits in register number, 2 * FIXSIZE + 2 }
        IDSIZE = 8;              { maximum identifier length }

   type
      crtcommand = (HOME, CLEAR, ERASEOL, ERASEOS, UP, DOWN, LEFT, RIGHT, BEEP);
      charset = set of char;
      fixed = integer[FIXSIZE];
      xreal = packed record
         expo: MINEXP..MAXEXP;
         frac: fixed
      end;
      register = integer[REGSIZE];
      xresult = (OK, OVERFLOW, UNDERFLOW, ZERODIVIDE);
      format = (FIXEDPOINT, SCIENTIFIC);
      identifier = string[IDSIZE];
      nodeptr = ^node;
      node = record
         name: identifier;
         value: xreal;
         left, right: nodeptr
      end;

   var
      alldone: boolean;
      s, xstr: string;
      valid: charset;
      i, ndigs, inpline: integer;
      x: xreal;
      result: xresult;
      root: nodeptr;
      ten: array [0..REGSIZE] of register;
      fmt: format;

   {------------------------------}
   { Modules to be inserted here: }
   {          crt                 }
   {          posstr              }
   {          getkey              }
   {          addchar             }
   {          chopchar            }
   {          getstring           }
   {          eraseline           }
   {          center              }
   {          getboolean          }
   {          ask                 }
   {          gchar               }
   {          gnbchar             }
   {          stof                }
   {          ftos                }
   {          wait                }
   {          remark              }
   {          initcalc            }
   {          xnorm               }
   {          xadd                }
   {          xtos                }
   {          evalstmt            }
   {          crtscroll           }
   {          disptitle           }
   {          getstmt             }
   {          findformat          }
   {------------------------------}
```

```
begin { calc }
   crt(CLEAR);
   disptitle('calc');
   initcalc;
   repeat
      while getstmt(s) do begin
         findformat(s, fmt, ndigs);
         posstr('=', length(s) + 1, inpline);
         i := 1;
         result := evalstmt(s, i, x);
         if result = OK then
            result := xtos(x, fmt, ndigs, xstr);
         if result = OK then
            posstr(xstr, length(s) + 3, inpline)
         else begin
            posstr('?', length(s) + 3, inpline);
            case result of
               OVERFLOW:
                  remark('Sorry: overflow');
               UNDERFLOW:
                  remark('Sorry: underflow');
               ZERODIVIDE:
                  remark('Sorry: division by zero')
            end
         end;
         crtscroll(1);
         disptitle('calc')
      end;
      alldone := ask('Exit?(Y/N):', MAXCRTROW - 1, FALSE, FALSE);
      eraseline(MAXCRTROW - 1)
   until alldone;
   crt(CLEAR)
end.
```

calc makes use of 16 procedures and functions developed in the two previous chapters. We are beginning to see the advantages of modular design: it cuts programming effort and makes our programs more uniform in appearance and function.

Initializing Global Variables

Most large programs contain quite a few global variables accessible to all parts of the program. We customarily initialize these variables in a separate routine; in this case, the routine is **initcalc**:

```
procedure initcalc;
{ Initialize global variables }
var
   i: integer;
begin { initcalc }
   valid := ['A'..'Z', '0'..'9', '+', '-', '*',
             '/', ' ', '.', '=', '(', ')', '[', ']'];
   root := NIL;
   ten[0] := 1;
```

```
    for i := 1 to REGSIZE do
      ten[i] := 10 * ten[i - 1];
    fmt := FIXEDPOINT;
    ndigs := 2;
    inpline := MAXCRTROW - 3
end;
```

initcalc initializes the following variables:

valid	The set of characters that may be entered by the user in an input statement.
root	The pointer to the root node of the binary tree in which the variables are to be stored. It is initialized to **NIL**, indicating the tree is initially empty.
ten	An array of powers of 10; **ten[1]** = 10, **ten[6]** = 1000000, and so on. The elements of the array are used in various calculations in the program.
fmt, ndigs	The format for displayed numbers is initially fixed-point with two digits after the decimal point.
inpline	The line on the CRT where the user enters statements.

Three Easy Modules

Three of the modules **calc** needs are relatively easy to design. First, the procedure **crtscroll** scrolls the CRT screen a specified number of lines:

```
procedure crtscroll(n: integer);
{ Scroll CRT n lines }
begin { crtscroll }
   gotoxy(0, MAXCRTROW);
   while n > 0 do begin
      writeln;
      n := n - 1
   end
end;
```

Second, the routine **disptitle** puts the name of the program in a box at the top of the screen:

```
procedure disptitle(s: string);
{ Display title in box at top of screen }

var
   i, nch: integer;

begin { disptitle }
```

```
      eraseline(0);
      eraseline(2);
      center(s, 1);
      crt(RIGHT);
      write('*');
      crt(DOWN);
      nch := length(s) + 4;
      for i := 1 to nch do begin
          crt(LEFT);
          write('*');
          crt(LEFT)
      end;
      crt(UP);
      write('*');
      crt(LEFT);
      crt(UP);
      for i := 1 to nch do
          write('*')
end;
```

Finally, the routine **getstmt** obtains the input statement from the user:

```
function getstmt(var s: string): boolean;
{ Get statement from user }
begin { getstmt }
   getstring(s, MAXCRTCOL - FIXSIZE - 8, 0, inpline, '', valid, TRUE);
   getstmt := (length(s) > 0)
end;
```

We set the maximum length of the user's input string to the value **MAXCRTCOL − FIXSIZE − 8**. This ensures that both the input statement and the result can fit on the same CRT line. **calc** displays an equal sign (with blanks on either side for cosmetic purposes) and the numeric result immediately following the input statement. This may take as many as 23 character positions.

This method severely restricts the room available for an input statement on 40-column displays like the Apple II's. If we set **MAXCRTCOL** to 39, this leaves the user with only 17 characters for an input statement. In this case, you may wish either to (1) modify the program to display the result on the following line and increase the maximum statement length to the full screen width, or (2) set **MAXCRTCOL** to 79 and use the Apple's screen-flipping feature to view separately the two halves of the screen.

getstmt uses **getstring**'s software shift lock feature to shift all input alphabetic characters to uppercase. This eliminates potential complications in other parts of the program and minimizes the user's possible confusion as to whether the identifier **apple** refers to the same variable as **APPLE**, or **Apple**, or even **aPpLe**. Instead of worrying about such questions while writing the variable storage and retrieval routines, we solve the problem at the input stage and in a manner obvious to the user.

getstmt returns **FALSE** as the function result if the user simply presses <RETURN> instead of entering a statement. Otherwise, it returns **TRUE**.

Extracting Formatting Directives

As outlined previously, **calc** extracts the formatting directives from the input string before evaluating the statement. Combining format directive interpretation with statement evaluation would needlessly complicate the program. As **calc** finds and interprets each format directive in the input statement, it replaces them with blanks; this ensures that the part of the program that does the arithmetic does not have to know about the format directives. And, obviously, the format directive interpreter does not have to know about arithmetic either.

Here is **findformat**:

```
procedure findformat(var s: string; var fmt: format; var ndigs: integer);
{ Find, extract, and erase formatting directives in string }

var
    i, j: integer;
    c: char;
    f: fixed;

begin { findformat }
    i := 1;
    while i <= length(s) do begin
        while not (gnbchar(s, i, c) in ['[', chr(0)]) do
            i := i + 1;
        if c = '[' then begin
            j := i;
            i := i + 1;
            if gnbchar(s, i, c) = 'F' then begin
                fmt := FIXEDPOINT;
                i := i + 1
            end
            else if c = 'S' then begin
                fmt := SCIENTIFIC;
                i := i + 1
            end;
            if gnbchar(s, i, c) in ['0'..'9'] then
                if stof(s, i, 0, f) then
                    if (f >= 0) and (f <= FIXSIZE - 1) then
                        ndigs := trunc(f);
            while not (gnbchar(s, i, c) in [']', chr(0)]) do
                i := i + 1;
            if c = ']' then
                i := i + 1;
            while j < i do begin
                s[j] := ' ';
                j := j + 1
            end
        end
    end
end;
```

Statement Syntax

We have been using an abstract term, *statement*, to describe the input strings **calc** evaluates, and we have given plenty of examples of such statements. When we begin to design the part of the program that evaluates statements, however, we need to be a little more precise in our description.

One natural and easily understood method for defining legal statement syntax is the *syntax diagram;* nearly every introductory Pascal text uses such diagrams to describe the language itself. But syntax diagrams are powerful tools for use in *any* application involving language analysis, including **calc**.

Figure 4-1 is the syntax diagram for a statement. The rules for interpreting such diagrams are simple. Each diagram has a single starting point and a single ending point. Arrows indicate legal directions (one-way streets) for traversing the diagram. Forks in the path show alternatives or repetitive structures. Rectangular boxes indicate language elements defined in other syntax diagrams. Circles show symbols that must be matched exactly. Notice that in Figure 4-1 the diagram contains a box labeled *statement*. This indicates that diagrams may be recursive, that is, refer to themselves. Thus, the diagram says that a statement may be an *expression* (which has yet to be formally defined) or a string of the form *identifier = statement* (which we call an *assignment*).

Note that syntax diagrams do not tell us anything about how to process language elements; they only tell us how to recognize the elements. What we do with the elements once they are recognized is left up to us.

Now that we know what statements look like, we can write the routine that evaluates them. When we talk about "evaluating" a statement, we simply

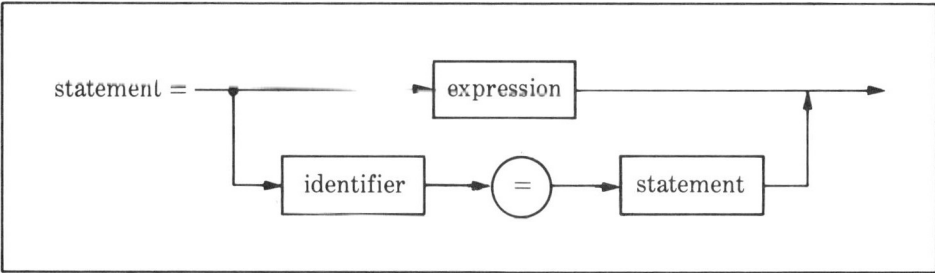

Figure 4-1. Statement syntax diagram

mean we calculate its numeric value. If the statement is an assignment, we also assign the statement's value to the specified identifier.

One complication arises when the first thing in the statement is an identifier. Even though we have not formally defined it, we know an expression may look something like

```
APPLE + ORANGE - PEAR
```

while an assignment may look like

```
APPLE = GRAPE - LEMON/LIME + 34
```

How do we distinguish between the two? If a statement leads off with an identifier, we look at the next (non-blank) character following the identifier. If the character is an <=>, we know we have an assignment. If the character is not an <=>, the statement must be an expression. (If the statement does not lead off with an identifier, it must be an expression.)

Using the syntax diagram, we first express our statement evaluation routine in pseudo-code:

```
begin
   renember beginning of statement
   if the first thing in the statement is an identifier then
      if the next (nonblank) character is an equals sign then
         skip over equals sign
         evaluate statement from this point
         if calculation OK then
            assign value to identifier
      else
         backtrack - evaluate expression from beginning
   else
      evaluate expression
end
```

The function **evalstmt** is called in the following manner:

```
result := evalstmt(s, i, x)
```

The input parameter **s** is the string that **evalstmt** is to evaluate. The **var** parameter **i** is both an input and an output parameter. On input, it tells **evalstmt** at what position in the string to begin evaluating the statement; on output, it tells the calling routine at what position the evaluation stopped by pointing to the next non-blank character in the string after the statement. The **var** parameter **x** is the numeric value of the statement seen. Finally, the calculation status is returned as the function result. If no fatal errors occurred, the status returned is **OK**; otherwise, the appropriate error code is returned. We customarily use this type of calling sequence when we evaluate other language elements. More examples will follow.

Here is the statement evaluation function in Pascal:

```
function evalstmt(var s: string; var i: integer; var x: xreal): xresult;
{ Evaluate input statement }

var
   id: identifier;
   c: char;
   isave: integer;
   result: xresult;

{-----------------------------}
{ Modules to be included here: }
{        findid               }
{        evalexpr             }
{        assign               }
{-----------------------------}
begin { evalstmt }
   isave := i;
   if findid(s, i, id) then
      if gnbchar(s, i, c) = '=' then begin
         i := i + 1;
         result := evalstmt(s, i, x);
         if result = OK then
            assign(id, x)
      end
      else begin
         i := isave;
         result := evalexpr(s, i, x)
      end
   else
      result := evalexpr(s, i, x);
   evalstmt := result
end;
```

The key to controlling complexity in a program module is to delegate responsibility to other program modules. If **evalstmt** sees an expression, it calls the routine **evalexpr** to calculate the expression's value. If it sees an assignment, it remembers the identifier and calls itself recursively to evaluate the substatement following the equal sign.

Identifier Recognition

Our next step is to build the routine that recognizes and returns identifiers. Figure 4-2 is the syntax diagram for an identifier.

We will not present diagrams for the elements *letter* and *digit;* we assume the reader knows what letters and digits are. Figure 4-2 matches our previous informal description of a legal identifier.

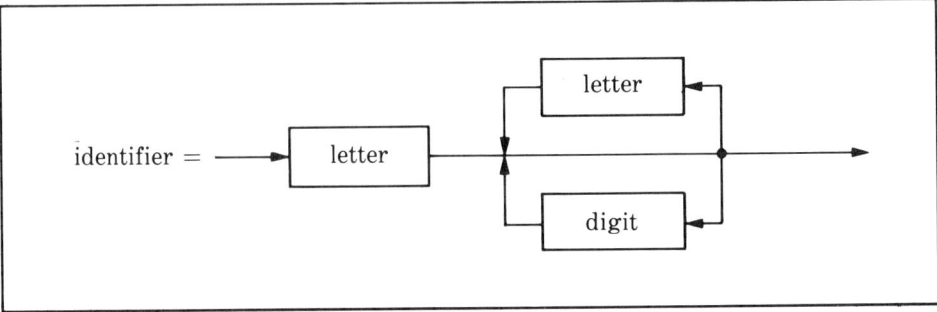

Figure 4-2. Identifier syntax diagram

The **findid** routine looks at a specified point in the string for an identifier. It is called in the following way:

```
idseen := findid(s, i, id)
```

The function returns the value **TRUE** if it sees a legal identifier at the specified position in the string; on exit, the variable **id** contains the identifier, and the parameter **i** points to the next non-blank character in the string following the identifier. If no identifier is seen at the specified position, the function returns **FALSE** and the value of **i** is unchanged.

```
function findid(var s: string; var i: integer; var id: identifier): boolean;
{ Get identifier from string }
var
    c: char;
begin { findid }
    id := '';
    if gnbchar(s, i, c) in ['A'..'Z', 'a'..'z'] then begin
        {$v-}
        addchar(id, c, IDSIZE);
        {$v+}
        i := i + 1;
        while gnbchar(s, i, c) in ['A'..'Z', 'a'..'z', '0'..'9'] do begin
            {$v-}
            addchar(id, c, IDSIZE);
            {$v+}
            i := i + 1
        end;
        findid := TRUE
    end
    else
        findid := FALSE
end;
```

The **findid** routine allows imbedded blanks inside an identifier; this is one

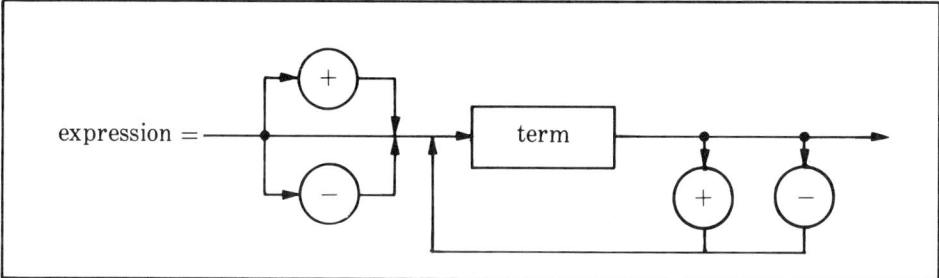

Figure 4-3. Expression syntax diagram

result of our previously mentioned desire to make **calc** as flexible as possible. For example, the user can legally enter the statement

```
PERIM = SIDE 1 + SIDE 2 + SIDE 3
```

Imbedding blanks in identifiers will not work in many computer languages; for many reasons, these languages must be somewhat stricter about syntax. But in **calc**, we can afford to be lenient. (Are there any hidden drawbacks to this scheme?)

Expression Evaluation

The next step is to evaluate expressions. Figure 4-3 is the syntax diagram for a valid expression. In English, the figure says an expression is a sequence of one or more *term*s separated by plus and minus signs; the first term may also have a leading sign. Again, the word "term" will be left undefined for now; all we need to know about terms is what is expressed in the syntax diagram.

The syntax diagram translates into Pascal in a natural manner:

```
function evalexpr(var s: string; var i: integer; var x: xreal): xresult;
{ Evaluate expression }
var
    c: char;
    x1: xreal;
    result: xresult;
    negterm: boolean;
{-----------------------------}
{ Modules to be included here: }
{        xsub                  }
{        evalterm              }
{-----------------------------}
```

```
begin { evalexpr }
   negterm := FALSE;
   if gnbchar(s, i, c) in ['+', '-'] then begin
      i := i + 1;
      negterm := (c = '-')
   end;
   result := evalterm(s, i, x);
   if negterm then
      x.frac := -x.frac;
   while (result = OK) and (gnbchar(s, i, c) in ['+', '-']) do begin
      i := i + 1;
      result := evalterm(s, i, x1);
      if result = OK then
         if c = '+' then
            result := xadd(x, x1, x)
         else { c = '-' }
            result := xsub(x, x1, x)
   end;
   evalexpr := result
end;
```

evalexpr first looks for the optional leading sign; the variable **negterm** is assigned the value **TRUE** if there is a leading minus sign. If the leading sign is a plus sign (or absent), **negterm** is **FALSE**. **evalexpr** then calls **evalterm** to evaluate the first term; if **negterm** is **TRUE**, the value of the first term is negated. The value of the first term becomes our sum.

Then **evalexpr** looks for additional terms. If the next non-blank character is a <+> or <−> it is noted and **evalterm** evaluates the next term. After each term is evaluated, it is either added to or subtracted from our sum, depending on whether the previous sign seen was <+> or <−>. The arithmetic is carried out by the routines **xadd** and **xsub**. The expression evaluation continues until no more signs are seen.

A fatal error (signaled by a non-**OK** result from **evalterm**, **xadd**, or **xsub**) terminates the evaluation.

Term Evaluation

Evaluating a term is even simpler than evaluating an expression. Figure 4-4 shows the syntax diagram for a term. A term is made up of one or more *factor*s separated by either asterisks or slashes. The translation of a term into Pascal is straightforward:

```
function evalterm(var s: string; var i: integer; var x: xreal): xresult;
{ Evaluate term of expression }

var
   x1: xreal;
   result: xresult;
   c: char;
```

```
{------------------------------}
{ Modules to be inserted here: }
{          evalfact            }
{          xmul                }
{          xdiv                }
{------------------------------}
begin { evalterm }
   result := evalfact(s, i, x);
   while (result = OK) and (gnbchar(s, i, c) in ['*', '/']) do begin
      i := i + 1;
      result := evalfact(s, i, x1);
      if result = OK then
         if c = '*' then
            result := xmul(x, x1, x)
         else { c = '/' }
            result := xdiv(x, x1, x)
   end;
   evalterm := result
end;
```

Again, **evalterm** delegates the responsibility of evaluating a specific language element, *factor*, into another module, **evalfact**; **evalterm** does not even know what a factor *is*. We also isolate the work of carrying out multiplications and divisions in the modules **xmul** and **xdiv**.

Factor Evaluation

The next step is evaluating factors. Figure 4-5 shows the syntax diagram. A factor is either a *statement* enclosed in parentheses, an identifier, or a number. It may have an optional leading sign. Here is the corresponding Pascal routine:

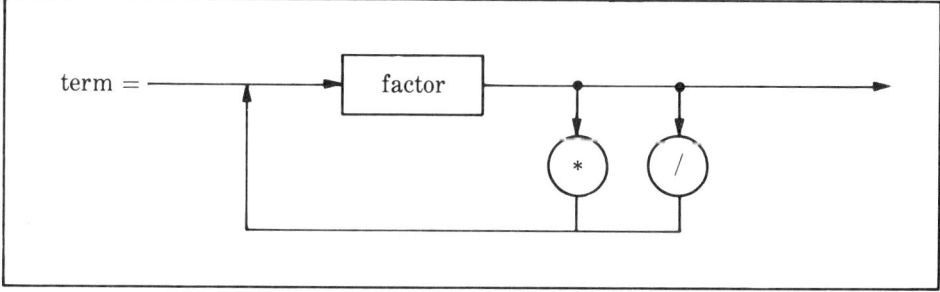

Figure 4-4. Term syntax diagram

```
function evalfact(var s: string; var i: integer; var x: xreal): xresult;
{ Evaluate factor }

var
   c: char;
   negfact:  boolean;

{-----------------------------}
{ Modules to be inserted here: }
{        stox                  }
{        evalid                }
{-----------------------------}
begin { evalfact }
   negfact := FALSE;
   if gnbchar(s, i, c) in ['+', '-'] then begin
      i := i + 1;
      negfact := (c = '-')
   end;
   if gnbchar(s, i, c) = '(' then begin
      i := i + 1;
      evalfact := evalstmt(s, i, x);
      if gnbchar(s, i, c) = ')' then
         i := i + 1
      else
         remark('Missing right parenthesis')
   end
   else if findid(s, i, id) then
      evalfact := evalid(id, x)
   else
      evalfact := stox(s, i, x);
   if negfact then
      x.frac := -x.frac
end;
```

This is a three-way branch: after noting and skipping over the optional sign, **evalfact** looks at the next non-blank character. If it sees a left paren-

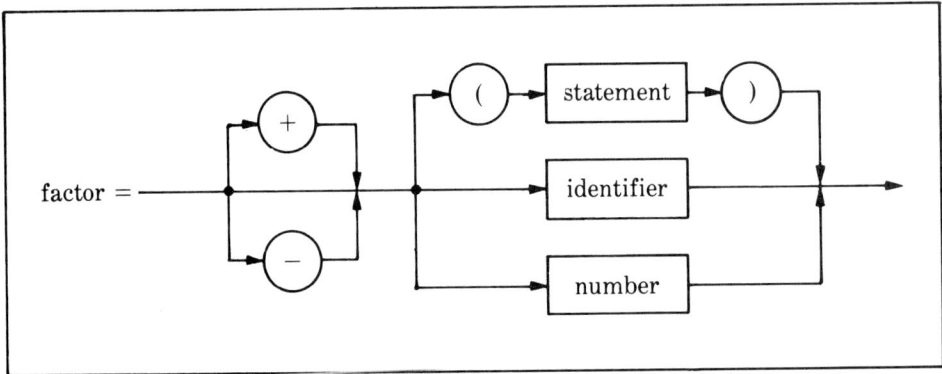

Figure 4-5. Factor syntax diagram

thesis, the routine skips over it and then calls **evalstmt** to evaluate the following statement. If instead **evalfact** sees an identifier, it calls **evalid** to evaluate the identifier. Otherwise, it calls **stox**, which tries to interpret the factor as a number.

Notice that **evalfact** is the place where the "missing right parenthesis" syntax error is detected. According to the syntax diagram, if a left parenthesis is seen, there must follow a statement and a balancing right parenthesis. After evaluating a statement led by a left parenthesis, **evalfact** expects to see the balancing right parenthesis as the next non-blank character. If it is there, it is skipped over; if it is not there, the error message is displayed.

Arithmetic

Before tackling the somewhat thorny problem of converting strings of characters into our extended real data type (and vice versa), we will design the routines to carry out arithmetic operations. It is beyond the scope of this book to prove the routines we design here are correct; such proofs involve more detailed analysis than we can give. The interested reader should refer to the bibliography at the end of this chapter for works on arithmetic.

Our first task (and the hardest) is addition. We want a routine to add two extended reals and return the result. The result should be properly rounded to a precision of **FIXSIZE** digits. We also want to know whether the addition results in overflow or underflow. Here is the **xadd** routine in Pascal:

```
function xadd(arg1, arg2: xreal; var x: xreal): xresult;
{ Add two extended reals }
var
   rawfrac: register;
   rawexpo: integer;
   temp: xreal;
begin { xadd }
   if arg1.expo < arg2.expo then begin { swap }
      temp := arg1;
      arg1 := arg2;
      arg2 := temp
   end;
   if arg1.expo - arg2.expo >= FIXSIZE + 2 then begin { |arg1| >> |arg2| }
      x := arg1;
      xadd := OK
   end
   else begin
      rawexpo := arg1.expo;
      rawfrac := arg1.frac * ten[FIXSIZE + 1] +
                 arg2.frac * ten[FIXSIZE + 1 - (arg1.expo - arg2.expo)];
      xadd := xnorm(rawexpo, rawfrac, x)
   end
end;
```

To begin, the routine ensures that the second argument's exponent is less than or equal to the first argument's exponent; if this is not so, the two arguments are swapped to make it so.

Next, **xadd** disposes of the case where there is a large difference in the two arguments' exponents, that is, so much difference that adding the second argument to the first would not change the first within the limits of our assumed precision. (For example, consider the result of adding the mass of an electron to the mass of the sun.) In this case, we can set our result to the value of the first argument and we have finished the calculation.

Usually, though, **xadd** must do the addition. The goal is to add the arguments to generate a *raw fraction* and a *raw exponent*. A separate routine (called **xnorm**) combines these two numbers into a properly normalized **xreal** variable. The raw fraction is a variable of the **register** type. As previously mentioned, a variable of the **register** type can hold integers of **2 * FIXSIZE + 2** digits. The raw exponent is an integer, but one not necessarily restricted to the range **MINEXP..MAXEXP**. The combination of the raw fraction and the raw exponent essentially forms a "double-precision" number, which **xnorm** rounds off and fits back into an **xreal** variable.

To do the addition, we first multiply the **frac** parts of our two arguments by the factor **ten[FIXSIZE + 1]**; then we "line up the decimal points" of the two arguments by dividing the second argument's **frac** by the appropriate power of ten. Finally, we add the two **frac**s, and this gives us our raw fraction. (Actually, this is all done in one statement in the **xadd** routine.) The raw exponent is set to the exponent of the first argument. (Skeptical readers are invited to work through a few examples by hand to convince themselves that all this legerdemain actually works.)

The raw fraction **rawfrac** passed to **xnorm** will contain *at most* **2 * FIXSIZE + 2** digits (why?). The normalization routine, **xnorm**, must round the raw fraction to **FIXSIZE** digits, adjusting the raw exponent accordingly. Then it must combine the raw fraction and exponent into an extended real, test the result for overflow or underflow, and return either the status **OK** or the appropriate error code.

A pseudo-code version of **xnorm** might look like this:

```
begin
   if raw fraction is zero
      set xreal to zero and return
   else
      if raw fraction is negative
         change its sign
         remember that it was negative
      end-if
      while raw fraction has fewer than (2 * FIXSIZE + 1) digits
```

```
            multiply it by 10 (scale left)
            decrease raw exponent by one
         end-while
         repeat
            if raw fraction has more than (2 * FIXSIZE + 1) digits
               divide by 10 (scale right)
               increase raw exponent by one
            end-if
            round raw fraction to FIXSIZE digits
               (by adding 5 * 10^FIXSIZE)
         until raw fraction has (2 * FIXSIZE + 1) digits
         if raw exponent > max exponent
            overflow!
         else if raw exponent < min exponent
            underflow!
         else
            set xreal exponent = raw exponent
            set xreal fraction = raw fraction/(10 ^ (FIXSIZE + 1))
               (xreal fraction will then have FIXSIZE digits, as required)
         end-else
         if original raw fraction was negative
            negate xreal fraction
      end-else
end
```

The Pascal version of **xnorm** follows the pseudo-code closely:

```
function xnorm(rawexpo: integer; rawfrac: register; var x: xreal): xresult;
{ Round and normalize extended real }
var
   negfrac: boolean;
begin { xnorm }
   with x do
      if rawfrac = 0 then begin
         frac := 0;
         expo := MINEXP;
         xnorm := OK
      end
      else begin
         negfrac := (rawfrac < 0);
         if negfrac then
            rawfrac := -rawfrac;
         while rawfrac < ten[2 * FIXSIZE] do begin
            rawfrac := ten[1] * rawfrac;
            rawexpo := rawexpo - 1
         end;
         repeat
            if rawfrac >= ten[2 * FIXSIZE + 1] then begin
               rawfrac := rawfrac div ten[1];
               rawexpo := rawexpo + 1
            end;
            rawfrac := rawfrac + 5 * ten[FIXSIZE]
         until rawfrac < ten[2 * FIXSIZE + 1];
         if rawexpo > MAXEXP then begin
            expo := MAXEXP;
            frac := ten[FIXSIZE] - 1;
            xnorm := OVERFLOW
         end
         else if rawexpo < MINEXP then begin
            expo := MINEXP;
            frac := ten[FIXSIZE - 1];
            xnorm := UNDERFLOW
```

```
            end
         else begin
            expo := rawexpo;
            frac := rawfrac div ten[FIXSIZE + 1];
            xnorm := OK
         end;
         if negfrac then
            frac := -frac
      end
end;
```

The remaining routines for doing arithmetic on extended reals are relatively easy. The **xsub** routine simply inverts the sign of its second argument and calls on **xadd** to do the calculation:

```
function xsub(arg1, arg2: xreal; var x: xreal): xresult;
{ Subtract two extended reals }

begin { xsub }
   arg2.frac := -arg2.frac;
   xsub := xadd(arg1, arg2, x)
end;
```

The multiplication routine is also simple, calling **xnorm** to do the complicated procedures:

```
function xmul(arg1, arg2: xreal; var x: xreal): xresult;
{ Multiply two extended reals }

var
   rawexpo: integer;
   rawfrac: register;

begin { xmul }
   rawexpo := arg1.expo + arg2.expo - EXCESS + 1;
   rawfrac := arg1.frac * arg2.frac;
   xmul := xnorm(rawexpo, rawfrac, x)
end;
```

Finally, the division routine is mainly concerned with handling division by 0 properly:

```
function xdiv(arg1, arg2: xreal; var x: xreal): xresult;
{ Divide two extended reals }

var
   rawfrac: register;
   rawexpo: integer;

begin { xdiv }
   if arg2.frac = 0 then begin
      if arg1.frac < 0 then
         x.frac := 1 - ten[FIXSIZE]
      else
         x.frac := ten[FIXSIZE] - 1;
      x.expo := MAXEXP;
      xdiv := ZERODIVIDE
```

```
      end
    else begin
      rawfrac := ((arg1.frac * ten[FIXSIZE+2]) div arg2.frac) * ten[FIXSIZE-2];
      rawexpo := arg1.expo - arg2.expo + EXCESS + 1;
      xdiv := xnorm(rawexpo, rawfrac, x)
    end
end;
```

On division by 0, **xdiv** returns a **ZERODIVIDE** status to its calling routine and also sets the result **x** to a very large positive or negative **xreal**, depending on the sign of **arg1** (although this is not required in **calc**, since calculation terminates and any results are thrown away on a division by 0).

Converting a String to an Extended Real

Now we need to build **stox**, a routine to convert a string of characters to an extended real. Again our goal is to maintain as much flexibility as possible in our syntax. The syntax diagram for a number (Figure 4-6) is our most complex one so far. In words, this figure says a number is made up of

- An optional leading sign.
- Zero or more digits.
- An optional decimal point, followed by zero or more digits.
- An optional exponent, consisting of the letter "E", an optional sign, and zero or more digits.

Notice that *all* parts of the number are optional—even a null string is a "legal" number. (What are the consequences of this design decision?)

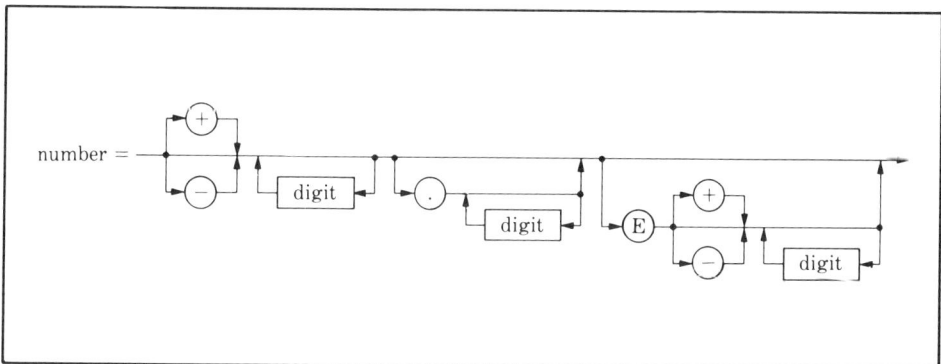

Figure 4-6. Number syntax diagram

The complex syntax diagram indicates **stox** is likely to be complex as well. We outline it first in extremely simple pseudo-code, following the syntax diagram and hiding most of the ugly details:

```
begin
   get optional leading sign
   get (zero or more) digits
   if decimal point is seen
      get digits after decimal point, if any
   if "E" is seen
      get exponent
   combine into extended real
end
```

Fortunately, most of the logic in **stox** is similar to that in the **stof** procedure in Chapter Three. If we are careful to keep track of the number of significant digits seen (**nsig**) and the number of digits seen after the decimal point (**nafter**), we can keep the apparent complexity under control.

```
function stox(var s: string; var i: integer; var x: xreal): xresult;
{ Convert string to extended real }
const
   HUGE = 9999;          { Limit on converted exponent }
var
   rawexpo, nsig, nafter, epart, nesig: integer;
   negepart, negnum: boolean;
   rawfrac: register;
   c: char;
   f: fixed;
begin { stox }
   rawfrac := 0;
   nsig := 0;
   nafter := 0;
   epart := 0;
   negnum := FALSE;
   negepart := FALSE;
   if gnbchar(s, i, c) in ['+', '-'] then begin
      negnum := (c = '-');
      i := i + 1
   end;
   while gnbchar(s, i, c) = '0' do
      i := i + 1;
   while gnbchar(s, i, c) in ['0'..'9'] do begin
      if nsig < REGSIZE - 1 then
         rawfrac := 10 * rawfrac + ord(c) - 48;
      nsig := nsig + 1;
      i := i + 1
   end;
   if c = '.' then begin
      i := i + 1;
      if nsig = 0 then
         while gnbchar(s, i, c) = '0' do begin
            nafter := nafter + 1;
            i := i + 1
         end;
      while gnbchar(s, i, c) in ['0'..'9'] do begin
```

```
              if nsig < REGSIZE - 1 then
                 rawfrac := 10 * rawfrac + ord(c) - 48;
              nsig := nsig + 1;
              nafter := nafter + 1;
              i := i + 1
           end
        end;
        if gnbchar(s, i, c) in ['E', 'e'] then begin
           i := i + 1;
           epart := HUGE;
           if stof(s, i, 0, f) then begin
              negepart := (f < 0);
              if negepart then
                 f := -f;
              if f < HUGE then
                 epart := trunc(f)
           end
        end;
        if (nsig < REGSIZE - 1) then
           rawfrac := rawfrac * ten[REGSIZE - 1 - nsig];
        if negnum then
           rawfrac := -rawfrac;
        if negepart then
           rawexpo := nsig - nafter + EXCESS - epart
        else
           rawexpo := nsig - nafter + EXCESS + epart;
        stox := xnorm(rawexpo, rawfrac, x)
end;
```

Somewhat surprisingly, the toughest part of **stox** is guarding against a situation where the user enters a huge trailing exponent part. **stox** uses a "brute-force" solution: it initializes the exponent **epart** to the large value **HUGE** (9999) and uses **stof** to accumulate the exponent. If **stof** fails to convert the exponent (by returning **FALSE**) or the exponent is bigger than **HUGE**, **epart** retains the value **HUGE**; otherwise, **epart** is assigned to the value actually seen. In any case, **xnorm** returns the appropriate error code whenever necessary.

Converting an Extended Real To a String

The **xtos** routine converts an extended real number into a string. It simply calls the appropriate routine depending on whether a fixed-point or scientific formatting mode is desired.

```
function xtos(x: xreal; fmt: format; ndigs: integer; var s: string): xresult;
{ Convert extended real to string }

{----------------------------}
{ Modules to be inserted here: }
{       xtosci               }
{       xtofix               }
{----------------------------}
```

```
begin { xtos }
   case fmt of
      FIXEDPOINT:
         xtos := xtofix(x, ndigs, s);
      SCIENTIFIC:
         xtos := xtosci(x, ndigs, s)
   end
end;
```

Since whatever rounding is done to the input **xreal** might cause overflow, **xtos** must return an **xresult** indicating to its caller whether the translation worked.

Fixed-point formatting is accomplished by the **xtofix** routine. The pseudo-code looks like this:

```
begin
   if number is too large to be presented compactly
      convert to scientific notation
   else if number is too small to be presented accurately
      convert to scientific notation
   else
      if number has more than ndigs digits after decimal
         round number to ndigs digits
      convert to fixed-point
end
```

Rounding is a matter of adding an appropriate factor to the number and then truncating to the appropriate number of digits. For example, if three digits after the decimal are desired, we add the number 0.0005 (after first converting it into an extended real). After the rounding factor is added, we divide the number's **frac** part by a factor of 10 large enough to truncate digits more than **ndigs** digits after the decimal point. Then we use the **ftos** routine from the previous chapter to convert the resulting number to a string.

This turns into the following Pascal code:

```
function xtofix(x: xreal; ndigs: integer; var s: string): xresult;
{ Convert extended real to fixed point format }

var
   negnum: boolean;
   result: xresult;
   round: xreal;

begin { xtofix }
   if x.expo - EXCESS > FIXSIZE - ndigs then { too big }
      result := xtosci(x, FIXSIZE - 1, s)
   else if (x.expo - EXCESS < 1 - ndigs) and (x.frac <> 0) then { too small }
      result := xtosci(x, FIXSIZE - 1, s)
   else begin
      result := OK;
      if x.expo - EXCESS < FIXSIZE - ndigs then begin { round }
         negnum := x.frac < 0;
         if negnum then
```

```
                x.frac := -x.frac;
            round.frac := 5 * ten[FIXSIZE - 1];
            round.expo := EXCESS - ndigs;
            result := xadd(x, round, x);
            if negnum then
                x.frac := -x.frac;
        end;
        if result = OK then
            ftos(x.frac div ten[FIXSIZE - ndigs - x.expo + EXCESS], 0, ndigs, s)
    end;
    xtofix := result
end;
```

A similar method is used in **xtosci** to convert a number to scientific notation. Here is the pseudo-code:

```
begin
    if fewer than FIXSIZE digits are desired in answer and number is non-zero
        round number to ndigs digits
    convert frac to string
    convert expo to string
    combine into final result
end
```

The **ftos** routine carries out the drudgery of converting numbers to strings. Here is the Pascal code:

```
function xtosci(x: xreal; ndigs: integer; var s: string): xresult;
{ Convert extended real to scientific notation }
var
    negnum: boolean;
    result: xresult;
    rawfrac: register;
    rawexpo: integer;
    s1, s2: string;
begin { xtosci }
    result := OK;
    if (ndigs < FIXSIZE - 1) and (x.frac <> 0) then begin { round }
        negnum := (x.frac < 0);
        if negnum then
            x.frac := -x.frac;
        rawfrac := x.frac * ten[FIXSIZE + 1] + 5 * ten[2 * FIXSIZE - ndigs - 1];
        rawexpo := x.expo;
        result := xnorm(rawexpo, rawfrac, x);
        if negnum then
            x.frac := -x.frac
    end;
    if result = OK then begin
        ftos(x.frac div ten[FIXSIZE - ndigs - 1], 0, ndigs, s1);
        if x.frac = 0 then
            s2 := '0'
        else
            ftos(x.expo - EXCESS - 1, 0, 0, s2);
        s := concat(s1, 'e', s2)
    end;
    xtosci := result
end;
```

Variable Storage and Retrieval

We have left the simplest task for last: storing and retrieving variables. Whenever an assignment statement is seen, **evalstmt** calls **assign** to assign to the identifier **id** the calculated value of the rest of the statement, **x**.

```
procedure assign(id: identifier; x: xreal);
{ Assign value to identifier }
{-----------------------------}
{ Modules to be inserted here: }
{          insertnode          }
{-----------------------------}
begin { assign }
   insertnode(root, id, x);
end;
```

assign is simply a call to **insertnode**, which searches the tree for a node containing the variable **id**. If **id** is not found in the tree, **insertnode** adds a new node to the tree containing **id** and its value **x**. If **id** *is* found in the tree, **insertnode** just changes the value of **id**'s node to **x**.

Since a binary tree is an inherently recursive data structure, **insertnode** is also recursive.

```
procedure insertnode(var p: nodeptr; var id: identifier; var x: xreal);
{ Add identifier to tree or change value of existing identifier }
begin { insertnode }
   if p = NIL then begin { id not in tree, add it by creating new node }
      new(p);
      p^.name := id;
      p^.value := x;
      p^.left := NIL;
      p^.right := NIL
      end
   else if id < p^.name then { search left subtree }
      insertnode(p^.left, id, x)
   else if id > p^.name then { search right subtree }
      insertnode(p^.right, id, x)
   else { Identifier found, change old value }
      p^.value := x
end;
```

Recursive routines are as close as programming gets to magic: they are extremely concise, simple routines that can accomplish complex results with seemingly little effort. You have to watch *very* carefully to see that what is really going on is not magic at all. As a result, most people find recursive routines either extremely beautiful or extremely confusing. If you are confused, read the following paragraphs carefully for an explanation of how **insertnode** works.

In English, **insertnode**'s logic works as follows: if **p**, the node pointer passed to **insertnode**, is **NIL** (points nowhere), the search has failed. Create a new node to which **p** points via the standard procedure **new**, and assign the new node's fields to the identifier's name and value. Also set the new node's **left** and **right** subtree pointers to **NIL**. (Note that since **p** is a **var** parameter, its new value is returned to the calling routine. What would happen if it was not returned? Remember that **root**, the binary tree's root, is initialized to **NIL**.)

If the node pointer passed to **insertnode** is not **NIL**, examine the node to which it points. If **id** is less than the identifier field of the node (**p^.name**), we have to search the left subtree (pointed to by **p^ .left**). This search can be done by simply calling **insertnode** recursively. Similarly, if **id** is *greater* than **p^ .name**, call **insertnode** to search further, starting at the node's *right* subtree.

If **id** is neither less than nor greater than **p^.name**, then it must *equal* **p^.name**. We have discovered that **id** was previously added to the tree at this point. In this case, the node's **value** field is set to the new value **x**.

That explains putting variables into the tree. But what about retrieving their values as required by **evalfact**? The function **evalid** does the job.

```
function evalid(id: identifier; var x: xreal): xresult;
{ Get value of identifier }
var
    p: nodeptr;
{-----------------------------}
{ Modules to be inserted here: }
{         searchtree          }
{-----------------------------}
begin { evalid }
   p := searchtree(root, id);
   if p = NIL then begin { not found }
      remark(concat('Undefined identifier: ', id));
      x.expo := MINEXP;
      x.frac := 0
   end
   else
      x := p^.value;
   evalid := OK
end;
```

evalid calls **searchtree** to look for the identifier **id** in the tree; if the identifier is not found, **searchtree** returns a **NIL** pointer. In this case, **evalid** informs the user that the variable is undefined and returns a value of 0 for the variable's value.

If the identifier *is* in the tree, **searchtree** returns a pointer to its node and **evalid** returns the node's value field as the value of the identifier:

```
function searchtree(p: nodeptr; var id: identifier): nodeptr;
{ Search tree for identifier }
begin { searchtree }
   if p = NIL then { not in tree }
      searchtree := NIL
   else if id < p^.name then { search left subtree }
      searchtree := searchtree(p^.left, id)
   else if id > p^.name then { search right subtree }
      searchtree := searchtree(p^.right, id)
   else { found it }
      searchtree := p
end;
```

As might have been expected, **searchtree**'s logic is similar to that of **insertnode**.

Note that both **insertnode** and **searchtree** rely on the fact that in Apple and UCSD Pascal, strings of arbitrary length can be directly compared with the relational operators (>, <, >=, <=, <>, and =). This is a non-standard extension of Standard Pascal's string comparisons. In Standard Pascal, two strings (**packed array**s **of char**) can be compared with relational operators only if they have the same declared length.

Suggestions

There are many different ways to improve the version of **calc** we have presented here.

Efficiency   There is no doubt that **calc** is not a lightning-quick calculator, although it is probably fast enough for most users' needs. Should you decide to improve **calc**'s efficiency, go about it systematically. Determine in which routines the program spends most of its time; these are the routines to consider optimizing. There is no point in speeding up a routine in which **calc** spends only a small percentage of its time. Sometimes this can be done with simple common sense and previous experience; other times it requires direct measurement.

Some versions of Pascal offer an option that automatically keeps track of how many times each of the routines in the program is called. This option can be of help in discovering which routines to try optimizing first. If your version does not provide such a feature, you can easily add statements to the code that accomplish the same thing; for example, a "brute-force" method would be to print the name of each routine as it is entered. Or the program could maintain an internal counter array, one element per measured routine. In this way, each routine would increment the corresponding element on entry.

If your system has a real-time clock that is readable from a program, you can accumulate the total amount of time spent in each routine.

After any modification to the code is made, measure the resulting increase in speed; this allows you to determine which methods work best for increasing efficiency.

Error Recovery As previously stated, **calc** simply scans the input string as far as it can and reports whatever numeric result it winds up with. You could improve **calc**'s handling of erroneous and nonsense input; for example, if **calc** stops evaluating a statement before its end, warn the user of this occurrence and somehow indicate where in the string the evaluation stopped.

Reliability Although **calc** is not affected by overflows or other calculation errors, there are problems with the way memory is handled. Each variable defined by the user takes up memory. Procedures and functions also use a certain amount of memory each time they are called (although the memory is freed again on exit from the subroutine). As a result, there is the possibility that **calc** may cause an out-of-memory execution error if a large number of variables are defined or a very complex expression is evaluated. The challenge to the programmer is to allow **calc** to handle such occurrences in a civilized manner.

Adding Features The most obvious drawback of **calc** is its lack of functions. As in most programming languages, the expression

```
SIN(X)
```

should evaluate to the sine of the variable **x**. Other trigonometric functions, logarithms, exponentials, square roots, and so forth should be added. **calc** could also use an exponentiation operator so the user could make calculations like

```
2 ^ 3 = 8.00
[S2] 8 ^ 8 = 1.68e7
```

The first step, of course, is to decide where any new function or operator would appear in the syntax diagrams. Then the appropriate section of code can be modified to add the new feature. Do not forget to add new error codes if the new features can generate errors not already considered (for example, taking the square root of a negative number).

Other features might be useful. An *adjustable radix* would be helpful to programmers, allowing them to express results in hexadecimal, octal, or other bases. An optional capability to carry out computations on *complex numbers* would be considered useful by some.

Additional possibilities could include adding a command that would cause **calc** to display all currently defined identifiers; adding a command that would send nicely formatted input formulas and results to the printer, making **calc** analogous to a printing calculator; adding an editing capability that would allow the user to recalculate the previous formula with slight changes; and adding commands to save and load currently defined variables to and from a disk file.

As a very open-ended project, a *programming capability* could be added to **calc** to allow the user to specify repetitive calculations, alternate decisions, and so on. You could also add the capability to load and save **calc** "programs" on disk.

Recommended Reading

Doing arithmetic on computers is thoroughly explained in *Seminumerical Algorithms* by D. Knuth (Addison-Wesley, 1981). All the arithmetic routines used in **calc** are based on algorithms given there. Readers interested in modifying these algorithms should consult Knuth's book.

The general subject of language analysis is covered in a more formal manner in Chapter 5 of *Algorithms + Data Structures = Programs* by N. Wirth (Prentice-Hall, 1976).

Nearly all introductory books on Pascal include some material on binary trees. *Data Structures Using Pascal* by A. Tenenbaum and M. Augenstein (Prentice-Hall, 1981) contains lots of information on binary trees and other popular data structures. Other books with material about binary trees include *Programming in Pascal* by P. Grogono (Addison-Wesley, 1981) and Wirth's book mentioned previously.

FIVE

Text File Tools

In this chapter we will develop a number of routines for manipulating *text files:* programs, documents, or other human-readable information stored on the computer. We will also build **print**, a utility program to print text files.

Most programmers, and even most computer users, have at least an intuitive idea that a text file is a file containing characters arranged into lines of arbitrary length. Text files are the primary method used by computers to store information that can be read by humans. As a result, many programs are designed to use text files: *editors* allow users to create and modify text files, *compilers* translate program text files into code the computer can more easily understand, *text formatters* rearrange text files into more eye-pleasing formats, and so on.

Since text files are so commonplace on computer systems, it is worth expending some effort to make our tools for working with them as good as possible. However, the limitations of both the Pascal language and our particular version of Pascal force us to make trade-offs between the different "goodness" criteria discussed in Chapter One.

Trade-Offs

One set of trade-offs results from Standard Pascal's built-in I/O procedures, which are not designed for interactive systems. As previously noted, Standard Pascal offers no way to access a file by its name from within a program; for example, this prevents us from writing a program that allows the user to specify interactively a certain file for input. As a further drawback, Standard Pascal provides no method to detect errors while reading or writing files; this prohibits portable code that allows users to recover from such errors.

Most versions of Pascal offer solutions to these Standard Pascal limitations, but these solutions are non-portable. This is the trade-off: in order to improve our programs' flexibility and reliability, we are forced to sacrifice a certain amount of portability.

A second set of trade-offs has to do with *efficiency*. Apple Pascal's text file I/O using the built-in procedures **read** and **write** is impossibly slow. Dramatic increases in efficiency are possible by using non-portable routines provided in Apple Pascal to read and write "blocks" of text instead of single characters or lines. Further gains are possible by recoding some Pascal routines in assembly language. (We will later present measurements on these gains.) Thus, this trade-off involves choosing between increased efficiency and decreased portability.

As an additional drawback, using such non-portable language features and programming "tricks" causes the program code to become much less clear than it would be if we had simply used the built-in **read** and **write** routines. Limitations and requirements of Apple Pascal cause an additional loss of clarity.

Our choice is to maximize the flexibility, reliability, and efficiency of our text file tools; unfortunately (but necessarily), this decreases their portability, and to a lesser extent, their clarity.

We will try to minimize our portability problems by limiting our tools to a small number of "primitive" routines that can be easily rewritten for different environments. Table 5-1 contains a list of our text file tools and an informal description of what each routine does.

Table 5-1. Text File Tools

Module	Purpose
tfopen	Open an existing text file for input
tfcreate	Create a new text file for output
tfread	Read a string from a text file
tfwrite	Write a string to a text file
tfclose	Close a previously opened or created text file
gettfname	Obtain the name of a text file from the user

Apple Pascal Text File Format

When we use Standard Pascal's **read** and **write** routines for text file I/O, we do not have to worry about the special format placed by the local operating system on text files. Instead, **read** and **write** are responsible for such considerations. Unfortunately, our decision to maximize efficiency requires us to learn the details of the way text files are represented by the Apple Pascal operating system. (Most, if not all, of the following details also apply to UCSD Pascal systems.)

- Apple Pascal disk files are made up of 512-byte *blocks*. Text files on disk are special cases of such data files. Each text file is made up of 1024-byte *pages*, with each page consisting of two blocks.
- The first page of the file contains no text; instead, it contains data used by the system editor. Apple Pascal's built-in text file routines handle this header page automatically.
- Each subsequent page of the text file contains the actual text. Individual lines are not split between pages; there is an integral number of lines on each page. Any leftover space at the end of a page is padded with <NUL> (ASCII 0) characters.
- The end of each line is marked by a <CR> (ASCII 13) character.
- Leading blanks at the beginning of a line are optionally encoded in the following way: the first character in the line is a <DLE> (ASCII 16); the next byte contains the number of leading blanks plus 32 (mod 256). The primary purpose of this leading blank encryption is to save space on the disk.

Text File Data Structures

Our primary concerns in designing our text file tools are flexibility, reliability, and efficiency. To ensure reliability, all the routines return some sort of error code to allow programs using them to recover from unpredictable errors. For efficiency's sake, Apple Pascal's **blockread** and **blockwrite** routines are used to read and write pages from text files on disk.

The following code defines the data types used by our text file routines:

```
<const>
  GOODIO = 0;
  ENDFILE = -1;
  PAGESIZE = 1024;
  MAXFNAME = 23;
```

```
<type>
   iostatus = integer;
   tfile = file;
   page = packed array [0..PAGESIZE] of char;
   tfrec = record
      buf: page;
      bufptr: integer;
      mode: (RDMODE, WRMODE);
   end;
   filename = string[MAXFNAME];
```

Our routines return error codes as variables of the type **iostatus**. A value of 0 (to which we give the mnemonic **GOODIO**) indicates no error. A value of −1 (to which we give the mnemonic **ENDFILE**) means the end of the input file was reached while reading. All other **iostatus** values are considered to indicate errors. We could also have defined **iostatus** this way:

```
<type>
   iostatus = (GOODIO, ENDFILE, ERR);
```

This method would have eliminated the constant declarations for **GOODIO** and **ENDFILE**; however, we would also have lost any information about what kind of error occurred. In our design, we allow the possibility of different error codes for different errors, so the calling program can take different actions depending on the specific error seen. We will present an example later.

blockread and **blockwrite** require us to use a special Apple Pascal file type called the *untyped* file. This file type (briefly used in Chapter Three) allows us to view any disk file as simply a sequence of 512-byte blocks; the operating system does not "know" whether we are accessing a text file, a data file, or some other kind of file.

We keep information concerning a text file in a record of type **tfrec**. The record contains a 1025-byte buffer (**buf**) that holds the current page of the file in memory. Only the first 1024 bytes of the buffer (elements 0 through 1023) are actually read or written. The 1025th byte (element 1024) is used as a *sentinel* signaling the end of the page for the text input routines. This sentinel byte always contains a <NUL>, thus guaranteeing that the page ends with at least one <NUL>. (This byte is required in the case where an input file page itself contains no <NUL> padding, that is, when the text lines exactly fill the 1024 bytes of the page.) An integer (the variable **bufptr**) holds the position in the buffer where the next line is to be either read or written. The variable **mode** indicates whether the file is currently being read (**RDMODE**) or written (**WRMODE**).

Our data structures would have been cleaner if we had been able to keep *all* the information about a given file in the record, as in the following:

```
<type>
   tfrec = record
      f: file;
      buf: page;
      bufptr: integer;
      mode: iomode
   end;
```

But we are unable to do this. This construction is illegal in Apple Pascal (although it is allowed in Standard Pascal) because Apple Pascal does not allow records to contain file types. Arrays of files and pointers to files are not permitted either.

Finally, file names are stored as strings with a maximum length of 23 characters, the upper limit imposed by the Apple Pascal operating system.

tfopen

The following routine opens a named text file for input:

```
function tfopen(var f: tfile; var tf: tfrec; name: filename;
                                    var status: iostatus): iostatus;
{ Open text file for input }
var
   nbr: integer;
begin { tfopen }
   {$i-}
   reset(f, name);
   status := ioresult;
   if status = GOODIO then
      with tf do begin
         nbr := blockread(f, buf, 2, 2);
         status := ioresult;
         if (status = GOODIO) and (nbr <> 2) then
            status := ENDFILE;
         buf[PAGESIZE] := chr(0);
         bufptr := 0;
         mode := RDMODE
      end;
   tfopen := status
   {$i+}
end;
```

We discussed the Apple Pascal built-in routines **reset** and **ioresult** as well as the compiler directives {$i+} and {$i−} in Chapter Three.

In addition, **tfopen** uses Apple Pascal's built-in **blockread** function to read the first page containing text from the file. (Remember that the first two blocks in the file do not contain any text.) The call

```
nbr := blockread(f, buf, i, j)
```

reads **i** blocks from the untyped file **f** into the buffer array **buf** starting with the **j**th block in the file (where the first block in the file is considered to be block number 0). The **buf** parameter may be subscripted to indicate a starting position in the array. The starting-block parameter **j** is optional; if it is absent, the next sequential block(s) in the file is read. The routine returns the number of blocks actually read as the function's result. When the last block of the file is read, the function **eof(f)** becomes **TRUE**; otherwise, it is **FALSE**.

After **tfopen** reads the page into memory, it sets the buffer pointer to point to the first character in the page. As mentioned previously, the last character in the buffer acts as a sentinel; **tfopen** sets it to <NUL>. Finally, the routine sets the mode to **RDMODE**, indicating we are reading from the file.

If an error occurs during either the **reset** or the **blockread** operations, **tfopen** returns the error code obtained from **ioresult** to the calling routine, both as the **var** parameter **status** and as the function's result. If, for some reason, no I/O error is signaled from **ioresult** but **blockread** tells us that it did not read two blocks as expected, **tfopen** returns an error code of **ENDFILE** to its calling routine.

tfcreate

The routine for creating a new file for output is very similar to **tfopen**:

```
function tfcreate(var f: tfile; var tf: tfrec; name: filename;
                                 var status: iostatus): iostatus;
{ Create new text file for output }

var
   nbw: integer;

begin { tfcreate }
   {$i-}
   rewrite(f, name);
   status := ioresult;
   if status = GOODIO then
      with tf do begin
         fillchar(buf, PAGESIZE, chr(0));
         nbw := blockwrite(f, buf, 2);
         status := ioresult;
         if (status = GOODIO) and (nbw <> 2) then
            status := 8; { No room }
```

```
        mode := WRMODE;
        bufptr := 0
      end;
  tfcreate := status
  {$i+}
end;
```

tfcreate must write the first two blocks of the text file in order to be compatible with Apple Pascal's text file format. We choose to fill these two blocks with <NUL> characters; fortunately, this simple solution works.

The built-in routine **rewrite(f, name)** attempts to create a new file called **name** associated with the file variable **f**. An error occurs if an illegal or inaccessible name is specified.

The built-in routine **blockwrite** is the inverse of **blockread**. The call

```
nbw := blockwrite(f, buf, i, j)
```

writes **i** blocks to the untyped file **f** from the **buf** array, starting at the **j**th block of the file. The **buf** parameter may be subscripted to indicate a starting position in the array. If the parameter **j** is absent, the next sequential block(s) in the file is written into. The number of blocks actually written is returned as the function's result.

We also use the built-in **fillchar** routine to fill the **buf** array quickly with <NUL> characters. The call

```
fillchar(buf, i, c)
```

assigns **i** bytes of the **buf** array to the character **c**. The **buf** parameter may be subscripted to indicate a starting position in the array. A more portable **for** loop could also be used here, but **fillchar** is much faster.

tfcreate returns any error code both as the **var** parameter **status** and as the function's result. If **ioresult** fails to signal an I/O error but **blockwrite** tells us two blocks were not written to the file, **tfcreate** returns a value of 8 as an error code. This is the Apple/UCSD Pascal error code for no room on the disk.

tfclose

When a program is finished using a text file, it closes the file by calling the **tfclose** routine.

```
function tfclose(var f: tfile; var tf: tfrec; var status: iostatus): iostatus;
{ Close text file }
var
   nbw: integer;
begin { tfclose }
   {$i-}
   status := GOODIO;
   with tf do
      if mode = WRMODE then begin
         if bufptr > 0 then begin
            fillchar(buf[bufptr], PAGESIZE - bufptr, chr(0));
            nbw := blockwrite(f, buf, 2);
            status := ioresult
         end;
         close(f, LOCK);
         if status = GOODIO then
            status := ioresult
      end
      else begin { Read mode }
         close(f);
         status := ioresult
      end;
   tfclose := status
   {$i+}
end;
```

If the file is being written, **tfclose** checks if the page in memory contains any lines not yet written to disk; if it does, the last page is padded with <NUL>s and written to the file. In any case, the file is closed using the Apple Pascal built-in procedure **close** with the second parameter set to **LOCK**; this action makes sure the new file appears in the disk directory.

If the file was being read, the **close** routine is called with no second parameter.

In either case, any error code is returned both as the **var** parameter **status** and as the function's result.

tfread

The routine **tfread** reads the next line of text from a text file into a string variable. This routine must check for two special situations in addition to normal error checking.

The first situation is the end-of-file, and the solution is relatively simple. After the last line of the file is read, subsequent calls to **tfread** return **ENDFILE** as the I/O status instead of the normal **GOODIO**.

The second situation is not as obvious but is almost as important. What happens if the text file line has more characters than can fit in the string? We do not want **tfread** to silently ignore any characters beyond the string's maximum length. Neither do we want **tfread** to return the too long line as two or more strings without any signal to the calling program about what is really going on.

Our solution is the following: normally, **tfread** appends characters from the page buffer to the end of the string until either the maximum length of the string is reached or the <CR> end-of-line character is seen. The <CR> is also appended to the end of the string if there is room for it. The routine calling **tfread** will thus be able to detect a line that is too long; such a line simply will not have a <CR> character at the end. The remainder of a too long line may be retrieved with additional calls to **tfread**; there may be as many calls as necessary to read the line's <CR> end-of-line marker.

Here is the **tfread** routine:

```
function tfread(var f: tfile; var tf: tfrec; var s: string; maxlen: integer;
                                             var status: iostatus): iostatus;
{ Read string from text file }
var
   nbr: integer;
begin { tfread }
   {$i-}
   status := GOODIO;
   with tf do begin
      grabline(buf, bufptr, s, maxlen);
      if length(s) = 0 then
         if eof(f) then
            status := ENDFILE
         else begin
            nbr := blockread(f, buf, 2);
            status := ioresult;
            if (status = GOODIO) and (nbr <> 2) then
               status := ENDFILE;
            bufptr := 0;
            grabline(buf, bufptr, s, maxlen)
         end
   end;
   tfread := status
   {$i+}
end;
```

The input string is returned as the **var** parameter **s**. The routine calling **tfread** specifies the maximum number of characters the string **s** can accept in the parameter **maxlen**. This allows the calling program to adjust the capacity of the input string depending on the application. As usual, any error code is returned both as the function's result and the **var** parameter **status**.

tfread first calls **grabline** to transfer the next line from the buffer **buf** into the string variable **s**. Most often, that is all that needs to be done. If the buffer is empty, **grabline** returns a null (zero-length) string. In this case, **tfread** checks the **eof** function to see if the last page of the file has already been read. If **eof(f)** is **TRUE**, the end-of-file has been reached; **tfread**

returns **ENDFILE** to the calling routine to signal that fact. If **eof(f)** is **FALSE**, there is at least one more page to read. In that case, **tfread** calls **blockread** to get the next page, resets the buffer pointer, and finally calls **grabline** again to get the first line from the new page into the string.

We will eventually code the **grabline** routine in the Apple II's 6502 assembly language. First, however, we present it in Pascal. This approach has a number of benefits: first, it enables us to design and debug the code's logic before it is translated into assembly language; second, readers with other computers can either use the Pascal routine directly or use it with the 6502 code as a stepping stone to code the routine in their own computers' assembly language.

grabline is sufficiently complex to warrant writing it in pseudo-code first. The primary complication in **grabline** is in turning any <DLE> blank encryption in the text file into actual blank characters in the returned string. The following first rough sketch of **grabline** ignores this detail:

```
begin
   set string = '' (null string)
   repeat
      get next character from buffer
      if character is not <NUL>
         append it to string
   until(character is <NUL>) or (character is <CR>) or (max length is reached)
end
```

grabline appends characters to the end of the string until either a <NUL> character is seen (indicating the end of the current page buffer), a <CR> character is seen (indicating the end of the line), or the maximum string length is reached.

The operation "get next character from buffer" is where the <DLE> encryption is handled. To make **grabline** as reliable as possible, we have to design it to correctly handle situations that "should never happen." Such situations could be (1) an encryption in the middle or at the end of a line, (2) two or more consecutive encryptions, or (3) an encryption specifying more blanks than can fit in the output string. When all these possibilities are taken into account, the pseudo-code for the "get next character" operation looks like this:

```
get next character from buffer:
   { Assume bp is current position in buffer, c is returned character }

   c = buf[bp]
   bp = bp + 1
   while c is a <DLE> character
```

```
        if buf[bp] is a <SPACE> (no more blanks in encryption)
            c = buf[bp + 1]
            bp = bp + 2 (point bp at next character)
        else (more blanks to decode)
            c = <SPACE>
            decrement buf[bp] (mod 256)
            bp = bp - 1 (point bp back at <DLE> for next time)
end-while
```

Here is **grabline** in Pascal:

```
procedure grabline(var buf: page; var i: integer; var s: string;
                                                   maxlen: integer);
{ Get line from page buffer, decode DLE encryption }
var
    len: integer;
    done: boolean;
    c: char;
begin { grabline }
    len := 0;
    s := '';
    repeat
        c := buf[i];
        i := i + 1;
        while c = chr(16) do
            if buf[i] = ' ' then begin
                c := buf[i + 1];
                i := i + 2
            end
            else begin
                buf[i] := chr((ord(buf[i]) + 255) mod 256);
                i := i - 1;
                c := ' '
            end;
        done := (c = chr(0));
        if not done then begin
            addchar(s, c, maxlen);
            len := len + 1;
            done := (c = chr(13)) or (len >= maxlen)
        end
    until done
end;
```

We coded the operation that decrements the buffer character in **grabline** as

```
buf[i] := chr((ord(buf[i]) + 255) mod 256)
```

instead of the more natural

```
buf[i] := chr((ord(buf[i]) - 1) mod 256)
```

This was done because Apple Pascal implements the **mod** operator in a non-standard manner. In Apple Pascal, the expression (-1) **mod** 256 evaluates to 1, not 255 as required by ISO Standard Pascal. To avoid this problem, we are always careful to ensure arguments to **mod** are nonnegative.

In an actual program source text, the **grabline** routine would probably be nested inside the **tfread** function.

tfwrite

The routine to write a string into the text file, **tfwrite**, is the inverse of **tfread**:

```
function tfwrite(var f: tfile; var tf: tfrec; var s: string;
                                  var status: iostatus): iostatus;
{ Write string to text file }
var
   nbw: integer;
begin { tfwrite }
   {$i-}
   status := GOODIO;
   crunch(s);
   with tf do begin
      if bufptr + length(s) > PAGESIZE then begin
         fillchar(buf[bufptr], PAGESIZE - bufptr, chr(0));
         nbw := blockwrite(f, buf, 2);
         status := ioresult;
         if (status = GOODIO) and (nbw <> 2) then
            status := 8;    { No room }
         bufptr := 0
      end;
      dropline(buf, bufptr, s)
   end;
   tfwrite := status
   {$i+}
end;
```

tfwrite first calls **crunch** to encode leading blanks in the output string. Then **tfwrite** checks if there is room in the current page buffer to hold the output line; if there is no room, it pads the page buffer with <NUL>s and writes the page to the output file. The buffer pointer is returned to the beginning of the buffer. **tfwrite** uses **dropline** to copy the characters from the string into the buffer.

Here is the **crunch** routine:

```
procedure crunch(var s: string);
{ Encode leading blanks in string }
var
   i: integer;
   c: char;
```

```
begin { crunch }
   i := 1;
   c := gnbchar(s, i, c);
   if i > 3 then begin
      s[1] := chr(16);
      s[2] := chr((i + 287) mod 256);
      moveleft(s[i], s[3], length(s) - i + 1);
      {$r-}
      s[0] := chr(length(s) - i + 3)
      {$r+}
   end
end;
```

Since the purpose of encoding the string's leading blanks is to save space on the disk, we only do so if there are three or more of them. Encoding zero or one leading blank actually makes the string longer; encoding two blanks leaves the string the same length as it was before. We will code **crunch** in assembly language later in this chapter.

crunch uses the Apple Pascal built-in routine **moveleft**, which moves an arbitrary number of bytes from one place in memory to another. The call

```
moveleft(source, destination, nbytes)
```

moves **nbytes** bytes starting at the location specified by **source** to the location specified by **destination**. The variables that specify **source** and **destination** may be any type (except a file type), and they may be subscripted to indicate starting positions. The copying begins with the first byte of the source range and works toward the end. As with **fillchar**, we could have used a portable **for** loop here, but **moveleft** is faster.

The **dropline** procedure moves the characters in the string to the page buffer and updates the buffer pointer to point to the next position available in the buffer. We will eventually code **dropline** in assembly language, as we did with **grabline** and **crunch**. Here is the procedure in Pascal:

```
procedure dropline(var buf: page; var i: integer; var s: string);
{ Put string in output buffer }
begin { dropline }
   if length(s) > 0 then begin
      moveleft(s[1], buf[i], length(s));
      i := i + length(s)
   end
end;
```

gettfname

Apple Pascal, like other operating systems, has unique and non-portable rules about legal file names. **gettfname** uses **getstring** to obtain a text file name from the user.

```
procedure gettfname(var name:filename; col, row:integer; default:filename);
{ Get text file name from user }
begin { gettfname }
   {$v-}
   getstring(name, MAXFNAME, col, row, default,
                    ['!'..'~'] - ['$', '[', '=', '?'], TRUE);
   {$v+}
   if (length(name) > 0) and (pos('.TEXT', name) = 0) and
                             (length(name) <= MAXFNAME - 5) then begin
      name := concat(name, '.TEXT');
      posstr(name, col, row)
   end
end;
```

gettfname also uses **pos**, a built-in Apple and UCSD Pascal routine we have not yet discussed. The function call

```
i := pos(sub, s)
```

searches the string **s** (from the beginning) for the first occurrence of the string **sub**. (In **gettfname**, **pos** searches for the string .TEXT in the entered file name.) If **pos** is successful, it returns the index in **s** where **sub** is seen. If **sub** does not appear in **s**, **pos** returns 0.

gettfname imposes the following rules on text file name input: the user is limited to **MAXFNAME** characters (23 in this case); all alphabetic characters are forced to uppercase; all printable characters except spaces, dollar signs, left brackets, equal signs, and question marks are allowed in the name. These restrictions reflect both the internal conversions Apple Pascal does itself and the rules of other programs in the system. Finally, if the normal Apple Pascal text file suffix .TEXT does not appear in the name and there is room for it, **gettfname** appends it to the end of the input string.

Interested readers might wish to modify **gettfname** to do more rigorous checking, thus making it more difficult for the user to enter an illegal file name. Specifically, the current version does no checking on the entered name's internal syntax, thus allowing the user to enter invalid names such as **WAYTOOLONGVOL:A.TEXT** or **N:O:N:S:E:N:S:E.TEXT**. Be sure, however, not to disallow any *legal* names. You will also want to consider what the most likely user input errors are.

(What input errors do *you* make? If you have ever observed other people using interactive programs, what input errors do *they* commonly make?)

Assembly Language

Our first step in translating **grabline**, **crunch**, and **dropline** into assembly language is to declare them in the Pascal host program as **external** functions or procedures. **grabline** is declared as

```
procedure grabline(var buf: page; var bufptr: integer; var s: string;
                                            maxlen: integer); external;
{ Get line from input buffer }
```

dropline is declared this way:

```
procedure dropline(var buf:page; var bufptr:integer; var s:string); external;
{ Put string in output buffer }
```

crunch is declared this way:

```
procedure crunch(var s: string); external;
{ Encode leading blanks in string }
```

The logical placement for these declarations would be to nest them inside the routines in which they are called. However, Apple Pascal does not allow declarations for external routines to be nested. The next best choice is to declare the routines just above the routines in which they are used.

We cannot consider all the many details of the methods used to incorporate assembly language routines in a Pascal program; most details would only apply to our particular version of Pascal. Specifically, we will not discuss the method used to assemble the routines and link them to our Pascal host program. (For similar reasons, we have not described how to go about compiling the Pascal programs we are presenting.) We assume that interested readers already know how to accomplish such feats, or that they can learn to carry them out.

Nor will we discuss the 6502's, or any other CPU's architecture or instruction set. Again we assume readers either know or can find out the relevant details for their own computer systems.

We will, however, discuss the method Apple Pascal uses to communicate with an assembly language routine; this information is vital to understanding the assembly code presented later in this chapter.

A calling program pushes parameters to an assembly language subroutine onto the 6502's stack in the order in which they are declared in the subroutine's parameter list. (Therefore, they must be popped off the stack in the reverse order.) Apple Pascal also pushes an additional four bytes onto the stack on top of these parameters if the assembly subroutine is declared as a function; these extra bytes must be discarded on entry to the function. The top two bytes of the stack contain the subroutine's return address (the memory location to which program control returns when the subroutine is finished).

On exit, if the assembly language subroutine is declared as a function, the function result must be pushed back onto the stack. The assembly language subroutine (whether declared as a procedure or a function) must also push the two bytes containing the subroutine's return address back onto the top of the stack.

The method used by the calling program to pass individual parameters to a subroutine depends on how the parameters are declared in the **external** declaration in the Pascal host. A **var** parameter is always passed by its address (more precisely, the stack contains the address of the variable's first byte). Record variables, array variables, and strings are also always passed by their addresses. Other data types (integers, Booleans, characters, reals, subrange types, scalar types, pointers, sets, and long integers) declared as value (non-**var**) parameters are passed by value (that is, their values are pushed onto the stack).

We will only be passing addresses or integers to our assembly routines; both take up two bytes and are stored in memory with the less significant byte preceding the more significant byte. They are stored on the stack with the less significant byte on top; the less significant byte is the first popped from the stack and the last pushed onto the stack.

The assembly language source text consists of optional *macro definitions* followed by the assembly language subroutines. The first macro definition is for **pop**, which takes a 16-bit (two-byte) value from the 6502's stack and stores it in two adjacent memory locations.

```
        .macro pop
;
;       macro to pop 16-bit argument
;
        pla
        sta %1
        pla
        sta %1+1
        .endm
```

Macro definitions are simply shorthand definitions of commonly occurring operations. Instead of repeatedly writing a long sequence of 6502 instructions to carry out a common operation, we instead use a previously defined macro. As an example, using the **pop** macro just defined, we could put the following line in our assembly language routine:

```
pop return
```

The assembler automatically translates this into the following sequence of 6502 instructions:

```
pla
sta return
pla
sta return+1
```

We also define a macro for the inverse operation **push**; it pushes a 16-bit argument onto the stack.

```
        .macro push
;
;       macro to push 16-bit argument
;
        lda %1+1
        pha
        lda %1
        pha
        .endm
```

The macro **inc16** increments a 16-bit value in memory:

```
        .macro inc16
;
;       macro to increment 16-bit argument
;
        inc %1
        bne $01
        inc %1+1
$01
        .endm
```

Finally, the **dec16** macro decrements a 16-bit value:

```
        .macro dec16
;
;       macro to decrement 16-bit argument
;
        inc %1
        dec %1
        bne $02
        dec %1+1
$02     dec %1
        .endm
```

The macro definitions are followed by the assembly language code for the subroutines. Here is **grabline**:

```
        .proc grabline,4
;
;       procedure to move a line from the input page buffer to string
;
;       declared in Pascal host as:
;
;       procedure grabline(var buf:page; var offset:integer; var s:string;
;                                       maxlen:  integer); external;
;
return  .equ 0          ; return address
buf     .equ 2          ; address of beginning of input page
offset  .equ 4          ; address of offset into input page
s       .equ 6          ; address of grabbed string
maxlen  .equ 8          ; maximum length of grabbed string
bp      .equ 0A         ; pointer to current position in buffer

        pop return      ; store return address
        pop maxlen      ; store maximum length
        pop s           ; store string address
        pop offset      ; store address of buffer pointer
        pop buf         ; store address of buffer
;
;       calculate buffer pointer = buf + offset
;
        clc             ; prepare for add
        lda buf         ; get low byte of buffer address
        ldy #0          ; index low byte of offset
        adc (offset),y  ; add low byte of offset
        sta bp          ; store low byte of buffer pointer
        lda buf+1       ; get high byte of buffer address
        iny             ; index high byte of offset
        adc (offset),y  ; add high byte of offset
        sta bp+1        ; store high byte of buffer pointer
;
;       Put characters into buffer
;
        ldx #0          ; keep a zero in x-reg
        ldy #0          ; initialize string index
nextch  lda (bp,x)      ; get character from buffer
        inc16 bp        ; increment buffer pointer
        cmp #10         ; is character a <DLE>?
        bne normch      ; no, handle normal character
        lda (bp,x)      ; <DLE> seen, get blank count
        cmp #20         ; is blank code a <SPACE>?
        bne decryp      ; no, handle blank encryption
        inc16 bp        ; done with encrypted blanks, increment pointer
        jmp nextch      ; back to check for another <DLE>-encryption
decryp  sec             ; prepare to subtract
        sbc #1          ; decrement character (one fewer blank)
        sta (bp,x)      ; return it to buffer
        dec16 bp        ; point bp at <DLE> for next time through
        lda #20         ; character is a <SPACE>
normch  cmp #0          ; is character a <NUL>?
        beq finish      ; yes, so exit
        iny             ; index next character in string
        sta (s),y       ; store character in string
        cmp #0D         ; was character a <CR>?
        beq finish      ; yes, so exit
        cpy maxlen      ; reached string limit?
        bne nextch      ; no, back for another character
;
```

```
;               Finish up
;
finish  tya                     ; get string pointer
        ldy #0                  ; index length byte of string
        sta (s),y               ; store length
;
;               Calculate new offset = bp - buf
;
        sec                     ; prepare to subtract
        lda bp                  ; get buffer pointer low byte
        sbc buf                 ; subtract buffer address low byte
        sta (offset),y          ; store in offset low byte
        iny                     ; index offset high byte
        lda bp+1                ; get buffer pointer high byte
        sbc buf+1               ; subtract buffer address high byte
        sta (offset),y          ; store in offset high byte
        push return             ; push return address
        rts                     ; and return
```

Here is the assembly language code for **dropline**:

```
        .proc dropline,3
;
;       Procedure to append line to output buffer
;
;       Declared in Pascal host as:
;
;       procedure dropline(var buf: page; var offset: integer; var s: string):
;                                                                    external;
return  .equ 0                  ; return address
buf     .equ 2                  ; address of buffer start
offset  .equ 4                  ; address of buffer offset
s       .equ 6                  ; address of string
len     .equ 8                  ; length of string

        pop return              ; store return address
        pop s                   ; store string address
        pop offset              ; store offset address
        pop buf                 ; store buffer address

        ldy #0                  ; index length byte of string
        lda (s),y               ; get length of string
        beq exit                ; if zero, there's nothing to do
        sta len                 ; store length
        inc16 s                 ; point s at first character of string
;
;       set buf to point to current buffer position by adding offset
;
        clc                     ; prepare to add
        lda buf                 ; get low byte of buffer address
        adc (offset),y          ; add low byte of offset
        sta buf                 ; store in low byte of buffer address
        iny                     ; index high byte
        lda buf+1               ; get high byte of buffer address
        adc (offset),y          ; add high byte of offset
        sta buf+1               ; store in high byte of buffer address
;
;       move string to buffer
;
        ldy #0                  ; index first character
nxtbyt  lda (s),y               ; get next byte from string
        sta (buf),y             ; store in buffer
        iny                     ; index next character
        cpy len                 ; compare with string length
        bne nxtbyt              ; if non equal, back for next character
;
```

124 Advanced Pascal Programming Techniques

```
;           finish up by updating offset
;
            tya             ; move string length to A
            clc             ; prepare to add
            ldy #0          ; index low byte of buffer offset
            adc (offset),y  ; add low byte of buffer offset to length
            sta (offset),y  ; store new low byte of buffer offset
            lda #0
            iny             ; index high byte of buffer offset
            adc (offset),y  ; add high byte of buffer offset to carry
            sta (offset),y  ; store new high byte of buffer offset
exit        push return     ; push return address
            rts             ; and return
```

Finally, here is the code for **crunch**:

```
            .proc crunch,1
;
;           procedure to encode leading blanks in string
;
;           declared in Pascal host as:
;
;           procedure crunch(var s: string); external;
;
return   .equ 0             ; return address
s        .equ 2             ; string address
len      .equ 4             ; string length
nbsaved  .equ 5             ; number of bytes saved by crunching
s1       .equ 6             ; temporary pointer

            pop return      ; store return address
            pop s           ; store string address
            ldy #0          ; index string length byte
            lda (s),y       ; get string length
            sta len         ; and store it
;
;           find first nonblank character in string
;
            lda #20         ; put a blank in accumulator
inchr       iny             ; index next string character
            beq havebl      ; if y=0, we've wrapped around (255 blanks)
            cpy len         ; if y > length, exit loop
            beq chkbl
            bcs havebl
chkbl       cmp (s),y       ; is character a blank?
            beq inchr       ; yes, go back for next character
;
;           y now contains (# of leading blanks) + 1
;           subtract 3 to get number of bytes saved by crunching
;           don't crunch if y = 1, 2, or 3
;
havebl      dey
            beq done
            dey
            beq done
            dey
            beq done
            sty nbsaved     ; store nbsaved
;
;           calcuate new length = old length - nbsaved
;
```

```
            sec                 ; prepare to subtract
            lda len             ; get old length
            sbc nbsaved         ; subtract nbsaved
            ldy #0              ; index length byte
            sta (s),y           ; store new length in string
            sta len             ; and in zero page
;
;           store blank encryption in string
;           s[1] := <DLE>
;           s[2] := 32 + (# of leading blanks) = 34 + nbsaved
;
            iny                 ; index first character
            lda #10             ; get a <DLE>
            sta (s),y           ; store it in string
            iny                 ; index second character
            clc                 ; prepare to add
            lda nbsaved         ; get nbsaved
            adc #22             ; add 34 (decimal)
            sta (s),y           ; store in string
;
;           move characters in string left
;
            lda s               ; get string address low byte
            clc                 ; prepare to add
            adc nbsaved         ; add nbsaved
            sta s1              ; store temp pointer low byte
            lda s+1             ; get string address high byte
            adc #0              ; add carry, if any
            sta s1+1            ; store temp pointer high byte
outch       iny                 ; index next character in string
            cpy len             ; if y > new length, we're done
            beq movech
            bcs done
movech      lda (s1),y          ; get character from string
            sta (s),y           ; store at new position
            jmp outch           ; back for next character
done        push return         ; push return address
            rts                 ; and return
```

We will later measure the improvements that result from translating these Pascal routines into assembly language.

Units and Libraries

By looking at programs like **calc** and **gaslog**, it becomes obvious that using a large number of programmer-defined data types and modules can rapidly make a program's source code large and difficult to handle. In our following programs, we will alleviate this problem by making use of two excellent features of Apple and UCSD Pascal: the ability to group related procedures, functions, data types, and constant declarations into separately compiled *units*, and the ability to combine such units into *libraries*.

We will not attempt to go into detail on the construction of such units and libraries and the method used to link them with our programs. Such details would merely duplicate information already available to Apple and UCSD

Pascal programmers and would not apply to users of other versions of Pascal.

A unit is made up of two parts: the *interface* section and the *implementation* section. The interface section contains **const, type,** and **var** declarations and "heading" declarations for procedures or functions. The implementation section contains the actual code and local variables for the routines declared in the interface section. The implementation section may also contain its own procedures and functions, as well as its own constant, type, and variable declarations.

From this point, we assume our most useful routines and declarations have been gathered into units and those units have been collected into a library shown in Table 5-2.

A program using a unit may refer to any of the items declared in the interface section of the unit. Items declared in the implementation section are "private" to the unit and cannot be accessed by the program. For instance, the **datestuff** unit mentioned in Table 5-2 includes the **stod** procedure (which converts a string to a date) in the implementation part of the unit, where it is called by **getdate**. But **stod** is inaccessible to programs using the **datestuff** unit. Similarly, the implementation part of the **textstuff** unit would contain the declarations for **grabline, crunch,** and **dropline,** and these routines could not be used directly by an application program.

Units and libraries are used in programs with the **uses** declaration. The program statement

```
uses
    {$u APPLE2:TOOLSTUFF.CODE } crtstuff, textstuff;
```

notifies the Pascal compiler that the program needs to call routines or use data types provided in the **crtstuff** and **textstuff** units and that the units may be found in the library file **APPLE2:TOOLSTUFF.CODE**.

Libraries and units have the following benefits: they allow programmers to isolate commonly used routines in one place rather than spreading them over a large number of application programs. Code in units need not be recompiled every time a modification is made to a program, which saves time. Finally, units provide a higher level of modularization than is available from procedures and functions alone. If our individual modules are considered tools, then units are toolboxes: sets of related tools. (To carry the analogy further, libraries could be thought of as collections of toolboxes or perhaps as toolsheds.)

A final note. Libraries and units are optional. If your version of Pascal does not offer a similar separate compilation feature, simply be sure the routines

Table 5-2. Contents of Units in Library

Unit Name	Contents (interface)

crtstuff	constant declarations:
	  MAXSTR, MAXCRTCOL, MAXCRTROW
	type declarations:
	  crtcommand, charset
	modules:
	  crt, posstr, getkey, addchar, chopchar, getstring, eraseline, center, wait, remark, disptitle, getboolean, ask, gchar, gnbchar

fixstuff	constant declarations:
	  FIXSIZE
	type declarations:
	  fixed
	modules:
	  stof, ftos, getfixed

datestuff	type declarations:
	  date
	modules:
	  dtos, getdate

textstuff	constant declarations:
	  PAGESIZE, GOODIO, ENDFILE, MAXFNAME
	type declarations:
	  iostatus, page, tfile, filename, tfrec
	modules:
	  tfopen, tfcreate, tfread, tfwrite, tfclose, gettfname

and declarations contained in the appropriate units are present in the program's source code.

Measurements

We will test our text file routines with **copy**, a simple program that copies an input text file to an output text file line by line with no changes. Here is the main routine of **copy**.

```
program copy;
{ Copy text files - benchmark program }
uses
   {$u apple2:toolstuff.code } crtstuff, textstuff;
var
   status: iostatus;
   margin: integer;
   inname, outname: filename;
   infile, outfile: tfile;
   intf, outtf: tfrec;
   done: boolean;
   s: string;
begin { copy }
   margin := (MAXCRTCOL - 35) div 2;
   crt(CLEAR);
   disptitle('copy');
   posstr(' Input file:', margin, 4);
   posstr('Output file:', margin, 6);
   repeat
      gettfname(inname,  margin + 12, 4, '');
      gettfname(outname, margin + 12, 6, '');
      remark('Ready to start timing');
      if tfopen(infile, intf, inname, status) = GOODIO then begin
         if tfcreate(outfile, outtf, outname, status) = GOODIO then begin
            repeat
               if tfread(infile, intf, s, MAXSTR, status) = GOODIO then begin
                  if tfwrite(outfile, outtf, s, status) <> GOODIO then
                     remark('Error writing output file')
               end
               else if status <> ENDFILE then
                  remark('Error reading input file')
            until status <> GOODIO;
            if tfclose(outfile, outtf, status) <> GOODIO then
               remark('Error closing output file')
         end
         else
            remark('Error creating output file');
         if tfclose(infile, intf, status) <> GOODIO then
            remark('Error closing input file')
      end
      else
         remark('Error opening input file');
      remark('Stop timing');
      done := not ask('Any more?(Y/N):', MAXCRTROW - 1, FALSE, FALSE);
      eraseline(MAXCRTROW - 1)
   until done;
   crt(CLEAR)
end.
```

To measure the effects of our various design decisions on efficiency, three different versions of **copy** were used to copy two different text files from one disk to another. The first text file was a Pascal program containing 10,722 characters in 511 lines; the second was a manuscript file with 16,975 characters in 488 lines. (The manuscript file also contained program segments and commands to a text formatter.) The elapsed time was measured between the pressing of the <RETURN> key in response to the remark **Ready to start timing** and the appearance of the remark **Stop timing** on the screen.

The first version of **copy**, **copy1**, uses "standard" text file access. The built-in **text** file type is used; **tfread** simply calls **readln** to read lines from the input file, and **tfwrite** calls **writeln** to write lines to the output file. Error checking is performed as described previously.

copy2 is the **copy** program just presented, using the Pascal versions of **grabline**, **dropline**, and **crunch**. Finally, **copy3** uses the assembly language versions of these routines.

The execution times for the three versions of **copy** on both files are shown in Table 5-3. Our decision to use Apple Pascal's block I/O routines and to code three routines in assembly language appears to have been more than adequately justified; the two improvements taken together cause an increase in speed of more than a factor of ten.

One final note on **copy**. It is simply meant as a benchmark program to measure the effect of changing our text file I/O routines—not as a "real" program for everyday use. A real file-copying routine would read in a large number of file blocks all at once and then write them to the output file. This routine would not bother to break the input file into lines, decode and re-encode <DLE> encryptions, and then reassemble the lines into the output file. In addition, there is little point in restricting a file-copying routine to text files; a flexible routine would be able to handle all types of files.

print

Our principal program in this chapter is **print**, a utility program for printing text files in a pleasing format. **print** splits the printed output into numbered pages; the program prints a header on each page showing the page number, the name of the file, and the current date.

Table 5-3. Measurements on **copy**

	Program (10,722 characters)	Manuscript (16,975 characters)
copy1	273 seconds	410 seconds
copy2	103 seconds	139 seconds
copy3	26 seconds	37 seconds

When **print** is started, it asks the user for the current date. After the date is entered, the program displays a number of "print parameters." The screen appears as in Figure 5-1.

After **print** displays the current values of the parameters, it asks the user if any changes are desired. If the user wants to make changes, the program asks for the new values of each parameter. As in Chapter Three's **gaslog** program, the default answers are the previous values; the user only needs to type in the answers he or she wants to change.

Many of these parameters are self-explanatory. The *page length* is the number of lines per page; it is initialized to 66. The *left margin* is the page column in which lines are to begin; it is initialized to 15. (Printed page columns are numbered from 0, just like CRT columns; a left margin of 0 says text begins in the first column.) No printing extends into the column specified by the *right margin,* which is initialized to 132.

Many Pascal compilers allow a single program's source text to be split up among several different text files. In Apple and UCSD Pascal, the compiler directive

```
{$I SPROCKET.TEXT }
```

```
                    ********
                    * print *
                    ********

            Current print parameters:

      Page length(lines):66
      Left margin:15          Right margin:132
      Print included files(Y/N):N
      Output to file or printer (F/P):P
      Output file name:
      Printer init. string:@eP
      Printer term. string:@eP

                  Any changes?(Y/N):__
```

Figure 5-1. **print**'s initial display

causes the compiler to "include" the **SPROCKET.TEXT** file at that point; the net effect is just as if the source code from **SPROCKET.TEXT** existed in the program text.

Since **print** may be used to print program source texts, it provides an option to print any files specified by include directives in the source file. To invoke this option, the **Print included files(Y/N)** parameter should be set to <Y>; otherwise, it should be set to <N>. **print** allows nesting of include directives; an included file can itself include files.

Since not all users have printers, **print** can optionally redirect its output to a text file. To take advantage of this, the user may specify an <F> value for the **Output to file or printer (F/P)** parameter; <P> sends the output to the printer, if present. If the output is to a text file, **print** asks for the file's name.

Finally, many printers (even inexpensive ones) provide features such as compressed print, boldface, italics, and so on. These features are accessed by special sequences of characters that the printer treats as commands instead of normal text to be printed. For example, the Epson MX-80 printer interprets the character sequence <ESC><P> (ASCII 27, ASCII 80) as a command to start printing compressed characters (16.5 characters per inch). The sequence <ESC><Q> causes normal-sized characters (10 characters per inch) to be printed. For obvious reasons, printer commands usually contain one or more non-printing characters unlikely to occur in normal text.

print allows the user to specify two printer command character sequences: the first is an initialization command sent to the printer before printing begins; the second is a "termination" command to return the printer to its normal state at the end of the printing run.

How do we represent the non-printing characters usually contained in such strings? We use a flexible method generally known as an *escape sequence*. First, we define <@> (at sign) as our escape character (do not confuse this with the ASCII character <ESC>). This character signals that the next few characters in the string are not to be interpreted as normal text. **print** uses the following rules to interpret escape sequences:

- The sequence **@e** (or **@E**) in the command string causes an <ESC> (ASCII 27) to be sent to the printer.

- The sequence **@c**<*char*> (or **@C**<*char*>), where <*char*> is an alphabetic character, sends a <Control-*char*> to the printer. For example, **@cf** is translated into a <Control-F> (ASCII 6); **@CS** turns into a <Control-S> (ASCII 19).

- The sequence **@h***nn* (or **@H***nn*), where *nn* is a hexadecimal value, sends the character with ASCII value *nn*. *nn* may be 0, 1, or 2 hex digits. For example, the string **@h1F** sends an ASCII 31 character to the printer (1F hex = 31 decimal).
- The sequence **@@** may be used to send a single <@> to the printer. This is just a special case of this rule: if the character following an <@> character is anything but an <e>, <c>, or <h> (or the uppercase equivalents) the decoding routine deletes the <@>. (Thus, **@zks** becomes **zks**).
- A null string may be specified by the sequence **@h00**; this causes no characters to be sent to the printer.

After the user has set all the parameters to their desired values, **print** asks for the names of the files to print. The user may enter as many as 14 file names. **print** stops asking for file names if the user simply presses <RETURN> when prompted for a file name. **print** also allows the user to correct any mistakes made in entering file names. The program asks **Any changes?(Y/N):;** if the user answers <Y>, **print** requests the file names again with the defaults set to the user's previous responses.

After the user enters the file names, **print** displays the message **Please check printer...** This message reminds the user to make sure the printer is ready to accept data and begin printing. As each file is printed, the message **<−Printing** is displayed next to its name on the screen. When printing is completed, this message is normally replaced with the message **<−Done**. If an error occurs while opening or printing the file, an appropriate error message is displayed instead. Figure 5-2 shows the screen's appearance while a number of files are being printed.

After all files in the list have been printed, **print** asks **All done?(Y/N):**. If the user answers <N>, **print** cycles back to the parameter-changing section, allowing files to be printed with different parameters without leaving the program.

Here is the main routine of **print**:

```
{$s+,v-}
program print;
{ Print textfiles }

uses
    {$u apple2:toolstuff.code } crtstuff, fixstuff, datestuff, textstuff;

const
    MAXPLEN = 999;        { Maximum lines on page }
```

```
   MAXFILES = 14;          { Maximum number of files user can specify per run }
   PCOMSIZE = 15;          { Max length of printer command strings }
   MARGIN1 = 2;            { # lines between top of page & header }
   MARGIN2 = 1;            { # lines between header & first text line }
   MARGIN3 = 3;            { # lines between last text line and bottom of page }
   DATEWID = 8;            { Width of date string }
   LSTRSIZE = 255;         { Long string size }
type
   pcommand = string[PCOMSIZE];

var
   name: array [1..MAXFILES] of filename;
   today: date;
   pagelen, rmarg, lmarg, nfiles, margin: integer;
   include, hardcopy: boolean;
   pinit, pterm: pcommand;
   outname: filename;

{-------------------------------}
{ Modules to be inserted here:  }
{       initprint               }
{       changeparams            }
{       getnames                }
{       printfiles              }
{-------------------------------}
begin { print }
   crt(CLEAR);
   disptitle('print');
   initprint;
   repeat
      changeparams;
      getnames;
      printfiles
   until ask('All done?(Y/N):', MAXCRTROW - 1, FALSE, FALSE);
   crt(CLEAR)
end.
```

```
                    ********
                    * print *
                    ********

            Enter up to 14 files to print.
            Press <RETURN> when done

            1:COLETTE.TEXT              ← Done
            2.KOALA.TEXT                ← Done
            3:ARCHIVE:FINDINCDIR.TEXT   ← Not Found
            4:APPLE2:CRTSTUFF.TEXT      ← Printing
            5:LIB2:INVOICE.TEXT
            6:LIB2:GAMESTATE.TEXT
```

Figure 5-2. **print** in action

The compiler directives {$s+,v—} at the top of the program turn on the compiler's swapping mode and turn off the compiler's string-length type checking. These options were described in Chapter Three.

The constant **LSTRSIZE** specifies the length of the longest string **print** can handle. We choose it to be the upper limit on the length of an Apple Pascal string, 255. **LSTRSIZE** limits the width of the output line, so we want it to be as long as possible to accommodate printers that can print very long lines.

Initializing Global Variables

The **initprint** procedure accepts the current date from the user and initializes **print**'s other global variables:

```
procedure initprint;
{ Initialize print's global variables }

var
    i: integer;

begin { initprint }
    i := (MAXCRTCOL - 20) div 2;
    posstr('Today''s Date?:', i, 4);
    getdate(today, i + 14, 4, today, FALSE);
    pagelen := 66;
    lmarg := 15;
    rmarg := 132;
    include := FALSE;
    pinit := '@eP';
    pterm := '@eQ';
    outname := '';
    hardcopy := TRUE;
    margin := (MAXCRTCOL - 39) div 2
end;
```

The values shown are suitable for printing text files on an Epson MX-80 printer. The printer command strings turn on the MX-80's compressed characters for printing the files and return the printer to normal-sized characters when printing is finished.

A more sophisticated version of **print** might be designed to "remember" parameter settings (and probably the date as well) from one session to the next by saving the parameter values in a small data file on disk. When started, **print** would read the data file to obtain the previous session's parameters; if any parameters are changed, **print** would save the new values in the data file. The primary difficulty (in Apple Pascal) is in specifying what disk drive **print** should use for such a data file: should the default disk or the disk on which the **print** program is contained be used?

Changing Print Parameters

We use **changeparams** to display the current parameters and accept any changes from the user. Here is the **changeparams** routine:

```
procedure changeparams;
{ Allow user to change global printing parameters }
var
   s: string;

{-----------------------------}
{ Modules to be inserted here: }
{        getint               }
{-----------------------------}
begin { changeparams }
   center('Current print parameters:', 4);
   crt(ERASEOS);
   ftos(pagelen, 0, 0, s);
   posstr(concat('Page length (lines):', s), margin, 6);
   ftos(lmarg, 0, 0, s);
   posstr(concat('Left margin:', s), margin, 8);
   ftos(rmarg, 0, 0, s);
   posstr(concat('Right margin:', s), margin + 23, 8);
   if include then
      s := 'Y'
   else
      s := 'N';
   posstr(concat('Print included files(Y/N):', s), margin, 10);
   if hardcopy then
      s := 'P'
   else
      s := 'F';
   posstr(concat('Output to file or printer (F/P):', s), margin, 12);
   posstr(concat('Output file name:', outname), margin, 14);
   posstr(concat('Printer init. string:', pinit), margin, 16);
   posstr(concat('Printer term. string:', pterm), margin, 18);
   while ask('Any changes(Y/N):', MAXCRTROW - 1, FALSE, TRUE) do begin
      pagelen := getint(margin + 20, 6, MARGIN1 + MARGIN2 + MARGIN3 + 3,
                                                  MAXPLEN, pagelen, TRUE);
      lmarg := getint(margin + 12, 8, 0, LSTRSIZE - (MAXFNAME + DATEWID + 1),
                                                        lmarg, TRUE);
      rmarg:= getint(margin + 36, 8, lmarg + MAXFNAME + DATEWID + 1, LSTRSIZE,
                                                        rmarg, TRUE);
      include := getboolean(margin + 26, 10, include, TRUE);
      getstring(s, 1, margin + 32, 12, s, ['P', 'F'], TRUE);
      hardcopy := (s = 'P');
      if hardcopy then begin
         getstring(pinit, PCOMSIZE, margin + 21, 16, pinit, [' '..'~'], FALSE);
         getstring(pterm, PCOMSIZE, margin + 21, 18, pterm, [' '..'~'], FALSE)
         end
      else { file output }
         gettfname(outname, margin + 17, 14, outname)
      end
end;
```

changeparams only asks for an output file name if the user specifies that output is to go to a file. It only asks for printer initialization and termination strings if the user specifies that the output is to go to the printer.

Integers are obtained from the user with the **getint** function:

```
function getint(col,row,mini,maxi,defi: integer; defaulted: boolean): integer;
{ Get integer from user }

var
   f: fixed;

begin { getint }
   getfixed(f, col, row, mini, maxi, defi, 0, defaulted);
   getint := trunc(f)
end;
```

Our previous work in making fixed-point numeric input as flexible as possible has paid off in making **getint** extremely simple to write.

Getting the File Names

The **getnames** routine gets the names of the files the user wants to print:

```
procedure getnames;
{ Get file names to print }

var
   i: integer;
   s: string;

begin { getnames }
   ftos(MAXFILES, 0, 0, s);
   center(concat('Enter up to ', s, ' files to print.'), 4);
   center('Press <RETURN> when done', 5);
   crt(ERASEOS);
   for i := 1 to MAXFILES do begin
      gotoxy(margin, i + 6);
      write(i: 2, ':');
      name[i] := ''
   end;
   repeat
      i := 0;
      repeat
         i := i + 1;
         gettfname(name[i], margin + 3, i + 6, name[i])
      until (name[i] = '') or (i = MAXFILES);
      if name[i] = '' then
         nfiles := i - 1
      else
         nfiles := MAXFILES
   until not ask('Any changes?(Y/N):', MAXCRTROW - 1, FALSE, TRUE);
   gotoxy(0, nfiles + 7);
   crt(ERASEOS)
end;
```

Printing the Files

The user-specified text files are printed with the **printfiles** routine:

```
procedure printfiles;
{ Print files }

const
   PRINTER = 6;          { Unit number of printer }
var
   junk, status: iostatus;
   outf: tfile;
   outrec: tfrec;
   pageno, lineno, i: integer;
{----------------------------}
{ Modules to be inserted here: }
{        decode              }
{        initoutput          }
{        termoutput          }
{        wrstr               }
{        wchars              }
{        skip                }
{        printfoot           }
{        fprint              }
{----------------------------}
begin { printfiles }
   if initoutput(status) = GOODIO then begin
      for i := 1 to nfiles do begin
         pageno := 1;
         lineno := 1;
         posstr('<- Printing ', margin + 27, i + 6);
         if fprint(name[i], pageno, lineno, status) = GOODIO then
            posstr('<- Done       ', margin + 27, i + 6)
         else if (status = 9) or (status = 10) then
            posstr('<- Not found', margin + 27, i + 6)
         else if status = 7 then
            posstr('<- Bad name ', margin + 27, i + 6)
         else { something else bad happened }
            posstr('<- I/O Error', margin + 27, i + 6);
         if lineno > 1 then
            junk := printfoot(pageno, lineno, pagelen, junk)
      end;
      junk := termoutput(junk)
   end
end;
```

This routine contains a simple example of doing different things depending on the type of I/O error seen by our text file routines. Apple Pascal's **ioresult** function returns a value of 9 if a program attempts to access a disk (or "volume") that is not present. A value of 10 is returned if the program attempts to access a nonexistent file. A value of 7 is returned if the file name is illegal. These will probably be the most common errors, and special error messages are returned if any of them occurs. Other kinds of errors are lumped together in an <-I/O Error message. (If you feel a blunt "I/O

Error" message is too unfriendly or does not contain enough information, change the code to reflect your preferences. One possible approach is to write a routine that accepts an I/O error number and returns a short string describing the error that can be passed along to the user.)

Output Initialization And Termination

The **printfiles** routine calls **initoutput** to initialize the "ouput device," which either sends the initialization string to the printer or opens the specified output file. After all files have been printed, **printfiles** calls **termoutput**, which either closes the output file or sends the termination string to the printer.

Here is **initoutput**:

```
function initoutput(var status: iostatus): iostatus;
{ Initialize printer or output text file }

{----------------------------}
{ Modules to be included here: }
{         initprinter          }
{----------------------------}

begin { initoutput }
   if hardcopy then begin
      if initprinter(pinit, status) <> GOODIO then
         remark('Can''t access printer')
   end
   else begin { file output }
      if tfcreate(outf, outrec, outname, status) <> GOODIO then
         remark(concat('Can''t create ', outname))
   end;
   initoutput := status
end;
```

This is a simple two-way decision, depending on the value of the Boolean variable **hardcopy**. It returns an error code in the usual manner, both as the function's result and the parameter **status**.

Here is **initprinter**:

```
function initprinter(pc: pcommand; var status: iostatus): iostatus;
{ Initialize printer }
begin { initprinter }
   remark('Please check printer...');
   {$i-}
   unitclear(PRINTER);
   status := ioresult;
   if status = GOODIO then begin
      decode(pc);
```

```
            if length(pc) > 0 then begin
                unitwrite(PRINTER, pc[1], length(pc), 0, 12);
                status := ioresult
            end
      end;
      initprinter := status
   {$i+}
end;
```

Apple and UCSD Pascal provide low-level I/O routines to control peripheral devices directly. These routines access devices by *unit numbers;* the system printer is unit number 6, which is defined here as the constant **PRINTER**. The call

```
unitclear(unitnum)
```

resets the specified unit to its "power-up" state. We use it in **initprinter** to test whether there is a printer in the system; if there is no printer, **ioresult** returns a non-zero value.

initprinter and **termprinter** use the **unitwrite** built-in procedure to send a sequence of characters to the printer. The procedure call

```
unitwrite(unitnum, buffer, length, blocknum, mode)
```

writes **length** bytes from **buffer** to unit number **unitnum**. The **buffer** argument may be subscripted to indicate a starting position for the transfer. The parameters **blocknum** and **mode** are optional; if they are absent, they are assumed to be 0. If the specified unit is a block-structured device, like a disk drive, the parameter **blocknum** tells **unitwrite** to which block of the unit the bytes are to be written; the parameter is ignored if the unit is a serial device, like a printer.

The **mode** parameter is more important for our purposes. This parameter is an integer controlling (among other things) handling of the infamous <DLE> encryption and end-of-line <CR> (ASCII 13) characters. If **mode** is 0, <DLE> encryptions are converted into the appropriate number of blank characters and <CR> characters are translated into <CR>-<LF> combinations. If **mode** is 12, neither of these translations is done. Thus, to avoid accidental conversion of characters in our printer command strings, we specify a **mode** of 12.

The **termoutput** routine undoes whatever **initoutput** did. It either closes the output file or sends the termination string to the printer.

```
function termoutput(var status: iostatus): iostatus;
{ Send termination command to printer or close output file }

{----------------------------}
{ Modules to be included here: }
{        termprinter          }
{----------------------------}

begin { termoutput }
   if hardcopy then begin
      if termprinter(pterm, status) <> GOODIO then
         remark('Can''t close printer')
   end
   else begin { file output }
      if tfclose(outf, outrec, status) <> GOODIO then
         remark('Can''t close output file')
   end;
   termoutput := status
end;
```

Here is **termprinter**:

```
function termprinter(pc: pcommand; var status: iostatus): iostatus;
{ Send termination string to printer }

begin { termprinter }
   status := GOODIO;
   decode(pc);
   if length(pc) > 0 then begin
      {$i-}
      unitwrite(PRINTER, pc[1], length(pc), 0, 12);
      status := ioresult
      {$i+}
   end;
   termprinter := status
end;
```

Decoding Escape Sequences

Both **initprinter** and **termprinter** call **decode**, which translates escape sequences in the printer command strings into the actual decoded characters and returns the translated string to the calling routine.

```
procedure decode(var pc: pcommand);
{ Decode printer command string }

var
   s: pcommand;
   i: integer;
   c: char;

{----------------------------}
{ Modules to be inserted here: }
{        gesc                 }
{----------------------------}
```

```
begin { decode }
    s := '';
    i := 1;
    while gesc(pc, i, c) <> chr(0) do begin
        addchar(s, c, PCOMSIZE);
        i := i + 1
    end;
    pc := s
end;
```

decode hands the responsibility of decoding individual escape sequences over to **gesc**. **gesc** looks at the ith character of the command string; if the character is not an <@> escape character, it simply returns the character. If the character *is* an <@>, it attempts to decode the following characters as a meaningful escape sequence. In order for **decode** and **gesc** to work together, **gesc** must leave **i** pointing to the last character of the escape sequence so the *next* time through the loop **gesc** will look at the character immediately following the sequence.

```
function gesc(var s: string; var i: integer; var c: char): char;
{ Get (possibly escaped) character from string }
const
    ESCAPE = '@';           { Printer command string escape }
var
    c1: char;
{-------------------------------}
{ Modules to be included here: }
{           htoc               }
{-------------------------------}
begin { gesc }
    if gchar(s, i, c) = ESCAPE then
        if gchar(s, i + 1, c) = chr(0) then
            c := ESCAPE
        else begin
            i := i + 1;
            if c in ['E', 'e'] then
                c := chr(27)
            else if c in ['C', 'c'] then begin
                if gchar(s, i + 1, c1) in ['A'..'Z'] then begin
                    c := chr(ord(c1) - 64);
                    i := i + 1
                end
                else if c1 in ['a'..'z'] then begin
                    c := chr(ord(c1) - 96);
                    i := i + 1
                end
            end
            else if c in ['H', 'h'] then
                c := htoc(s, i)
        end;
    gesc := c
end;
```

gesc does most of the escape sequence interpretation itself, but it hands the job of decoding hexadecimal digits into characters over to the **htoc** function. Like **gesc**, **htoc** leaves **i** pointing to the last character in the sequence.

```
function htoc(var s: string; var i: integer): char;
{ Convert zero, one, or two hex digits into a character }
var
   n, nd: integer;
   c: char;
begin { htoc }
   n := 0;
   nd := 0;
   while (gchar(s, i+1, c)in['0'..'9','A'..'F','a'..'f'])and(nd<2) do begin
      if c in ['0'..'9'] then
         n := 16 * n + ord(c) - 48
      else if c in ['A'..'F'] then
         n := 16 * n + ord(c) - 55
      else { c in ['a'..'f'] }
         n := 16 * n + ord(c) - 87;
      nd := nd + 1;
      i := i + 1
   end;
   htoc := chr(n)
end;
```

htoc decodes a maximum of two characters beyond the **@h** sequence. It terminates when it reaches this limit or when it sees a character that cannot be interpreted as a hexadecimal digit.

Printing Individual Files

A file is printed by the **fprint** routine, which is complex enough to present in pseudo-code first:

```
begin
   open input file
   while not end of file
      get line from file
      if at top of page
         print header
      print line
      if line didn't have a <CR> at end
         print a <CR> (fold long lines)
      if at bottom of page
         advance to top to next page
      if we're printing included files
         check line for include directives & print files if present
   end-while
   close input file
end
```

Most of the differences between this outline and the Pascal code involve our exhaustive error checking. If an error occurs while reading the input or writing the output, **fprint** should exit immediately without attempting to do any more I/O.

fprint calculates the maximum length of a string that fits between our specified margins and passes the value to **tfread**. As we discussed when we designed **tfread**, any input string without a <CR> character at its end is longer than this specified maximum length. When this happens, **fprint** writes its own <CR> to the output so the remainder of the long input string appears on the following line(s) on the printed output. (You may want to satisfy yourself that this works even for very narrow margins and very long input strings.)

fprint's handling of included files also deserves a little explanation. If the Boolean print parameter **include** is **TRUE**, **fprint** checks the input string for one or more include directives. As each directive is found, **fprint** calls itself recursively to print the specified file. If an error occurs while an included file is printed, it is handled by directing a remark to the user at the bottom of the screen. This method seems more useful than terminating printing altogether or simply ignoring the error.

Here is the **fprint** routine itself:

```
function fprint(var name: filename; var pageno, lineno: integer;
                                    var status: iostatus): iostatus;
{ Print a file -- calls itself recursively for included files }
type
    lstring = string[LSTRSIZE];
var
    intf: tfile;
    inrec: tfrec;
    lmstr, s: lstring;
    i, max: integer;
    newname: filename;
    c: char;
    junk: iostatus;

{------------------------------}
{ Modules to be inserted here: }
{       findincdir             }
{       printhead              }
{------------------------------}
begin { fprint }
    max := rmarg - lmarg;
    {$r-}
    fillchar(lmstr[1], lmarg, ' ');
    lmstr[0] := chr(lmarg);
    {$r+}
    if tfopen(intf, inrec, name, status) = GOODIO then begin
        while status = GOODIO do
            if tfread(intf, inrec, s, max, status) = GOODIO then begin
```

```
            s := concat(lmstr, s);
         if lineno <= 1 then
            status:=printhead(today,pageno,rmarg,lmarg,name,lineno,status);
         if status = GOODIO then
            if wrstr(s, status) = GOODIO then begin
               lineno := lineno + 1;
               if gchar(s, length(s), c) <> chr(13) then
                  status := skip(1, status);
            end;
         if (status = GOODIO) and (lineno >= pagelen - MARGIN3) then
            status := printfoot(pageno, lineno, pagelen, status);
         if (status = GOODIO) and include then begin
            i := lmarg + 1;
            while findincdir(s, i, newname) do
               if fprint(newname, pageno, lineno, junk) <> GOODIO then
                  remark(concat('Error including ', newname))
         end
      end;
      if status = ENDFILE then { normal result }
         status := tfclose(intf, inrec, status)
      else { something bad happened }
         junk := tfclose(intf, inrec, junk)
   end;
   fprint := status
end;
```

The code

```
{$r-}
fillchar(lmstr[1], lmarg, ' ');
lmstr[0] := chr(lmarg);
{$r+}
```

is a fast way to initialize **lmstr** to a string of **lmarg** blanks. (See the description of **fillchar** earlier in this chapter.)

A possible bug in **fprint** involves its recursive call to itself. If the include files are nested too deeply (or if a file includes itself directly or indirectly) the program will eventually run out of memory and crash. You may want to solve this problem either by limiting the depth of recursion or by checking the amount of memory remaining before calling **fprint** recursively.

One simple improvement to **fprint** would be to avoid splitting a long line in the middle of a word. Instead, save the partial word at the end of the long line and print it with its end on the continuation line. (What is a good way to define "word" in this context? Do you have to impose a restriction on the maximum length of a word?)

Another improvement would allow the user to *interrupt* printing by pressing a key. The program would then ask if the user wanted to continue printing the current file, to skip to the next file, or to quit printing altogether.

String and Character Output

As we saw in the **initoutput** and **termoutput** routines, the Boolean variable **hardcopy** may be used to direct output easily to a text file or to the printer. Another example is **wrstr**, which sends a string to one or the other.

```
function wrstr(var s: string; var status: iostatus): iostatus;
{ Write string to printer or output file }
{-----------------------------}
{ Modules to be included here: }
{      lprint                   }
{-----------------------------}
begin { wrstr }
   if hardcopy then
      wrstr := lprint(s, status)
   else { file output }
      wrstr := tfwrite(outf, outrec, s, status)
end;
```

If the string is to be sent to the printer, **wrstr** simply calls **lprint** to do the job.

```
function lprint(var s: string; var status: iostatus): iostatus;
{ Write string to printer }
begin { lprint }
   {$i-}
   status := GOODIO;
   if length(s) > 0 then begin
      unitwrite(PRINTER, s[1], length(s));
      status := ioresult
   end;
   lprint := status
   {$i+}
end;
```

fprint also calls **skip**, which sends a specified number of <CR> characters to the output device:

```
function skip(n: integer; var status: iostatus): iostatus;
{ Skip n lines on output }
begin { skip }
   skip := wchars(n, chr(13), status)
end;
```

skip calls **wchars** to do the actual output. **wchars** is a general-purpose routine that repeatedly sends any single character a specified number of times to the output device.

```
function wchars(n: integer; c: char; var status: iostatus): iostatus;
{ Write n characters to output }
var
   s: string[1];
begin { wchars }
   s := '';
   addchar(s, c, 1);
   status := GOODIO;
   while (n > 0) and (status = GOODIO) do begin
      status := wrstr(s, status);
      n := n - 1
   end;
   wchars := status
end;
```

Page Formatting

At the beginning of each output page, **fprint** calls **printhead** to print the header information at the beginning of each page:

```
function printhead(today: date; pageno,rmarg,lmarg: integer; name: filename;
                   var lineno: integer; var status: iostatus): iostatus;
{ Print page header }
var
   dstr, pstr: string;
   n: integer;
begin { printhead }
   dtos(today, dstr);
   ftos(pageno, 0, 0, pstr);
   pstr := concat('Page ', pstr);
   n := rmarg - length(dstr) - length(name) - lmarg;
   if skip(MARGIN1, status) = GOODIO then
      if wchars(lmarg, ' ', status) = GOODIO then
         if wrstr(name, status) = GOODIO then
            if wchars(n, ' ', status) = GOODIO then
               if wrstr(dstr, status) = GOODIO then
                  if skip(1, status) = GOODIO then
                     if wchars(rmarg - length(pstr), ' ', status)=GOODIO then
                        if wrstr(pstr, status) = GOODIO then begin
                           status := skip(MARGIN2 + 1, status);
                           lineno := lineno + MARGIN1 + MARGIN2 + 2
                        end;
   printhead := status
end;
```

There is nothing very complicated about **printhead**: it simply prints out each item in the header separated by the appropriate number of spaces and <CR> characters. It continually checks to be sure no further I/O is done if an error occurs.

At the end of each output page, **fprint** calls **printfoot** to skip to the beginning of the next page. (**printfoot** is also called by **printfiles** after each file is printed so the following file starts printing at the top of a page.) Most printers respond to a form feed (<FF>, ASCII 12) character by advancing to the top of the next page. If output is to a file instead, **printfoot** calls **skip**, which sends an equivalent number of blank lines to the file.

```
function printfoot(var pageno, lineno: integer; pagelen: integer;
                                      var status: iostatus): iostatus;
{ Print bottom of page }
begin { printfoot }
   if hardcopy then { send formfeed to printer }
      printfoot := wchars(1, chr(12), status)
   else
      printfoot := skip(pagelen - lineno + 1, status);
   if status = GOODIO then begin
      pageno := pageno + 1;
      lineno := 1
   end
end;
```

Finding Include Directives

The **findincdir** routine is called by **fprint** to look for an include directive in a string. The call

```
found := findincdir(s, i, name);
```

searches the string **s** for an include directive beginning with the ith character in the string. If an include directive is found, the function returns **TRUE** as its result, the parameter **name** contains the name of the file to be included, and **i** points one character beyond the end of the directive. If an include directive is not found, the function returns **FALSE** and **i** points to one character beyond the end of the string.

Here is **findincdir**:

```
function findincdir(var s: string; var i: integer; var name: filename):boolean;
{ Find include directive in string, return text file name }
var
   comment: string;
   c: char;
   j: integer;
   found: boolean;

{-----------------------------}
{ Modules to be included here: }
{         findcomment          }
{-----------------------------}
```

```
begin { findincdir }
   name := '';
   found := FALSE;
   repeat
      if findcomment(s, i, comment) then
         if gchar(comment, 1, c) = '$' then
            if gchar(comment, 2, c) in ['I', 'i'] then
               if not (gchar(comment, 3, c) in ['+', '-']) then begin
                  j := 3;
                  while gnbchar(comment, j, c) <> chr(0) do begin
                     addchar(name, c, MAXFNAME);
                     j := j + 1
                  end;
                  found := (length(name) > 0);
                  if found and (length(name) <= MAXFNAME - 5) then
                     if (pos('.TEXT', name)=0) and (pos('.text', name)=0) then
                        name := concat(name, '.TEXT')
               end
   until found or (i > length(s));
   findincdir := found
end;
```

findincdir uses **findcomment** to search for and extract comments from the string. **findcomment** returns the contents of any comment it finds, stripping off the comment delimiters.

To be a legal include directive, a comment's first character must be a <$>, and the second an upper- or lowercase <I>. The third character must not be a <+> or <−>; in those cases we have an I/O error-checking directive ({$i+} or {$i−}) instead of an include directive.

If all these conditions are fulfilled, **findincdir** moves the file name from the string into the variable **name**. Like **gettfname**, **findincdir** adds a **.TEXT** suffix to the end of the file name if one is not there and there is room for it.

The **findcomment** routine works this way: the call

```
found := findcomment(s, i, comment)
```

starts looking for a comment at the **i**th character of the string **s**. If a comment is found, **findcomment** returns **TRUE**, the variable **comment** contains the text of the comment, and **i** points to the character following the comment. If a comment is not seen, **findcomment** returns **FALSE** and **i** points to one character beyond the end of the string.

Here is **findcomment**:

```
function findcomment(var s:string; var i:integer; var comment:string):boolean;
{ Find Pascal comment in string }

var
   found: boolean;
   c1, c2: char;
   eoc, eos: boolean;
```

```
begin { findcomment }
   comment := '';
   found := FALSE;
   repeat
      if (gchar(s, i, c1) = '(') and (gchar(s, i + 1, c2) = '*') then begin
         i := i + 2;
         found := TRUE;
         repeat
            eoc := (gchar(s, i, c1) = '*') and (gchar(s, i + 1, c2) = ')');
            eos := (gchar(s, i, c1) = chr(0));
            if not (eoc or eos) then begin
               addchar(comment, c1, MAXSTR);
               i := i + 1
            end
         until eoc or eos;
         if eoc then
            i := i + 2
         else { end of string }
            i := i + 1
      end
      else if gchar(s, i, c1) = '{' then begin
         i := i + 1;
         found := TRUE;
         while not (gchar(s, i, c1) in ['}', chr(0)]) do begin
            addchar(comment, c1, MAXSTR);
            i := i + 1
         end;
         if c1 = '}' then
            i := i + 1
      end
      else
         i := i + 1
   until (i > length(s)) or found;
   findcomment := found
end;
```

Note that **findcomment** detects comments enclosed either in brackets or parentheses and asterisks. Note also that **findcomment** does not handle multi-line comments. Interested readers may want to look for ways to improve it.

Suggestions

In addition to the suggestions mentioned previously, you might want to consider adding the following features to **print**:

- Depending on the speed of your printer and its interface, you may notice that the printer pauses between printing individual lines. This is a signal that the printer is printing lines faster than the computer generates them. Improve **print**'s efficiency by recoding "bottleneck" routines in assembly language or adopting improved algorithms.

- Display some indication of **print**'s progress in printing individual files. It would be simple to display, say, every tenth line on the screen as it is printed. Or continuously display the current page and line number as the file is printing. Somewhat more useful would be for **print** to estimate the size of the file and display continuously how many lines or pages *remain* to be printed. (Even more useful would be an estimate of the *time* needed to print each file.)

- Allow the user the option of inserting single sheets into the printer by hand and pressing <**RETURN**> to signal **print** to print the next page. Similarly, add an option to pause between printing each file to allow the user to insert a different form or paper type.

Recommended Reading

print is a fancier version of the program of the same name from *Software Tools in Pascal* by B. Kernighan and P. J. Plauger (Addison-Wesley, 1981). You will find a number of suggestions there for making the program more flexible. You will also find a number of other valuable programs making use of text files for input and output.

6502 Assembly Language Programming by Lance Leventhal (Osborne/McGraw-Hill, 1981) and *6502 Assembly Language Subroutines* by Lance Leventhal and Winthrop Saville (Osborne/McGraw-Hill, 1982) are two books that are quite useful for converting Pascal routines into 6502 instructions.

SIX

Games and Strategy

There is no denying the popularity of computer games. There are thousands of game programs available for nearly all popular computer systems, from large mainframes to even the smallest microcomputers. These games are of all possible types: games requiring fast reflexes, sharp wits, simple good luck, or any combination thereof. The computer may play actively against one or more opponents, or it may act as a neutral referee between two or more users, judging which moves are legal and keeping score.

A large number of games pit the computer against its human user in a contest of mental skill. There seems to be some urge in many programmers' psyches to turn a powerful machine into a competitor. Perhaps it should be dubbed the Frankenstein syndrome: the urge to create an artificial and (at least in some sense) superior intelligence that can beat the average human player.

In some areas, attempting to "outwit" a computer can be as hopeless as a footrace against a Ferrari. Any computer can easily outdo any human in traditional data processing or other tasks of computation. How challenging would it be to program a "game" that pits a computer against a human in a race to sort 500 names into alphabetical order or to multiply 100 pairs of 10-digit numbers? You can easily think of many other competitions in which a human would have no chance of winning against a computer.

Because of its great computational speed, there are even traditional games, like tic-tac-toe or nim, which the computer can be programmed to play "perfectly." In such games, the computer can rapidly analyze all possible combinations of moves, determining which moves lead to victories, ties, or defeats. Since the eventual outcome of any move is determined, the computer can play flawlessly; given a fair game in the first place, the best result a human can hope for is a tie.

More complex games often have so large a number of possible outcomes that even the fastest computers have no hope of examining them all fully.

Human opponents can then bring their superior powers of pattern recognition and tacit knowledge into play. (These skills are not so easily programmed or even quantified.) Such is the case in games like chess or go. To a lesser extent, it is also true in *Reversi,* the game we will design in this chapter.

The origin of *Reversi* is unclear; one version was developed in England in the 1880s, although there are claims that the game was previously invented in China and was known as Fan Mien. The game has also been known as Friends. It has recently been popularized as the board game Othello, which is sold by Ideal.

The Rules of *Reversi*

Reversi is a simple game, and the rules can be learned in a matter of minutes. The game is played on an 8×8 board, like a chessboard. The game pieces are discs that are white on one side and black on the other. The initial board position is shown in Figure 6-1; two discs of each color are placed on the four central squares, with each color occupying a diagonal.

Players choose either black or white as their colors, either by a coin flip or

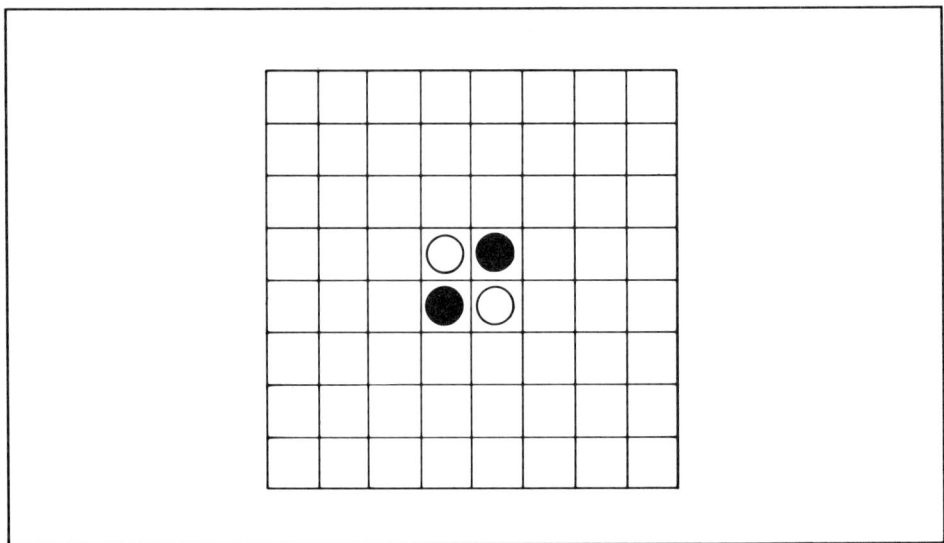

Figure 6-1. Initial board position

an agreement to switch colors for each game. By convention, black moves first.

A player moves by placing a disc of his or her own color uppermost on an empty square so that one or more of the opponent's pieces are *outflanked;* there must be at least one continuous horizontal, vertical, or diagonal row of the opponent's pieces between the disc being played and a previously placed disc of the player's color. All the opponent's outflanked discs in all possible directions are then flipped over to the player's own color. (See Figures 6-2 and 6-3.)

The two players move in turn until neither player can make a legal move either because there are no empty squares or because neither can outflank the other on the remaining empty squares. If only one player cannot make a legal move, the player's turn is skipped. The winner is the player who winds up owning the greatest number of discs on the board; ties are possible.

This is all you need to know to play *Reversi;* further details and examples may be found in the references at the end of the chapter.

Running the Program

Our primary goal in designing our **reversi** program is to make the computer a worthy opponent of an average human player. We need to arrive at some method by which the computer can make good moves and avoid bad ones. In addition, **reversi** should be as fast as possible for two reasons: first, a fast program is more interesting to play because the user does not have to wait for the computer to make its move, and second, a fast program may play better than a slower one because it can examine more possible moves in the same amount of time.

Nearly as important as the quality of the program's play is the program's ease of use. The human player should be able to concentrate as much as possible on *playing* the game, not on the details of running the program. Good game programs often make playing more enjoyable than the equivalent board game, because they eliminate illegal moves, keep score, and even point out moves the user may not have thought of.

We will design two versions of **reversi**: one that can be played on a normal CRT text screen and another that uses graphics for the board display. Other than the display, the two versions play identically; the following description applies to both.

To maximize ease of use, **reversi** differs slightly from our previous programs in its method of getting input from the user. All responses are single-key only; the program takes the first valid key the user presses and considers

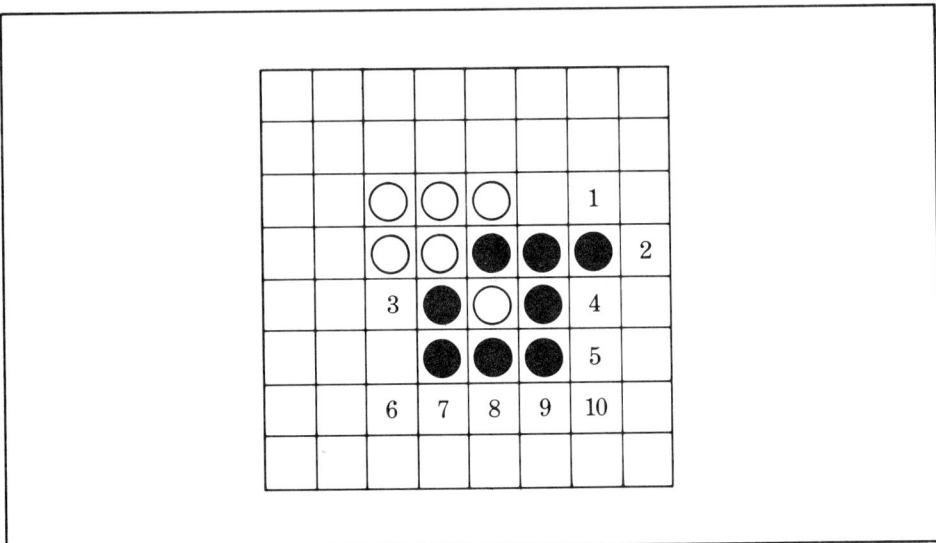

Figure 6-2. Numbered squares show white's legal moves

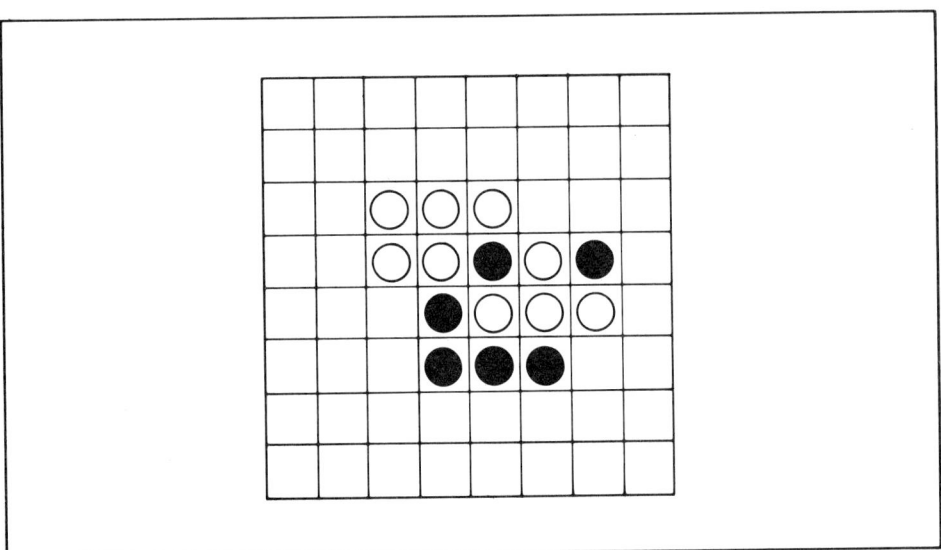

Figure 6-3. Board after white moves to position 4

it to be the user's response. The <RETURN> key is not used to terminate input, and the <BACKSPACE> key is not used to correct a mistake.

The computer displays the initial board position and then asks **Do you want white or black?(W/B):**. The user answers <W> for white discs or <B> for black. All other keys pressed are illegal; the computer beeps until the user presses either <W> or <B>.

reversi then asks **Enter lookahead for computer(1-6):**. *Lookahead* refers to how many moves ahead the computer looks to determine its best move. The larger this number, the better the computer plays; this is true at least in theory. We'll discuss lookahead in more depth later. First-time players should choose an initial lookahead of 1 and later increase it if the computer is too easy to beat at that level.

After the user answers these two questions the game begins. The computer and the human user alternate turns until neither one can make a legal move. As each move is made, **reversi** updates the display to reflect the new pattern of discs on the board and the current score. When the game is over, the computer declares one player or the other to be the winner.

How does the user make a move? When it is the human's turn, **reversi** displays an asterisk <*> in one of the squares to which the human has a legal move. The asterisk acts as a cursor. The user presses the <→> key on the Apple's keyboard (other computers may use a different key) to move the asterisk to another legal square. As the user keeps pressing the <→> key, **reversi** places the cursor on each square on which the user has a legal move, skipping back to the first move as necessary. The <←> key on the Apple (again, other computers can use a different key) may be used to cycle through the legal moves in the opposite direction. This scheme ensures that the user cannot enter illegal moves; the asterisk only appears in legal squares.

When the cursor occupies the square to which the user wants to move, the user presses the <RETURN> key. The display is quickly updated to reflect the result of the move.

At the end of each game, **reversi** asks **Play again?(Y/N):**; the user answers <Y> to start another game or <N> to exit from the program.

Data Structures

Our first problem in writing **reversi** is how to represent the game board in the computer's memory.

For reasons of efficiency, it is useful to wrap an additional layer of squares around the 8×8 board to act as *border* squares. These border squares act as sentinels to permit the program to scan the board squares in different directions without continually checking whether the board's array limits have been exceeded. (We will see how this works later.)

The addition of these border squares turns the 8×8 board into a 10×10 board. How do we represent this in Pascal? The most obvious solution is to represent the board as a 10×10 two-dimensional array, as follows:

```
<type>
   board = array [0..9, 0..9] of <something>;
```

Generally you should represent a real-world situation with a similar data structure; such an arrangement is easier for you to understand and debug. For this reason, early versions of the **reversi** program used a two-dimensional array to represent the board in memory.

Even though using a two-dimensional array is a simple and natural solution, in this case it significantly complicates other matters. Typically, the computer must work harder to access an individual element of a two-dimensional array than it does to access an element of a one-dimensional array. On the Apple II, it takes nearly two and one-half times longer to retrieve an element from a two-dimensional array of integers than it does to retrieve an element from a one-dimensional array of the same size. This difference translates into a loss of efficiency for the program as a whole.

In addition, we want to be able to access a given square's neighbor quickly; this also turns out to be easier with a one-dimensional array. For these reasons, the version of **reversi** presented here uses a one-dimensional array to represent the board.

We start our data structure definition by setting up the **contents** and **player** data types:

```
<type>
   contents = (LIGHT, DARK, EMPTY, BORDER);
   player = LIGHT..DARK;
```

We use **LIGHT** and **DARK** to represent a square occupied by a white or black disc. (We do not use the more natural **WHITE** and **BLACK** because these identifiers are already used by the Apple's graphics routines.) An empty square is represented by the value **EMPTY**, and the border squares have the value **BORDER**. The type **player** is defined to be either **LIGHT** or **DARK**.

Board squares are numbered from 0 to 99. (See Figure 6-4 for the arrangement.) This allows us to define the **squarenum** data type:

0	1	2	3	4	5	6	7	8	9
10	11	12	13	14	15	16	17	18	19
20	21	22	23	24	25	26	27	28	29
30	31	32	33	34	35	36	37	38	39
40	41	42	43	44	45	46	47	48	49
50	51	52	53	54	55	56	57	58	59
60	61	62	63	64	65	66	67	68	69
70	71	72	73	74	75	76	77	78	79
80	81	82	83	84	85	86	87	88	89
90	91	92	93	94	95	96	97	98	99

Figure 6-4. Board numbering scheme

```
<type>
    squarenum = 0..99;
```

At a number of places in **reversi**, it is necessary to store a list of moves to be examined by the program. This is accomplished by record variables of the type **movelist**, which is defined as follows:

```
<const>
    MAXMOVES = 60;
<type>
   movelist = record
       nmoves: 0..MAXMOVES;
       move: array [1..MAXMOVES] of squarenum
   end;
```

A variable of the type **movelist** holds the number of moves in the list in the integer **nmoves** and each individual move in the array **move**. The constant declaration for **MAXMOVES** says that there is room for a maximum of 60 moves in a list. This value of **MAXMOVES** is certainly higher than necessary, since we will never come across a board with 60 possible moves. On the other hand, it is hard to calculate a "theoretical" maximum list size. Thus, we choose to be overly careful in specifying **MAXMOVES**; this care allows us to add moves to a list without checking that the list gets too large.

We can define the data structure used to keep track of the board as follows:

```
<type>
   board = record
      sq: array [squarenum] of contents;
      ndiscs: array [player] of integer;
      possible: movelist
   end;
```

Here the array **sq** holds the contents of the board squares and the array **ndiscs** contains the number of discs currently owned by each player. The board record also contains **possible**, a list of *possible* legal moves. A square is defined as a possible move if it is empty and there is at least one square adjacent to it that contains either a white or black disc. It should be clear that either player's legal moves are a subset of these possible moves. When looking for a player's legal moves, **reversi** only needs to consider moves in this **possible** list. Whenever a move is made to the board, **reversi** modifies the list to reflect the new arrangement of possible moves.

There is also a **direction** type that represents all eight possible horizontal, vertical, and diagonal directions from any given square. We use the compass directions as mnemonics:

```
<type>
   direction = (NORTH, NORTHEAST, EAST, SOUTHEAST,
                SOUTH, SOUTHWEST, WEST, NORTHWEST);
```

reversi — The Main Routine

We will design the text version of **reversi** first. This will allow us to concentrate on getting the program to work properly before making the modifications for graphics. While designing the text version, we will keep in mind that we plan to use graphics eventually; this might save us from coding in design features that would require extensive rewriting when developing the graphics modifications.

Given the data definitions we have developed, the main routine of **reversi** is relatively simple:

```
{$s+}
program reversi;
{ The game of Reversi }
```

```
uses
   {$u apple2:toolstuff.code } crtstuff;
const
   MAXMOVES = 60;
type
   contents = (LIGHT, DARK, EMPTY, BORDER);
   player = LIGHT..DARK;
   squarenum = 0..99;
   movelist = record
      nmoves: 0..MAXMOVES;
      move: array [1..MAXMOVES] of squarenum
   end;
   board = record
      sq: array [squarenum] of contents;
      ndiscs: array [player] of integer;
      possible: movelist
   end;
   direction = (NORTH, NORTHEAST, EAST, SOUTHEAST,
                SOUTH, SOUTHWEST, WEST, NORTHWEST);
var
   accept, fwdkey, backey, ch: char;
   delta: array [direction] of integer;
   sqord: array [squarenum] of integer;
   sqchar: array [contents] of char;
   corner, poison1, good1: array [1..4] of squarenum;
   poison2, good2: array [1..4, 1..2] of squarenum;
   edge: array [1..4, 1..4] of squarenum;
   xmarg, ymarg: integer;

{---------------------------------}
{ Modules to be included here:    }
{       initrev                   }
{       dispgrid                  }
{       playagame                 }
{---------------------------------}
begin { reversi }
   crt(CLEAR);
   disptitle('reversi');
   initrev;
   dispgrid;
   repeat
      playagame;
      center('Play again?(Y/N):', ymarg + 18);
      ch := getkey(ch, ['Y', 'N'], TRUE);
      eraseline(ymarg + 18)
   until ch = 'N';
   crt(CLEAR)
end.
```

Initializing reversi's Global Variables

As in most of our programs, we set aside a separate routine to initialize **reversi**'s global variables. The routine is split into two parts because of a restriction of the Apple Pascal compiler that limits the size of the object code generated for any single procedure to 1200 bytes. Here is **initrev**:

160 Advanced Pascal Programming Techniques

```
procedure initrev;
{ Initialize reversi global variables }

procedure initrev1;
{ Initialize globals, part 1 }

var
   i, j, sv: integer;
begin { initrev1 }
   accept := chr(13);
   backey := chr(8);
   fwdkey := chr(21);
   xmarg := (MAXCRTCOL - 32) div 2;
   ymarg := 4;
   sqchar[DARK] := 'B';
   sqchar[LIGHT] := 'W';
   sqchar[EMPTY] := ' ';
   sqchar[BORDER] := '*';
   sqord[11] := 1; sqord[12] := 7; sqord[13] := 2; sqord[14] := 2;
                   sqord[22] := 8; sqord[23] := 6; sqord[24] := 5;
                                   sqord[33] := 3; sqord[34] := 4;
                                                   sqord[44] := 0;
   for j := 1 to 4 do
      for i := j to 4 do begin
         sv := sqord[10 * j + i];
         sqord[10 * i + j] := sv;
         sqord[10 * (9 - i) + j] := sv;
         sqord[10 * (9 - j) + i] := sv;
         sqord[10 * j + 9 - i] := sv;
         sqord[10 * i + 9 - j] := sv;
         sqord[10 * (9 - i) + 9 - j] := sv;
         sqord[10 * (9 - j) + 9 - i] := sv
      end;
   delta[NORTH] := -10;
   delta[NORTHEAST] := -9;
   delta[EAST] := 1;
   delta[SOUTHEAST] := 11;
   delta[SOUTH] := 10;
   delta[SOUTHWEST] := 9;
   delta[WEST] := -1;
   delta[NORTHWEST] := -11
end;

procedure initrev2;
{ Initialize globals, part 2 }

var
   i: integer;
begin { initrev2 }
   corner[1]    := 11; poison2[1, 1] := 12; good2[1, 1] := 13;
   poison2[1, 2] := 21; poison1[1]   := 22;
   good2[1, 2]  := 31;                      good1[1]    := 33;

   corner[2]    := 18; poison2[2, 1] := 17; good2[2, 1] := 16;
   poison2[2, 2] := 28; poison1[2]   := 27;
   good2[2, 2]  := 38;                      good1[2]    := 36;

   corner[3]    := 81; poison2[3, 1] := 82; good2[3, 1] := 83;
   poison2[3, 2] := 71; poison1[3]   := 72;
   good2[3, 2]  := 61;                      good1[3]    := 63;

   corner[4]    := 88; poison2[4, 1] := 87; good2[4, 1] := 86;
   poison2[4, 2] := 78; poison1[4]   := 77;
   good2[4, 2]  := 68;                      good1[4]    := 66;
```

```
      for i := 1 to 4 do begin
         edge[1, i] := 12 + i;
         edge[2, i] := 28 + 10 * i;
         edge[3, i] := 21 + 10 * i;
         edge[4, i] := 82 + i
      end
   end;

begin { initrev }
   initrev1;
   initrev2
end;
```

initrev initializes the following variables:

- **accept**, **fwdkey**, and **backey** are the keys the user presses to accept the cursor-displayed move, to move the cursor to the next move in the legal move list, and to move the cursor to the previous move in the legal move list, respectively. **accept** is set so the move is accepted by the <RETURN> key. **fwdkey** is set to the Apple's <→> key (<Control-U>, ASCII 21), and **backey** is set to the <←> key (<BACKSPACE>, ASCII 8). These keys can be chosen to reflect any particular keyboard arrangement the user has. The keys chosen here have obvious mnemonic significance on the Apple, which is an advantage. They are also grouped closely together on the Apple II's keyboard, which may be a disadvantage: the user might accidentally press the <RETURN> key while meaning to press one of the others.

- **xmarg** and **ymarg** are the CRT coordinates of the upper left-hand corner of the board as it is displayed on the screen. The choice of **xmarg** centers the board horizontally on the screen. **ymarg** may have to be changed for CRT screens with fewer than 24 lines.

- **sqchar** is an array containing the characters **reversi** uses to display each board square on the (text) screen: a square occupied by a black disc is represented by the letter <B>, a white disc by the letter <W>; empty squares are represented by blanks. The asterisk character, <*>, is used as the cursor.

- **sqord** is an array controlling the order in which the computer evaluates moves. We will discuss the usefulness of this feature later when we talk about how the computer arrives at its moves. Until then, we will simply point out that **initrev** only directly assigns the values of ten squares, using the game board's eightfold symmetry to assign values to the other squares.

- **delta** is an array containing amounts to add to a board square's index to get the index of the adjacent square in the specified direction. For example, the square in the **SOUTHEAST** direction from square 44 is

```
44 + delta[SOUTHEAST] = 44 + 11 = 55
```

This method is simple and reasonably efficient.

- **corner, poison1, poison2, good1, good2,** and **edge** are all arrays used to group various squares into classes. The variable **corner[2]**, for example, is the number of the second corner square, 18. **poison1** squares (22, 27, 72, and 77) are the squares diagonally adjacent to corner squares. **good1** squares (33, 36, 63, and 66) are those two squares diagonally away from corner squares. **poison2** squares (12, 17, 21, 28, 71, 78, 82, and 87) are the squares horizontally and vertically adjacent to corners. **good2** squares (13, 16, 31, 38, 61, 68, 83, and 86) are those two squares away from the corner squares in horizontal and vertical directions. Finally, the **edge** array contains the numbers of the four central squares on each of the four edges of the board.

All these board square arrays are used to help judge the strategic merits of the various board positions when the computer calculates its move. Generally, moves to **corner**, **good1**, and **good2** squares are considered good moves, and moves to **poison1** and **poison2** squares are considered bad. It is also a good idea to control **edge** squares. We will discuss *Reversi* strategy in greater detail later.

Displaying the Board

The board grid only needs to be put onto the screen once, at the beginning of the program. This is accomplished with **dispgrid**:

```
procedure dispgrid;
{ Display board grid - text version }

var
    i: integer;
begin { dispgrid }
    center('---------------------------------', ymarg);
    for i := 1 to 15 do
        if odd(i) then
            center('!   !   !   !   !   !   !   !   !', ymarg + i)
        else
            center('!---!---!---!---!---!---!---!---!', ymarg + i);
    center('---------------------------------', ymarg + 16)
end;
```

Playing a Single Game

The procedure **playagame** plays individual games against the user. The logic for deciding whether the game is over or not is slightly tricky and is best described first in the following pseudo-code:

```
begin
   initialize variables for game
   set current player to black
   set game-over flag to FALSE
   set previous-player-moved flag to TRUE
   repeat
      display current score
      if current player has a legal move
         get move from current player
         make move
         set previous-player-moved flag to TRUE
      else if previous player moved
         set previous-player-moved flag to FALSE
      else { neither player can move }
         set game over flag to TRUE
      set current player to other player
   until game over
end
```

The "previous-player-moved" flag indicates whether the previous player moved; it is set to **TRUE** whenever a player makes a legal move and set to **FALSE** whenever a player does not have a legal move. The game is over when the current player has no legal move and the previous-player-moved flag indicates the other player had no legal move on the previous turn.

```
procedure playagame;
{ Play one game }
var
   mainboard: board;
   list: movelist;
   gameover, moved: boolean;
   computer, human, currentplayer: player;
   lookahead: integer;
   k: squarenum;

{-----------------------------}
{ Modules to be inserted here: }
{         dispsquare          }
{         setsquare           }
{         other               }
{         initgame            }
{         itos                }
{         dispscore           }
{         flanking            }
{         makelist            }
{         addmove             }
{         delmove             }
{         getmove             }
{         makemove            }
{         declarewinner       }
{-----------------------------}
```

```
begin { playagame }
   initgame;
   currentplayer := DARK;
   gameover := FALSE;
   moved := TRUE;
   repeat
      dispscore;
      if makelist(list, currentplayer, mainboard) > 0 then begin
         moved := TRUE;
         k := getmove(list, currentplayer);
         makemove(k, currentplayer)
      end
      else if moved then
         moved := FALSE
      else { Neither player able to move }
         gameover := TRUE;
      currentplayer := other(currentplayer)
   until gameover;
   declarewinner
end;
```

We will refer to the board on which the game is played as the *main board;* it is represented by the variable **mainboard** in the preceding routine. We are careful to distinguish the main board from those generated later in the program to test the results of the computer's hypothetical moves.

Initializing Game Variables

Each time a new game is started, **playagame** calls **initgame** to set up the initial conditions.

```
procedure initgame;
{ Initialize game variables }
var
   i, j: integer;
   ch: char;
begin { initgame }
   eraseline(ymarg + 17);
   with mainboard do begin
      for i := 0 to 9 do begin
         sq[i] := BORDER;
         sq[i + 90] := BORDER;
         sq[10 * i] := BORDER;
         sq[10 * i + 9] := BORDER
      end;
      ndiscs[LIGHT] := 2;
      ndiscs[DARK] := 2;
      with possible do begin
         nmoves := 12;
         move[ 1] := 33;
         move[ 2] := 34;
         move[ 3] := 35;
         move[ 4] := 36;
         move[ 5] := 43;
         move[ 6] := 46;
         move[ 7] := 53;
```

```
              move[ 8] := 56;
              move[ 9] := 63;
              move[10] := 64;
              move[11] := 65;
              move[12] := 66
           end
     end;
     for i := 1 to 8 do
        for j := 1 to 8 do
           setsquare(10 * i + j, EMPTY);
     setsquare(44, LIGHT);
     setsquare(55, LIGHT);
     setsquare(45, DARK);
     setsquare(54, DARK);
     center('Do you want white or black?(W/B):', ymarg + 18);
     case getkey(ch, ['W', 'B'], TRUE) of
        'W': begin
                human := LIGHT;
                posstr('Computer is black', xmarg, ymarg + 17)
             end;
        'B': begin
                human := DARK;
                posstr('Computer is white', xmarg, ymarg + 17)
             end
     end;
     center('Enter lookahead for computer(1-6):', ymarg + 18);
     lookahead := ord(getkey(ch, ['1'..'6'], FALSE)) - 48;
     eraseline(ymarg + 18);
     posstr('Lookahead:', xmarg + 22, ymarg + 17);
     write(ch);
     posstr('Computer:', xmarg, ymarg + 18);
     posstr('Human:', xmarg + 24, ymarg + 18);
     computer := other(human)
end;
```

initgame initializes the main board by setting the border squares to **BORDER** and the interior squares to **EMPTY**. It then places two **LIGHT** and two **DARK** initial discs on the four central squares. It also initializes the main board's **possible** move list to the twelve squares immediately surrounding the four central squares. These are the only squares we need to examine initially for legal moves for either player.

After initializing the main board, **initgame** asks the user to choose colors and to enter the lookahead value. Since single-key user input is used throughout **reversi**, **initgame** uses **getkey** to accept the user's input instead of **getstring**. Note that the parameters passed to **getkey** ensure that the user types a valid response (although, unfortunately, single-key input does not allow the user to correct a valid but mistaken response).

Miscellaneous Simple Routines

The main board's squares are initialized in **initgame** with the simple procedure **setsquare**. In setting a square to a new value, it also calls **dispsquare** to reflect the new arrangement on the CRT screen.

```
procedure setsquare(k: squarenum; c: contents);
{ Put piece on square }
begin { setsquare }
   mainboard.sq[k] := c;
   dispsquare(k, c)
end;
```

We also call **setsquare** throughout **reversi** to change the squares' contents as the game progresses.

Keeping in mind that we will be modifying the program for graphics later, we isolate the code that displays a square's contents in the **dispsquare** procedure:

```
procedure dispsquare(k: squarenum; c: contents);
{ Display square contents on text screen }
begin { dispsquare }
   gotoxy(xmarg + 4 * (k mod 10 - 1) + 2,
          ymarg + 2 * (k div 10 - 1) + 1);
   write(sqchar[c]);
   crt(HOME)
end;
```

The **other** function is used in **initgame** to find the computer's color once the human's choice of color is known. If **other** is fed the argument **LIGHT**, it returns the value **DARK**, and vice versa:

```
function other(pl: player): player;
{ Return other player's color }
begin { other }
   if pl = LIGHT then
      other := DARK
   else
      other := LIGHT
end;
```

other points out one advantage and one disadvantage of the use of scalar types to represent a small number of distinct values. The advantage is one of clarity. When the programmer sees the code

```
currentplayer := other(currentplayer)
```

it is obvious that the program is indicating that the current player is now the other player.

The disadvantage is one of efficiency. **other** must be called *every* time we want to know what the "other player's color" is. We could have avoided this by defining the squares' contents as constants instead of scalars, as follows:

```
<const>
   LIGHT = 0;
   DARK = 1;
   EMPTY = 2;
   BORDER = 3;
<type>
   contents = LIGHT..BORDER;
   player = LIGHT..DARK;
```

Then we could have avoided the **other** procedure entirely; for example, switching the current player could be coded as

```
currentplayer := 1 - currentplayer;
```

But this is much less clear than calling **other**. For now, we opt for the additional clarity of using the scalar type, although we will note this as a potential change to increase the program's efficiency.

playagame calls **dispscore** before every move to display the number of discs each player owns:

```
procedure dispscore;
{ Display current score }
var
   s: string;
begin { dispscore }
   with mainboard do begin
      itos(ndiscs[computer], 2, s);
      posstr(s, xmarg + 10, ymarg + 18);
      itos(ndiscs[human], 2, s);
      posstr(s, xmarg + 31, ymarg + 18)
   end
end;
```

dispscore makes use of **itos**, which converts an integer into a string. **itos** is similar to the **ftos** routine described in Chapter Three. We could have used **ftos** instead, but that approach would involve inserting all the declarations for the **fixed** data type, details that are irrelevant to **reversi**.

```
procedure itos(n, wid: integer; var s: string);
{ Convert integer to string }
var
   negnum: boolean;
   i, j: integer;
   ch: char;
begin { itos }
   negnum := (n < 0);
   n := abs(n);
   s := '';
   repeat
```

```
            addchar(s, chr(n mod 10 + 48), MAXSTR);
            n := n div 10
         until n = 0;
         if negnum then
            addchar(s, '-', MAXSTR);
         while length(s) < wid do
            addchar(s, ' ', MAXSTR);
         i := 1;
         j := length(s);
         while i < j do begin
            ch := s[i];
            s[i] := s[j];
            s[j] := ch;
            i := i + 1;
            j := j - 1
         end
   end
end;
```

Finding Legal Moves

Before getting each move, **playagame** calls **makelist** to compose a list of legal moves for the player whose move it is. This involves scanning the main board's **possible** move list to sift out the moves that are legal for the current player. **makelist** performs this function, returning a list of the legal moves as a **var** parameter and the number of legal moves as its result.

```
function makelist(var legal: movelist; pl: player; var bd: board): integer;
{ Make list of legal moves, return number of legal moves }
var
   i: integer;

{------------------------------}
{ Modules to be inserted here: }
{       legalmove              }
{------------------------------}
begin { makelist }
   legal.nmoves := 0;
   with bd.possible do
      for i := 1 to nmoves do
         if legalmove(move[i], bd, pl) then begin
            legal.nmoves := legal.nmoves + 1;
            legal.move[legal.nmoves] := move[i]
         end;
   makelist := legal.nmoves
end;
```

The **movelist** structure is similar to a string: both structures have an arbitrary number of elements (moves for **movelist**s or characters for strings) up to a certain maximum number. There is also an indicator of the current number of elements in the structure (the length of the string or the variable **nmoves** in the **movelist**). To simplify things, an additional restriction is imposed on the list: it must not contain any duplicate moves. This restriction ensures, for example, that possible moves are not examined for legality more than once. Since there are no duplicate moves in the **possible** list, **makelist** can just append each legal move it finds to the end of the **legal** list.

The Boolean function **legalmove** called by **makelist** tests whether a specific move is legal. It returns **TRUE** if it is legal and **FALSE** if it is not.

```
function legalmove(k: squarenum; var bd: board; pl: player): boolean;
{ Test if move is legal }
var
   ok: boolean;
   dir: direction;
begin { legalmove }
   dir := NORTH;
   ok := flanking(k, dir, bd, pl);
   while (dir <> NORTHWEST) and not ok do begin
      dir := succ(dir);
      ok := flanking(k, dir, bd, pl)
   end;
   legalmove := ok
end;
```

legalmove uses **flanking** to look at successive directions from the specified square until it either discovers that the opponent is outflanked along a certain direction (in which case the move is legal) or runs out of directions to check (in which case the move is illegal). The call

```
ok := flanking(k, dir, bd, pl);
```

checks whether the player **pl** would outflank the opponent in the direction **dir** by moving to square **k** on the board **bd**. Here is **flanking**:

```
function flanking(k: squarenum; dir: direction; var bd: board; pl: player):
                                                                    boolean;
{ Return whether player flanks opponent from given square in given direction }
var
   ok: boolean;
   opponent: player;
   del: integer;
begin { flanking }
   ok := FALSE;
   opponent := other(pl);
   del := delta[dir];
   k := k + del;
   with bd do
      if sq[k] = opponent then begin
         repeat
            k := k + del
         until sq[k] <> opponent;
         ok := (sq[k] = pl)
      end;
   flanking := ok
end;
```

Expressed in words, **flanking** checks the neighboring square in the specified direction. If it does not belong to the opponent, the player does not outflank in that particular direction. If the neighboring square *does* belong to the opponent, **flanking** looks at successive squares in the same direction until it comes across a square not belonging to the opponent; if that square belongs to the player, the player outflanks the opponent in that direction. If, instead, the square is empty or it is a border square, the player does not outflank the opponent in that direction.

It is important that **flanking** be relatively efficient; it may be called as many as eight times to determine whether a given square is one of the legal moves for a player. You may want to consider how **flanking** would change for a different data structure. (What if we were using a two-dimensional array to represent the board? What if we did not use our sentinel border squares to prevent ourselves from going off the board and used explicit checks in the program instead?)

Getting Players' Moves

Once a list of player's legal moves has been compiled, **playagame** calls the **getmove** function to obtain the player's choice of one of these moves. This function is a simple two-way switch that calls different routines to get either the human's move or the computer's move:

```
function getmove(var list: movelist; pl: player): squarenum;
{ Get current player's move }

{------------------------------}
{ Modules to be included here: }
{         gethuman             }
{         getcomputer          }
{------------------------------}
begin { getmove }
   if pl = computer then
      getmove := getcomputer(list)
   else
      getmove := gethuman(list)
end;
```

Of the two, the simpler routine by far is **gethuman**; it allows the user to scan through all the legal moves with the <←> and <→> keys and to select one with the <RETURN> key:

```
function gethuman(var list: movelist): squarenum;
{ Get human's move }

var
```

```
      i: integer;
      ch: char;
begin { gethuman }
   i := 1;
   crt(BEEP);
   with list do begin
      repeat
         dispsquare(move[i], BORDER);
         ch := getkey(ch, [accept, backey, fwdkey], FALSE);
         dispsquare(move[i], EMPTY);
         if ch = backey then begin
            i := i - 1;
            if i < 1 then
               i := nmoves
         end
         else if ch = fwdkey then begin
            i := i + 1;
            if i > nmoves then
               i := 1
         end
      until ch = accept;
      gethuman := move[i]
   end
end;
```

For completeness, we should also specify **getcomputer**, the routine that calculates the computer's "best" move. Instead, we will use the following temporary routine, which allows us to test the remainder of the program:

```
function getcomputer(var list: movelist): squarenum;
{ Get computer's move - interim version }
begin
   getcomputer := list.move[1]
end;
```

This version of **getcomputer** simply picks the first move in the move list. We do not expect such a simple algorithm to generate very intelligent play, but it enables us to test the program easily to verify that everything else works right.

Making the Move

Once either player picks a move, the **makemove** routine is called to update the main board, reflecting the new arrangement of discs:

```
procedure makemove(k: squarenum; pl: player);
{ Make move on main board }
var
   dir: direction;
   k1: squarenum;
```

```
      opponent: player;
      del: integer;
begin { makemove }
   setsquare(k, pl);
   opponent := other(pl);
   with mainboard do begin
      ndiscs[pl] := ndiscs[pl] + 1;
      delmove(k, possible);
      for dir := NORTH to NORTHWEST do begin
         del := delta[dir];
         if flanking(k, dir, mainboard, pl) then begin
            k1 := k + del;
            repeat
               setsquare(k1, pl);
               ndiscs[pl] := ndiscs[pl] + 1;
               ndiscs[opponent] := ndiscs[opponent] - 1;
               k1 := k1 + del
            until sq[k1] = pl
         end
         else if sq[k + del] = EMPTY then
            addmove(k + del, possible)
      end
   end
end;
```

makemove first places the player's disc on the specified square and then deletes the move from the main board's **possible** move list (because the square is no longer empty). Then it examines all eight directions, flipping over all the opponent's disks that the new move outflanks. If a square next to the new move is empty, **makemove** adds it to the main board's **possible** move list.

The **addmove** routine adds a move to a list.

```
procedure addmove(k: squarenum; var list: movelist);
{ Add move to list, unless already present }

var
   i: integer;

begin { addmove }
   with list do begin
      move[nmoves + 1] := k;
      i := 1;
      while move[i] <> k do
         i := i + 1;
      if i = nmoves + 1 then
         nmoves := nmoves + 1
   end
end;
```

Note that **addmove** carries out a sequential search of the elements already in the list to ensure there is no duplication.

delmove is the inverse of **addmove**; it deletes a move from a list:

```
procedure delmove(k: squarenum; var list: movelist);
{ Delete move from list }
```

```
var
   i: integer;
begin { delmove }
   with list do begin
      move[nmoves + 1] := k;
      i := 1;
      while move[i] <> k do
         i := i + 1;
      if i < nmoves + 1 then begin
         while i <= nmoves - 1 do begin
            move[i] := move[i + 1];
            i := i + 1
         end;
         nmoves := nmoves - 1
      end
   end
```

delmove does not assume that the move to be deleted actually appears in the list. Instead, it searches for the move to be deleted; if it is found, the moves above it are moved down one position in the list and **nmoves** is decreased by one.

Finishing Up

After the game is over, **playagame** calls **declarewinner**, which (as you might expect) tells the user which side won:

```
procedure declarewinner;
{ Tell who won }
var
   diff: integer;
   s: string;
begin { declarewinner }
   with mainboard do
      diff := ndiscs[computer] - ndiscs[human];
   if diff > 0 then begin
      itos(diff, 0, s);
      center(concat('I won by ', s), ymarg + 17)
   end
   else if diff < 0 then begin
      itos(-diff, 0, s);
      center(concat('You won by ', s), ymarg + 17)
   end
   else
      center('We have tied!', ymarg + 17)
end;
```

Although the computer's move-generation algorithm needs to be improved, this finishes **reversi**.

Game Theory

How will **reversi** decide which one of its legal moves is the best one for it to make against its human opponent? Before dealing with the question of an effective strategy for our specific game, we will look at the problem in general and describe a method that can be applied to *any* game of this type.

In theory, the computer could examine all possible move sequences for white and black, discovering which sequences end up in won games for either color. If such an analysis were achievable, the computer could always play a "perfect" game, forcing a win if possible. Such an analysis is feasible for very simple games.

For *Reversi* and most other complex games, such complete solutions are very impractical and may be impossible with current computer technology. There are simply too many move sequences to examine. As a result, the computer must base its moves on incomplete information and consider only a limited number of possible future positions.

To see how such move selection works, let's assume that two players named Maxie and Minnie are playing a game and that Maxie wants to find his best move. We will also assume that we can somehow assign a *score* to any given game position, reflecting how good that position is for Maxie; that is, the larger the number, the better his chances are for victory.

Maxie's simplest strategy is to evaluate the position resulting from each of his legal moves; his best move is the one that results in the board position with the highest score. Simply stated, Maxie tries to make the move that *maximizes* his score.

We have just described Maxie's best strategy if he "looks ahead" one move. We can expect Maxie's judgment of his best move would be improved if he took Minnie's *possible responses* into account, that is, if he looked ahead two moves. After all, she may have laid a trap and may have a devastating reply to the move he had originally calculated to be his best. In that case, he might have been better off to choose some other move.

To take Minnie's responses into account, Maxie could use the following method: generate all of Minnie's possible responses to each of his possible moves, pick the most favorable position, and choose the move leading to it. This method, while intuitively attractive, is *not* the best strategy, because it assumes Minnie will *cooperate* in making the move leading to Maxie's most favorable position. Assuming Minnie is reasonably intelligent (or lucky), she is more likely to choose a move leading to the *least* favorable position for

Maxie. Thus, the best strategy for Maxie is to choose the move to which Minnie can make the least damaging response.

We can express this idea more clearly in pictures. Consider the *game tree* shown in Figure 6-5. The root node at the top represents the initial board position. The nodes at the next level represent the board positions resulting from each of Maxie's possible moves. The nodes at the bottom level represent the board positions resulting from Minnie's possible responses. (For simplicity, we will assume Maxie has four legal moves and Minnie has four legal responses to any of those moves.) The numbers in the 16 nodes at the bottom level represent the scores calculated for the resulting board positions.

Consider what happens if Maxie makes the move represented by the first (leftmost) branch in Figure 6-5. Minnie has the choice of moves resulting in scores of 2, 9, 7, or 9. Since a higher score reflects a better position for Maxie, Minnie will choose her first move, winding up with a score of 2.

If Maxie instead chooses the second branch from the left, Minnie will pick from moves resulting in scores of 8, 5, 3, or 5; she will choose to give Maxie the lowest score of 3. Similarly, Minnie will "stick" Maxie with a score of 2 if he chooses the third branch and a score of 1 if he takes the fourth branch.

So what is Maxie's best choice? Obviously, it is the second branch. His strategy is to maximize his score, given that Minnie is trying to minimize it. By choosing the second branch, he can guarantee himself at least a score of 3, no matter what Minnie's response is.

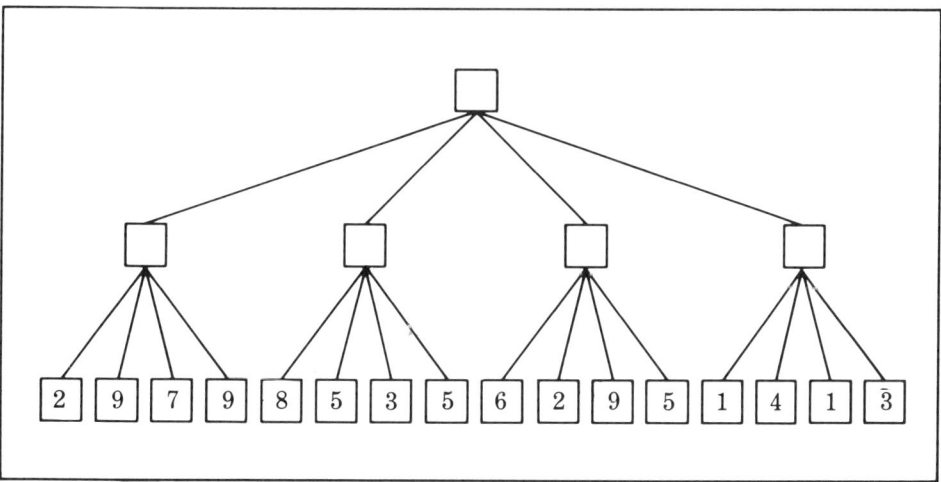

Figure 6-5. Hypothetical game tree

Table 6-1. Dependence of Number of Positions Evaluated on Lookahead

Lookahead	Number of Positions Evaluated
1	8
2	64
3	512
4	4096
5	32768
6	262144

This strategy is known as *minimax*. We have described the process for lookaheads of 1 and 2 respectively. Generalization to higher values of lookahead is straightforward although somewhat dizzying. For a lookahead of 3, we must look at each of Maxie's responses to each of Minnie's responses to each of Maxie's possible initial moves. Clearly, this is a job only a computer could love.

It should also be clear that increasing the lookahead can greatly increase the time it takes to find the best move. For example, assuming each player has an average of eight moves to consider per turn, the number of positions can become quite large. Table 6-1 shows the number of board positions evaluated for different lookahead values. Fortunately, there is a shortcut that can significantly decrease the computation time necessary for the minimax procedure. This shortcut is called *alpha-beta pruning*; it applies when using lookaheads of 2 or greater.

To see how alpha-beta pruning works, consider again the game tree in Figure 6-5. Assume Maxie is examining it from left to right to find his best move. After Maxie has looked at Minnie's responses to his first two possible moves, he knows he can achieve at least a score of 3 if he chooses the second branch. When he sees that Minnie's second response to his third choice results in a score of 2, Maxie knows *at that point* that he should not choose the third branch; Minnie will be able to put him in a worse position than she would if he made his second choice. As a result, Maxie need not evaluate the results of Minnie's last two responses to his third choice. These branches of the game tree are said to be *pruned*.

Similarly, when Maxie discovers that the score resulting from Minnie's first response to his fourth move is 1, he knows that he need not evaluate the positions resulting from Minnie's other responses. Once again, he knows that his second choice is better than his fourth without doing any further work. Thus, he has avoided looking at five of the 16 branches.

Perhaps an easier way to verify that alpha-beta pruning works correctly is to observe that Maxie's best move is totally independent of the scores resulting from the pruned branches. No matter what values we put in the boxes corresponding to Minnie's third and fourth responses to Maxie's third move, or Minnie's second, third, and fourth responses to Maxie's fourth move, Maxie's best move remains his second.

In general, Maxie can stop evaluating Minnie's possible moves at any level of the game tree whenever the result from one node falls below a previously established *cutoff value*. (The cutoff value is 3 in the example we just examined.) The cutoff value is the maximum of the minimum values seen so far in previous nodes at the same level.

If this is not enough to confuse you thoroughly, note that Maxie can use an analogous pruning strategy when evaluating his own responses to Minnie's moves (at lookaheads of 3 or more). Here Maxie can avoid evaluating whenever the result from a node rises above the minimum of the maximum values seen so far in previous nodes at the same level, since he knows that Minnie will choose the previous node instead of the current one. Interested readers may want to draw their own game trees to see how this process works or to consult one of the references at the end of this chapter.

The savings resulting from alpha-beta pruning can be dramatic, but the

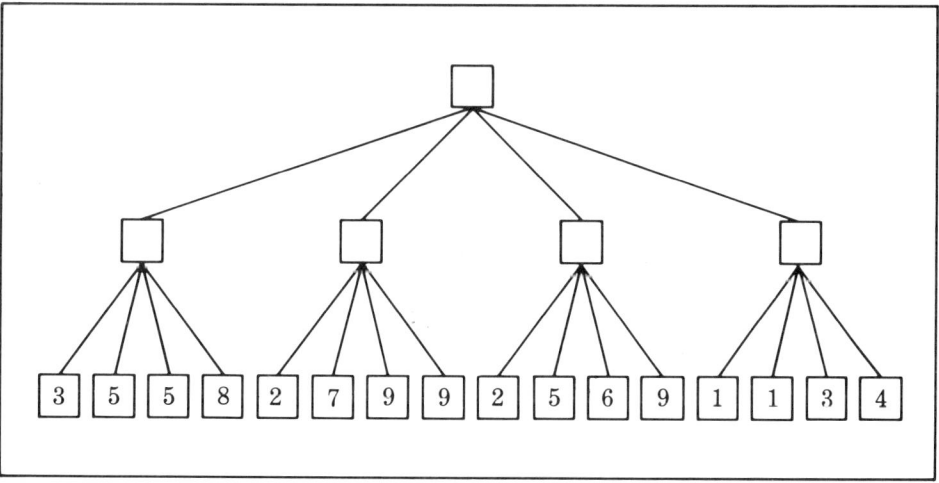

Figure 6-6. Game tree with its nodes sorted

actual gains depend critically on the order in which moves are evaluated. To verify this, consider what happens if Maxie evaluates the game tree from Figure 6-5 in a right-to-left order. In this case, *no* pruning is done. To get the most benefit from pruning, it helps to evaluate both players' best moves first. For example, consider the game tree in Figure 6-6, where we have simply rearranged the order of the nodes from our original tree. In this case, Maxie can avoid evaluating *nine* final positions: he only has to consider Minnie's four responses to his first move and her first response to each of his other three moves.

Getting the Computer's Move

Now we have a general idea of how the computer playing *Reversi* against a human can arrive at its "best" move by following the minimax algorithm. The computer simply plays the role of Maxie in the scenario just described. To find the computer's best move we will write two functions, **findmax** and **findmin**. **findmax** finds the computer's best move from a given position, choosing the move that results in the maximum score. Similarly, **findmin** determines the *human's* best move from a given position, choosing the move that minimizes the resulting score. Essentially, **findmax** follows Maxie's strategy, while **findmin** follows Minnie's strategy. (More accurately, **reversi** uses **findmin** to determine the human player's best moves in order to avoid them.) **findmax** and **findmin** call each other when necessary to travel down the levels of the game tree.

The new version of **getcomputer** looks like this:

```
function getcomputer(var list: movelist): squarenum;
{ Get computer's move }

var
    max: integer;
    best: squarenum;

{------------------------------}
{ Modules to be inserted here: }
{       eval                   }
{       trymove                }
{       sortlist                }
{       findmin fwd decl.       }
{       findmax                }
{       findmin                }
{------------------------------}

begin { getcomputer }
    if list.nmoves = 1 then { only one legal move }
        getcomputer := list.move[1]
    else begin
```

```
      max := findmax(lookahead, list, mainboard, MAXINT, best);
      getcomputer := best
   end
end;
```

If the computer has only one move, there is no point in evaluating the game tree to any level; **getcomputer** simply returns the only move it can make. Otherwise, the routine calls **findmax** to choose the best move for the computer.

The arguments passed to **findmax** are the lookahead to tell it how far ahead to look in the game tree, a list of the computer's legal moves, the current board, and the cutoff value. The best move is returned in the **var** parameter **best**. When **findmax** is called by **getcomputer**, the cutoff value is set to **MAXINT**, which is the same as having no cutoff at all. Cutoff only occurs in **findmax** when it is called by **findmin** at lookaheads of three or greater.

Here is **findmax** in pseudo-code:

```
begin
   sort move list
   if there are legal moves
      repeat
         make next move in list
         if lookahead <= 1
            evaluate board
         else
            generate human's possible responses
            find score of human's best move
               (with one less move lookahead & cutoff of current maximum score)
         if score > previous maximum
            save new best move & maximum score
      until (last move has been considered) or (score is >= cutoff)
   else { no legal moves }
      if lookahead <= 1 then
         evaluate board, set max score to result
      else
         generate human's possible responses
         set max score to score of human's best move
            (with one less move lookahead & no cutoff)
   return maximum score and best move
end
```

The operation "sort move list" is as yet unspecified, but it refers to putting the moves in order so that the computer's best moves are considered first. As we mentioned previously, this will improve the efficiency of our search; we will have more to say on this later.

The pseudo-code outline translates into the following Pascal code:

```
function findmax(look: integer; var list: movelist; var bd: board;
                 cutoff: integer; var bestmove: squarenum): integer;
{ Get computer's best move }

var
```

```
      newlist: movelist;
      newbd: board;
      i, maxscore, score, nm: integer;
      junk: squarenum;
   begin { findmax }
      sortlist(list);
      with list do
         if nmoves > 0 then begin
            maxscore := -MAXINT;
            i := 1;
            repeat
               newbd := bd;
               trymove(move[i], computer, newbd);
               if look <= 1 then
                  score := eval(newbd, human)
               else begin
                  nm := makelist(newlist, human, newbd);
                  score := findmin(look - 1, newlist, newbd, maxscore, junk)
               end;
               if score > maxscore then begin
                  maxscore := score;
                  bestmove := move[i]
               end;
               i := i + 1
            until (i > nmoves) or (maxscore >= cutoff)
         end
         else begin { no legal move }
            if look <= 1 then
               maxscore := eval(bd, human)
            else begin
               nm := makelist(newlist, human, bd);
               maxscore := findmin(look - 1, newlist, bd, -MAXINT, junk)
            end
         end;
      findmax := maxscore
   end;
```

findmax evaluates each of the computer's moves by making a temporary copy of the current board in the variable **newbd**, and then makes the move in question to the temporary board by calling the procedure **trymove**. (This procedure will be described presently.) If the current lookahead value is 1, **findmax** then calls the **eval** function to return a "score" for the new board position. Otherwise it generates a list of legal moves for the human player from the new board and calls **findmin** to return the score of the human's best move.

Since **findmax** and **findmin** call each other, we have to specify one as a **forward** procedure; we choose to do so with **findmin**. The declaration goes before the body of **findmax**:

```
function findmin(look: integer; var list: movelist; var bd: board;
                 cutoff: integer; var bestmove: squarenum): integer; forward;
```

Not surprisingly, **findmin** looks just like **findmax**. The only differences are that **findmin** looks for a minimum score rather than a maximum score and has a reverse logic for cutoff. (It stops evaluating when a node falls below the specified cutoff value.) Here is **findmin**:

```
function findmin;
{ Get human's best move }
var
   newlist: movelist;
   newbd: board;
   i, minscore, score, nm: integer;
   junk: squarenum;
begin { findmin }
   sortlist(list);
   with list do
      if nmoves > 0 then begin
         minscore := MAXINT;
         i := 1;
         repeat
            newbd := bd;
            trymove(move[i], human, newbd);
            if look <= 1 then
               score := eval(newbd, computer)
            else begin
               nm := makelist(newlist, computer, newbd);
               score := findmax(look - 1, newlist, newbd, minscore, junk)
            end;
            if score < minscore then begin
               minscore := score;
               bestmove := move[i]
            end;
            i := i + 1
         until (i > nmoves) or (minscore <= cutoff)
      end
      else begin { no legal moves }
         if look <= 1 then
            minscore := eval(bd, computer)
         else begin
            nm := makelist(newlist, computer, bd);
            minscore := findmax(look - 1, newlist, bd, MAXINT, junk)
         end
      end;
   findmin := minscore
end;
```

Both **findmin** and **findmax** use **trymove**, which makes a specified move to a board. It is similar to **makemove**, except that the move is not made to the main board but rather to the temporary boards created by **findmax** and **findmin**. And of course the result of the hypothetical move is not displayed on the screen:

```
procedure trymove(trysq: squarenum; pl: player; var bd: board);
{ Try move, updating board }
var
   dir: direction;
   k1: squarenum;
```

```
      opp: player;
      del: integer;
begin { trymove }
   opp := other(pl);
   with bd do begin
      sq[trysq] := pl;
      ndiscs[pl] := ndiscs[pl] + 1;
      delmove(trysq, possible);
      for dir := NORTH to NORTHWEST do begin
         del := delta[dir];
         if flanking(trysq, dir, bd, pl) then begin
            k1 := trysq + del;
            repeat
               sq[k1] := pl;
               ndiscs[pl] := ndiscs[pl] + 1;
               ndiscs[opp] := ndiscs[opp] - 1;
               k1 := k1 + del
            until sq[k1] = pl
         end
         else if sq[trysq + del] = EMPTY then
            addmove(trysq + del, possible)
      end
   end
end;
```

Evaluating a Board Position

The major remaining problem is to design **eval**, the function that accepts a board position and returns a numeric score. The only requirement is that **eval** return a greater score for board positions that are more favorable for the computer.

As previously discussed, the winner in *Reversi* is the player who owns the larger number of discs at the end of the game. This suggests one possible method for assigning a score to a board position: simply count the number of discs the computer has on the board. That solution, while having the virtue of simplicity, is far from the best. *Reversi* positions are so volatile that often a player with a huge numerical superiority in discs at one point in the game winds up losing the game only a few moves later. Thus, there are other factors governing whether a player has a good position.

One of these factors is the *strategic value* of the squares each player owns. Although we cannot go into great detail on the subject here, it is relatively easy to discover that the most valuable squares on the board are the corner squares. Once a player's disc is placed on a corner square, it cannot be outflanked and therefore cannot be flipped to the opponent's color. As a result, corner discs are used as immovable bases to flip over large numbers of the opponent's discs.

Since corner squares are so valuable, it follows that a player will want to avoid squares *adjacent* to the corners if possible. The only way a player can capture a corner square is for the other player to move to a square neighboring that corner. Moving to these squares can be deadly: these are the **poison1** or **poison2** squares described in our discussion of **initrev**.

Working backward, it follows that squares adjacent to these "poison" squares are relatively desirable for the player to occupy; owning them increases the likelihood the opponent will take a poison square.

Edge squares are also important. Since a disc occupying an edge square can only be flipped by another square on the edge, it is desirable for a player to take over edge squares and exclude his or her opponent from footholds on the edges.

In addition to considering the number of discs and strategic values of the squares each player owns, it is important to take each player's *mobility* into account: as in chess, the more moves a player can make, the better his or her position. One common method of winning a game is to force an opponent to take one of the poison squares by eliminating all other possible moves.

In designing our evaluation function, we will try to take all three of these factors into account. Remember, the more favorable the position is for the computer, the higher the score returned by **eval** should be.

The disc advantage is easiest to calculate: you simply subtract the number of discs owned by the human from the number owned by the computer.

The mobility factor is also easy to put into numeric terms: find the number of legal moves available to whichever player has the move in the given position. This number will be handled differently depending on whether it is the computer's or the human's turn to move. From the computer's point of view, the computer's mobility is "good," and the human's "bad."

The strategic factors are hardest to quantify; we will take the easiest possible way out by assigning numeric scores to the various good and bad situations previously described. For example, the strategic score is increased by n points for every corner square the computer owns and *decreased* by n points for every corner square the user owns. If any corner square is empty, the function looks at the ownership of the poison squares adjacent to the corner, subtracting points if the square is owned by the computer and adding points if it is owned by the human. If any poison squares are empty, it then looks at the corresponding "good" squares, adding points if they are owned by the machine and subtracting them if they are owned by the human.

Finally, the four edges are considered: if an edge only has the computer's discs on it, it is considered a plus factor; if an edge is occupied only by the user's discs, it is considered a minus factor.

The combination of all these factors into a single numeric score is somewhat arbitrary. We choose to multiply the computer's disc advantage and the mobility factor by program-specified constants and add them together with the different point values assigned to the good and bad strategic situations described previously.

All this is probably easiest to understand by looking at the **eval** function:

```
function eval(var bd: board; pl: player): integer;
{ Evaluate board position }
const
    K1 = 1;        { weighting factor for disc advantage }
    K2 = 3;        { weighting factor for mobility }
    K3 = 200;      { score for owning corner }
    K4 = -100;     { penalty for owning poison1 square }
    K5 = 50;       { score for owning good1 square }
    K6 = -25;      { penalty for owning poison2 square }
    K7 = 15;       { score for owning good2 square }
    K8 = 10;       { score for having only discs on edge }
    K9 = 20;       { score for occupying edge }
var
    list: movelist;
    i, j, score: integer;
    c: contents;
    sideset: set of contents;
begin { eval }
    with bd do
        if ndiscs[human] = 0 then { Human wiped out }
            eval := MAXINT
        else if ndiscs[computer] = 0 then { Computer wiped out }
            eval := - MAXINT
        else begin
            score := K1 * (ndiscs[computer] - ndiscs[human]);
            if pl = computer then
                score := score + K2 * makelist(list, pl, bd)
            else
                score := score - K2 * makelist(list, pl, bd);
            for i := 1 to 4 do begin
                c := sq[corner[i]];
                if c = computer then
                    score := score + K3
                else if c = human then
                    score := score - K3
                else begin { corner empty, check poison squares }
                    c := sq[poison1[i]];
                    if c = computer then
                        score := score + K4
                    else if c = human then
                        score := score - K4
                    else begin
                        c := sq[good1[i]];
                        if c = computer then
                            score := score + K5
                        else if c = human then
                            score := score - K5
                    end;
                    for j := 1 to 2 do begin
                        c := sq[poison2[i, j]];
                        if c = computer then
                            score := score + K6
```

```
                    else if c = human then
                        score := score - K6
                    else begin
                        c := sq[good2[i, j]];
                        if c = computer then
                            score := score + K7
                        else if c = human then
                            score := score - K7
                    end
                end
            end
        end;
        for i := 1 to 4 do begin
            sideset := [];
            for j := 1 to 4 do
                sideset := sideset + [sq[edge[i, j]]];
            if sideset = [computer] then
                score := score + K9
            else if sideset = [computer, EMPTY] then
                score := score + K8
            else if sideset = [human, EMPTY] then
                score := score - K8
            else if sideset = [human] then
                score := score - K9
        end;
        eval := score
    end
end;
```

In addition to following the previous discussion, **eval** looks for an immediate win or loss by checking whether either player has no discs left on the board. The immediate loss for the human is assigned the score **MAXINT**, and the immediate loss for the computer is assigned the score **−MAXINT**.

Sorting the Move Lists

We said that the efficiency gain using alpha-beta pruning depends on the order in which moves are evaluated; the best performance occurs when the best moves for each player are evaluated first. The problem with this is that we do not know in advance which moves are the best; if we did, we would not have to search the game tree.

Fortunately, even a rough guess at the best order is better than nothing. From our previous discussion, we know that a move to the corner is very likely to be a good move for either player and that a move to a poison square is likely to be a bad move. Thus, based on our judgment of the strategic value of each square, we choose to evaluate corner moves first, poison moves last, and other squares in between. **sortlist** sorts the moves into the order specified by the **sqord** array specified back in the **initrev** initialization procedure.

sortlist uses an algorithm known as the *Shell sort* to rearrange the moves in the list. Although we cannot present a discussion of various sorting methods, the Shell sort is a good choice for sorting small numbers of elements. Here is **sortlist**:

```
procedure sortlist(var list: movelist);
{ Sort move list to put good moves first }
var
   i, j, jg, gap, k: integer;
begin { sortlist }
   with list do begin
      gap := nmoves div 2;
      while gap > 0 do begin
         for i := gap + 1 to nmoves do begin
            j := i - gap;
            while j > 0 do begin
               jg := j + gap;
               if sqord[move[j]] <= sqord[move[jg]] then
                  j := 0
               else begin
                  k := move[j];
                  move[j] := move[jg];
                  move[jg] := k
               end;
               j := j - gap
            end
         end;
         gap := gap div 2
      end
   end
end;
```

Some Pascals may have a built-in or easily accessible general-purpose sorting routine faster than **sortlist**.

Measurements

We previously stated that alpha-beta pruning and sorting the move list improved the efficiency of the computer's move-searching routine. But by how much? To find out, **reversi** was modified slightly to play games against itself: the **gethuman** routine was altered to call **findmin** to find the best reply to the moves generated by **getcomputer**.

The speed of the version of **reversi** presented here was compared with the speeds of slightly changed versions that (1) found the best move by straight minimaxing without alpha-beta pruning and (2) used pruning but did not sort the move list. We measured the amount of time these two versions of the program and the original version took to play complete games against themselves with lookahead values of 1, 2, and 3.

At a lookahead of 1, both alpha-beta pruning and sorting *increase* the game-playing time slightly. This stands to reason since alpha-beta pruning has no effect on the minimax algorithm with one-move lookahead; the extra test only adds overhead. But the increase in running time is insignificant: the program version using alpha-beta pruning ran only 0.2% slower than the pure minimax version. And the version that sorted the move list into order ran only 2% slower than the pure minimax version.

The real benefits appear at lookaheads of 2 and 3. At a lookahead of 2, alpha-beta pruning improved the run time by 42% over pure minimax. Sorting the move list before pruning saved 65% over pure minimax. At a lookahead of 3, alpha-beta pruning saved 67% over pure minimax. Sorting combined with pruning resulted in a savings of 79%.

Because alpha-beta pruning decreases the number of positions evaluated, the percentages reported here depend strongly on the relative speed of the **eval** function compared to that of the rest of the program. For example, if **eval** were speeded up, the resulting relative percentage savings would probably *decrease*, although the absolute efficiency of the program would improve.

That is the good news. The bad news is that, even with our improvements, **reversi** is relatively sluggish at higher lookaheads. At a lookahead of 3, the program takes an average of approximately two minutes to decide on its move (on the Apple II). This is simply too slow for interactive play.

There are probably two profitable approaches to improving efficiency at this point: the first is to improve the move-finding algorithm to consider even fewer moves in the game tree. There are a number of possible methods for doing this; see the readings at the end of the chapter for ideas.

The second method is our old standby, which is to recode one or more of our routines in assembly language. **reversi** has a number of modules that are possible candidates for this treatment. We will limit ourselves here to translating one, **flanking**. As previously noted, the function is called a number of times whenever the program makes a move (in **makemove**), tries a move (**trymove**), or decides whether a move is legal (**legalmove**).

Here is **flanking** in 6502 assembly language:

```
        .func flanking,4
;
;       Routine to test whether player outflanks other in given direction
;       from given square.
;
;       declared in Pascal host as:
;
;       function flanking(k: squarenum; dir: direction; var bd: board;
;                                       pl: player): boolean; external;
;
return  .equ 0          ; return address
k       .equ 2          ; square number
dir     .equ 4          ; direction
```

188 Advanced Pascal Programming Techniques

```
bd      .equ 6          ; board address
pl      .equ 8          ; player color (0 or 1)
result  .equ 0A         ; function result
other   .equ 0C         ; other player's color
del     .equ 0D         ; increment for specified direction

        pop return      ; store return address
        pla             ; discard stack bias
        pla
        pla
        pla
        pop pl          ; store player's color
        pop bd          ; store board address
        pop dir         ; store direction
        pop k           ; store square number
;
;       store FALSE result
;
        lda #0
        sta result
        sta result+1
;
;       calculate other player's color = 1 - pl
;
        sec
        lda #1
        sbc pl
        sta other
;
;       get increment for specified direction
;
        ldx dir         ; put direction in x-reg
        lda delta,x     ; get increment
        sta del         ; and store it
;
;       calculate offset of neighboring square, store in y
;
        lda k           ; get initial square number
        asl a           ; multiply by two
        clc             ; prepare to add
        adc del         ; add increment to get offset
        tay             ; move it to y

        lda (bd),y      ; get contents of neighboring board square
        cmp other       ; is it other player?
        bne exit        ; no, exit
nextsq  tya             ; get old offset
        clc             ; prepare to add
        adc del         ; add increment
        tay             ; move new offset to y
        lda (bd),y      ; get contents of board square
        cmp other       ; does square contain other player's piece?
        beq nextsq      ; yes, go back to look at next square
        cmp pl          ; does square contain player's piece?
        bne exit        ; no, exit (border or empty square)
        lda #1          ; store TRUE
        sta result      ; in low byte of result
exit    push result     ; push result
        push return     ; push return address
        rts             ; and return
;
;       Table of increments (in hexadecimal)
;
delta   .byte -14,-12,2,16,14,12,-2,-16
```

Note that this code uses the **push** and **pop** macros defined in Chapter Five. This assembly language version of **flanking** makes use of the following (not necessarily portable) features of Apple Pascal.

- Apple Pascal stores the **sq** array at the beginning of a **board** record so that the location to which the address **bd** points contains the element **bd.sq[0]**; each element of the **sq** array takes up two bytes.

- The **delta** array corresponds to the **delta** array in the Pascal code except that each corresponding element in the assembly routine is multiplied by 2 (since elements in the **sq** array take up two bytes).

- Scalar types in Apple Pascal are actually two-byte integers. The first element is 0, the second is 1, and so on. Thus, the assembly language routine uses the fact that the identifiers **LIGHT** and **DARK** are 0 and 1, respectively, in calculating the variable **other**. In looking up the increment for the specified direction, the routine assumes that **NORTH** is 0, **NORTHEAST** is 1, and so on.

- Boolean **TRUE** values are represented by the integer 1 (or any non-zero integer); Boolean **FALSE** values are represented by 0. A single Boolean variable takes up two bytes, just like an integer.

We measured the speed improvement when using the assembly language version of **flanking** instead of the Pascal version; the percentage savings were approximately 60%, thus cutting the average move time from two minutes to about 45 seconds at a lookahead of 3. Similar percentage savings are seen at other lookaheads. The reader is invited to determine which other routines are good candidates for recoding.

Apple Graphics Primer

Not surprisingly, graphics commands used in a Pascal program are even less portable than the other non-portable features we have seen so far. Graphics functions provided by computer hardware vary widely, and unfortunately there is as yet no guarantee that the graphics routines described here for the Apple II will work on other computers—even if the computers have similar graphics capabilities. Those wishing to modify the routines to their hardware can get some pointers from the discussion here.

Apple Pascal provides a number of routines that allow a Pascal program to take advantage of the Apple II's graphics. The routines are not built-in in the sense that, for example, the **length** function is built-in; instead, the routines are available in a compiled unit called **turtlegraphics**, which is contained in the System Library.

The Apple's graphics screen is a rectangle providing a resolution of 280 dots in the x (horizontal) direction by 192 dots in the y (vertical) direction. The origin ($x = 0$, $y = 0$) is in the lower-left corner of the screen. (Note that this differs from the origin of the text screen.) The screen can display six different colors: white, black, orange, blue, violet, and green. (We will only use white and black here.)

The Apple Pascal graphics procedures we will be using can be split up into four parts:

Initialization/Termination Procedures   Calling the procedure **initturtle** switches the CRT display from the normal text screen to the graphics screen; this command also clears the graphics screen to black. To return to the text screen, a program calls the procedure **textmode**.

Line-Drawing Procedures   Lines are drawn by moving an imaginary *turtle* around the graphics screen. The turtle has a position specified by the coordinates x and y. The turtle also can be thought of as facing in a certain direction. This direction is specified by an angle measured counterclockwise in degrees; an angle of 0 degrees means the turtle is facing right, parallel to the horizontal x axis.

Lines are drawn on the screen by moving the turtle. The command **move(d)** will move the turtle **d** units in the direction in which the turtle is facing. The command **moveto(x, y)** moves the turtle from its current position to the point (x, y).

The turtle can be turned to face in another direction with the procedures **turn** and **turnto**. The **turn** procedure is a *relative* turn; **turn(t)** causes the turtle to pirouette t degrees in a counterclockwise direction. The **turnto** procedure, on the other hand, specifies an *absolute* turn; **turnto(t)** causes the turtle to turn *to* an angle of **t** degrees regardless of the direction it was previously facing.

The color plotted by the turtle when it moves is controlled with the procedure **pencolor**. The command **pencolor(WHITE)** causes the turtle to draw white lines on the screen. A call of **pencolor(NONE)** will cause the movements of the turtle to be invisible. These are the only two options we will be using here, although the turtle can be commanded to draw in any available color.

As an example, the following procedure (not used in **reversi**) draws a rectangular frame around the boundaries of the graphics screen:

```
procedure frame;
{ Draw frame around boundary of screen }
begin { frame }
   pencolor(NONE);
   moveto(0, 0);
   turnto(0);
   pencolor(WHITE);
   move(279);
   turn(90);
   move(191);
   turn(90);
   move(279);
   turn(90);
   move(191)
end;
```

Picture-Drawing Procedure   In addition to drawing lines, the graphics routines provide a method to draw rectangular "pictures" on the screen. The procedure is called **drawblock**; the call

```
drawblock(pic, rowsize, xskip, yskip, width, height, x, y, mode);
```

puts the picture specified by **pic** at the position (x, y) on the screen. Typically, the variable **pic** is a two-dimensional packed array of Boolean values; the individual elements of the array make up individual dots in the picture. A **TRUE** value "turns on" the dot in the picture (displays it as white), and a **FALSE** value turns it off (displays it as black).

The parameters **xskip** and **yskip** allow the routine to start copying the array to the screen from a position other than the beginning of the array. The parameters **width** and **height** allow the calling routine to specify how many dots of the array are to be copied to the screen. When we use **drawblock** we will always copy a full array from its beginning.

The **rowsize** parameter tells **drawblock** how many bytes are contained per row of the array. This number is calculated from the number of dots per row by the following formula:

```
rowsize := 2 * ((rowdots + 15) div 16);
```

Finally, the **mode** parameter is an integer between 0 and 15. The usual value of **mode** we will be using is 10, which simply copies the **pic** array to the screen, replacing whatever is there.

Text-Display Procedures   Apple Pascal also provides procedures to display text on the graphics screen. The call **wchar(ch)** places the character **ch** at the turtle's current position on the screen. The call **wstring(s)** does the same for the string **s**.

There are a few other routines provided in the **turtlegraphics** unit, but these are the only ones we will use here.

Modifying reversi for Graphics

Instead of completely reprinting all the sections of the program changed by our switch to graphics, we will simply describe the changes themselves. Because of our sensible design, the modifications only affect the initialization routines and the parts of the program that perform output, leaving the remainder of the program unchanged. Once we have designed some graphics tools corresponding to our text-screen tools, most of the changes are simple one-to-one substitutions. These changes are

- Inform the compiler the program will be using the graphics routines by changing the **uses** statement from

    ```
    uses
        {$u apple2:toolstuff.code } crtstuff;
    ```

    to

    ```
    uses
        turtlegraphics, {$u apple2:toolstuff.code } crtstuff;
    ```

- Add the global **const** declarations:

    ```
    <const>
        XMAX = 279;            { Maximum screen x-coordinate }
        YMAX = 191;            { Maximum screen y-coordinate }
        SQSIZ = 18;            { Board square size in dots   }
        PICSIZE = 17;          { Picture size in dots        }
        CHARWID = 7;           { Character width in dots     }
        ROWSIZE = 4;           { Picture width in bytes      }
    ```

- Add the global **type** declaration:

    ```
    <type>
        picture = packed array [1..PICSIZE, 1..PICSIZE] of boolean;
    ```

- Add the global **var** declarations:

    ```
    <var>
        sqpic: array [contents] of picture;
        xorg, yorg: integer;
    ```

The **sqpic** array holds the pictures used to display the square's contents. The variables **xorg** and **yorg** contain the coordinates of the lower left-hand corner of the game board on the graphics screen.

- This next step adds code to the initialization procedure **initrev2** to set up the **sqpic** Boolean arrays and to initialize the variables **xorg** and **yorg**. First add the following constant declarations:

```
<const>
   R1SQ = 54;
   R2SQ = 44;
   R = 9;
```

We also need to declare the following two additional variables in **initrev2**:

```
<var>
   j, i2, r2: integer;
```

Finally, the following section of code can be inserted in **initrev2** just before the final **end** statement:

```
xorg := (XMAX - 8 * SQSIZ) div 2;
yorg := (YMAX - 8 * SQSIZ) div 2;
for i := 1 to PICSIZE do begin
   i2 := sqr(i - R);
   for j := 1 to PICSIZE do begin
      r2 := i2 + sqr(j - R);
      sqpic[EMPTY, i, j] := FALSE;
      sqpic[LIGHT, i, j] := (r2 < R1SQ);
      sqpic[DARK, i, j] := (r2 < R1SQ) and (r2 > R2SQ);
      sqpic[BORDER, i, j] := (r2 < R1SQ) and
         ((i = R) or (j = R) or (i = j) or (i = PICSIZE + 1 - j))
   end
end
```

Initializing the picture arrays may be a little confusing. For each picture array element [i,j] the program calculates the integer value **r2**, which is the square of the "distance" of the element from the "center" of the array, the element [9,9].

All elements of the Boolean array for **sqpic[EMPTY]** are set to **FALSE**. This simply means empty squares on the screen will be filled with black.

A dot in the **LIGHT** square picture is turned on (set to **TRUE**) if its value of **r2** is less than 54; otherwise, it is turned off (set to **FALSE**). This results in a round white disc on the screen.

Similarly, a dot in the picture for the **DARK** squares is turned on only if its value of **r2** lies between 45 and 53; this appears on the screen as a ring of white dots around a dark center, indicating a black disc.

Finally, the **BORDER** picture is used as a move-selection cursor as in the text version. A dot in this picture is set to **TRUE** if its value of **r2** is less than 54 and it lies either on the central horizontal line through the square, the central vertical line, or either diagonal. This results in an asterisk-like display on the graphics screen.

- Replace the text version of **dispgrid** with the following graphics version:

```
procedure dispgrid;
{ Display board grid - graphics }
var
    i, x, y, d: integer;
begin { dispgrid }
    d := 8 * SQSIZ;
    turnto(0);
    y := YORG;
    for i := 0 to 8 do begin
        pencolor(NONE);
        moveto(xorg, y);
        pencolor(WHITE);
        move(d);
        y := y + SQSIZ
    end;
    turn(90);
    x := xorg;
    for i := 0 to 8 do begin
        pencolor(NONE);
        moveto(x, yorg);
        pencolor(WHITE);
        move(d);
        x := x + SQSIZ
    end
end;
```

- After the procedure **dispgrid**, add the following six procedures. The first procedure, **initgraphics**, switches the screen display from text to graphics:

```
procedure initgraphics;
{ Initialize graphics screen }
begin { initgraphics }
    initturtle
end;
```

Apple II 80-column board users might need to add some code here and send some hardware-dependent commands to the board or direct the user to perform some action. For example, the ALS Smarterm 80-column board requires the additional line

```
write(chr(20), 'A1')
```

to be included in the procedure to switch display from the board's video signal to the Apple's normal video signal.

The second procedure, **termgraphics**, switches back to the text screen from the graphics screen:

```
procedure termgraphics;
{ Back to text screen }
begin { termgraphics }
   textmode
end;
```

termgraphics undoes whatever **initgraphics** did. Again, 80-column board programmers might have to insert code here depending on their situation. For example, the ALS Smarterm requires the additional line

```
write(chr(20), 'B1')
```

The remaining four procedures perform common text manipulation functions on the graphics screen. **geraseline** erases a horizontal line of text from the graphics screen:

```
procedure geraseline(y: integer);
{ Erase line of text from graphics screen }
var
   i: integer;
begin { geraseline }
   pencolor(NONE);
   moveto(0, y);
   for i := 0 to XMAX div CHARWID do
      wchar(' ')
end;
```

gposstr puts a string at a specified position on the graphics screen:

```
procedure gposstr(s: string; x, y: integer);
{ Put string on graphics screen }
begin { gposstr }
   pencolor(NONE);
   moveto(x, y);
   wstring(s)
end;
```

gcenter centers a string on the graphics screen:

```
procedure gcenter(s: string; y: integer);
{ Center string on graphics screen }

begin { gcenter }
  geraseline(y);
  gposstr(s, (XMAX - length(s) * CHARWID - 1) div 2, y)
end;
```

Finally, **gdisptitle** puts the program's title in a box at the top of the graphics screen:

```
procedure gdisptitle(s: string);
{ Display title on graphics screen }

var
   ht, wd: integer;

begin { gdisptitle }
   ht := 10;
   wd := (length(s) + 1) * CHARWID;
   gcenter(s, YMAX - 10);
   pencolor(NONE);
   moveto((XMAX - (length(s) + 1) * CHARWID - 3) div 2, YMAX - 11);
   turnto(0);
   pencolor(WHITE);
   move(wd);
   turn(90);
   move(ht);
   turn(90);
   move(wd);
   turn(90);
   move(ht)
end;
```

- Replace the text version of **dispsquare** with this version, which uses **drawblock** to display our previously defined pictures:

```
procedure dispsquare(k: squarenum; c: contents);
{ Put picture in square on graphics screen }

begin { dispsquare }
   drawblock(sqpic[c], ROWSIZE, 0, 0, PICSIZE, PICSIZE,
            xorg + SQSIZ * (k div 10 - 1) + 1,
            yorg + SQSIZ * (k mod 10 - 1) + 1, 10)
end;
```

- In the **initgame** procedure, the program must request information and display it on the graphics screen instead of the text screen. The following six modifications accomplish this feat:

    a. Change the first line in **initgame** from

    ```
    eraseline(ymarg + 17);
    ```

    to

```
      geraseline(yorg - 10);
```

b. Change the line

```
center('Do you want white or black?(W/B):', ymarg + 18);
```

to

```
gcenter('Do you want white or black?(W/B):', yorg - 20);
```

c. Change the line

```
posstr('Computer is black', xmarg, ymarg + 17)
```

to

```
gposstr('Computer is black', 0, yorg - 10)
```

d. Similarly, change the line

```
posstr('Computer is white', xmarg, ymarg + 17)
```

to

```
gposstr('Computer is white', 0, yorg - 10)
```

e. Change the line

```
center('Enter lookahead for computer(1-6):', ymarg + 18);
```

to

```
gcenter('Enter lookahead for computer(1-6):', yorg - 20);
```

f. Finally, change the five lines

```
eraseline(ymarg + 18);
posstr('Lookahead:', xmarg + 22, ymarg + 17
write(ch);
posstr('Computer:', xmarg, ymarg + 18);
posstr('Human:', xmarg + 24, ymarg + 18);
```

to

```
geraseline(yorg - 20);
gposstr('Lookahead:', XMAX - 11 * CHARWID, yorg - 10);
wchar(ch);
gposstr('Computer:', 0, yorg - 20);
gposstr('Human:', XMAX - 8 * CHARWID, yorg - 20);
```

- The **dispscore** procedure must also be modified to display the score on the graphics screen. Change the line

  ```
  posstr(s, xmarg + 10, ymarg + 18);
  ```

  to

  ```
  gposstr(s, 9 * CHARWID, yorg - 20);
  ```

  And change the line

  ```
  posstr(s, xmarg + 31, ymarg + 18)
  ```

  to

  ```
  gposstr(s, XMAX - 2 * CHARWID, yorg - 20)
  ```

- The **declarewinner** routine must be modified as well. Change the lines

  ```
  center(concat('I won by ', s), ymarg + 17)
  ...
  center(concat('You won by ', s), ymarg + 17)
  ...
  center('We have tied!', ymarg + 17)
  ```

  to

  ```
  gcenter(concat('I won by ', s), yorg - 10)
  ...
  gcenter(concat('You won by ', s), yorg - 10)
  ...
  gcenter('We have tied!', yorg - 10)
  ```

- Finally, make the following four changes to **reversi**'s main routine:

  a. Change the line

```
crt(CLEAR);
disptitle('reversi');
```

to

```
initgraphics;
gdisptitle('reversi');
```

b. Change the line

```
center('Play again?(Y/N):', ymarg + 18);
```

to

```
gcenter('Play again?(Y/N):', yorg -20);
```

c. Change the line

```
eraseline(ymarg + 18);
```

to

```
geraseline(yorg - 20);
```

d. Change the final occurrence of the line

```
crt(CLEAR)
```

to

```
termgraphics
```

Suggestions

There are a number of possible improvements to **reversi** that vary greatly in difficulty. The first priority is to improve the program's efficiency; an interactive game program can never be too fast. As previously suggested, you will want to measure where the program spends most of its time to determine where improvements can be the most beneficial.

One possibility worth investigating is to combine **findmax** and **findmin** into one non-recursive function, maintaining its own stack-like data structure for storing game boards and move lists at each level of the game tree. Generally, a non-recursive routine is faster than the equivalent recursive one because the bookkeeping associated with procedure calling is eliminated, although the gain in efficiency is not always worth the increased complexity in the program's logic.

You might also consider modifying the data structures or rewriting routines in assembly language to improve efficiency. Also check the suggested readings at the end of this chapter for further tricks that might help decrease the work done by the move-generation algorithm.

Another avenue of improvement is to refine the program's quality of play. Although this version of **reversi** can beat novices, it is no match for more experienced players. The simplest way to improve the strategy is to adjust the constant values Ki in the **eval** function. You might also want to make the weighting factors move-dependent. It makes sense to emphasize mobility and strategic value at early stages of the game, but at later stages the best procedure is probably to grab as many discs as possible. Of course, you might also be able to invent a completely different method for determining the best move.

To judge whether any change you make in the move generator is really an improvement, you could play one version of the program against another and see which version wins; or you could set up a tournament between a number of competing strategies to determine the best. The challenge is to make such a tournament as automatic as possible, thereby making it easy to create a large number of "players," each using a different strategy. Then a few hours (or days, or even weeks) later, the overall winner is declared.

The program's aesthetics could also be improved. You could modify the program to take advantage of any special hardware present on the computer you are using, making use of sound, graphics, input devices other than the keyboard, and so on. One valuable improvement to the current version of **reversi** would be to somehow inform the user of the computer's last move and the discs it flipped.

Add a command to allow the user to print out the current board state on the printer; if your printer has the capability, do it in high-resolution graphics. Add a command to make the computer display its ranking of the user's legal moves from best to worst. Allow the user to change the computer's strategy, possibly by altering the parameters Ki. Add an option to force the computer to take only its second best move (or third best, fourth best, and so on).

Depending on your efficiency improvements, a game may simply take too long to be played in one session with higher lookahead values. Add commands to load and save partially played games from and to disk.

Allow the user to set an upper limit on the time the computer can spend considering its moves. (This is easy if your computer hardware contains a real-time clock.) How might you adjust the minimax strategy if such a time limit is imposed?

Finally, you may want to program other games. Good luck!

Recommended Reading

Additional information on *Reversi* may be obtained from a number of sources. *Scarne's Encyclopedia of Games* by J. Scarne (Harper and Row, 1973) describes *Reversi* and many other games.

A good reference on computer-game programming is David Levy's monthly "Intelligent Computer Games" column in the magazine *Creative Computing*. The column began in the February 1980 issue and terminated in the March 1982 issue. The column in the June 1981 issue explained *Reversi*.

A clear and somewhat more formal description of game-tree searching and alpha-beta minimaxing is given in the book *Etudes for Programmers* by C. Wetherell (Prentice-Hall, 1978). Also presented in this book is a description of the game of Kalah. You may also want to investigate references in the field of artificial intelligence for more ideas on improving the program's play. One good textbook covering this subject is *Principles of Artificial Intelligence* by N. Nilsson (Tioga Publishing, 1980).

For those interested in chess, the book *Sargon: A Computer Chess Program* by Dan and Kathe Spracklen (Hayden, 1978) describes a chess program and provides the program's source code in Z-80 assembly language. One rich source of ideas for new games to program is the popular magazine *Games*.

The Shell sort algorithm used in **sortlist** was copied nearly verbatim from *Software Tools in Pascal* by B. Kernighan and P. J. Plauger (Addison-Wesley, 1981). This book is an excellent source of useful techniques.

SEVEN

Simulation and Animation

When not used for playing games, computers are often employed for more serious applications. A large number of these uses may be grouped under the general term *simulation*. A simulation is an effort to make a realistic *model* of some "real-world" system in order to discover how the system behaves under various conditions.

Simulations may be used for *prediction:* to establish, under certain given conditions, what is going to happen (to the weather, the economy, the pollutants in Lake Erie, the population of Omaha, and so on) in a given period of time. Simulations may also be used for *explanation*; if the model correctly describes the actual behavior of the real-world system, the assumptions that went into making the model are tentatively verified. Finally, simulations may be used for *experimentation*: changing the parameters of the model and observing its resulting behavior can indicate how the real-world system would behave under analogous conditions. This last aspect is very useful in situations where experimentation on the real-world system itself is impossible, prohibitively expensive, or otherwise impractical.

Simulations sometimes involve actual physical models of the system being simulated. For example, there are scale models of the Mississippi River and Chesapeake Bay used to study flooding and currents in those bodies of water. Another well-known example is the testing of aircraft and automobile models in wind tunnels.

More often the model is an *abstract* one consisting entirely of mathematical formulas and logical decisions. Such models, especially complex ones, are natural candidates for computer simulation. Computer simulation is used both in the "hard" sciences (such as physics, chemistry, and engineering) and the social sciences (such as economics, psychology, and anthropology).

Most large businesses use computer modeling to predict the behavior of their enterprises under different pricing or marketing strategies or to predict different features of the economic climate. The Congressional Budget Office uses a computer model of the national economy to predict (with varying degrees of sucess) the effect of legislation on unemployment, inflation, and economic growth. Nuclear engineers simulate the behavior of different reactor designs under emergency conditions. Ecologists model the relationships between a number of interacting biological species and their environment to predict trends in the species' populations and their effects on natural resources.

One feature all simulations have in common is *simplification*. In translating the real-world system into the model, certain assumptions are always made in order to keep the complexity of the model under control. The most common method of simplification is simply to neglect aspects of the real-world system that are not important to the results of the simulation. Clearly, good judgment is necessary when choosing which elements to neglect. For example, a video game manufacturer will probably not include the effects of unusual weather in its sales projections.

Another method of simplification is seen when concrete numeric values or relationships are assigned to system components that are inherently intangible. For example, a vital part of a business simulation may be an assumption that x additional dollars spent on advertising will generate y additional dollars of revenue, where y is a (presumably) complex mathematical function of x. Behind this complex mathematical function, however, lies a myriad of even more complex details and questionable assumptions, such as what kind of advertising to use, where to place it, and how people will react to it.

Because of such simplifications, the results of simulations are never exactly right. Poor judgment, ideological bias, or simple bad luck in designing a model may make the model totally incorrect, so that its results bear no relation to reality. For example, prolonged rainy weather could well cause a number of bored families to buy a video game they would not otherwise have purchased. An unusually offensive television commercial may cause sales of the advertised product to decrease. Thus, we must keep in mind that while simulations are useful, they are only as good as their designers.

Our discussion so far has been extremely general. In the remainder of the chapter, we will design two simulations of relatively simple systems from the world of physics. The first, **bouncer**, simulates the behavior of a number of balls in a closed box. The second, **isaac**, models the motion of bodies acting under mutual gravitational attraction.

Both programs use *animation* to display the progress of the simulation. Instead of printing out page after page of numbers representing positions and velocities, the programs translate these quantities into pictures and display them continuously on the computer's screen. As a result, the programs presented here are directly runnable only on an Apple II computer since they use Apple Pascal's non-portable graphics routines. They may, however, be modified to run on other computers with comparable graphics abilities.

If your computer lacks graphics capabilities, you might modify these programs to display their results on other types of graphics devices; for example, many models of printers can generate high-resolution graphics. Likewise, these programs could be easily changed to work on the normal CRT text screen, albeit at considerably lower resolution.

Data Structures — Coordinates and Vectors

In both **bouncer** and **isaac** we will be concerned with describing the *positions*, *velocities*, and *accelerations* of a number of objects. You no doubt already have at least an intuitive feel for what these three quantities are. Unfortunately, intuitive knowledge is not enough to tell us how to best represent such quantities in our simulation programs. Instead, we need to digress slightly into mathematics.

First, consider how to describe positions. Of course, an object's position simply describes "where it is" at a certain time. With a little thought, it is easy to see that the position of an object can be *completely described by three numbers*. For example, at a given instant we could observe a mosquito to be flying 0.58 meters above the floor of a room, 2.72 meters from the west wall, and 3.14 meters from the north wall. As another example, an airplane's position may be specified by its latitude, longitude, and altitude above sea level. In mathematical language, the three numbers used to specify the position of an object are called the *coordinates* of the object and the method by which these coordinates are assigned is called a *coordinate system*.

The most familiar coordinate system is called the *Cartesian* coordinate system which we used in describing the location of the mosquito. To set up a Cartesian system, all that is necessary is to specify three flat surfaces (or *planes*) at right angles to each other; the position of any point is specified by the three numbers giving the point's distance from the three planes. By convention, the three numbers are usually designated as x, y, and z, and positions are specified by writing them in the form (x, y, z).

In the mosquito example, we used the room's floor and its north and west walls as our planes. Thus, the letter x is simply shorthand for "the distance from the north wall," the letter y stands for "the distance from the west wall," and z means "the distance above the floor." Instead of a long sentence describing the mosquito's position, we could say "the mosquito is at (3.14, 2.72, 0.58)" and anyone knowing the coordinate system and the unit of measurement would understand. The point where the three planes intersect is called the *origin*, the point (0,0,0); in our example, the origin is the northwest corner of the room's floor.

The three numbers x, y, and z together are said to make up a *vector*. Each number is said to be a *component* of the vector. What we have just seen is that "position" is a *vector quantity*. This is just another way of saying that we need three numbers to describe where an object is. To emphasize this, a vector is sometimes said to have three *dimensions*.

In many cases, however, we can choose to ignore one component of a vector quantity. For example, if we were describing the position of an ocean liner (instead of an airplane), we could safely neglect reporting its "altitude above sea level" and describe its position using only two numbers: latitude and longitude. Similarly, if we were describing the location of a mouse on the floor of a room (instead of a mosquito in the air), we need only give the two numbers x and y. To use another familiar example, the CRT screen is a two-dimensional system; we can describe the position of a character on the screen by specifying its column and row.

We can go even further in some situations, restricting the position vector to one dimension. For example, if we know a car is traveling along Interstate 80 between New York and San Francisco, its position can be described by just *one* number (for example, its distance in miles from the George Washington Bridge).

Now consider velocity. Intuitively, we know velocity describes "how fast" something is going. In our more precise approach, we are going to define velocity as *the rate at which a position vector is changing*. Note that each component of a position vector can change independently of the other components. This means we need one number to measure how fast the x-component of the position vector is changing, one number to measure how fast the y-component is changing, and one number to measure how fast the z-component is changing. Thus, velocity must also be considered a vector quantity: the x-component of a velocity vector measures how fast the x-component of a position vector is changing, and the same is true for y and z.

Again using our mosquito for an example, assume that its velocity is the vector (0.11, 0.39, −0.55), where the numbers given have the units "meters per second." One second after being at the position (3.14, 2.72, 0.58) the mosquito will be at the position (3.14+0.11, 2.72+0.39, 0.58−0.55) or (3.25, 3.11, 0.03)—assuming, of course, that the mosquito's velocity remains constant during that second.

If a position vector is restricted to two dimensions, the corresponding velocity vector also has two dimensions. Since the third component of the position vector is ignored, there is no way to calculate the third component of the velocity vector.

Finally, consider acceleration: we define acceleration as the rate at which the velocity of an object is changing (just like we defined velocity to be the rate at which the object's position was changing). It is relatively easy to see that acceleration must also be a vector quantity—we need one number to measure the rate of change for each component of the corresponding velocity vector.

Vectors are often interpreted as "arrows" of a certain length that point in a certain direction. For example, a position vector (x, y, z) can be drawn as an arrow pointing from the origin of the coordinate system to the point (x, y, z). The length of a vector arrow is called the vector's *magnitude*. It is calculated by summing the squares of each component of the vector and taking the square root of the result. (Note that the magnitude of a vector is a *number*, not a vector.) The magnitude of a vector nearly always has an easily understandable physical significance: the magnitude of a position vector is the distance of the specified point from the origin. The magnitude of an object's velocity vector is the object's *speed*.

Keeping this discussion in mind, we find that representing vectors in Pascal is straightforward. In the three-dimensional case we could say

```
<type>
   coordinate = (X, Y, Z);
   vector = array [coordinate] of real;
```

For example, we could declare the mosquito's position and velocity as the following vectors:

```
<var>
   mosqpos, mosqvel: vector;
```

and assign numbers to each vector component:

```
...
mosqpos[X] := 3.14;
mosqpos[Y] := 2.72;
mosqpos[Z] := 0.58;
```

```
...
mosqvel[X] := 0.11;
mosqvel[Y] := 0.39;
mosqvel[Z] := -0.55;
...
```

We could write the following simple Pascal function to calculate the magnitude of a vector:

```
function magnitude(var v: vector): real;
 { Calculate magnitude of a vector }

begin { magnitude }
   magnitude := sqrt(sqr(v[X]) + sqr(v[Y]) + sqr(v[Z]))
end;
```

where **sqr** and **sqrt** are the standard Pascal routines to calculate a number's square and square root, respectively.

In both **bouncer** and **isaac**, we will choose to neglect the z-coordinate, restricting our simulations to two dimensions. Thus, all our vectors will have only x- and y-components. The reason behind this decision is simple: a two-dimensional model is easier to display on the graphics screen. In the programs, we will change the definition of the **coordinate** type slightly from that shown previously to

```
<type>
   coordinate = (X, Y);
```

Vectors are powerful tools for carrying out calculations that would otherwise be *very* complex. Although further discussion of the subject would be beyond the scope of the book, interested readers can look at the suggested reading material at the end of this chapter for more information.

Real Numbers

You may have noticed that in the definition of the **vector** type, we defined the vector components to be the Pascal built-in type **real**. You may ask why we have used reals here.

In Chapters Three and Four we developed the **fixed** and **xreal** data types to avoid using reals. Our reasons for doing so were the lack of control over the precision of calculations using real numbers and the inability to recover from overflow or underflow errors. In simulations, however, neither of these problems is quite so serious.

Typically, simplifying assumptions made in modeling real-world systems cause much more inaccuracy in the results of the simulation than that introduced from the imprecision of floating-point arithmetic. If we are programming a simulation of a business, it is probably safe to assume it does not matter whether the hypothetical business makes ten million dollars or ten million and one dollars, even though accounting standards in an actual business are more stringent.

Neither is the possibility of overflow and underflow so critical in a typical simulation. A simulation program that results in an overflow or underflow error usually reveals some flaw in the model itself. Again using the business simulation as an example, if the model shows the firm taking in 10^{40} dollars per week (causing an overflow error), the programmer should probably change the model's assumptions or internal workings rather than design a data type that will handle such large numbers.

One powerful argument for using reals in a simulation program is the relative ease of doing calculations with them. Mathematical details like keeping track of decimal points and signs are automatically handled by the language. The built-in transcendental functions (**sin**, **exp**, and so on) are designed to accept reals as arguments and return reals as results.

We will presently design an interactive-input routine for reals.

bouncer

The goal of our first simulation, **bouncer**, is to show the motion of a number of balls in a closed box. Each execution of **bouncer** allows the user to generate an arbitrary number of *runs* of the simulation. For each individual run of the simulation, the user supplies a number of parameters governing the conditions of the run.

The four run parameters are

- The number of balls in the box. The user may tell the program to display the motion of as many as 40 balls in a single run. Of course, the more balls used, the slower the program runs. In **bouncer**, this parameter is represented by the integer variable **nballs**.

- A time interval. This parameter governs the "coarseness" of the simulation's calculations; it is often called *delta-t* or *dt*. *dt* specifies the time between successive estimates of the balls' positions and velocities.

(**bouncer** uses a ball's position and velocity at a given instant to calculate its position and velocity a short time later. Then this new position and velocity are used to calculate the ball's position and velocity a short time after that, and so on.) Generally speaking, a large time interval decreases the simulation's accuracy, while a short time interval increases the simulation's accuracy (but also decreases the program's speed). The user may enter this parameter as a real number between 0.0001 and 1.0. In **bouncer**, this parameter is represented by the real variable **dt**.

- An acceleration vector. Balls in the box are assumed to be subjected to a constant acceleration (which may be zero). This is meant to show the effects of gravity on the balls. Since acceleration is a vector, the user specifies two numbers, one for acceleration in the x-direction and one for acceleration in the y-direction. For either number, the user enters a real number between −1.0 and 1.0. In **bouncer**, this parameter is represented by **acc**, a variable of the **vector** type.

- Whether or not to show the balls' paths. **bouncer** can optionally draw the balls' paths on the screen, giving a better idea of how the balls move. In **bouncer**, this parameter is represented by the Boolean variable **showpath**.

The version of **bouncer** presented here assigns each ball a random initial position within the box and, within certain limits, a random initial velocity. We also could have required the user to enter this information by typing in two numbers for each ball's initial position and two more specifying each initial velocity.

After the user enters the required run parameters, **bouncer** switches over to the graphics screen and shows how the balls move under the given assumptions. Figure 7-1 shows a "snapshot" of a typical run for three balls; the run parameters specified an x-acceleration of 0.0, a y-acceleration of −1.0, and a time interval of 0.1.

The simulation continues until the user presses any key; then the program switches back to the text screen and asks the user for parameters for another run. Entering 0 for the number of balls ends the program.

Here is the main routine of **bouncer**:

```
{$s+}
program bouncer;
{ Bouncing ball simulation }
uses
    applestuff,         { for note, random, and keypress }
    turtlegraphics,     { for graphics routines }
    {$u apple2:toolstuff.code }
    crtstuff;
```

```
const
   MAXBALLS = 40;        { Maximum # of balls in box }
   PICSIZE = 5;          { Picture size in dots }
type
   coordinate = (X, Y);
   vector = array [coordinate] of real;
   picture = packed array [1..PICSIZE, 1..PICSIZE] of boolean;
var
   ballpic: picture;
   i, margin, nballs: integer;
   showpath: boolean;
   acc: vector;
   dt: real;
   prompt: array [1..5] of string;

{-----------------------------}
{ Modules to be inserted here: }
{          initbounce         }
{          getbparams         }
{          runbouncer         }
{-----------------------------}
begin { bouncer }
   crt(CLEAR);
   disptitle('bouncer');
   initbounce;
   for i := 1 to 5 do
      posstr(prompt[i], margin, 8 + 2 * i);
   repeat
      getbparams;
      if nballs > 0 then
         runbouncer
   until nballs <= 0;
   crt(CLEAR)
end.
```

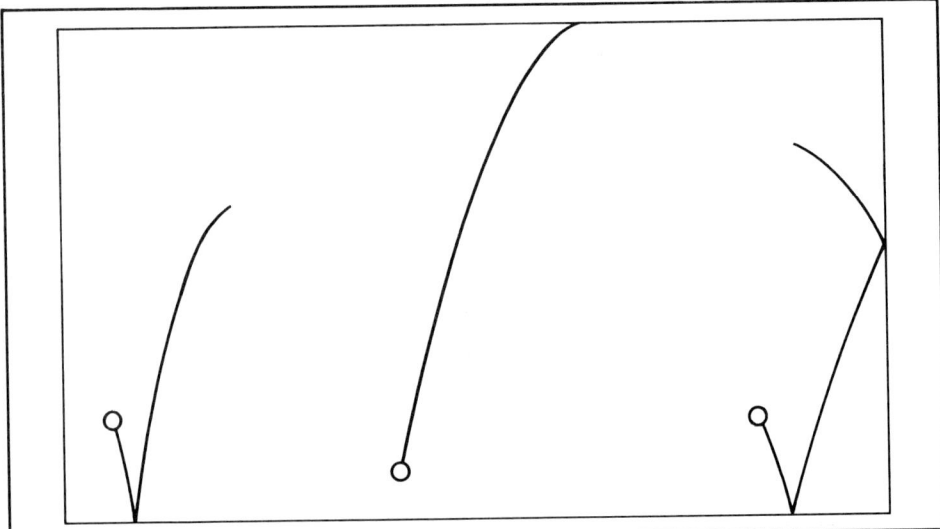

Figure 7-1. "Snapshot" of typical **bouncer** run

Note that the **picture** data type used here in **bouncer** was also used in the graphics version of **reversi** in Chapter Six. The only difference is the size of the picture array specified by the constant **PICSIZE**; in **reversi**, PICSIZE was 17, and here it is 5. We used **picture**s to draw game pieces in **reversi**; in **bouncer**, we will use the same trick to draw and erase our bouncing balls.

Initializing Global Variables

As usual, we use a separate routine to initialize our program's global variables:

```
procedure initbounce;
{ Initialize bouncer globals }
var
   i, j: integer;
begin { initbounce }
   prompt[1] := 'Number of balls (0 to exit):';
   prompt[2] := 'Time interval:';
   prompt[3] := 'X-acceleration(-1.0 - +1.0):';
   prompt[4] := 'Y-acceleration(-1.0 - +1.0):';
   prompt[5] := 'Show ball paths(Y/N):';
   margin := (MAXCRTCOL - 29) div 2;
   for i := 1 to 5 do
      for j := 1 to 5 do
         ballpic[i, j] := ((i in [1, 5]) and (j in [2..4])) or
                         ((j in [1, 5]) and (i in [2..4]))
end;
```

initbounce initializes the following three variables:

- **prompt** is an array of five strings used to hold the prompts for the run parameters previously described.

- **margin** controls the horizontal positioning of the prompts on the CRT screen; the calculation shown ensures that the prompts are reasonably centered on either a 40- or 80-column screen.

- **ballpic** is the picture array used to display the balls on the screen. Initializing the array is simply a matter of setting each individual array element to **TRUE** if the corresponding dot on the graphics screen is to be lit and **FALSE** if it is to be dark.

getbparams

The next step is to design the code that accepts the run parameters. There is nothing new or difficult here; **getbparams** simply calls interactive input routines to get the parameters.

```
procedure getbparams;
{ Get parameters for bouncer run }

type
   format = (FIXEDPOINT, SCIENTIFIC);

{----------------------------}
{ Modules to be included here: }
{       stoi                 }
{       itos                 }
{       getint               }
{       getreal              }
{----------------------------}

begin { getbparams }
   nballs := getint(margin + length(prompt[1]), 10, 0,MAXBALLS, 0, FALSE);
   if nballs > 0 then begin
      dt := getreal(margin + length(prompt[2]), 12, 0.0001, 1.0, 0.0,
                                          FIXEDPOINT, 6, 4, FALSE);
      acc[X] := getreal(margin + length(prompt[3]), 14, -1.0, 1.0, 0.0,
                                          FIXEDPOINT, 6, 2, TRUE);
      acc[Y] := getreal(margin + length(prompt[4]), 16, -1.0, 1.0, 0.0,
                                          FIXEDPOINT, 6, 2, TRUE);
      showpath := getboolean(margin + length(prompt[5]), 18, FALSE, FALSE)
   end
end;
```

Integer Input

You may recall that we wrote a small integer-input routine in Chapter Five for **print**. That routine simply used **getfixed** to get a value of the **fixed** data type from the user and then converted that value to an integer. We now want to write a version of **getint** that does not depend on using the **fixed** data type; this will allow us to use integers in a program without bringing in all the **fixed** declarations and conversion routines.

The new version of **getint** follows the same logic as all our other interactive input routines; it uses the same calling sequence as the version presented in Chapter Five:

```
function getint(col,row,mini,maxi,defi:integer; defaulted: boolean):integer;
{ Get integer from user }

var
   mins, maxs, defs, s: string;
   maxlen, i, int: integer;
   booboo, good: boolean;

begin { getint }
   itos(mini, 0, mins);
   itos(maxi, 0, maxs);
   if length(mins) > length(maxs) then
      maxlen := length(mins)
   else
      maxlen := length(maxs);
   if defaulted then
      itos(defi, 0, defs)
```

```
      else
         defs := '';
      booboo := FALSE;
      repeat
         getstring(s, maxlen, col, row, defs, ['0'..'9', '+', '-'], FALSE);
         good := (length(s) > 0);
         if good then begin
            i := 1;
            good := stoi(s, i, int)
         end;
         if good then { still ok }
            good := (int >= mini) and (int <= maxi);
         if good then begin
            itos(int, maxlen, s);
            posstr(s, col, row)
         end
         else begin
            booboo := TRUE;
            crt(BEEP);
            center('Please enter a number between', MAXCRTROW - 1);
            center(concat(mins, ' and ', maxs), MAXCRTROW)
         end
      until good;
      if booboo then begin
         gotoxy(0, MAXCRTROW - 1);
         crt(ERASEOS)
      end;
      getint := int
end;
```

getint makes use of **itos**, which converts an integer to a string. (We designed this routine in Chapter Six). We also need a string-to-integer conversion routine, **stoi**, which we have not designed yet.

For **stoi** we will use a design similar to the one used for **stof** in Chapter Three. The call

```
good := stoi(s, i, int);
```

starts looking for an integer at the ith character of the string s. The integer seen is returned as the parameter **int**, and the returned parameter **i** points to the string character that made conversion stop — either a non-digit or the end of the string. **stoi** returns a Boolean value as its result, indicating whether or not the conversion went smoothly. If **stoi** returns **TRUE**, the string contained a valid integer. If it returns **FALSE**, the string contained an integer that would have been greater than **MAXINT** or less than −**MAXINT**.

Here is **stoi**:

```
function stoi(var s: string; var i, int: integer): boolean;
{ Convert string to integer }
const
   MDIV10 = 3276;        { MAXINT div 10 }
   MMOD10 = 7;           { MAXINT mod 10 }
```

```
var
   ok, negnum: boolean;
   digit: integer;
   c: char;
begin { stoi }
   int := 0;
   ok := TRUE;
   negnum := FALSE;
   if gnbchar(s, i, c) in ['+', '-'] then begin
      negnum := (c = '-');
      i := i + 1
   end;
   while gnbchar(s, i, c) in ['0'..'9'] do begin
      if ok then begin
         digit := ord(c) - 48;
         if (int > MDIV10) or ((int = MDIV10) and (digit > MMOD10)) then
            ok := FALSE
         else
            int := 10 * int + digit
      end;
      i := i + 1
   end;
   if negnum then
      int := -int;
   stoi := ok
end;
```

You should note that the constants **MDIV10** and **MMOD10** are set to the values **MAXINT div 10** and **MAXINT mod 10**, respectively. We need to know these values in order to protect the calculation

```
int := 10 * int + digit
```

from overflow. The values shown here are based on a value of **MAXINT** of 32767; a version of Pascal with another value of **MAXINT** will require different values here.

The routines **stoi** and **itos** can be used instead of **stof** and **ftos** in some of our previous programs.

Real Number Input

Our next step is to design **getreal**, a routine that accepts a real number from the user.

As previously mentioned, the precision, range, and storage requirements of the built-in real data type vary from one implementation of Pascal to another. Some versions of Pascal even offer more than one "flavor" of the real data type and allow the programmer to pick the one most suitable to the application at hand. In order to write a reliable interactive input tool for real numbers, it is necessary to know (at least approximately) the applicable implementation-defined limits on reals. This information should be available in the implementation's documentation.

In Apple Pascal, the real data type has approximately 7.2 decimal digits (24 bits) of precision. The largest positive real is approximately 3.4e38 (2^{128}) and the smallest positive real is approximately 1.2e−38 (2^{-126}). Each real variable requires four bytes of memory. The routines we will build will use this information to convert reals to strings and strings to reals while avoiding overflow and underflow errors. It should be relatively easy to modify the routines to work correctly for versions of Pascal with different real implementations.

Like our previous **get** interactive input tools, **getreal** uses **getstring** to accept the user's input as a string variable and then converts the string to the desired data type. **getreal** is called in the following way:

```
r := getreal(col, row, minr, maxr, defr, fmt, width, ndigs,
                                                    defaulted);
```

The calling parameters have the following customary meanings:

- **col** and **row** specify at what position on the CRT screen the input takes place.

- **minr** and **maxr** are the lower and upper limits for the input number. If the number entered by the user does not fall within these limits (or the user makes some other mistake), **getreal** displays a helpful error message at the bottom of the screen and allows the user another try.

- **defr** is the default answer. It is used only if the Boolean parameter **defaulted** is **TRUE**; otherwise no default is provided.

- **fmt** is a parameter controlling the display format of the numbers. It is a variable of the type **format**, either **FIXEDPOINT** or **SCIENTIFIC**, as defined in Chapter Four.

- **width** governs the input field length; in entering the number, the user may type in a maximum of **width** characters.

- **ndigs** controls the number of digits displayed after the decimal point in the number.

If the number the user types in passes all the validity checks, it is returned to the calling program as the function's result.

getreal looks much like **getfixed** from Chapter Three. It follows the same logic.

```
function getreal(col, row: integer; minr, maxr, defreal: real;
                 fmt: format; width, ndigs: integer; defaulted: boolean): real;
{ Get real number from user }

type
   calcstatus = (OK, OVERFLOW, UNDERFLOW, ZERODIVIDE);

var
   s, mins, maxs, defs: string;
   good, booboo: boolean;
   i: integer;
   r: real;
   okset: charset;

{-------------------------------}
{ Modules to be included here: }
{         stor                 }
{         rtos                 }
{-------------------------------}

begin { getreal }
   okset := ['0'..'9', '.', '+', '-', 'E', 'e'];
   rtos(minr, fmt, 0, ndigs, mins);
   rtos(maxr, fmt, 0, ndigs, maxs);
   if defaulted then
      rtos(defreal, fmt, 0, ndigs, defs)
   else
      defs := '';
   booboo := FALSE;
   repeat
      getstring(s, width, col, row, defs, okset, FALSE);
      good := (length(s) > 0);
      if good then begin
         i := 1;
         good := (stor(s, i, r) = OK)
      end;
      if good then
         good := (r >= minr) and (r <= maxr);
      if good then begin
         rtos(r, fmt, width, ndigs, s);
         posstr(s, col, row)
      end
      else begin
         booboo := TRUE;
         crt(BEEP);
         center('Please enter a number between', MAXCRTROW - 1);
         center(concat(mins, ' and ', maxs), MAXCRTROW)
      end
   until good;
   if booboo then begin
      gotoxy(0, MAXCRTROW - 1);
      crt(ERASEOS)
   end;
   getreal := r
end;
```

Like most of our previous **get<type>** routines, **getreal** requires separate routines to translate back and forth between strings and our desired data type.

Let's consider **rtos** first. This routine translates a real number into a string according to a specified format. The following call converts the real number **r** into the string **s**.

```
rtos(r, fmt, width, ndigs, s);
```

If the parameter **fmt** is **FIXEDPOINT**, the string is formatted in fixed-point format. If it is **SCIENTIFIC**, scientific notation is used. In either case, there are **ndigs** digits displayed after the decimal point and the string is padded with blanks on the left, if necessary, to a length of **width** characters. If more than **width** characters are needed for the number, they are used, making the string longer.

rtos is a simple two-way switch depending on the value of **fmt**:

```
procedure rtos(r: real; fmt: format; width, ndigs: integer; var s: string);
{ Convert real to string }
{------------------------------}
{ Modules to be included here: }
{       rtofix                 }
{       rtosci                 }
{       rightjust              }
{------------------------------}
begin { rtos }
   case fmt of
      FIXEDPOINT:
         rtofix(r, ndigs, s);
      SCIENTIFIC:
         rtosci(r, ndigs, s)
   end;
   rightjust(s, width)
end;
```

rtofix is a procedure that translates a real number into a string in the **FIXEDPOINT** format as follows:

```
procedure rtofix(r: real; ndigs: integer; var s: string);
{ Convert real to string, fixed point format }
const
   MAXPWR = 37;         { Maximum # of digits to round }
var
   i, digit, nbefore: integer;
begin { rtofix }
   if r < 0.0 then begin
      s := '-';
      r := -r
   end
   else
      s := '';
   if (ndigs >= 0) and (ndigs <= MAXPWR) then
      r := r + 0.5/pwroften(ndigs);
   nbefore := 1;
   while r >= 10.0 do begin
      r := r/10.0;
      nbefore := nbefore + 1
   end;
```

```
      for i := 1 to nbefore + ndigs do begin
        if i = nbefore + 1 then
          addchar(s, '.', MAXSTR);
        digit := trunc(r);
        addchar(s, chr(48 + digit), MAXSTR);
        r := 10.0 * (r - digit)
      end
end;
```

In words, **rtofix** works like this: if **r** (the number to be converted) is negative, the string **s** is initialized to "−" and **r** is set to −**r**; otherwise, **s** is set to the null string and **r** is left as is.

Then **r** is rounded to **ndigs** digits after the decimal point by adding a rounding factor. If **ndigs** is 0, the rounding factor is 0.5; if **ndigs** is 1, the rounding factor is 0.05; and so on. **rtofix** checks the value of **ndigs** to make sure the rounding factor can be calculated without generating an underflow error. Based on the value of Apple Pascal's smallest positive real, we can see that attempting to calculate a rounding factor for a value of **ndigs** greater than 37 would result in underflow.

After rounding, **rtofix** counts the number of digits preceding the decimal point by successively dividing the number by 10 until the number falls below 10. This also serves to normalize the number, making sure it lies in the range

```
0.0 <= r < 10.0
```

The variable **nbefore** keeps track of the number of digits before the decimal point. Note that there is always at least one, even if it is only a leading zero.

At this point we know the output string will contain **nbefore** + **ndigs** digits: **nbefore** digits before the decimal point and **ndigs** after. The **for** loop generates these digits one at a time by "chopping off" the leading digit of **r**, converting it to a character and adding it to the end of the string **s**. The decimal point is added to the string at the correct point after **nbefore** digits have been generated. (If you are doubtful, work an example or two by hand.)

In calculating the rounding factor, **rtofix** makes use of **pwroften**, a routine built into Apple Pascal (also present in UCSD Pascal). The call

```
x := pwroften(n)
```

simply sets x to the **n**th power of 10. The parameter **n** must be in the range 0 to 38 (for Apple Pascal). See Appendix A for a "portable" version of **pwroften** if your Pascal lacks it.

When using **rtofix**, you may notice that it sometimes generates nonsense digits in its output string if the calling routine specifies more significant digits to be displayed than available in the actual precision of the number. For example, if **r** is exactly 11.0 and **ndigs** is 10, the output string might look something like

```
11.0000002384
```

This error—while very small—is bothersome, and you may want to modify **rtofix** to avoid it. (But be careful; doing so correctly is not quite as simple as sounds at first.)

It might be useful for **rtofix** to round on the *left* side of the decimal point well as the right. This could be done by specifying a negative value of **ndigs**. For example, if *ndigs* is -2, the number would be rounded to the nearest multiple of 100.

After designing **rtofix**, writing **rtosci** is relatively easy. We want the output string returned by **rtosci** to be in the form

```
<optional sign><fraction part>e<exponent part>
```

where the fraction part is a number in the range

```
1.0 <= <fraction part> < 10.0
```

if the input real number is non-zero. The exponent part is a (possibly signed) integer.

Thus, our approach is to "split" the input number **r** into a fraction part, **frac**, and an exponent part, **expo**, and then separately convert each part into a string. This is actually not too difficult to accomplish. At the start of the routine, we initialize **frac** to **r** and **expo** to 0. If **frac** is not less than 10, we divide **frac** successively by 10 until it *is* less than 10, incrementing **expo** for each division. For example, if the input number is 4892.45, at the end of this process **frac** will be 4.89245 and **expo** will be 3.

If, on the other hand, the initial value of **frac** is less than 1.0 (but not 0) we *multiply* it successively by 10 until it is greater than or equal to 1.0, *decrementing* **expo** for each multiplication. For example, if the input number **r** is 0.0423, after this manipulation **frac** will be 4.23 and **expo** will be -2.

We then use **rtofix** to convert **frac** to a string (which takes care of rounding to **ndigs** digits) and use **itos** to convert **expo** to a string. Then we use **concat** to put the whole thing together.

This is probably most clearly expressed by the following Pascal code.

```
procedure rtosci(r: real; ndigs: integer; var s: string);
{ Convert real to string, scientific notation }
var
   frac: real;
   expo: integer;
   s1, s2: string;
begin { rtosci }
   frac := r;
   expo := 0;
   if abs(frac) >= 10.0 then
      repeat
         frac := frac/10.0;
         expo := expo + 1
      until abs(frac) < 10.0
   else if (abs(frac) < 1.0) and (r <> 0.0) then
      repeat
         frac := 10.0 * frac;
         expo := expo - 1
      until abs(frac) >= 1.0;
   rtofix(frac, ndigs, s1);
   itos(expo, 0, s2);
   s := concat(s1, 'e', s2)
end;
```

Note that **rtosci** properly handles negative and zero values of **r**, which we did not explicitly consider in the previous description.

The only remaining code needed for **rtos** is **rightjust**, which pads the string returned by **rtofix** or **rtosci** with blanks on the left to expand it to **width** characters. (If the string is already **width** characters or more in length, no padding is done.)

```
procedure rightjust(var s: string; width: integer);
{ Pad string with blanks on left to expand to specified width }
var
   nblanks: integer;
begin { rightjust }
   nblanks := width - length(s);
   if nblanks > 0 then begin
      {$r-}
      moveright(s[1], s[nblanks + 1], length(s));
      fillchar(s[1], nblanks, ' ');
      s[0] := chr(width)
      {$r+}
   end
end;
```

This routine first calculates **nblanks**, the number of blanks needed to expand the string to **width** characters. **rightjust** then uses the Apple and UCSD Pascal built-in routine **moveright** to move the characters in the string **nblanks** spaces to the right. **moveright** is nearly the same as **moveleft**, described in Chapter Five. The call

```
moveright(source, destination, nbytes)
```

moves **nbytes** bytes beginning at the location specified by **source** to the location specified by **destination**. The only difference between **moveleft** and **moveright** is that **moveright** starts moving bytes from the *end* of the source range and works toward its beginning, while **moveleft** starts from the beginning of the source range and works toward its end. This distinction is important when the source and destination ranges *overlap*, as they may here. We must be careful to move a byte before it is overwritten.

After the characters in the string have been moved, **nblanks** blanks are added to the front of the string using the Apple and UCSD Pascal built-in routine **fillchar** (described in Chapter Five). Finally, the string's length byte is changed to indicate the new length of the string.

stor

The last routine we need for interactive real input is **stor**, the routine that converts a string into a real number. Common sense dictates that this routine is where we must be most careful to guard against overflow and underflow errors; if the user accidentally enters a number that is too large or too small, **stor** must detect and report the error, rather than simply cause the program to crash.

Our design for **stor** is similar to that used for **stox** in Chapter Four. The call

```
status := stor(s, i, r);
```

starts looking at the ith character of the string **s** for the number. On output, **r** contains the number extracted from the string and **i** points to the character in the string where conversion stopped. **stor** returns a variable of type **calcstatus** as its result. This will be **OK** if the conversion succeeded and **OVERFLOW** or **UNDERFLOW** if the string contained a number that was too large or too small. (We distinguish between overflow and underflow errors on the chance that a routine calling **stor** would want to take different actions for these different conditions.)

As we saw in Chapter Four, it is helpful to work from a syntax diagram in designing string-interpretation routines. For **stor** we will use the "number" syntax diagram presented in Chapter Four. This makes sense since we do not need to distinguish between real and **xreal** string representations. (More importantly, how could we expect the programs' user to distinguish between them?)

As usual, our biggest problem is *controlling complexity*. The best way to do so in **stor** is to keep track of two things: the number of significant digits seen in the number (**nsig** in the following code) and the number of digits seen after the decimal point (**nafter** in the following code).

As the digits in the string are scanned, we will use them to accumulate **frac**, the "fraction part" of the number previously discussed. If we see an "E" scaling factor in the string, we will use **stoi** to convert it to an exponent part **expo**; if there is no scaling factor, **expo** is set to 0. After the string has been scanned, we adjust **expo** based on **nsig** and **nafter** and then combine **frac** and **expo** into the output real.

The pseudo-code for **stor** is shown here:

```
begin
   initialize
   get optional leading sign
   skip over leading non-significant zeros (if any)
   get (zero or more) digits, accumulate fraction
      - accumulate fraction
      - keep track of significant digits seen
   if there's a decimal point
      skip over it
      if no significant digits seen yet
         skip over zeros
            - keep track of # of digits after decimal
      get (zero or more) significant digits after decimal
                                                         point
         - continue to accumulate fraction
         - keep track of # of digits after decimal
         - continue to count significant digits
   if "E" or "e" is seen
      skip over it
      get exponent
   combine fraction and exponent into real
end
```

This turns into the following Pascal code:

```
function stor(var s: string; var i: integer; var r: real): calcstatus;
{ Convert string to real }

const
   MAXRSIG = 10;        { Maximum significant digits in real }
   MAXEXP = 38;         { Maximum real's exponent }
   MAXFRAC = 3.4;       { Maximum real's fraction (approx.) }
   MINEXP = -38;        { Minimum real's exponent }
   MINFRAC = 1.2;       { Minimum real's fraction (approx.) }
```

```
    var
        negnum: boolean;
        c: char;
        frac, p10: real;
        expo, nsig, nafter: integer;
        status: calcstatus;
    begin { stor }
        negnum := FALSE;
        frac := 0.0;
        p10 := 1.0;
        expo := 0;
        nsig := 0;
        nafter := 0;
        status := OK;
        if gnbchar(s, i, c) in ['+', '-'] then begin
            negnum := (c = '-');
            i := i + 1
        end;
        while gnbchar(s, i, c) = '0' do
            i := i + 1;
        while gnbchar(s, i, c) in ['0'..'9'] do begin
            if nsig < MAXRSIG then begin
                frac := frac + p10 * (ord(c) - 48);
                p10 := p10/10.0
            end;
            nsig := nsig + 1;
            i := i + 1
        end;
        if c = '.' then begin
            i := i + 1;
            if nsig = 0 then
                while gnbchar(s, i, c) = '0' do begin
                    i := i + 1;
                    nafter := nafter + 1
                end;
            while gnbchar(s, i, c) in ['0'..'9'] do begin
                if nsig < MAXRSIG then begin
                    frac := frac + p10 * (ord(c) - 48);
                    p10 := p10/10.0
                end;
                nsig := nsig + 1;
                nafter := nafter + 1;
                i := i + 1
            end
        end;
        if c in ['E', 'e'] then begin
            i := i + 1;
            if not stoi(s, i, expo) then
                status := OVERFLOW
        end;
        if status = OK then begin
            expo := expo + nsig - nafter - 1;
            if (expo > MAXEXP) or ((expo = MAXEXP) and (frac > MAXFRAC)) then
                status := OVERFLOW
            else if (expo < MINEXP) or ((expo = MINEXP) and (frac < MINFRAC)) then
                status := UNDERFLOW
            else if expo >= 0 then
                r := frac * pwroften(expo)
            else
                r := frac/pwroften(-expo)
        end;
        if negnum then
            r := -r;
        stor := status
    end;
```

(The best way to verify and understand this routine is to work through one or two examples by hand.)

Note that after a certain number of significant digits have been seen in the string, it is pointless to include any *additional* digits in the conversion calculation. This "certain number" depends on the precision of the real data type; in Apple Pascal, for example, if the input string is "35.00000000383," the digits "383" are unimportant to the final value returned by **stor**.

Thus, **stor** skips over significant digits after **MAXRSIG** significant digits have been converted. The constant **MAXRSIG** is set large enough so that neglecting these additional digits can have no effect on the calculation; if reals have a precision of n digits, setting **MAXRSIG** to the smallest integer greater than or equal to $n + 2$ is safe. In the preceding code, we chose **MAXRSIG** to be 10.

You may wish to attempt to think up "pathological" input strings that will cause **stor** to give incorrect results or even crash. This is one of the most valuable techniques you can use to ensure a routine is reliable. (Note that the values shown for **MINFRAC** and **MAXFRAC** are only approximate.) Is it worth fixing **stor** to handle such cases correctly? Can you do it without introducing other bugs?

runbouncer

Finally, we can return to designing our simulation. The next step is to write **runbouncer**, which sets up and carries out each individual run of the simulation.

First, we will present a short description of the data structure. We need to keep track of each ball's position and velocity during the run. As we discussed, these quantities are both vectors. The natural way to represent this in Pascal is to keep the information for each ball in a record and to hold each individual record in an array, as in the following:

```
<type>
   ballrec = record
       pos, vel: vector
       end;

<var>
   ball: array [1..MAXBALLS] of ballrec;
```

Thus, the x-component of ball number 5's position is **ball[5].pos[X]** and the y-component of ball 10's velocity is **ball[10].vel[Y]**.

With that taken care of, here is **runbouncer**:

```
procedure runbouncer;
{ Run bouncer simulation }
const
   XMAX = 279;          { Graphics screen maximum x-coordinate }
   YMAX = 191;          { Graphics screen maximum y-coordinate }
type
   ballrec = record
      pos, vel: vector
   end;
var
   ball: array [1..MAXBALLS] of ballrec;
   max, min: vector;
   ch: char;
{------------------------------}
{ Modules to be inserted here: }
{         initgraphics         }
{         plotball             }
{         initbrun             }
{         moveballs            }
{         termgraphics         }
{------------------------------}
begin { runbouncer }
   initgraphics;
   initbrun;
   repeat
      moveballs
   until keypress;
   ch := getkey(ch, [chr(0)..chr(127)], FALSE);
   termgraphics
end;
```

runbouncer first calls **initgraphics**, which prepares the graphics screen for use, and **initbrun**, which sets up the initial conditions for the run. It then continually calls **moveballs**, which moves the balls on the screen according to the initial conditions, parameters, and assumptions.

After each call to **moveballs, runbouncer** checks to see if the user has pressed a key. This is accomplished with the **boolean** function **keypress**, a routine provided by Apple Pascal in the standard unit **applestuff. keypress** returns **TRUE** if the user has pressed a key on the keyboard; otherwise it returns **FALSE**. It is important to remember that **keypress** does not *wait* for a key to be pressed, nor does it read the character typed in. It simply tells us whether a character is "waiting" to be read.

keypress is especially useful when we want to interrupt a program "on the fly"; that is why it was provided with Apple Pascal. Designing **keypress** for a version of Pascal that does not provide it will, in general, require knowledge of the computer's operating system or I/O hardware, or both. (See Appendix A.)

When **runbouncer** detects a pressed key, it reads the typed character using **getkey**; otherwise, the character would "hang around" waiting to be read until the next user input was requested, which is not a desirable situation. Finally, **termgraphics** is called to return to the text screen.

We presented **initgraphics** and **termgraphics** in Chapter Six, so we will not consider them further here.

initbrun

The **initbrun** routine sets up a number of variables for the run; it also displays the box and initial arrangement of balls on the graphics screen:

```
procedure initbrun;
{ Initialize bouncer ball positions and velocities, box boundaries }

const
    VMAX = 5;              { Maximum abs. val. for ball velocity component }

var
    i: integer;
{------------------------------}
{ Modules to be inserted here: }
{         frame                }
{         randreal             }
{------------------------------}
begin { initbrun }
    frame;
    min[X] := 2.0;
    max[X] := XMAX - 2.0;
    min[Y] := 2.0;
    max[Y] := YMAX - 2.0;
    for i := 1 to nballs do
        with ball[i] do begin
            pos[X] := randreal(min[X], max[X]);
            pos[Y] := randreal(min[Y], max[Y]);
            plotball(pos);
            vel[X] := randreal(-VMAX, +VMAX);
            vel[Y] := randreal(-VMAX, +VMAX);
        end
end;
```

initbrun calls **frame** (shown in Chapter Six) to draw the walls of the box on the screen. We assume the box fills the whole screen. The variables **min** and **max** describe where the walls of the box are: **min[X]** is the lower limit for a ball's x-position, **max[X]** is the upper limit, and the same is true for **Y**. Note that a ball's position is the position of the *center* of the ball and that each ball has a "radius" of two screen dots. Thus, the **min** and **max** limits are two screen units away from the walls.

For each ball, **initbrun** assigns a random position within the box. This is accomplished by selecting a random x-coordinate between **min[X]** and **max[X]** and a random y-coordinate between **min[Y]** and **max[Y]**. A random initial velocity is similarly calculated for each ball, with each component of the velocity assigned a random value between −**VMAX** and +**VMAX**; **VMAX** is a constant, chosen here as 5.0. Finally, **initbrun** calls **plotball** to display each ball's initial position.

Random real numbers are obtained using the **randreal** function:

```
function randreal(a, b: real): real;
{ Return random real between specified limits }
begin { randreal }
   randreal := a + (b - a) * random/32767.0
end;
```

This function makes use of **random**, which we used in Chapter Two. As you may remember, it is a routine in Apple Pascal's standard unit **applestuff**, and it returns a random integer in the range 0 to 32767.

The other routine we need is **plotball**:

```
procedure plotball(pos: vector);
{ Draw or erase ball on screen }
const
   ROWSIZE = 2;            { 2 * ((PICSIZE + 15) div 16) - picture size in bytes }
begin { plotball }
   drawblock(ballpic, ROWSIZE, 0, 0, PICSIZE, PICSIZE, round(pos[X] - 2.0),
                                                       round(pos[Y] - 2.0), 6)
end;
```

plotball calls **drawblock** to display the previously defined **ballpic** picture array on the screen. Two points are worth noting. First, **drawblock** requires us to specify where the picture is to be plotted by passing the x- and y-positions of the picture array's *lower left-hand corner* as integer values. The **pos** vector is the position of the center of the ball, so we substract 2.0 from each component of **pos** and round to the nearest integer before passing them to **drawblock**.

The second point is more subtle: we not only use **plotball** to draw a ball at a specified position, but we also use it to *erase* a previously drawn ball at a specified position. The key to this behavior is the last parameter to **drawblock**, the "mode" parameter. It governs the method used to move the elements of the picture array to the screen. We have selected a value of 6, which is the "exclusive-or" mode. Exclusive-or works like this: for each element in the picture array, the corresponding screen dot is examined. If the screen dot is on *or* the picture array element is **TRUE** *but not both*, the screen dot is turned on. Otherwise the screen dot is turned off.

This is exactly what we want. If the area on the screen is empty (all dots off), the picture array is simply copied to the screen. If the screen area already contains a copy of the picture array, the screen dots are turned off. This process also does sensible things in the more general case where the screen area is not initially empty. Making two successive calls to **plotball** at the same position simply leaves the screen as it was before the calls.

moveballs

Now it is time to design **moveballs**. We have deliberately tried to concentrate the special assumptions and calculations of the model into this routine, thus hiding them from the rest of the program. It should be clear that this is more sensible than scattering such model details throughout the program.

The **moveballs** routine, given each ball's position (**pos**) and velocity (**vel**) as well as the constant acceleration applied to each ball (**acc**), must calculate a projected "new" position and velocity a short time interval (**dt**) later. Then it must erase the ball from the graphics screen at the old position and redraw it at the new position.

Our "simplifying assumptions" come into play here. First, we are going to assume the balls in the box do not interact with each other—either they pass through each other like ghosts or they are too small for collisions between them to happen very often. This saves us from having to calculate the distances between each pair of balls at each time interval to see if they were close enough to affect each other.

A second simplifying assumption governs how the balls bounce off the walls of the box. Let's say a ball bounces off the "bottom" of the box. We will assume that this collision does not affect the ball's x-velocity (the component parallel to the box bottom) and it simply "turns around" the y-component of the velocity (the component perpendicular to the bottom) so that it is now heading upward at the same speed at which it was heading downward.

Elementary physics gives us enough information to calculate each ball's new position and velocity from its original position and velocity and the given constant acceleration. Each component of the ball's motion is *independent* of the others; we can do calculations for the x-components without considering the y-components.

Let's assume **p(t)** is one component of a ball's position vector at a given time. The new position component at a later time, **t + dt**, is given by

```
p(t + dt) := p(t) + dt * <average velocity between t and
                                                       t + dt>
```

We will use a "pseudo-Pascal" notation to present mathematical formulas. In English, this formula simply says "the ball's new position (at time **t + dt**) can be calculated by taking the ball's old position (at time **t**) and adding **dt** times the ball's average velocity during the interval."

Thus, we have reduced our problem to calculating the average velocity during the time interval. We will estimate the average velocity as the velocity *halfway between* time **t** and time **t + dt**, as follows:

```
<average velocity between t and t + dt> := v(t + dt/2)
```

This estimate is accurate when there is a constant acceleration during the time interval, as we have here. It ceases to be accurate if the acceleration changes a great deal during the time interval. But since we have a constant acceleration, the new velocity is simply related to the old velocity

```
v(t + dt/2) := v(t) + a * dt/2
```

where **a** is the acceleration. Thus, the formula for the new position becomes

```
p(t + dt) := p(t) + dt * (v(t) + a * dt/2)
```

The only thing left to do is to calculate the ball's new velocity at time **t +dt**. Since we have a constant acceleration, this is

```
v(t + dt) := v(t) + a * dt
```

Remember that these calculations apply to each component of the position, velocity, and acceleration. For each ball we do this calculation *twice*, once for each vector component. That is exactly what we do in **moveballs**.

```
procedure moveballs;
{ Move balls on screen }
var
   i: integer;
   j: coordinate;
   newpos: vector;
```

```
{------------------------------}
{ Modules to be inserted here: }
{        line                  }
{------------------------------}
begin { moveballs }
    for i := 1 to nballs do
        with ball[i] do begin
            for j := X to Y do begin
                newpos[j] := pos[j] + dt * (vel[j] + acc[j] * dt/2.0);
                if (newpos[j] < min[j]) or (newpos[j] > max[j]) then begin
                    note(2, 2);
                    newpos[j] := pos[j];
                    vel[j] := -vel[j]
                end
                else
                    vel[j] := vel[j] + acc[j] * dt
            end;
            plotball(pos);
            if showpath then
                line(pos, newpos);
            plotball(newpos);
            pos := newpos
        end
end;
```

Note carefully the order of the calculations. We first calculate the ball's projected new position. If the ball's new position component is beyond one of the walls (less than **min** or greater than **max**), we bring the ball back to its previous position and send it heading in the opposite direction by switching the sign of the velocity component. If the ball did not hit the wall, the new value of the velocity component is calculated normally.

After this calculation is carried out for both x- and y-components, we erase the ball from its previous position and redraw it in its new position. If the parameter **showpath** is **TRUE**, we also draw a line between old and new positions. Finally, the value of **pos** is updated to **newpos** so that the next time **moveballs** is called it will work with the ball's new position.

The procedure **note** used in **moveballs** is called whenever a ball bounces off a wall. This procedure is provided in Apple Pascal's **applestuff** unit, and it simply sounds the Apple's speaker. A variety of different sounds can be generated by **note**. The call

```
note(p, d)
```

sounds a note of "pitch" **p** and "duration" **d** (**p** must be an integer between 0 and 50, and **d** an integer between 0 and 255). The call **note(2, 2)** generates an appropriate brief "bouncing" sound. Clearly, this feature will not be available on some computers and on others it may be superseded by much more sophisticated sound abilities.

The only routine left to specify is **line**, which draws a line between two points on the graphics screen.

```
procedure Line(v1, v2: vector);
{ Plot line between two points }
begin { line }
   pencolor(NONE);
   moveto(round(v1[X]), round(v1[Y]));
   pencolor(WHITE);
   moveto(round(v2[X]), round(v2[Y]))
end;
```

Suggestions

Once you have **bouncer** running, the natural thing to try is modifying the model's assumptions. If you add the assumption that the balls *do* interact with each other, you will have to specify the mathematical details of the interaction. This might be easier if you have taken a good physics course. You might also want to change the way balls bounce off the wall. You could, for example, specify that a ball loses a certain amount of energy whenever it collides with the wall. Or you could give each ball a spin, which will greatly change the balls' interactions with each other and with the walls, as any billiards player will attest. Again, the mathematical details are up to you.

We avoided talking about units in our development of **bouncer**. You may want to specify positions in meters, velocities in meters per second, and accelerations in meters per second per second, or whatever your favorite units are. In this case, you will also need to be able to specify the dimensions of the box in whatever units you select.

You may also allow the user to enter numbers specifying the size of the box. Can you think of a good way for the user to easily specify different *shapes* of the box?

Next, allow the user to place obstacles like walls, revolving doors, or arbitrary shapes *within* the box. This could easily develop into a good game. Allow the user to manipulate a movable wall (customarily called a "paddle") to cause the balls to hit a target or some other goal.

If you go this far, you will probably need to develop general-purpose graphics routines that allow any size or shape of box or obstacle to be represented on the graphics screen. This brings in the idea of scaling, windowing, clipping, and so on.

Add a command to allow the user to "freeze" the screen temporarily. You might also add a command that will cause the graphics screen to be printed on the system printer or stored on disk if your hardware allows it.

Finally, you may want to represent the analogous three-dimensional problem accurately on the screen. The details of the model need not be much more complex in this case; it is a matter of adding the proper calculations for the third dimension. The complexity lies in the mathematics of the necessary graphics routines.

isaac

Our second simulation is **isaac**, named after Isaac Newton. Newton discovered the law of gravitation, which we will explore in this simulation. Our purpose is to show how a number of objects move under their mutual gravitational attraction.

The general structure of **isaac** is much like **bouncer**'s: each execution consists of a number of individual runs, and for each run the user specifies a number of parameters. For **isaac**, the user must specify the number of objects, a time interval between successive calculations, and whether to show the objects' paths. Unlike **bouncer**, the user also enters initial positions and velocities for each object. In addition, the user must enter a *mass* for each object, since the gravitational attraction between any two objects depends on their masses.

Like **bouncer**, **isaac** displays the animated behavior of the model until the user presses a key. The user can either exit from the program by entering 0 for the number of objects or enter the parameters for another run. Successive "snapshots" of a sample run of **isaac** are shown in Figures 7-2, 7-3, and 7-4. (Parameters used to generate this run are shown later.)

Here is the main routine of **isaac**:

```
{$s+}
program isaac;

uses
    applestuff,         { for keypress }
    turtlegraphics,     { for graphics routines }
    transcend,          { for square root }
    {$u apple2:toolstuff.code }
    crtstuff;

const
    MAXOBJECTS = 10;    { Maximum number of objects per run }
    PICSIZE = 5;        { Size of picture array in dots }

type
    coordinate = (X, Y);
    vector = array [coordinate] of real;
    objectrec = record
        mass: real;
        pos, vel: vector
```

```
      end;
    picture = packed array [1..PICSIZE, 1..PICSIZE] of boolean;
var
    object: array [1..MAXOBJECTS] of objectrec;
    i, margin, nobjects: integer;
    prompt: array [1..9] of string;
    dt: real;
    showpath: boolean;
    ballpic: picture;
{-----------------------------}
{ Modules to be inserted here: }
{        initisaac            }
{        getiparams           }
{        runisaac             }
{-----------------------------}
begin { isaac }
   crt(CLEAR);
   disptitle('isaac');
   initisaac;
   for i := 1 to 9 do
      posstr(prompt[i], margin, 2 + 2 * i);
   repeat
      getiparams;
      if nobjects > 0 then
         runisaac
   until nobjects <= 0;
   crt(CLEAR)
end.
```

Note that an additional unit is specified in the **uses** statement, **transcend**. Apple Pascal puts "transcendental" functions in this unit instead of building them into the compiler. **isaac** uses the square root function, **sqrt**, from this unit.

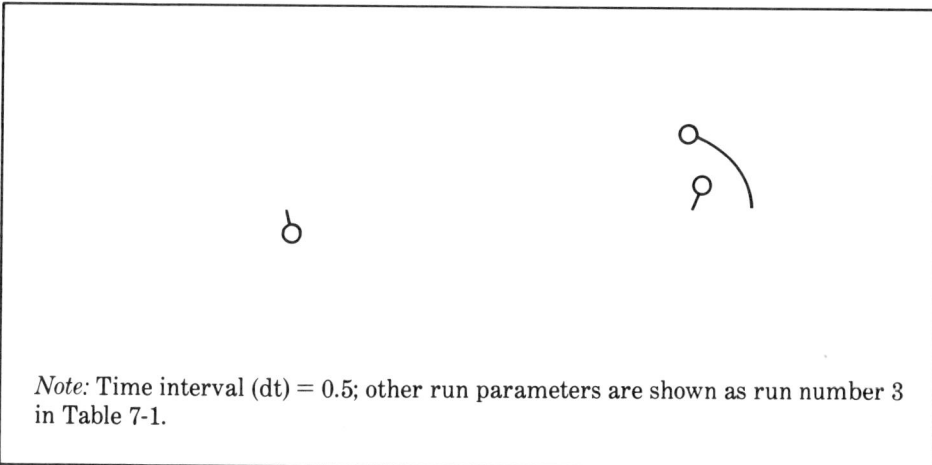

Note: Time interval (dt) = 0.5; other run parameters are shown as run number 3 in Table 7-1.

Figure 7-2. Typical **isaac** run after 12 iterations

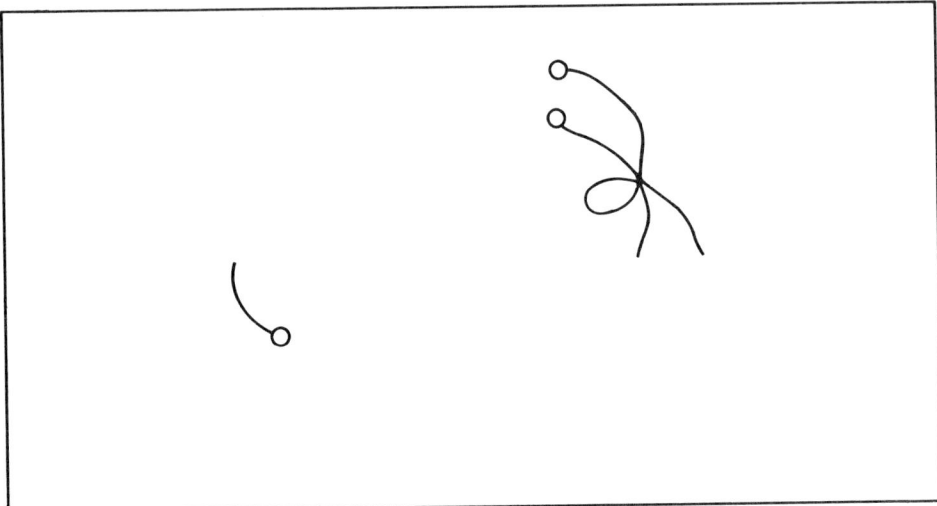

Figure 7-3. The same run after 64 iterations

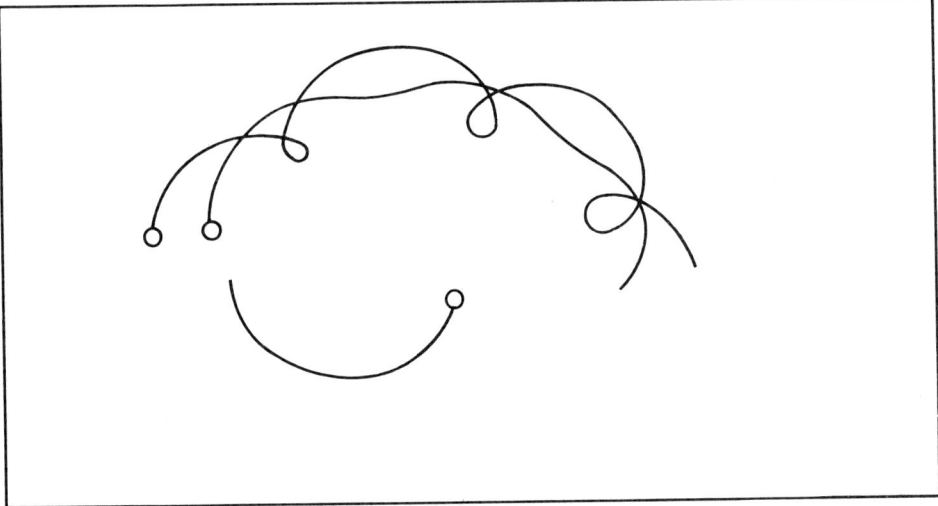

Figure 7-4. The same run after 175 iterations

Note also that the declaration for the **objectrec** type serves the same purpose as the **ballrec** type in **bouncer**. The only difference is that **objectrec** contains a field for **mass**, the object's mass.

The routine **initisaac** is also very similar to the analogous routine in **bouncer**; it initializes the **prompt** array, **margin**, and **ballpic**.

```
procedure initisaac;
{ Initialize isaac's globals }
var
   i, j: integer;
begin { initisaac }
   prompt[1] := 'Number of objects (0 to exit):';
   prompt[2] := 'Time interval:';
   prompt[3] := 'Show object paths(Y/N):';
   prompt[4] := '   Object No. ';
   prompt[5] := 'Mass:';
   prompt[6] := 'Initial x-position:';
   prompt[7] := 'Initial y-position:';
   prompt[8] := 'Initial x-velocity:';
   prompt[9] := 'Initial y-velocity:';
   margin := (MAXCRTCOL - 29) div 2;
   for i := 1 to 5 do
      for j := 1 to 5 do
         ballpic[i, j] := ((i in [1, 5]) and (j in [2..4])) or
                          ((j in [1, 5]) and (i in [2..4]))
end;
```

The procedure **getiparams** accepts the run parameters from the user.

```
procedure getiparams;
{ Accept parameters for isaac run }
const
   VMAX = 10.0;     { Maximum abs. val. of initial velocity component }
   XMIN = 0.0;      { Minimum initial x-position }
   XMAX = 279.0;    { Maximum initial x-position }
   YMIN = 0.0;      { Minimum initial y-position }
   YMAX = 191.0;    { Maximum initial y-position }

type
   format = (FIXEDPOINT, SCIENTIFIC);

var
   i: integer;
   s: string;

{-----------------------------}
{ Modules to be inserted here: }
{        itos                 }
{        stoi                 }
{        getint               }
{        getreal              }
{-----------------------------}

begin { getiparams }
   nobjects := getint(margin + length(prompt[1]), 4, 0, MAXOBJECTS, 0, FALSE);
   if nobjects > 0 then begin
      dt := getreal(margin + length(prompt[2]), 6, 0.0001, 1.0, 0.0,
                                            FIXEDPOINT, 6, 4, FALSE);
      showpath := getboolean(margin + length(prompt[3]), 8, FALSE, FALSE);
      for i := 1 to nobjects do begin
         itos(i, 0, s);
         posstr(s, margin + length(prompt[4]), 10);
```

```
            with object[i] do begin
                mass := getreal(margin + length(prompt[5]), 12, 0.0, 1000.0, 0.0,
                                                   FIXEDPOINT, 6, 1, FALSE);
                pos[X] := getreal(margin + length(prompt[6]), 14, XMIN, XMAX, 0.0,
                                                   FIXEDPOINT, 5, 1, FALSE);
                pos[Y] := getreal(margin + length(prompt[7]), 16, YMIN, YMAX, 0.0,
                                                   FIXEDPOINT, 5, 1, FALSE);
                vel[X] := getreal(margin + length(prompt[8]), 18,-VMAX, VMAX, 0.0,
                                                   FIXEDPOINT, 6, 2, FALSE);
                vel[Y] := getreal(margin + length(prompt[9]), 20,-VMAX, VMAX, 0.0,
                                                   FIXEDPOINT, 6, 2, FALSE)
            end
        end
    end
end;
```

The procedure **runisaac** sets up and carries out an individual run. It is very similar to **runbouncer** and uses some of the same routines.

```
procedure runisaac;
{ Run isaac simulation }

var
    ch: char;

{----------------------------}
{ Modules to be inserted here: }
{         initgraphics        }
{         plotball            }
{         initirun            }
{         moveobjs            }
{         termgraphics        }
{----------------------------}

begin { runisaac }
    initgraphics;
    initrun;
    repeat
        moveobjs
    until keypress;
    ch := getkey(ch, [chr(0)..chr(127)], FALSE);
    termgraphics
end;
```

How Gravity Works

Before we design the remainder of **isaac**, we need to digress briefly to describe the law of gravitation.

Newton discovered that an object placed a distance **r** from another object of mass **m** underwent an acceleration toward that object and that the magnitude of the acceleration was easily expressed in a formula. In a Pascal format, the formula can be written as

```
acc := G * m/sqr(r);
```

Here **G** is a constant that depends on the units used to express the quantities **acc**, **m**, and **r**. (For the rest of this chapter, we will assume we have chosen our units so that **G** = 1.)

Knowing the magnitude of the object's acceleration vector (given by the preceding formula) and the direction of the acceleration vector (toward the attracting object), we can calculate each component of the acceleration vector by using a little bit of mathematics.

Let's call the attracting object Object 1 and say it is at the position (x1, y1, z1). We will call the other object—the one for which we want to calculate the acceleration—Object 2 and say it is at (x2, y2, z2). The first step is to calculate **r**, the distance between the two objects. First we calculate the *vector difference* between the two positions by subtracting one position vector from the other, component by component, as follows:

```
(x1, y1, z1) - (x2, y2, z2) = (x1 - x2, y1 - y2, z1 - z2)
```

This new vector may be interpreted as a vector that describes the position of Object 1 *relative to* Object 2: it is just as if we had moved the origin of our coordinate system to Object 2. The distance then is simply the magnitude of this difference vector.

```
r := sqrt(sqr(x1 - x2) + sqr(y1 - y2) + sqr(z1 - z2))
```

This is a general formula that yields the distance between *any* two points in a Cartesian coordinate system. We will not formally prove this here, but you may recognize it as a form of the Pythagorean theorem. Knowing **r** allows us to calculate **acc**, the magnitude of the acceleration vector, with Newton's formula.

The next step is to calculate the individual components of the acceleration vector, **x-acc**, **y-acc**, and **z-acc**. Notice that the acceleration is in the direction of Object 1 relative to Object 2, the same direction as the vector difference in the positions calculated previously. This means the individual components of the acceleration vector and its magnitude, **acc**, must be in the same ratio as the individual components of the difference vector and *its* magnitude, **r**. In mathematical language this becomes

```
x-acc/(x1 - x2) = y-acc/(y1 - y2) = z-acc/(z1 - z2) = acc/r
```

Thus, the x-component of the acceleration is given by

```
x-acc := acc * (x1 - x2)/r
```

Similar equations hold for the y- and z-accelerations, as follows:

```
y-acc := acc * (y1 - y2)/r
z-acc := acc * (z1 - z2)/r
```

Notice that Object 2 also attracts Object 1. Calculating the acceleration of Object 1 is simply a matter of following through the same calculation, substituting the mass of Object 2 where we previously had the mass of Object 1 and interchanging x1 for x2, y1 for y2, and z1 for z2.

These formulas give us all we need to know about calculating the acceleration of one object due to the gravitational force exerted by another. What about the more complex situation where we have more than one other object? In this case we simply calculate the x-accelerations caused by *each* individual object and add them up to get the *total* x-acceleration. We do the same for the y- and z-accelerations.

Although we have discussed the three-dimensional case here, we will ignore the z-components in **isaac**, just as we did in **bouncer**.

Calculational Methods

The method we use in **isaac** to calculate an object's "new" position at the time **dt** after the "old" position differs slightly from the one we used in **bouncer**. We still use the same basic equation

```
p(t + dt) := p(t) + dt * v(t + dt/2)
```

The problem is that the acceleration is no longer a constant but changes as the objects move in relation to each other. How do we calculate the factor **v(t + dt/2)**? We will use a formula analogous to the one we used for position:

```
v(t + dt/2) := v(t - dt/2)
             + dt * <average acceleration between t - dt/2
                                             and t + dt/2>
```

Assuming that the object's acceleration changes relatively slowly and smoothly, we can estimate the "average acceleration between t − dt/2 and t + dt/2" as the acceleration halfway between the two times, **a(t)**. Thus, the formula becomes

```
v(t + dt/2) := v(t - dt/2) + dt * a(t)
```

This method of calculation requires that we keep track of the objects' velocities at time periods halfway between our position estimates. Therefore, for each run we must make an initial calculation once to estimate the velocity at a time **dt**/2 *before* the initial conditions at **t** = 0, as follows:

```
v(-dt/2) := v(0) - (dt/2) * a(0)
```

In summary, we use the following method to update the objects' positions:

```
begin
   calculate relative position vectors
       (using position vectors at time t, p(t))
   for each object
       calculate acceleration vector at time t, a(t)
           (using relative position vectors calculated above)
       calculate "average" velocity vector, v(t + dt/2)
           (using old velocity, v(t - dt/2) and a(t),
                                           calculated above)
       calculate new position vector at time (t+dt), p(t+dt)
           (using old position, p(t), and average velocity
                                           calculated above)
       update graphics screen
   end-for
end
```

We have to perform the following initialization to get things started correctly.

```
begin
   calculate relative position vectors
       (using initial position vectors at time 0, p(0))
   for each object
       calculate acceleration vector at time 0, a(0)
       use it to estimate velocity vector at time (-dt/2),
                                                  v(-dt/2)
   end-for
end
```

More Data Structures

It is important to realize we must perform the operations just described in the order shown. First calculate *all* the relative position vectors at time t, and then (and only then) use them to calculate the new positions at time **t** + **dt**. If we instead calculated the acceleration and updated the position of each object one at a time, inaccuracies would creep in because the acceleration of an object at a given time depends on the relative positions of the other objects *at the same time.* We cannot update the position of any object until we have calculated the relative positions of all the objects. Therefore, we need a data structure to hold all these relative positions.

The natural way to accomplish this in Pascal is to use a matrix. We declare

```
<type>
    relpos: array [1..MAXOBJECTS, 1..MAXOBJECTS] of vector;
```

The **relpos** matrix then holds the relative position vectors. For example, the element **relpos[2, 4]** is the vector difference between the position vectors of Object 2 and Object 4, with x-component **relpos[2, 4][X]** and y-component **relpos[2, 4][Y]**. We can write these more compactly as **relpos[2, 4, X]** and **relpos[2, 4, Y]**.

Remember that the acceleration calculations use both **r** (the distance between each pair of objects) and **sqr(r)** (its square). As long as we are accumulating relative position vectors, we might as well use them to calculate these quantities at the same time. Again, we use a matrix to hold the numbers:

```
<type>
    r, rsq: array [1..MAXOBJECTS, 1..MAXOBJECTS] of real;
```

For example, the number **r[3,1]** is the distance between Object 3 and Object 1. The square of the distance between Objects 5 and 6 is **rsq[5, 6]**.

The following relations hold between the elements of each array, as can be seen from the symmetry of the calculations:

```
relpos[j, i, k] = -relpos[i, j, k]
r[j, i] = r[i, j]
rsq[j, i] = rsq[i, j]
```

The first relation is true because the relative position **relpos** is calculated by subtracting the coordinates of the two objects; switching **i** and **j** reverses the sign of the result, as follows:

```
relpos[j, i, k] :=   (object[j].pos[k] - object[i].pos[k]);
               := - (object[i].pos[k] - object[j].pos[k]);
               := - relpos[i, j, k]
```

The other two relations are more obvious. The distance between Object **i** and Object **j** (**r[i, j]**) is the same as the distance between Object **j** and Object

i (r[j, i]); the same argument goes for the square of the distance.

We will use these three relations to eliminate some of the calculations.

initirun

Now we are ready to write **initirun**. This routine must plot the initial position of each object, which is a simple call to **plotball**. As we described previously, this routine must also estimate each object's velocity at time $-dt/2$. Doing so is a matter of translating all our discussion into the following equivalent Pascal code:

```
procedure initirun;
{ Initialize isaac run, do initial velocity estimate }
var
   relpos: array [1..MAXOBJECTS, 1..MAXOBJECTS] of vector;
   r, rsq: array [1..MAXOBJECTS, 1..MAXOBJECTS] of real;
   i, j: integer;
   k: coordinate;
   acc: vector;
   temp: real;
begin { initirun }
   for i := 1 to nobjects - 1 do
      for j := i + 1 to nobjects do begin
         for k := X to Y do begin
            relpos[i, j, k] := object[j].pos[k] - object[i].pos[k];
            relpos[j, i, k] := -relpos[i, j, k]
         end;
         rsq[i, j] := sqr(relpos[i, j, X]) + sqr(relpos[i, j, Y]);
         r[i, j] := sqrt(rsq[i,j]);
         rsq[j, i] := rsq[i, j];
         r[j, i] := r[i, j]
      end;
   for i := 1 to nobjects do begin
      acc[X] := 0.0;
      acc[Y] := 0.0;
      for j := 1 to nobjects do
         if i <> j then begin
            temp := object[j].mass/rsq[i, j]/r[i, j];
            acc[X] := acc[X] + temp * relpos[i, j, X];
            acc[Y] := acc[Y] + temp * relpos[i, j, Y]
         end;
      with object[i] do begin
         vel[X] := vel[X] - acc[X] * dt/2.0;
         vel[Y] := vel[Y] - acc[Y] * dt/2.0;
         plotball(pos)
      end
   end
end;
```

Note that in the calculation of the **relpos**, **r**, and **rsq** matrices, **initirun** only directly calculates half the elements, using the "symmetry" relations described here to generate the others.

moveobjs

Finally, the **moveobjs** routine carries out the task of figuring out "new" positions and velocities from their old values and moves the objects on the graphics screen:

```
procedure moveobjs;
{ Calculate new positions and velocities, move balls on screen }
var
    relpos: array [1..MAXOBJECTS, 1..MAXOBJECTS] of vector;
    r, rsq: array [1..MAXOBJECTS, 1..MAXOBJECTS] of real;
    i, j: integer;
    k: coordinate;
    acc, newpos: vector;
    temp: real;

{-----------------------------}
{ Modules to be inserted here: }
{          line               }
{-----------------------------}
begin { moveobjs }
    for i := 1 to nobjects - 1 do
        for j := i + 1 to nobjects do begin
            for k := X to Y do begin
                relpos[i, j, k] := object[j].pos[k] - object[i].pos[k];
                relpos[j, i, k] := -relpos[i, j, k]
            end;
            rsq[i, j] := sqr(relpos[i, j, X]) + sqr(relpos[i, j, Y]);
            r[i, j] := sqrt(rsq[i,j]);
            rsq[j, i] := rsq[i, j];
            r[j, i] := r[i, j]
        end;
    for i := 1 to nobjects do begin
        acc[X] := 0.0;
        acc[Y] := 0.0;
        for j := 1 to nobjects do
            if i <> j then begin
                temp := object[j].mass/rsq[i, j]/r[i, j];
                acc[X] := acc[X] + temp * relpos[i, j, X];
                acc[Y] := acc[Y] + temp * relpos[i, j, Y]
            end;
        with object[i] do begin
            for k := X to Y do begin
                vel[k] := vel[k] + acc[k] * dt;
                newpos[k] := pos[k] + vel[k] * dt
            end;
            plotball(pos);
            plotball(newpos);
            if showpath then
                line(pos, newpos);
            pos := newpos
        end
    end
end;
```

In running **isaac**, it is not easy at first to choose run parameters that cause "interesting" situations to appear on the screen. Table 7-1 shows values of input parameters that demonstrate behavior worthy of attention.

Table 7-1. Interesting **isaac** Run Parameters

Run No.	Object No.	Mass	Position X	Position Y	Velocity X	Velocity Y
1	1	1000.0	140.0	95.0	0.0	−0.002
	2	1.0	275.0	95.0	0.0	2.0
2	1	1000.0	5.0	95.0	0.0	0.5
	2	500.0	275.0	95.0	0.0	−1.0
3	1	1000.0	80.0	95.0	0.0	−1.0
	2	400.0	209.0	95.0	0.0	1.0
	3	100.0	229.0	95.0	0.0	6.0
4	1	1000.0	5.0	95.0	0.0	1.0
	2	1000.0	275.0	95.0	0.0	−1.0
	3	1.0	140.0	95.0	0.0	0.0
5	1	1000.0	140.0	95.0	0.0	−0.03
	2	10.0	230.0	95.0	0.0	3.33
	3	0.1	185.0	173.0	−2.89	1.67

Run 1 is the case of a light object in orbit around a much heavier one. This is analogous to the motion of the Earth around the Sun.

Run 2 shows how two objects of comparable mass orbit each other; a comparable real-world situation is a binary star system.

Run 3 is a three-object simulation: a light body in orbit around a heavier one, while these two orbit in turn around an even heavier object. This run is the one shown in Figures 7-2, 7-3, and 7-4. An analogous system is the Sun-Earth-Moon system, although the masses used in this example are much closer to each other than are the solar, terrestrial, and lunar masses.

Run 4 is a an example of *unstable equilibrium*. Two heavy masses orbit each other with a light object initially at rest halfway between them. Although there is "ideally" no net acceleration felt by the light object, imprecisions in **isaac**'s calculations eventually cause it to move ever so slightly off center. But moving even slightly toward one of the heavy objects causes *additional* acceleration in the same direction; eventually the light object moves completely away from its initial position.

Run 5, on the other hand, is an example of *stable equilibrium*. A light object (for example, an asteroid) precedes a heavier object (a planet) in its roughly circular orbit around a much heavier object (a star). The three objects form an approximately equilateral triangle, with the asteroid leading the planet in its orbit by an angle of about 60 degrees. One might justifiably expect the planet to attract the asteroid and either capture it or throw it into another orbit. However, that is not what happens; the asteroid always stays ahead of the planet. The light object is said to be at the stable *Lagrangian Point L4*. A second stable Lagrangian Point, called L5, *follows* the planet in its orbit by 60 degrees.

There is at least one analogy to Run 5 in our own backyard: the Sun-Jupiter system. Groups of asteroids have been observed in stable orbits at points corresponding to both L4 and L5, leading and following Jupiter in its orbit by approximately 60 degrees, as predicted.

Readers who know a little physics may notice that all the examples in Table 7-1 have one thing in common: the total vector momentum of each system adds up to 0 (approximately, in Run 5). Without this restriction, the system would eventually move off the screen. This is the reason most of the examples in Table 7-1 have no initial x-velocities. It is easier to set up a zero-momentum system by setting one component of all the objects' velocities to 0.

More Suggestions

Nearly all the suggestions made for experimenting with **bouncer** can also apply to **isaac**. In addition, you may want to allow the masses of the objects to change over time. (What would happen in the Sun-Earth-Moon system if the Sun somehow lost half its mass?)

One problem with **isaac** is that an object may occasionally move off the screen, causing the user to lose track of it. (Fortunately, trying to plot off the screen does not cause an execution error in Apple Pascal, so no explicit checks for offscreen objects are necessary in the program.) You could devise a method that will automatically keep all the objects on the screen. If one object moves off the screen, the picture is automatically rescaled. As a further step, you could automatically scale the other way if all the objects occupy only a small area of the screen.

Another problem with **isaac** occurs when two objects pass very close to one another. The calculated acceleration is then huge and varies greatly over the time period **dt**. This is in direct contradiction to our previous assumption that the acceleration only changes relatively slowly and smoothly during the time interval. As a result, the simulation loses accuracy. A possible improvement would be to detect this situation automatically and decrease **dt** by an appropriate amount to maintain a certain degree of accuracy. (Conversely, you could *increase* **dt** if it makes no difference to the accuracy of the simulation.)

The speed of the simulation as presented here is limited by all the calculations that need to be done. If desired, you could separate the calculations from the animation. Simply do all the calculations first and then display the results with the animation routines. Of course, this limits the duration of the animation. (Must it?)

You may wish to experiment with different laws for calculating accelerations. Be sure to investigate laws that have a different dependence on the distance between two objects. You could also add the effects of other interactions such as electromagnetism. In the real world, many heavenly bodies have their own magnetic fields, although they usually have negligible effects on orbits compared to gravitational fields. An entirely different situation occurs if you are calculating the motion of an electrically charged particle in an electromagnetic field; then the *gravitational* effects are usually negligible.

Recommended Reading

An introductory text that explores the topic of computer simulation in many different fields is *Introduction to Computer Simulation* by N. Roberts, D. Andersen, R. Deal, M. Garet, and W. Shaffer (Addison-Wesley, 1983). A good reference for physics simulations is the fascinating book *Scientific and Engineering Problem-Solving with the Computer* by W. R. Bennett, Jr. (Prentice-Hall, 1976).

An excellent introductory text that covers the material presented here in greater depth is *The Feynman Lectures on Physics, Volume 1* by R. Feynman, R. Leighton, and M. Sands (Addison-Wesley, 1963). Chapter 9 discusses the calculational methods we used here.

Should you want to improve the graphics display routines as suggested, a good place to start would be *Microcomputer Graphics* by R. Myers (Addison-Wesley, 1982). This book provides valuable mathematical tools for both two- and three-dimensional graphics displays, with examples in a computer language called Applesoft BASIC.

EIGHT

The Plane Truth: An Electronic Worksheet

In this chapter we will design **pascalc**, an "electronic worksheet" program similar to *VisiCalc, SuperCalc, CalcStar, Multiplan,* and many other commercially available programs.

Worksheet programs usually have the following features in common. The worksheet is a rectangular matrix of *cells*, organized into columns and rows. The CRT screen acts as a *window* displaying a section of the worksheet (the worksheet is normally too large to fit on the screen all at once). Simple commands scroll the window in any direction, allowing any part of the sheet to be viewed. The program's user "writes" on the worksheet by moving the CRT cursor to the desired cell and typing in information. Into any cell the user may write a *label* (any character string), a *number*, or a *formula* (a calculation with a numeric result).

A cell formula may refer to the values contained in other cells; its value then *depends* on the values of those other cells. This makes worksheet programs especially useful for answering "what-if" questions. For example, a worksheet could hold the results of an extensive loan amortization calculation based on an assumed interest rate. Getting the results for another interest rate can be accomplished by simply changing the cell containing the interest rate to another value; the rest of the worksheet is then recalculated under the new assumption.

Worksheet programs allow the computer to be used for problems like balancing a checkbook, budgeting, and figuring taxes, which otherwise would be solved with a calculator or pencil and paper. Of course, the computer makes complex manipulation of the entered data possible—something not as easily done with pencil and paper.

pascalc differs in a number of ways from commercially available worksheet programs. It is relatively slow, it is relatively inefficient in its use of available memory, and it does not offer a large number of functions and features. On the other hand, **pascalc** is more flexible than many commercially available programs. In addition, **pascalc** is modifiable; you may add, delete, or change its features to your heart's content.

How pascalc Works

The following is a short description of the operation of **pascalc**; more complete descriptions will be given as we design the program later. In the following discussion we assume a CRT size of 80 columns by 24 lines. Adapting **pascalc** to smaller or larger screen sizes is primarily a matter of displaying a smaller or larger number of columns and rows on the screen at one time.

When **pascalc** is started, the screen appears as shown in Figure 8-1. The

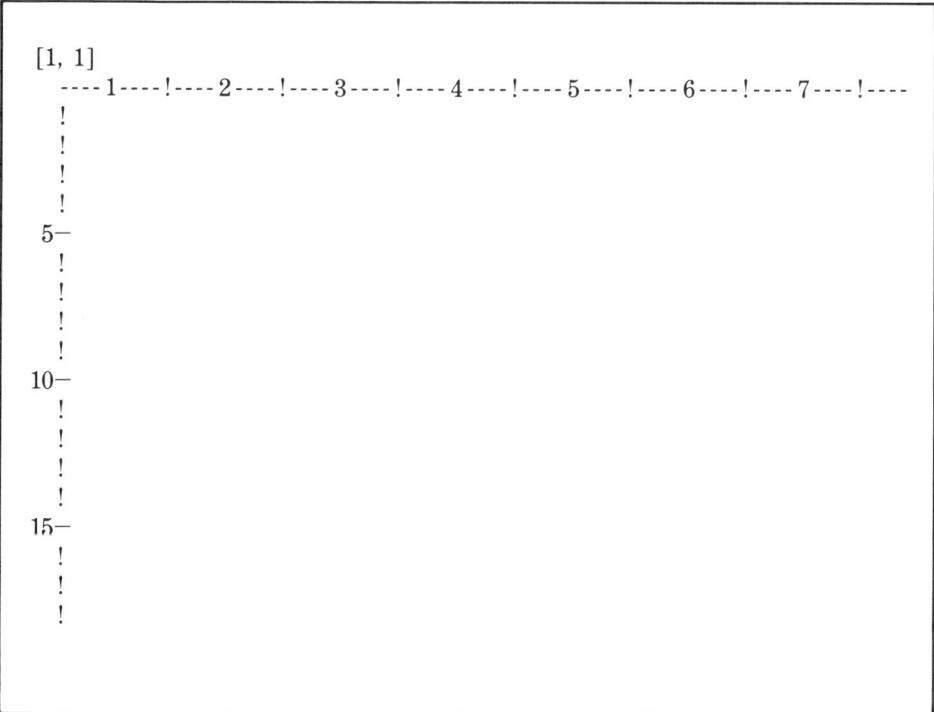

Figure 8-1. Initial **pascalc** screen display

CRT displays the first seven sheet columns and part of an eighth; these columns are labeled across the top of the screen. (Be careful to distinguish between sheet columns and CRT columns. A sheet column can occupy a number of CRT columns. Figure 8-1 shows each screen column made up of ten CRT columns, which is the normal set-up.) Rows are numbered down the left side of the screen; initially, the first 18 rows are displayed. The cursor occupies the cell in column 1, row 1; this is indicated by the **[1,1]** in the upper-left corner of the screen.

From this initial position, you can do any of the following four things in any order:

MOVE THE CURSOR You may move the cursor to an adjacent cell by typing one of four cursor-movement keys. You can get to any cell on the sheet from any other cell by typing a combination of cursor-movement keys. The sheet is automatically scrolled to keep the cursor on the screen. The only error is trying to move off the sheet; in this case, the cursor-movement command is ignored and the computer beeps.

ENTER A LABEL After moving the cursor to a cell, you may place a label at that point in the sheet. You signal your desire to enter a label by typing either a letter or a double-quote character <">. If you type a letter, **pascalc** assumes it is the first character of the label you want to enter; the program requests you to enter the label, automatically inserting the letter you typed as the first character of the label. The double-quote key is used where you want to enter a label *not* beginning with a letter; in this case, **pascalc** asks for a label, but does not use the quote as the first character.

Our usual rules for entering strings also apply to entering labels. <BACKSPACE> or <DELETE> erases the last character entered, and <RETURN> signals the computer that you are done typing. Labels may contain any printable character. After the label has been entered, it appears at the cell currently occupied by the cursor. The entire label is displayed, even if it extends beyond the current width of the column. (Strictly speaking, only the part of the label fitting into the current CRT window is displayed; the front or rear of the string may not be displayed if it extends out of the window.)

ENTER A NUMBER OR FORMULA Instead of a label, you may enter a number or a formula at the cursor's current position. Actually, **pascalc** does not distinguish between numbers and formulas; **pascalc** regards a number as a formula, albeit a simple one. You signal your desire to enter a formula by typing any character that might conceivably begin one: a digit, <0> to

<9>, a sign, <+> or <−>, a decimal point, <.>, a left parenthesis, <(>, or a left bracket, <[>.

Formulas are entered much as in the **calc** program in Chapter Four. Normal algebraic precedence is used, with parentheses indicating subexpressions to be evaluated first. The primary difference is in specifying "identifiers"; in **calc**, identifiers were alphanumeric strings (**APPLE**, **SIDE1**, and so on) allowing previously calculated results to be used in expressions. In **pascalc**, *cells* are used to hold "previously calculated results." Thus, instead of identifier names, a **pascalc** formula uses *cell references*, indicating that the value of the referenced cell is to be used at that point in the expression.

There are two types of cell reference, *absolute* and *relative*. An absolute cell reference is entered in the form [<**column**>,<**row**>]; the referenced cell's column and row coordinates are enclosed in square brackets and separated by a comma. For example, the cell reference [**4,9**] tells **pascalc** to use the value of the cell at column 4, row 9.

A relative cell reference, on the other hand, specifies the referenced cell in terms of its location with respect to the cell containing the formula. Relative cell referencing is indicated by signs preceding the column number, the row number, or both. For example, assume the formula at cell [**19,12**] contains the relative cell reference [**−3,+5**]. This says, "Use the value from the cell three columns to the *left* and five rows *below* the current cell." Thus, the value of the cell at [**16,17**] is used at that point in the formula.

To make relative cell referencing easier when entering a formula, you may use cursor-movement keys to "point" to the cell you want to reference. Details on how this is done are given in the discussion of the **getformstr** and **getrcc** routines later in this chapter.

One "function" is supported by **pascalc**: the **SUM** function, which is used to add together an arbitrary number of elements. For example, the expression **SUM([1,1]:[1,10])** may be used in a formula instead of the longer [**1,1**] + [**1,2**] + ... + [**1,10**]. A more detailed description of **SUM** is given later in the chapter.

ENTER A COMMAND   **pascalc** provides a number of commands that allow the user to change the sheet's formatting, erase cells or groups of cells from the sheet, copy cells from one point in the sheet to another, and many other things. A list of **pascalc** commands with brief descriptions of their functions is shown in Table 8-1. For more detail, see the relevant code design discussion.

That is all there is to **pascalc**. On the surface, at least, it is not too complex a program.

Table 8-1. **pascalc** Commands

Command	Key Sequence	Description
Recalculate	!	Recalculate sheet
Go To	>	Move cursor to user-specified cell
Copy	/C	Copy cells from one part of the sheet to another
Erase	/E	Erase one cell, one or more rows, one or more columns, or the entire sheet
Format	/F	Display and optionally change formatting parameters for sheet, column, or cell
Insert	/I	Insert one or more blank columns or rows into the sheet
Load	/L	Load previously saved sheet into memory from disk
Memory	/M	Display free memory remaining
Print	/P	Print sheet on printer
Quit	/Q	Quit from the program
Save	/S	Save sheet in memory to disk
Toggle	/T	Toggle recalculation parameters

Data Structures—The Sparse Matrix

The **pascalc** sheet is made up of 63 columns, each consisting of 255 rows of cells. The "natural" way to represent the sheet in memory would be to declare it as a two-dimensional array, as follows:

```
<var>
    cell: array [1..MAXCOLS, 1..MAXROWS] of cellrec;
```

where the **cellrec** data type is a record containing all the information pertaining to a single cell. But this array has **MAXCOLS** * **MAXROWS** elements, a total of over 16,000. If each **cellrec** record takes up ten bytes (which is probably an unrealistically low estimate) the matrix would require over 160,000 bytes of memory. This is simply more memory than many computers have.

We could, of course, make the sheet smaller, decreasing **MAXCOLS** and **MAXROWS** until the **cell** array fit into the available memory. Instead, we use an alternate method of representing the cells in memory, a data structure called the *sparse matrix*.

A sparse matrix is one in which most of the elements are "empty," that is, they contain no information. When many elements are empty, there is no reason to use memory to store them. Instead, the following arrangement is used: each column of the matrix has a *column header*, a pointer to the topmost non-empty element in the column. If there are no non-empty elements in the column, the pointer is **NIL**, that is, it points nowhere. Each element in the column also contains a pointer to the next non-empty element below it in the matrix; this pointer is **NIL** if the element is the last non-empty one in the column.

The same thing is done for rows. An array of "row header" pointers point to the leftmost cells in each row and are **NIL** if there are no cells in the row. Each element has a "right pointer" pointing to the next cell to the right in the row.

Figure 8-2 shows this arrangement on a hypothetical 5×5 matrix with non-

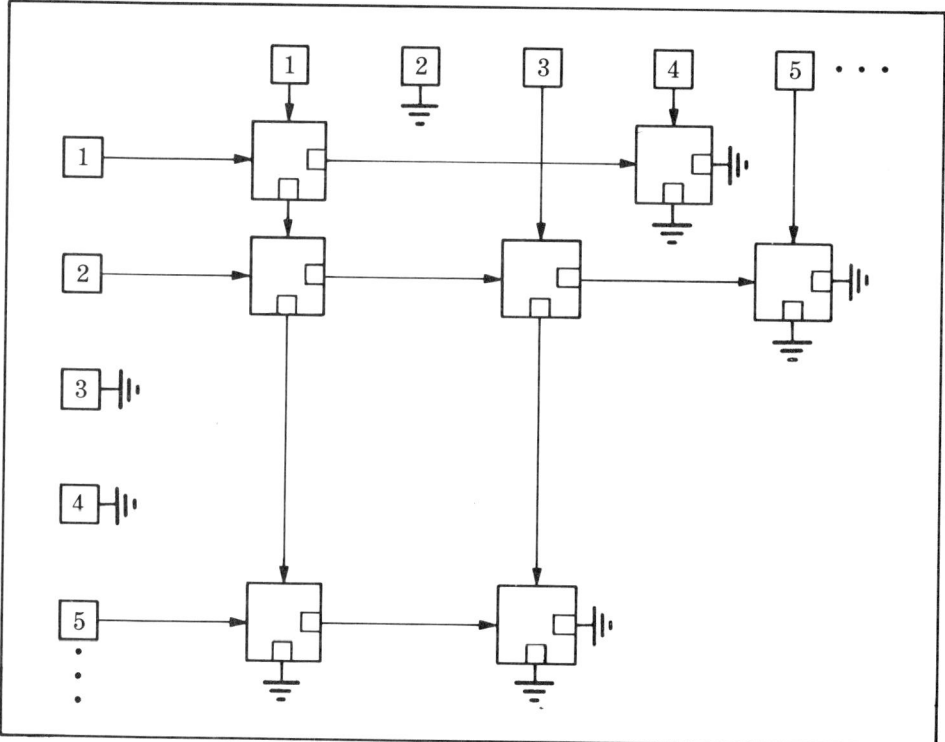

Figure 8-2. Sparse matrix data structure

empty cells [1,1], [1,2], [1,5], [3,2], [3,5], [4,1], and [5,2]. Column header pointers are shown as numbered boxes across the top of the figure, and row headers are down the left side. An electrical ground symbol is used to indicate a **NIL** pointer. Each cell has two pointers pointing to it, one down the column and one to the right across the row.

In Pascal, we can set up this data structure as follows. First, we define the **cellptr** and **cellrec** types:

```
<type>
   cellptr = ^cellrec;
   cellrec = packed record
      cellcol: 1..MAXCOLS;
      cellrow: 1..MAXROWS;

      { other stuff }

      rightptr, downptr: cellptr
   end;
```

In addition to right and down pointers to other cells, each cell record contains fields for its own column and row coordinates. If we were to approach a cell from the left, through the row pointers, we would not otherwise have any way to find out *which column* a given cell is in. Similarly, if we approach a cell from above, through the column pointers, it is difficult to otherwise discover the cell's row. The {other stuff} comment indicates the cell fields we have not yet defined.

The last step is to define the column headers and row headers, as follows:

```
<var>
   colptr: array [1..MAXCOLS] of cellptr;
   rowptr: array [1..MAXROWS] of cellptr;
```

Given this data structure with its column and row coordinates, we can write a routine to find a cell on the sheet. The **findcell** function accomplishes this:

```
function findcell(c, r: integer): cellptr;
{ Find cell on sheet, return pointer to it or NIL if not there }
var
   cp: cellptr;
   done: boolean;
begin { findcell }
   if (c < 1) or (c > MAXCOLS) or (r < 1) or (r > MAXROWS) then { off sheet }
      findcell := NIL
   else begin
      cp := rowptr[r];
```

```
        done := FALSE;
        while (cp <> NIL) and not done do
            if cp^.cellcol < c then
                cp := cp^.rightptr
            else begin
                done := TRUE;
                if cp^.cellcol <> c then
                    cp := NIL
            end;
        findcell := cp
    end
end;
```

This routine returns a pointer to the cell specified by its column **c** and row **r**. If there is no such cell defined on the sheet (or the coordinates given are outside the sheet boundaries), **findcell** returns a **NIL** pointer. The strategy **findcell** uses is to search the specified row **r** for a cell with a **cellcol** value of **c**; it starts at the cell pointed to by **rowptr[r]** and moves to the right across the row until either the desired cell is found or the search fails. (We could have written **findcell** to search column **c** for a cell with a **cellrow** value of **r**.)

Memory saved by using the sparse matrix data structure is used up rather quickly if the assumption that the sheet is "mostly empty" is violated. As the sheet fills up, there is a crossover point where the simple two-dimensional array structure would require less memory than the sparse matrix. (You may want to investigate this phenomenon more completely.)

Cell Records

We vaguely defined the **cellrec** data type to contain {**other stuff**}, symbolizing the other fields in the record containing the actual cell data. Our next step is to describe the contents of the cell record.

From our previous discussion, we know a non-empty cell contains either a label or a formula. In either case, though, a cell needs to contain a field describing *what is to be displayed on the screen*. In the case where the cell contains a label, this display field is simply the label itself. When the cell contains a formula, the field contains the properly formatted string representation of the numeric value of the formula.

One way to do this would be as follows:

```
<type>
    cellrec = packed record
        cellcol: 1..MAXCOLS;
        cellrow: 1..MAXROWS;

        { other stuff }
```

```
        display: string;

        rightptr, downptr: cellptr
    end;
```

Here we have added a field **display** containing the string to be displayed at the cell's position. This approach is *not* the one we use because it takes up too much memory. Each string we declare in our program uses 81 bytes (assuming we use the "default" string size of 80 characters, plus 1 for the length byte). But our *typical* requirement for the **display** field is probably *much* less than 80 characters. If, for example, our average label is 10 characters long, we waste 70 bytes of memory every time we create a new cell.

What if we declared a smaller maximum string size for the **display** field? This would decrease the storage requirement, as desired. But we want to allow the *possibility* of using 80 characters in the display field. If the user wants to use an 80-character label on the worksheet, the program should not prohibit it.

This dilemma crops up all the time in designing Pascal programs. In Pascal, each variable we define has a fixed memory requirement that cannot be changed during a program's execution. In designing data structures that handle variables of different "sizes" (like strings), we must define them to hold the *largest possible* size, even if on the average they actually require much less storage.

Our escape from this dilemma has two parts; the first part is *not* to define the display string in the **cellrec** data type, but instead to define a *pointer* to the string there:

```
<type>
   cellrec = packed record
      cellcol: 1..MAXCOLS;
      cellrow: 1..MAXROWS;

      { other stuff }

      display: stringptr;

      rightptr, downptr: cellptr
   end;
```

where we have previously defined the **stringptr** type as a pointer to a string.

```
<type>
   stringptr = ^string;
```

This does not solve the problem, but it allows us to *delay* solving the problem, which is sometimes nearly as good a strategy. We will present the second part of the solution later in the chapter.

Formatting

If we were only storing labels, the data structure we have just shown would be adequate. But a cell might also contain a formula, so we need additional storage in this case. Before we design the data structure used to store formula cells, however, we need to consider how the numeric values of formula cells are translated into display strings; that is, how they are to be formatted.

First, we must consider how to specify the formatting for a value. In previous chapters, we have seen that it is nearly always useful to be able to display a variable number of digits after the decimal point. It is also useful to allow display in both fixed-point and scientific format, as we saw in Chapter Four's **calc** program. We also want a field width parameter specifying the minimum number of characters used to display the number.

Putting all three parameters together in a Pascal record is simple. The **formatrec** is

```
<type>
   formatrec = packed record
      fmt: format;
      width: MINWIDTH..MAXWIDTH;
      ndigs: MINDIGS..MAXDIGS
   end;
```

where we have previously defined the **format** type as in **calc**:

```
<type>
   format = (FIXEDPOINT, SCIENTIFIC);
```

These three parameters are sufficient to display numbers in many useful formats. For example, monetary values may be displayed in a dollars-and-cents format by setting the **ndigs** parameter to 2 and **fmt** to **FIXEDPOINT**. If **ndigs** is 0, displayed numbers will be rounded to the nearest integer. Right-justification of a column of numbers can be accomplished by formatting them all with a **width** parameter large enough to accommodate the longest one; this will also align the decimal points in the column. Left-justification, if desired, can be carried out by setting the **width** parameter to 0.

Flexibility is one of our goals in describing how numeric values are displayed on the sheet. The user should be able to specify that *any* number on the sheet be displayed in *any* possible format. Thus, we would like to allow each cell to be formatted independently of any other. However, another of our design goals is ease of use: the user should not have to specify the formatting parameters for every formula cell on the sheet.

Our approach is the following: the user *may* specify formatting for any formula cell. If the user does not so specify, the cell defaults to the current *column format*. That is, the cell's value is formatted in the same way as all the other numbers in that column.

Column formats are handled in a similar way. The user may specify a certain format to be used for a column. If not, the numbers in the column are displayed according to the current *sheet format*.

The sheet column widths are controlled by the format widths; you can change the width of a sheet column by changing the width parameter of the column's format. And you can change the width of *all* sheet columns by changing the width parameter of the default sheet format.

Formula Storage

Now we can consider the storage method for formula cells. In the **cellrec** data type, we define a pointer **fp** to a record containing all the formula information:

```
<type>
   cellrec = packed record
      cellcol: 1..MAXCOLS;
      cellrow: 1..MAXROWS;
      fp: formptr;
      display: stringptr;
      rightptr, downptr: cellptr
   end;
```

where the **formptr** type has been defined as

```
<type>
   formptr = ^forminfo;
```

This allows **pascalc** to distinguish easily whether a given cell contains a label or a formula. If it is a label, the pointer **fp** is **NIL**; otherwise, **fp** points to a valid **forminfo** record. This arrangement has the additional benefit that extra memory need not be used to store formula information if the cell contains a label.

The **forminfo** record structure is as follows:

```
<type>
   forminfo = packed record
      usecolfmt: boolean;
      cellstat: xresult;
      cellfmt: formatrec;
      cellval: xreal;
      formula: stringptr
   end;
```

The Boolean field **usecolfmt** is **TRUE** if the cell's value is to be displayed according to the current column format; if it is **FALSE**, the formatting described in the **cellfmt** field is used.

The **cellstat** field is used to indicate whether an error occurred during evaluation of the cell's formula. The field is of the **xresult** type, which we previously used in **calc** to indicate overflow, underflow, and division by 0.

The **cellval** field contains the calculated value of the entered formula. We choose the **xreal** data type to represent numeric quantities because we can control the range and precision of the data type, and because we can easily avoid overflow and underflow errors. An additional good reason is that we can "filch" a number of routines from the **calc** program for use in **pascalc**.

Finally, the **formula** field contains a pointer to a string containing the formula entered by the user. We use a string pointer instead of the string itself for the same reasons explained with respect to the **display** field in the **cellrec** record: it allows us to make more efficient use of memory.

pascalc — the Main Routine

Now that we have defined most of the major data types used in **pascalc**, we can present the program's main routine:

```
{$s+}
program pascalc;
{ Electronic Spreadsheet }

uses
   {$u apple2:toolstuff.code } crtstuff, fixstuff, intstuff, textstuff;
const
   { Sheet constants }
   MAXROWS = 255;          { Number of rows on sheet }
   MAXCOLS = 63;           { Number of columns on sheet }
   XORG = 4;               { CRT column of first displayed sheet column }
```

```pascal
      YORG = 2;                { CRT row of first displayed sheet row }

    { Memory management constants }
      RESERVE = 1950;          { Number of words to not allocate }
      HDRSIZE = 4;             { Size of header in bytes }

    { Constants from calc }
      MINEXP = 0;              { xreal minimum exponent }
      MAXEXP = 127;            { xreal maximum exponent }
      EXCESS = 64;             { xreal exponent excess }
      REGSIZE = 26;            { 2 * FIXSIZE + 2 }
      IDSIZE = 8;              { Maximum identifier length }

    { Formatting constants }
      MINWIDTH = 0;            { Minimum format width }
      MAXWIDTH = 76;           { Maximum format width, MAXCRTCOL - XORG + 1 }
      MINDIGS = 0;             { Minimum format digits }
      MAXDIGS = 11;            { Maximum format digits, FIXSIZE - 1 }

    { Printing constants }
      PCOMSIZE = 15;           { Printer command string size }
      MAXPLEN = 999;           { Maximum page length }
      MTOP = 2;                { # of blank lines between top of page & 1st line }
      MBOT = 2;                { # of blank lines between last line & bottom }

type
    { Types from calc }
    xreal = record
       expo: MINEXP..MAXEXP;
       frac: fixed
    end;
    register = integer[REGSIZE];
    format = (FIXEDPOINT, SCIENTIFIC);
    identifier = string[IDSIZE];
    xresult = (OK, OVERFLOW, UNDERFLOW, ZERODIVIDE);

    { Printing types }
    pcommand = string[PCOMSIZE];

    { Formula information types }
    stringptr = ^string;
    formatrec = packed record
       fmt: format;
       width: MINWIDTH..MAXWIDTH;
       ndigs: MINDIGS..MAXDIGS
    end;
    formptr = ^forminfo;
    forminfo = packed record
       usecolfmt: boolean;
       cellstat: xresult;
       cellfmt: formatrec;
       cellval: xreal;
       formula: stringptr
    end;

    { Cell information types }
    cellptr = ^cellrec;
    cellrec = packed record
       cellcol: 1..MAXCOLS;
       cellrow: 1..MAXROWS;
       fp: formptr;
       display: stringptr;
       rightptr, downptr: cellptr
    end;

    { Memory management types }
```

```
         headerptr = ^header;
         header = record
            size: integer;
            next: headerptr
         end;

var
         { Sheet variables }
         autocalc, colcalc: boolean;
         sheetfmt: formatrec;
         curscol, cursrow, firstrow, lastrow, firstcol, lastcol: integer;
         nrows, inpline, statline: integer;
         curcp: cellptr;
         colptr: array [1..MAXCOLS] of cellptr;
         rowptr: array [1..MAXROWS] of cellptr;
         dashes: string;

         { Column variables }
         colpos: array [1..64] of integer;              { 64 = MAXCOLS + 1 }
         colfmt: array [1..MAXCOLS] of formatrec;
         usesheetfmt: packed array [1..MAXCOLS] of boolean;

         { Calculation variables }
         zero: xreal;
         ten: array [0..REGSIZE] of register;

         { Command characters & sets }
         upkey, downkey, leftkey, rightkey: char;
         cursorkeys, labelkeys, formkeys, cmdkeys, legalkeys: charset;
         cmdchars, formchars: charset;

         { Printing variables }
         pagelen, lmarg, rmarg, printx1, printx2, printy1, printy2: integer;
         pinit, pterm: pcommand;

         { Memory management variables }
         freelist: headerptr;

         { Control-flow variables }
         alldone: boolean;
         ch: char;

         { Scalar-type to text conversion variables }
         fmtchar: array [format] of char;
         boochar: array [boolean] of char;
         statchar: array [xresult] of char;

{------------------------------}
{ Modules to be inserted here: }
{        initpc                }
{        drawsheet             }
{        labelrows             }
{        labelcols             }
{        setcolpos             }
{        min                   }
{        max                   }
{        disprow                }
{        dispsheet             }
{        findcell              }
{        setcursor             }
{        movecursor            }
{        memout                }
{        ungetkey              }
{        initalloc             }
{        alloc                 }
{        free                  }
```

```
{          storestr            }
{          erasestr            }
{          storeform           }
{          eraseform           }
{          storecell           }
{          erasecell           }
{          getlabel            }
{          setparam            }
{          stoc                }
{          ctos                }
{          xnorm               }
{          xadd                }
{          calccell            }
{          recalc              }
{          formatcell          }
{          reformat            }
{          getformula          }
{          docommand           }
{-------------------------------}

begin { pascalc }
   initpc;
   drawsheet;
   setcolpos;
   labelcols(1);
   labelrows(1);
   dispsheet(1, 1);
   setcursor(1, 1);
   if initalloc(RESERVE) then
      repeat
         if getkey(ch, legalkeys, FALSE) in cursorkeys then
            movecursor(ch)
         else if ch in labelkeys then
            getlabel(ch)
         else if ch in formkeys then
            getformula(ch)
         else if ch in cmdkeys then
            docommand(ch)
      until alldone
   else
      remark('Not enough memory to run program');
   crt(CLEAR)
end.
```

The **uses** statement refers to **intstuff**, a unit we have not yet defined. The **intstuff** unit contains the routines **itos**, **stoi**, and **getint** from earlier chapters. As previously mentioned, if your version of Pascal does not provide for separately compiled groups of procedures and data declarations, they must be included in the source file and compiled with the rest of the program.

Since **pascalc** is a relatively large program, it makes sense to divide constant, type, and variable declarations into families and to comment each major division. Tables 8-2, 8-3, and 8-4 contain brief descriptions of the major global variables. Table 8-2 describes the sheet variables that **pascalc** uses to keep track of the display, the cursor, and so on. Table 8-3 describes the column variables that control column formatting. Table 8-4 describes the command characters and sets used by **pascalc** for input checking and user commands.

Table 8-2. Sheet Variables

Name	Type	Description
autocalc	Boolean	**TRUE** if sheet is automatically recalculated after each formula change, **FALSE** if recalculation is done manually
colcalc	Boolean	Controls the order in which sheet recalculation is done: **TRUE** if by column, **FALSE** if by row
sheetfmt	formatrec	Default formatting parameters for cells
curscol cursrow	integer	Column and row coordinates of current cursor position
firstrow lastrow	integer	First and last sheet rows currently displayed on screen
firstcol lastcol	integer	First and last sheet columns fully displayed on screen (right side of screen may show a partially displayed column)
nrows	integer	Number of sheet rows displayed on screen
inpline	integer	CRT line on which user input is requested
statline	integer	CRT line on which "program status" is displayed
curcp	cellptr	Pointer to cell on which cursor currently lies (**NIL** if cell is empty)
colptr rowptr	array of cellptr	Sheet column and row headers
dashes	string	String of dashes used for displaying column label line

Table 8-3. Column Variables

Name	Type	Description
colpos	array of integer	Relative starting position for each column
colfmt	array of formatrec	Formatting parameters for each column
usesheetfmt	array of Boolean	Array element is **TRUE** if column uses default sheet format parameters, otherwise **FALSE**

Table 8-4. Command Characters and Sets

Name	Type	Description
upkey	char	Key to move cursor up one sheet row
downkey	char	Key to move cursor down one sheet row
leftkey	char	Key to move cursor left one sheet column
rightkey	char	Key to move cursor right one sheet column
cursorkeys	charset	Set of the four cursor-moving keys
labelkeys	charset	Set of legal label-initiating keys
formkeys	charset	Set of legal formula-initiating keys
cmdkeys	charset	Set of legal command-initiating keys
legalkeys	charset	Union of the four previous sets
cmdchars	charset	Set of "slash" command characters
formchars	charset	Set of legal formula characters

The large number of declarations and modules required by **pascalc** should not be allowed to complicate the logic of the main routine's code, which is fairly simple. After initializing global variables, setting up and displaying the initial sheet, and so on, **pascalc** enters a loop that accepts an input character typed by the user and performs an action based on which class the character falls into. The four possible actions are the ones previously described: the **movecursor** routine moves the cursor to an adjacent cell on the sheet, **getlabel** accepts a label from the user, **getformula** accepts a formula, and **docommand** carries out one of the commands listed in Table 8-1. The loop continues until the flag **alldone** becomes **TRUE**; this is accomplished by the quit command.

Initializing Global Variables

As usual, **pascalc** uses a separate routine to initialize the variables common to the entire program. Here is that routine:

```
segment procedure initpc;
{ Initialize global variables }

var
    i: integer;

begin { initpc }
    crt(CLEAR);
```

```
    inpline := MAXCRTROW - 2;
    statline := MAXCRTROW - 3;
    center('Initializing...', statline);
    alldone := FALSE;
    ten[0] := 1;
    for i := 1 to REGSIZE do
       ten[i] := 10 * ten[i - 1];
    {$r-}
    fillchar(dashes[1], MAXWIDTH, '-');
    dashes[0] := chr(MAXWIDTH);
    {$r+}
    nrows := MAXCRTROW - YORG - 3;
    sheetfmt.fmt := FIXEDPOINT;
    sheetfmt.width := 10;
    sheetfmt.ndigs := 2;
    for i := 1 to MAXCOLS do begin
       colptr[i] := NIL;
       usesheetfmt[i] := TRUE
    end;
    for i := 1 to MAXROWS do
       rowptr[i] := NIL;
    autocalc := TRUE;
    colcalc := TRUE;
    zero.frac := 0;
    zero.expo := MINEXP;
    upkey := chr(15);
    downkey := chr(12);
    leftkey := chr(8);
    rightkey := chr(21);
    cursorkeys := [upkey, downkey, leftkey, rightkey];
    labelkeys := ['A'..'Z', 'a'..'z', '"'];
    formkeys := ['0'..'9', '+', '-', '.', '(', '['];
    cmdkeys := ['/', '!', '>'];
    legalkeys := cursorkeys + labelkeys + formkeys + cmdkeys;
    formchars := formkeys + ['A'..'Z', '*', '/', ']', ',', ')', ':', ' '];
    cmdchars := ['C', 'E', 'F', 'I', 'L', 'M', 'P', 'Q', 'S', 'T'];
    fmtchar[FIXEDPOINT] := 'F';
    fmtchar[SCIENTIFIC] := 'S';
    boochar[TRUE] := 'Y';
    boochar[FALSE] := 'N';
    statchar[OK] := ' ';
    statchar[OVERFLOW] := 'O';
    statchar[UNDERFLOW] := 'U';
    statchar[ZERODIVIDE] := 'Z';
    pagelen := 66;
    lmarg := 10;
    rmarg := 70;
    printx1 := 1;
    printx2 := 6;
    printy1 := 1;
    printy2 := pagelen - MTOP - MBOT - 1;
    pinit := '';
    pterm := '';
    eraseline(statline)
end;
```

The only unusual thing about **initpc** is its first line, **segment procedure initpc**;. In Apple and UCSD Pascal, a procedure or function may be designated as a "segment." The code corresponding to a segment routine is not loaded from disk into memory until the routine is called. After the routine is finished, it is "forgotten"; the memory used by the code is returned to the system for other uses.

initpc is a good choice for a segment routine. It is only called once, at the beginning of the program, so it is wasteful to keep it in memory for the entire program's execution. If your version of Pascal does not offer such an option, simply leave out the word **segment** in the code and everything will work normally.

The cursor-movement keys are initialized to the ones used by the Apple II Pascal Editor; users of different computers can (and should) change these values to whatever keys they customarily use for cursor movement.

Sheet Display Routines

pascalc uses a number of routines that control how the sheet is displayed on the CRT screen. The first routine **pascalc** calls after **initpc** is **drawsheet**, which displays a "skeleton" sheet; that is, it draws unlabeled horizontal and vertical axes and a blank cursor position indicator.

```
procedure drawsheet;
{ Draw sheet axes }
var
   i: integer;
begin { drawsheet }
   crt(CLEAR);
   posstr(dashes, XORG, YORG - 1);
   gotoxy(XORG - 1, YORG);
   for i := 1 to nrows do begin
      if i mod 5 = 0 then
         write('-')
      else
         write('!');
      crt(LEFT);
      crt(DOWN)
   end;
   posstr('[..,...]', 0, 0)
end;
```

We choose to label every fifth row on the sheet; the **labelrows** procedure accomplishes this. **labelrows** is called with one parameter, the row number to be placed at the top row of the sheet.

```
procedure labelrows(r1: integer);
{ Label rows }
var
   r, y: integer;
begin { labelrows }
   firstrow := r1;
   lastrow := firstrow + nrows - 1;
   r := firstrow + 4;
```

```
      y := YORG + 4;
      while r <= lastrow do begin
         gotoxy(0, y);
         write(r: 3);
         r := r + 5;
         y := y + 5
      end
end;
```

Calling **labelrows** updates the global variables **firstrow** and **lastrow**, which keep track of the first and last rows currently displayed on the sheet.

The **labelcols** procedure carries out the analogous job of labeling the sheet columns. Since each sheet column takes up a number of CRT columns, the task is slightly more complicated.

```
procedure labelcols(c1: integer);
{ Label columns }
var
   c, crtcol, wid: integer;
begin { labelcols }
   posstr(dashes, XORG, YORG - 1);
   firstcol := c1;
   c := firstcol;
   repeat
      crtcol := colpos[c + 1] - colpos[firstcol] + XORG - 1;
      if crtcol <= MAXCRTCOL then begin
         posstr('!', crtcol, YORG - 1);
         lastcol := c;
         wid := colpos[c + 1] - colpos[c];
         if wid > 2 then begin
            gotoxy(crtcol - (wid + 1) div 2, YORG - 1);
            write(c)
         end
      end;
      c := c + 1
   until (crtcol > MAXCRTCOL) or (c > MAXCOLS)
end;
```

This procedure destroys any previous column labeling by putting the **dash** string at the appropriate place on the screen. Exclamation points are put on this "ruler line" to mark the last CRT column of each sheet column. If a column is wide enough, it is labeled with the column number, approximately centered within it. **labelcols** updates the global variables **firstcol** (which contains the number of the first sheet column displayed on the screen) and **lastcol** (which contains the number of the last fully displayed sheet column).

The **colpos** array used in **labelcols** contains the relative "starting position" of each column on the worksheet. Using the **colpos** array simplifies the task of calculating the beginning and ending CRT screen columns of a given sheet column and of deciding whether a given cell's contents appear on the screen. For example, if sheet column **c1** starts in CRT column **x**, then sheet column **c2** starts in CRT column **colpos[c2]−colpos[c1]+x**.

The **colpos** array is initialized by the **setcolpos** procedure:

```
procedure setcolpos;
{ Set column positions from format widths }
var
   c: integer;
begin { setcolpos }
   colpos[1] := 0;
   for c := 1 to MAXCOLS do
      if usesheetfmt[c] then
         colpos[c + 1] := colpos[c] + sheetfmt.width
      else
         colpos[c + 1] := colpos[c] + colfmt[c].width
end;
```

The element **colpos[1]** is arbitrarily set to 1. To see how the remainder of the **colpos** array is calculated, observe that the difference between two adjacent elements of the array, **colpos[c+1]** and **colpos[c]**, is simply the width of column c: either the sheet-format width (if the column has not been assigned a special format) or the column-format width (if it has). Thus, to calculate any element of **colpos**, the routine simply adds the relevant column width to the previous element. Besides setting initial values for **colpos**, **setcolpos** is called to modify the **colpos** array whenever the default sheet format or any column format is changed.

The **dispsheet** procedure displays the sheet. It is called with two parameters, **c1** and **r1**, specifying the coordinates of the cell to be displayed in the upper-left corner of the CRT window. Although it is also called from **pascalc**'s main routine for initialization purposes, it is called from many other routines either to display the sheet after it has been changed or to move the window to display another section of the sheet.

```
procedure dispsheet(c1, r1: integer);
{ Display sheet }
var
   r: integer;
begin { dispsheet }
   if r1 <> firstrow then
      labelrows(r1);
   if c1 <> firstcol then
      labelcols(c1);
   for r := firstrow to lastrow do
      disprow(r)
end;
```

dispsheet first relabels the sheet rows and columns if the window has been moved (reflected by a value of **c1** different from **firstcol**, or a value of **r1**

different from **firstrow**, or both.) Then the contents of the windowed section of the sheet are displayed row by row.

The **disprow** procedure is responsible for displaying a single sheet row on the CRT screen; it is the place where our "screen is a window onto the worksheet" analogy is implemented. **disprow** must somehow decide whether a given cell's display string appears in the window or not. This decision is somewhat complicated by the fact that a cell's display string may *partially* appear in the window, clipped by the window's edge either on the right side, the left side, or possibly *both* sides.

The pseudo-code for **disprow** might look something like this:

```
begin
    calculate CRT row for display
    erase old display on CRT row
    check cell pointed to by row header pointer
    while (cell exists) and (we haven't moved off right edge
                                               of screen)
        calculate CRT column where display string should begin
        if CRT column > MAXCRTCOL
            we've moved off right edge of screen
        else
            check for clipping on left
               (calculate index of first displayed string
                                                character)
            check for clipping on right
               (calculate index of last displayed string
                                                character)
            if any part of string can be displayed
                display it at correct position
        end-else
        check next cell in row
    end-while
end
```

This pseudo-code translates into the following Pascal routine:

```
procedure disprow(r: integer);
{ Display single row }

var
   cp: cellptr;
   done: boolean;
   crtrow, crtcol, c1, c2: integer;

begin { disprow }
   crtrow := YORG + r - firstrow;
   gotoxy(XORG, crtrow);
   crt(ERASEOL);
   cp := rowptr[r];
   done := FALSE;
   while (cp <> NIL) and not done do begin
      with cp^ do begin
         crtcol := colpos[cellcol] - colpos[firstcol] + XORG;
```

```
              if crtcol > MAXCRTCOL then
                 done := TRUE
              else if display <> NIL then begin
                 c1 := max(1, XORG - crtcol + 1);
                 c2 := min(length(display^), MAXCRTCOL - crtcol + 1);
                 if c2 >= c1 then
                    posstr(copy(display^, c1, c2 - c1 + 1), crtcol + c1 - 1,
                                                                       crtrow)
              end
           end;
           cp := cp^.rightptr
        end
end;
```

In this code, the variable **c1** holds the index of the first displayed string character, and **c2** holds the index of the last displayed string character.

disprow uses the **copy** function, a routine built into Apple and UCSD Pascal. The call

```
substr := copy(s, i, n);
```

copies **n** characters from the string **s** starting at the **i**th character into the string **substr**. (The function returns a string result, something that is not allowed in programmer-written routines.)

disprow also uses the functions **min** and **max**; they are simple and useful routines returning the lesser and greater of their two integer arguments, respectively. Here are these two routines:

```
function min(i1, i2: integer): integer;
{ Return lesser of two integers }

begin { min }
   if i1 <= i2 then
      min := i1
   else
      min := i2
end;

function max(i1, i2: integer): integer;
{ Return greater of two integers }

begin { max }
   if i1 >= i2 then
      max := i1
   else
      max := i2
end;
```

Cursor Placement and Movement

Our next major goal is to design the routines dealing with the cursor: putting it in a specific sheet location and moving it from one place on the sheet to another.

The **setcursor** procedure places the cursor on a cell specified by its column and row coordinates.

```
procedure setcursor(c, r: integer);
{ Put cursor at specified spot }
var
   c1, r1: integer;
begin { setcursor }
   if c < firstcol then
      c1 := c
   else if c > lastcol then begin
      c1 := c;
      while (colpos[c + 1] - colpos[c1] <= MAXWIDTH) and (c1 > 1) do
         c1 := c1 - 1;
      if colpos[c + 1] - colpos[c1] > MAXWIDTH then
         c1 := c1 + 1
   end
   else
      c1 := firstcol;
   if r < firstrow then
      r1 := r
   else if r > lastrow then
      r1 := r - nrows + 1
   else
      r1 := firstrow;
   if (r1 <> firstrow) or (c1 <> firstcol) then
      dispsheet(c1, r1);
   gotoxy(1, 0);
   write(c: 2);
   crt(RIGHT);
   write(r: 3);
   curscol := c;
   cursrow := r;
   curcp := findcell(curscol, cursrow);
   eraseline(statline);
   if curcp <> NIL then
      with curcp^ do
         if (fp = NIL) and (display <> NIL) then
            posstr(concat('Label:', display^), 0, statline)
         else if fp <> NIL then
            if fp^.formula <> NIL then
               posstr(concat('Formula:', fp^.formula^), 0, statline);
   gotoxy(XORG + colpos[c] - colpos[firstcol], YORG + r - firstrow)
end;
```

If the cell is currently not displayed on the screen, **setcursor** scrolls the window to keep the cursor on the screen, either by adjusting the first displayed sheet column, or the first displayed sheet row, or both. The only slightly complex part of this adjustment occurs when the cursor moves off the right edge of the old window; then we have to find a new value of **firstcol** so that the new cursor sheet column is now the *last* fully displayed sheet column on the screen. **setcursor** figures this out by working backward from the new cursor sheet column in the **colpos** array.

setcursor then updates the cursor position indicator in the upper-left corner to reflect the new cursor position. If the cell the cursor lands on is not empty, **setcursor** also displays the contents of the cell (either a label or a formula) on the program status line below the window. (This is important since it is the only convenient way to find out a cell's formula if you have forgotten it.) The routine discovers whether the cell is empty or not by calling the **findcell** function.

Finally, **setcursor** places the CRT cursor at the cell's first character position on the screen. The order is important: **setcursor** must *leave* the CRT cursor at the correct position on the screen.

Once **setcursor** is designed, writing a routine to move the cursor is easy.

```
procedure movecursor(ch: char);
{ Move cursor in direction specified by user }
begin { movecursor }
   if (ch = upkey) and (cursrow > 1) then
      setcursor(curscol, cursrow - 1)
   else if (ch = downkey) and (cursrow < MAXROWS) then
      setcursor(curscol, cursrow + 1)
   else if (ch = rightkey) and (curscol < MAXCOLS) then
      setcursor(curscol + 1, cursrow)
   else if (ch = leftkey) and (curscol > 1) then
      setcursor(curscol - 1, cursrow)
   else { attempt to move off sheet }
      crt(BEEP)
end;
```

Based on the character typed by the user, **movecursor** moves the sheet cursor in the specified direction by calling **setcursor** to put the cursor on the appropriate adjacent cell. If the user tries to move off the sheet, **movecursor** sounds a warning beep.

Incremental Testing

Few large programs are designed "all at once," and **pascalc** is no exception. It is nearly always a good idea to test a program *as it is being built* in order to catch mistakes, bugs, and design flaws as soon as possible. Most of the benefits of incremental testing are obvious.

- *It is easier to test a small part of a program than to test the whole thing.* Testing is a long and usually not very interesting process of ensuring that the program compiles correctly and behaves as expected under different inputs. When a large program is tested "all at once" it is all too easy to forget to test one or two important features or to fail to test the features thoroughly. Tests of manageable pieces of the program soon after they are designed can be more rigorous and complete.

- *Debugging is easier when it is spread out over the program-development process.* Incremental testing allows the programmer to confront a small number of bugs that are usually isolated in the part of the program just designed. Since the program section is relatively fresh in the programmer's mind, the bugs will be easier to fix than if testing is delayed until the whole program is completed.
- *Design flaws should be detected as early as possible.* Just like bugs, program design flaws are easiest to fix soon after they are incorporated in the program. If, for example, we had discovered that **pascalc**'s method of cursor movement was clumsy, we could have redesigned the code *immediately,* before the remainder of the program was written to depend on that method.
- *The program "works" at an early stage.* A programmer's morale can be considerably improved by seeing tangible results of his or her programming effort and by observing the progress toward the final product.

At this point we have designed enough of **pascalc** to test what has been written so far. Write simple "stub" routines for the other procedures called from **pascalc**'s main routine, compile the program, and run it to make sure the initial sheet is displayed as expected and that cursor movement works correctly.

Entering Labels

Now **pascalc** can display a sheet (at least an empty one) and move the cursor around to any cell. It is time to write **getlabel**, which accepts a label from the user and inserts it into the sheet. Here is **getlabel**:

```
procedure getlabel(ch: char);
{ Get label from user }
var
    s: string;
    cp: cellptr;
begin { getlabel }
    if ch <> '"' then
        ungetkey(ch);
    eraseline(inpline);
    posstr('Label:', 0, inpline);
    getstring(s, MAXCRTCOL - 6, 6, inpline, '', [' '..'~'], FALSE);
    eraseline(inpline);
    if s <> '' then begin
        if curcp <> NIL then
            erasecell(curcp);
```

```
          if not storecell(curscol, cursrow, curcp) then
             memout
          else if not storestr(s, curcp^.display) then
             memout
    end;
    disprow(cursrow);
    setcursor(curscol, cursrow)
end;
```

In general, **getlabel** accepts a label from the user and then stores it in memory by creating a new cell in the sheet's sparse matrix structure. (If there is already a non-empty cell at the current cursor position, the old cell is "erased" before the new cell data is stored.) It then updates the sheet display (using **disprow**) to show the new label.

If there is no room in memory to store the new cell or the label string, **getlabel** calls **memout** to make this fact known to the user. Since this routine is so simple, we will design it first:

```
procedure memout;
{ Report lack of memory }
begin { memout }
   remark('OUT OF MEMORY')
end;
```

Un-Input

Remember that the main routine of **pascalc** discovers that the user wants to enter a label by looking for either a letter or a double quote. If the user types a letter, the letter is used as the first character of the label. The problem is that we want to use **getstring** to receive the label from the user, but **getstring** has no way to accept the first character of the label; the character has already been read from the keyboard.

There are a number of possible solutions to this problem. We could write a new version of **getstring** that accepts an initial input string as an input parameter. But it seems wasteful to completely rewrite a routine to add a minor feature.

Our solution, as shown in **getlabel**, is to call a routine called **ungetkey**. The **ungetkey** routine is the *inverse* of **getkey**. For example, the call

```
ungetkey(ch);
```

puts the character **ch** "back into the input buffer." What that means is the *next* time **getkey** is called, it will return the character **ch** to the calling routine instead of waiting for the user's input. *Subsequent* calls to **getkey**, however, will return the user's keyboard input as usual.

This can be accomplished rather easily by modifying **getkey** to check an "input buffer" before it looks for keyboard input. This approach requires that the input buffer be defined as a global variable and that "read" and "write" pointers into the buffer be maintained. We could define these items in the following way:

```
<var>
   inpbuf: packed array [0..BUFSIZE] of char;
   readptr, writeptr: 0..BUFSIZE;
```

inpbuf is an array that holds characters "waiting" to be read. The variable **readptr** indicates what element in the array was last read from the buffer, and the variable **writeptr** indicates what element was last written to the buffer. If the two pointers are equal, there are no characters waiting to be read in the input buffer.

Every program using this new method would have to initialize the pointers, as follows:

```
...
readptr := 0;
writeptr := 0;
...
```

Then the **ungetkey** routine would look something like this:

```
procedure ungetkey(ch: char);
{ Put character into input buffer }
begin { ungetkey }
   newptr := (writeptr + 1) mod (BUFSIZE + 1);
   if newptr <> readptr then begin
      inbuf[newptr] := ch;
      writeptr := newptr
   end
   else { buffer is full }
      crt(BEEP)
end;
```

Next, the **getkey** routine would be modified to check for a character in the input buffer before it checks keyboard input, as in the following:

```
function getkey(var ch:char;valid:charset;shiftlock:boolean);
{ Get valid key typed at keyboard or present in input buffer }
```

```
var
   ok: boolean;
begin { getkey }
   repeat
      if readptr <> writeptr then begin
         readptr := (readptr + 1) mod (BUFSIZE + 1);
         ch := inbuf[readptr]
      end
      else begin
         read(keyboard, ch);
         if eoln(keyboard) then
            ch := chr(13)
      end;
      if shiftlock and ...

      { as before }
      ...
end;
```

The **mod** operator is used in **getkey** and **ungetkey** to make **inpbuf[0]** the next element used after **inpbuf[BUFSIZE]**, resulting in a *circular* or *ring* buffer. It helps to think of the elements of **inpbuf** as arranged in a circle with **inpbuf[BUFSIZE]** wrapping around to be adjacent to **inpbuf[0]**. The technical term for this data structure is a *first-in first-out* (FIFO) buffer.

Given enough room in the buffer, we can even "unget" an entire string of characters. The **ungetstr** routine does just that.

```
procedure ungetstr(s: string);
{ Put string into console input buffer }
var
   i: integer;
begin { ungetstr }
   for i := 1 to length(s) do
      ungetkey(s[i])
end;
```

The advantage of this method is that it is easily implemented and relatively portable. Its disadvantage is that it requires modification of **getkey**. This is particularly painful because we have long since put **getkey** in a separately compiled unit, and modifying it would require modification and recompilation of the unit. Ideally, we would like to write an **ungetkey** routine that does not require **getkey** to be modified.

We *can* write such a routine, at least in Apple Pascal. We make use of the fact that the Apple Pascal operating system stores characters typed at the keyboard in a "type-ahead" buffer at a fixed address in memory (location

3B1 (hex), 945 (decimal)). Whenever the user types a key, the operating system takes it from the keyboard and puts it in this buffer. And whenever a Pascal program uses **read** to accept keyboard characters, the operating system gets the characters from the type-ahead buffer, not directly from the keyboard.

The Apple Pascal type-ahead buffer is *exactly* the same as the **inpbuf** array we used previously. It is a circular buffer with room for 79 characters. The system maintains both a read pointer and a write pointer into the buffer: the read pointer is a single byte at address BF18 (hex), 48920 (decimal), and the write pointer is a single byte at BF19 (hex), 48921 (decimal).

If we can access the type-ahead buffer and its read and write pointers, we can write a version of **ungetkey** that would duplicate the action of the operating system in putting a character into the buffer. This would be an easy task to accomplish in assembly language; here we will do it in Pascal.

Keep in mind that the method shown here is *extremely* non-portable. The code for **ungetkey** will only work under Apple Pascal version 1.1; it might not even work on a different version of the Apple Pascal operating system, which could conceivably put the type-ahead buffer at a different location, change its size, move the pointers, or eliminate the buffer altogether. In general, users of other versions of Pascal will have to use the "portable" **ungetkey** and modify **getkey** as indicated.

Our first step is to write **peek** and **poke** routines in Pascal. You may recognize the terminology, which is used in BASIC. **peek** is used to examine a given memory location. The function call

```
membyte := peek(addr)
```

returns the byte at the memory location **addr** and assigns it to the variable **membyte**. **poke**, on the other hand, is used to change the value of a given memory location. The procedure call

```
poke(addr, membyte);
```

changes the memory location **addr** to the value **membyte**. (Obviously, careless use of **poke** can be dangerous to your program.)

In general, **peek** and **poke** cannot be written in a portable way in Pascal; Pascal was simply not designed to access memory locations by their addresses. We can get around this shortcoming by setting a *pointer* variable to point to the desired memory location; then the location can be either examined or changed through the pointer.

In most versions of Pascal, a pointer variable simply contains the address of whatever it points to. In Apple Pascal, pointers are actually two-byte unsigned integers adequate for addressing any byte in a 65,536-byte memory space. But we cannot simply assign the address to a pointer: integer addresses and pointers are different types, and Pascal prevents a variable of one type from being assigned a value of another type.

However, we are not beaten yet. Assigning a pointer variable to point to a given address can be accomplished in most versions of Pascal by using a *variant* record type. First, consider the following two type declarations:

```
<type)
   byte = 0..255;
   twobytes = packed array [0..1] of byte;
```

These declarations say that a **byte** variable is a number in the range 0 to 255 and that a variable of the type **twobytes** is a packed array of two bytes. (Declaring the type as **packed** forces each element to take up one byte; omitting **packed** would cause each element to be stored as an integer, each taking two bytes.)

The next step is to declare a variant record type, **trixrec**, which contains either an integer or a pointer to a variable of type **twobytes**, as follows:

```
<type>
   trixrec = record
      case boolean of
         TRUE:
            (ptr: ^twobytes);
         FALSE:
            (adr: integer)
   end;
```

Variant records were included in Pascal as a way to save memory; different variable types can use the same storage space. If we declare a variable of type **trixrec** as follows:

```
<var>
   trix: trixrec;
```

then **trix** contains either an integer or a pointer to a **twobytes** variable: **trix.adr** is the integer and **trix.ptr** is the pointer. The key is that these two names refer to *the same region of memory;* both the integer and the pointer fields occupy the same two bytes.

Use of the variant record structure makes both **peek** and **poke** very easy to write. For **peek**, we initialize a variable of type **trix** to contain the (integer) address of the memory location at which we want to peek by assigning the address to the field **trix.adr**. Then the pointer field **trix.ptr** points to the memory location, and we can retrieve the contents of the memory location by accessing **trix.ptr^[0]**.

```
function peek(addr: integer): byte;
{ Basic-like peek function }
var
   trix: trixrec;
begin { peek }
   trix.adr := addr;
   peek := trix.ptr^[0]
end;
```

For **poke**, we initialize the **trix** variable with the address of the memory location, and then alter the memory location **trix.ptr** points to.

```
procedure poke(addr: integer; val: byte);
{ Basic-like poke }
var
    trix: trixrec;
begin { poke }
   trix.adr := addr;
   trix.ptr^[0] := val
end;
```

The **trixrec** variant record structure is called a *free type-union*. During program execution, Pascal has no way to determine whether we have stored an integer or a pointer in a **trixrec** variable. Although this trick "should" be treated as an error (because it violates Pascal's canons against type intermixing), as a practical matter the error will never be detected.

Given **peek** and **poke**, we can immediately write **ungetkey**:

```
procedure ungetkey(ch: char);
{ Put character into console input buffer }
const
   RPTR = -16616;        { address of console buffer read pointer }
   WPTR = -16615;        { address of console buffer write pointer }
   CONBUF = 945;         { address of console buffer }
   CBUFLEN = 78;         { length of console buffer - 1 }
type
   byte = 0..255;
   twobytes = packed array [0..1] of byte;
   trixrec = record
      case boolean of
         TRUE:
            (ptr: ^twobytes);
```

```
        FALSE:
            (adr: integer)
        end;
var
    newp: byte;

{-----------------------------}
{ Modules to be inserted here: }
{         peek                 }
{         poke                 }
{-----------------------------}
begin { ungetkey }
    newp := (peek(WPTR) + 1) mod CBUFLEN;
    if newp <> peek(RPTR) then begin
        poke(WPTR, newp);
        poke(CONBUF + newp, ord(ch));
    end
    else { buffer is full }
        crt(BEEP)
end;
```

The declared constants **RPTR** and **WPTR** represent the addresses of the console-buffer read pointer and write pointer, respectively. It is necessary to represent the addresses as negative integers; in Apple Pascal, integers are held in memory as *signed* 16-bit integers. Memory addresses, on the other hand, are *unsigned* 16-bit integers. The only difference arises when we want to represent an address greater than 32767; in that case, we have to convert the unsigned integer to a signed integer with the formula

```
<signed integer> := <unsigned integer> - 65536
```

Dynamic Memory Allocation

Our next step is to solve the problem we previously delayed: how to store variables of differing length (like strings) without wasting memory. Ideally, we would like to be able to store such data items in memory for as long as they are needed; when they are no longer needed, the memory they used should be returned to the system for other purposes. This process is termed *dynamic memory allocation;* the term "dynamic" is used because the memory requirements are determined while the program is running.

Standard Pascal *nearly* provides us with what we need. Suppose the variable **sp** is of the type **stringptr**, that is, it is a pointer to a string. Then the call to the standard Pascal built-in routine **new**

```
new(sp);
```

allocates storage in memory for a string and assigns the address of the storage to the pointer variable **sp**.

Standard Pascal also offers a method for deallocating the memory allocated by **new**; the call

```
dispose(sp);
```

disassociates the pointer **sp** from the string to which it points. In many Pascal implementations, the storage pointed to by **sp** is "freed," that is, returned to the system so that it may be reused for other purposes.

This approach, although close, does not solve our problem either, for two reasons. The first reason is that **new** allocates fixed-sized blocks of memory; in the case shown previously, the call **new(sp)** reserves in memory room enough to store an 80-character string, even though our actual requirements may be much less. This is the same inefficiency problem we had before.

The second reason is that Apple Pascal does not offer a **dispose** function. Even if we could efficiently allocate variable-sized storage areas, Apple Pascal does not provide a method to free them for other uses.

(If you are well-versed in Pascal, you probably know you *can* allocate variable-sized storage with **new** by using pointers to variant records and telling **new** the values of the tag fields. This "solution" is relatively clumsy, however, and Apple Pascal's lack of the analogous **dispose** function makes this method unusable for us.)

What the language does not provide for us we can build ourselves. We will design two routines, **alloc** and **free**, that allocate and deallocate specified sizes of memory. The call

```
addr := alloc(nbytes);
```

finds **nbytes** consecutive (and unused) bytes of memory and allocates them for use. **alloc** returns the address of the first byte of the block of memory as its function result. If **alloc** cannot find a large enough block of unused memory, it returns a value of 0 to signal failure.

Memory allocated by **alloc** can be deallocated by **free**. The call

```
free(addr, nbytes);
```

frees the area of memory **nbytes** bytes in length beginning at address **addr** for possible reuse. **alloc** and **free** are partners: attempting to call **free** with an address not allocated by **alloc**, or with a different value of **nbytes** from the number of bytes actually allocated by **alloc**, is dangerous at best. (After you fully understand how **alloc** and **free** work, however, you may want to consider whether such dangerous practices might occasionally be useful.)

Memory Management Data Structures

In order for **alloc** to do its job, we must invent some way of "marking" currently unused memory; otherwise, **alloc** would not be able to distinguish between free and reserved memory. In general, free memory will be broken up into an arbitrary number of different-sized blocks, alternating with blocks of memory currently in use. **alloc** searches through these free blocks trying to find one large enough to accommodate the request for **nbytes** bytes. Our strategy will be to keep a *circular list* of the available free space in memory. And we will use some of the free memory *itself* to store the list.

In our arrangement, each free memory block contains (1) an integer giving the size of the block, (2) a pointer to the next block in the chain, and (3) the remainder of the free space itself. The fields containing the size of the block and the pointer to the next block are together called the *block header*, which takes up four bytes of each free block. This structure is shown in Figure 8-3. The free list shown there contains four free blocks of 500 bytes, 344 bytes, 208 bytes, and 1012 bytes. The size field in each header is measured in header-sized units; to get the total number of bytes in the block, multiply the size field by 4. (This arrangement requires each free block to be a multiple of four bytes in length.)

In addition to the four large blocks shown in Figure 8-3, there is a block containing *just* a header with a size field of 0. In the following discussion, we will call this block the *list header*.

Finally, we define a pointer to some element in the list; this pointer will be used by the program to access the list. This is indicated by the "freelist" pointer in Figure 8-3.

Although it is not indicated in Figure 8-3, we put an additional restriction on the free memory list: the blocks in the list are in order by their location in memory. The list header is at a lower memory location than any free memory block, and the block highest in memory points back to the list header.

The free list structure is easy to define in Pascal. First, we can declare the block header structure as follows:

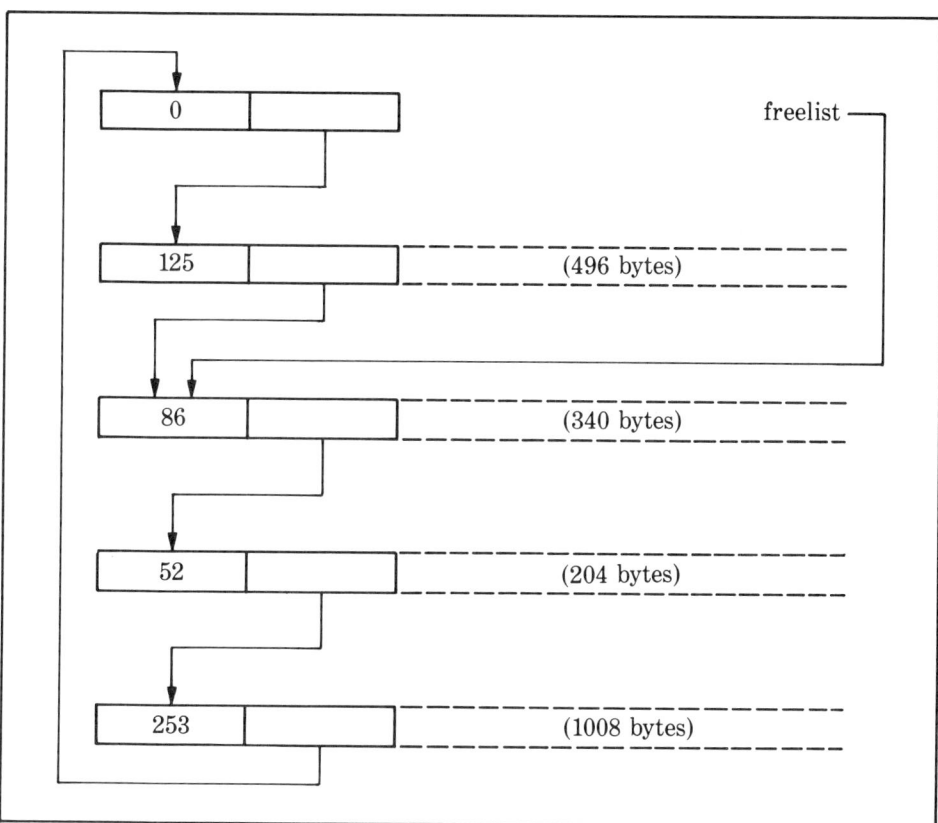

Figure 8-3. Free memory list data structure

```
<type>
   headerptr = ^header;
   header = record
      size: integer;
      next: headerptr
   end;
```

We also need to declare the pointer into the list as a global variable, as follows:

```
<var>
   freelist: headerptr;
```

In designing **alloc**, we will assume the free memory list has been set up with an initialization routine and that the **freelist** pointer points to any of the free memory block headers. Then **alloc** has to search the list, block by block, looking for a large enough block to contain **nbytes** bytes. If it finds one, it must somehow "unhook" the required number of bytes from the free list, returning their address to the calling routine. Equally as important, **alloc** must leave the free list structure in good shape, with correct size fields and pointers.

Here is **alloc**:

```
function alloc(nbytes: integer): integer;
{ Find and allocate nbytes unused bytes of memory }

var
   lastblk, currblk: headerptr;
   nunits: integer;
   done: boolean;

begin { alloc }
   nunits := (nbytes + HDRSIZE - 1) div HDRSIZE;
   lastblk := freelist;
   currblk := lastblk^.next;
   done := FALSE;
   repeat
      if currblk^.size >= nunits then begin { success }
         if currblk^.size = nunits then begin
            lastblk^.next := currblk^.next;
            alloc := ord(currblk)
         end
         else begin
            currblk^.size := currblk^.size - nunits;
            alloc := ord(currblk) + currblk^.size * HDRSIZE
         end;
         freelist := lastblk;
         done := TRUE
      end
      else if currblk = freelist then begin { failure }
         done := TRUE;
         alloc := 0
      end
      else begin { try next block }
         lastblk := currblk;
         currblk := currblk^.next
      end
   until done
end;
```

Since free memory blocks are stored in multiples of four bytes, **alloc** first translates the request for **nbytes** bytes into a request for **nunits** header-sized units, rounding up to the nearest multiple of four bytes. (The constant **HDRSIZE** is 4, the size of a header in bytes.) For example, if **nbytes** is 23, **alloc** needs to search for a block of memory containing at least six header-sized units, or 24 bytes.

Then **alloc** searches through the free list, using pointer variables **lastblk** and **currblk**. **lastblk** "lags behind" **currblk** in the search, always pointing to the list element preceding the one to which **currblk** points.

The **size** field of each block pointed to by **currblk** is examined in the search to see if it can satisfy the request for **nunits** units. If a block exactly big enough is found (**currblk^.size = nunits**), the block is simply unhooked from the free list by pointing the previous block's **next** pointer to the block *following* the current block; **alloc** returns the address of the unhooked block.

If the current block is *bigger* than required (**currblk^**.size > **nunits**), **alloc** simply decreases the block's **size** field by **nunits**; the net effect is to "chop off" the last **nunits** units of the block. **alloc** then returns the address of the chopped-off part.

The search fails whenever **alloc** has examined all the free blocks without finding one large enough. This happens when **currblk** wraps around to where the search started, the block to which **freelist** points.

One "trick" used in **alloc** is the non-standard use of the Standard Pascal **ord** function, a use available in both Apple and UCSD Pascal. When **ord** is called with a pointer variable as its argument, it returns the integer address as its result. The call

```
adr := ord(ptr)
```

returns the address pointed to by **ptr**. We could have used the free-union trick described previously to accomplish the same thing, but using **ord** is considerably more concise.

Now that we have designed **alloc**, what about **free**? In general, all **free** must do is return the freed block to the circular free list structure. First, the first four bytes of the freed block must be converted into a block header with the appropriate **size** field. Then the block must be relinked into the free list: its **next** pointer field must point to the "next" free block, and the "previous" free block's **next** pointer must point to the just-freed block.

We want to do slightly more than this, however. If the block to be freed is adjacent to a currently free block on either side, the two blocks are coalesced into a single, larger block. And if there are free blocks on *both* sides of the freed block, then *all three* blocks are merged into a single block. This approach permits a more efficient use of memory when different-sized blocks are continually allocated and freed, as in **pascalc**.

Thus, **free** uses the following strategy: it scans through the free list looking for the proper place to insert the freed block, either between two currently free blocks or at one "end" of the list. Once the proper place for the block is found, the block is linked into the list and combined with its neighboring blocks, if possible. Here is **free**:

```
procedure free(addr, nbytes: integer);
{ Return block of memory to free list }
```

```
var
   done: boolean;
   prevblk, nextblk, freeblk: headerptr;
begin { free }
   moveleft(addr, freeblk, 2);
   freeblk^.size := (nbytes + HDRSIZE - 1) div HDRSIZE;
   prevblk := freelist;
   nextblk := prevblk^.next;
   repeat
      done := (ord(freeblk) > ord(prevblk)) and (ord(freeblk) < ord(nextblk));
      if not done then
         if ord(prevblk) >= ord(nextblk) then
            done := (ord(freeblk) > ord(prevblk)) or
                    (ord(freeblk) < ord(nextblk));
      if not done then begin
         prevblk := nextblk;
         nextblk := nextblk^.next
      end
   until done;
   if ord(freeblk) + freeblk^.size * HDRSIZE = ord(nextblk) then begin
      freeblk^.size := freeblk^.size + nextblk^.size;
      freeblk^.next := nextblk^.next
   end
   else
      freeblk^.next := nextblk;
   if ord(prevblk) + prevblk^.size * HDRSIZE = ord(freeblk) then begin
      prevblk^.size := prevblk^.size + freeblk^.size;
      prevblk^.next := freeblk^.next
   end
   else
      prevblk^.next := freeblk;
   freelist := prevblk
end;
```

Now you can see why we required that the free list be kept in order by address: we can more easily determine whether two blocks are adjacent to each other.

free makes heavy use of the **ord** trick previously described in the discussion of **alloc** in order to compare block addresses and to calculate whether two blocks are adjacent in memory. In addition, it uses yet another trick to translate the address passed to **free** into a block header pointer. The call

```
moveleft(addr, freeblk, 2);
```

moves the two bytes of the integer variable **addr** into the header pointer variable **freeblk** so that **freeblk** now points to the address **addr**. This "works" because **moveleft** simply moves bytes from one point in memory to another without type checking. **moveleft** can also be used to translate pointers to addresses in the same way. (We could have used **moveleft** instead of the free union variant records in **peek** and **poke**; conversely, we could have used the variant record trick here in **free**.)

Apple Pascal Memory Management

Our only remaining problem is to initialize the free memory list structure used by **alloc** and **free**. As a first step, we need to investigate how the computer's memory is used during the execution of a program so we will know where we can safely set up the list. The details given here apply to Apple Pascal. Many versions of Pascal use similar memory management schemes.

During the execution of a Pascal program, the computer's memory is put to a number of uses: the program's code and data storage, the operating system, I/O buffers, and so on. It is not important for our purposes to know where any of these memory areas are; in general, they may be anywhere in available memory. In Apple Pascal, however, all system memory usage lies in either the bottom of memory (low addresses) or the top (high addresses). The region of memory in between is free memory available for use by the program. The size of this free memory region depends on the size of the program.

In Apple Pascal, the system keeps track of the locations of both the bottom and top of the free memory area. The bottom of the free memory area is called the *heap* and the top is called the *stack*. Figure 8-4 shows this simple arrangement.

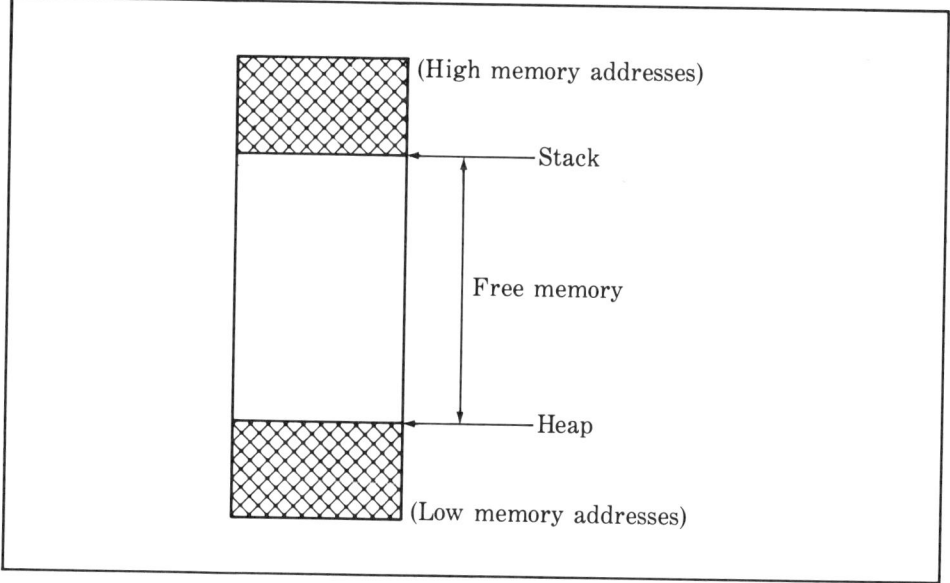

Figure 8-4. Apple Pascal memory layout

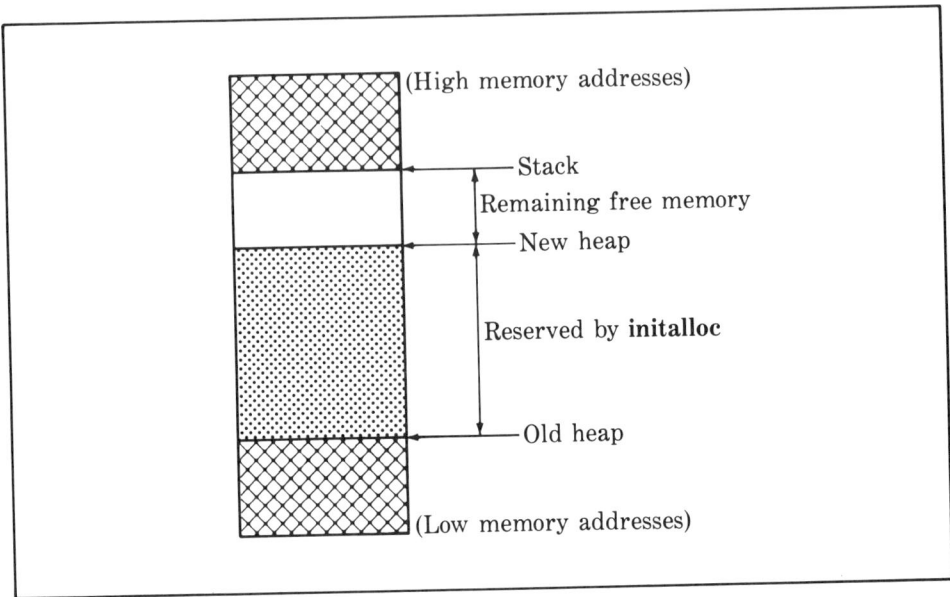

Figure 8-5. Memory layout after free list initialization

    The stack is used by the system to obtain the temporary storage necessary for calling routines. Whenever a procedure (or function) is called, a certain amount of memory is needed to store the procedure's local variables, return address, and other "bookkeeping" information. So whenever a procedure is called, the stack "grows" downward in memory. And when the procedure exits, the memory is freed, with the stack "shrinking" back upward in memory.

    The heap, on the other hand, is used for allocating dynamic variables with **new**: whenever **new** allocates a dynamic variable, the heap moves upward in memory.

    When the heap and the stack "collide," that is, the free memory shrinks to nothing, the program exits with a "stack overflow" execution error: the system is out of memory.

    Our strategy in setting up our initial free memory list will be to reserve a large block of memory when the program starts, leaving a relatively small free memory space for the system to use for procedure calls and other uses. The location of this large block will be on "top" of the initial heap position; the heap will then be relocated above the block. The net effect is to protect this large block of memory from use by the system. Figure 8-5 shows how the memory layout is altered by this free list initialization.

Reserving the large block is then a question of moving the heap; this can be done with three procedures built into Apple and UCSD Pascal: **mark**, **release**, and **memavail**. Assume that the variable **hptr** has been declared a pointer to an integer, as follows:

```
<var>
   hptr: ^integer;
```

Then the call

```
mark(hptr);
```

sets the variable **hptr** to point to the current heap, that is, it contains the address of the heap. On the other hand, the call

```
release(hptr);
```

sets the system's heap pointer to point to the address contained in **hptr**. Briefly, **mark** allows us to find out where the heap is, and **release** allows us to change its location.

The built-in function **memavail** is used to determine the amount of free memory at any given time during the execution of a program. The call

```
freewords := memavail;
```

returns the number of two-byte words between the heap and the stack.

Once we have reserved the large block, we can set up the free list within it. All this is accomplished by the **initalloc** function. The call

```
success := initalloc(leave);
```

attempts to set up an initial free list; it returns the value **TRUE** if successful and **FALSE** if not enough memory is available. The argument **leave** is the number of two-byte words of free memory **initalloc** is to allow the system to keep for calling routines. This parameter should be set just large enough so the system does not run out of memory with a stack overflow during program execution. In practice, setting the parameter correctly is a matter of trial and error.

Here is **initalloc**:

```
function initalloc(leave: integer): boolean;
{ Initialize dynamic allocation scheme }

var
   heap: ^integer;
```

```
      nunits, addr: integer;
      listhead, bigblock: headerptr;
begin { initalloc }
      nunits := (memavail - leave) div 2;
      if nunits < 2 then
         initalloc := FALSE
      else begin
         initalloc := TRUE;
         mark(heap);
         addr := ord(heap);
         moveleft(addr, listhead, 2);
         addr := addr + HDRSIZE;
         moveleft(addr, bigblock, 2);
         addr := addr + HDRSIZE * (nunits - 1);
         moveleft(addr, heap, 2);
         release(heap);
         with listhead^ do begin
            size := 0;
            next := bigblock
         end;
         with bigblock^ do begin
            size := nunits - 1;
            next := listhead
         end;
         freelist := listhead
      end
end;
```

The routine first calculates the size of the block to reserve as **nunits**, the number of header-sized units, based on the current **memavail** and the amount of memory to leave to the system. The absolute minimum size of the block is two headers: one for the list header and one for the header for the remainder of the free list. If there is not enough room for at least two headers in the block, **initalloc** reports failure to the main routine. Otherwise, **initalloc** calls **mark** and **release** to move the heap above the block and then sets up the initial free memory list structure. It uses both **ord** and **moveleft** to translate between pointer and integer types.

A final note on our memory-allocation tools: many versions of Pascal have built-in routines that accomplish essentially what we have built here. For example, UCSD Pascal versions IV.0 and later provide the routines **varnew** and **vardispose** used for allocating and freeing variable-sized blocks of memory. In such cases, it is probably desirable to use the built-in routines rather than the ones presented here.

Dynamic Storage of Strings

Our dynamic memory-allocation tools are usually not used directly, but instead are used through routines that "store" and "erase" variables of different types by calling **alloc** and **free**. For example, **storestr** is used to store a string in dynamic memory.

```
function storestr(var s: string; var sp: stringptr): boolean;
{ Store string in dynamic memory, return pointer to it }
var
   saddr: integer;
begin { storestr }
   saddr := alloc(1 + length(s));
   if saddr = 0 then begin
      sp := NIL;
      storestr := FALSE
      end
   else begin
      moveleft(saddr, sp, 2);
      sp^ := s;
      storestr := TRUE
      end
end;
```

This routine uses **alloc** to find and allocate space for the string s. The number of bytes requested from **alloc** is **length(s)+1**: the number of characters in the string plus 1 for the length byte. If there is no room to store the string (**alloc** returns 0), **storestr** returns a string pointer of **NIL** and a function result of **FALSE** to its caller, signifying failure. Otherwise, it stores the string at the allocated location, returning a pointer to the string as the **var** parameter **sp** and a function result of **TRUE**.

A stored string is erased from dynamic memory with **erasestr**:

```
procedure erasestr(sp: stringptr);
{ Erase string from dynamic memory }
begin { erasestr }
   if sp <> NIL then
      free(ord(sp), length(sp^) + 1)
end;
```

erasestr simply calls **free** to return the space previously reserved by **alloc** to the free list.

Cell Storage

We can now design routines to store and erase cells to and from our sparse matrix structure. Our first step is to store cells with **storecell**. The call

```
success := storecell(col, row, cp);
```

attempts to create a cell in memory with column and row coordinates **col** and

row. The **var** parameter **cp** returns a pointer to the created cell; the function result is a Boolean, reflecting whether or not the cell was successfully created.

storecell is slightly more complex than **storestr**. In addition to allocating space for the cell, **storecell** must link the cell into the existing sparse matrix structure. Here is **storecell**:

```
function storecell(col, row: integer; var cp: cellptr): boolean;
{ Create new cell at specified position, return pointer to it }

var
   celladdr: integer;
   cp1, cp2: cellptr;
   done: boolean;

begin { storecell }
   celladdr := alloc(sizeof(cellrec));
   if celladdr = 0 then begin
      cp := NIL;
      storecell := FALSE;
   end
   else begin
      moveleft(celladdr, cp, 2);
      with cp^ do begin
         cellcol := col;
         cellrow := row;
         display := NIL;
         fp := NIL;
         cp1 := NIL;                            { Link into column }
         cp2 := colptr[col];
         done := FALSE;
         while (cp2 <> NIL) and not done do
            if cp2^.cellrow <= row then begin
               cp1 := cp2;
               cp2 := cp2^.downptr
            end
            else
               done := TRUE;
         downptr := cp2;
         if cp1 = NIL then
            colptr[col] := cp
         else
            cp1^.downptr := cp;
         cp1 := NIL;                            { Link into row }
         cp2 := rowptr[row];
         done := FALSE;
         while (cp2 <> NIL) and not done do
            if cp2^.cellcol <= col then begin
               cp1 := cp2;
               cp2 := cp2^.rightptr
            end
            else
               done := TRUE;
         rightptr := cp2;
         if cp1 = NIL then
            rowptr[row] := cp
         else
            cp1^.rightptr := cp
      end;
```

```
        storecell := TRUE
      end
end;
```

storecell uses the **sizeof** function, which is available in Apple and UCSD Pascal. It is a function returning the storage requirement in bytes of the type specified in its argument. (It can also be called with the name of a variable, in which case it gives the amount of memory used by the variable.) There is no portable way to write a version of **sizeof** if your Pascal lacks it. Instead, replace the call to **sizeof** with the number of bytes used by the variable or type in question. The documentation for your Pascal implementation should contain sufficient information to determine such storage requirements.

The **erasecell** routine removes (unlinks) a specified cell from the sparse matrix and frees the memory previously allocated to the cell. Here is **erasecell**:

```
procedure erasecell(cp: cellptr);
{ Delete cell from sheet }
var
   cp1: cellptr;
begin { erasecell }
   if cp <> NIL then begin
      with cp^ do begin
         eraseform(fp);
         erasestr(display);

         { Unlink from column }
         if colptr[cellcol] = cp then
            colptr[cellcol] := downptr
         else begin
            cp1 := colptr[cellcol];
            while cp1^.downptr <> cp do
               cp1 := cp1^.downptr;
            cp1^.downptr := downptr
         end;

         { Unlink from row }
         if rowptr[cellrow] = cp then
            rowptr[cellrow] := rightptr
         else begin
            cp1 := rowptr[cellrow];
            while cp1^.rightptr <> cp do
               cp1 := cp1^.rightptr;
            cp1^.rightptr := rightptr
         end
      end;
      free(ord(cp), sizeof(cellrec))
   end
end;
```

In addition, **erasecell** calls **erasestr** to erase the cell's display string and **eraseform** (presented later) to erase the cell's formula data, if any.

Formula Storage

Our final example illustrates the storage and deletion of formula information records. Both are relatively easy to accomplish. **storeform** allocates space for a **forminfo** record and returns a pointer to it. Here is **storeform**:

```
function storeform(var fp: formptr): boolean;
{ Create formula info record }
var
   fadd: integer;
begin { storeform }
   fadd := alloc(sizeof(forminfo));
   if fadd = 0 then begin
      fp := NIL;
      storeform := FALSE
   end
   else begin
      moveleft(fadd, fp, 2);
      fp^.cellval := zero;
      fp^.usecolfmt := TRUE;
      fp^.cellstat := OK;
      fp^.formula := NIL;
      storeform := TRUE
   end
end;
```

eraseform calls **erasestr** to erase the formula string, then calls **free** to return the **forminfo** record to free memory. Here is **eraseform**:

```
procedure eraseform(fp: formptr);
{ Delete formula info record from dynamic memory }
begin { eraseform }
   if fp <> NIL then begin
      erasestr(fp^.formula);
      free(ord(fp), sizeof(forminfo))
   end
end;
```

The routines presented so far allow the insertion of labels on the worksheet. This is a good point to test what has been written up to now, before moving on to the next step.

Entering Formulas

Our next major goal in designing **pascalc** is to write the part of the program that does the number crunching: accepting formulas from the user, calculating values, and formatting the results. The natural place to begin is with **getformula**:

```
procedure getformula(ch: char);
{ Get formula from user }
var
   s: string;
   success: boolean;
{-----------------------------}
{ Modules to be inserted here: }
{        getformstr            }
{-----------------------------}
begin { getformula }
   ungetkey(ch);
   eraseline(inpline);
   posstr('Formula:', 0, inpline);
   getformstr(s);
   eraseline(inpline);
   if s <> '' then begin
      if curcp <> NIL then
         erasecell(curcp);
      success := storecell(curscol, cursrow, curcp);
      if success then
         success := storeform(curcp^.fp);
      if success then
         success := storestr(s, curcp^.fp^.formula);
      if not success then
         memout
      else if autocalc then begin
         recalc;
         reformat;
         dispsheet(firstcol, firstrow)
      end
      else begin
         calccell(curcp);
         formatcell(curcp);
         disprow(cursrow)
      end
   end;
   setcursor(curscol, cursrow)
end;
```

Much of **getformula** is already familiar. The first thing it does is call **ungetkey** to place the first character of the formula back into the type-ahead buffer. After accepting the formula as the string s, it erases any previous cell information at the cursor position by calling **erasecell**. **getformula** then creates a new cell at the present cursor position by calling **storecell** and creates a formula information record for the cell by calling **storeform**. Finally, it stores the formula string by calling **storestr**.

Any one of these dynamic memory allocations could possibly cause an out-of-memory error. Thus, **getformula** checks after each allocation to make sure it went well; if any step fails, the user is informed of the problem via **memout**.

Assuming all the allocations were successful, **getformula** does one of two things, depending on the value of the Boolean global parameter **autocalc**: if **TRUE**, **getformula** recalculates, reformats, and redisplays the entire sheet. Otherwise, **getformula** affects just the entered cell, calculating the value of the entered expression, formatting it, and displaying it on the screen at the current position.

The first thing to consider is how to get the formula string from the user. We could use **getstring** to accept formulas, as we used it to accept labels in **getlabel**. However, we want to add a major feature that is not available in **getstring**. As previously mentioned, relative cell references can be entered into a formula by using the cursor-movement keys to "point" to the referenced cell. (This is much more considerate than the alternate method of forcing the user to count cells.)

Thus, instead of **getstring**, **getformula** calls **getformstr** to input the formula string. The general design of **getformstr** is similar to **getstring**; you may wish to compare the two routines:

```
procedure getformstr(var s: string);
{ Get pascalc formula string }

const
    BS = 8;             { ASCII backspace key }
    CAN = 24;           { ASCII cancel key }
    ESC = 27;           { ASCII escape key }
    CR = 13;            { ASCII return key }
    DEL = 127;          { ASCII delete key }
    FLDCHR = '_';       { Input field marker }
    INPCOL = 8;         { Column where input starts }

var
    ch: char;
    okset: charset;
    relcol, relrow, i: integer;
    s1: string;

{----------------------------}
{ Modules to be inserted here: }
{        getrcc              }
{----------------------------}

begin { getformstr }
    s := '';
    okset := formchars + [chr(BS), chr(CR), chr(CAN), chr(ESC), chr(DEL)];
    gotoxy(INPCOL, inpline);
    for i := 1 to MAXCRTCOL - INPCOL do
        write(FLDCHR);
    gotoxy(INPCOL, inpline);
    while getkey(ch, okset, TRUE) <> chr(CR) do
        if (ch in [chr(BS), chr(DEL)]) and (length(s) > 0) then begin
            crt(LEFT);
            write(FLDCHR);
            crt(LEFT);
            chopchar(s)
        end
```

```
      else if (ch = chr(CAN)) and (length(s) > 0) then begin
         for i := length(s) downto 1 do begin
            crt(LEFT);
            write(FLDCHR);
            crt(LEFT)
         end;
         s := ''
      end
      else if ch = chr(ESC) then
         getrcc(INPCOL + length(s), inpline)
      else if (ch in formchars) and (length(s) < MAXCRTCOL - INPCOL) then
                                                                       begin
         addchar(s, ch, MAXSTR);
         write(ch)
      end
      else { Illegal character typed }
         crt(BEEP);
   for i := length(s) + 1 to MAXCRTCOL - INPCOL do
      write(' ')
end;
```

The "new feature" is the following code:

```
...
else if ch = chr(ESC) then
   getrcc(INPCOL + length(s), inpline)
else
...
```

getformstr uses the <ESC> key as a signal that the user wants to enter a relative cell reference via cursor movement. Other than that, **getformstr** acts just like **getstring** in error checking and editing. It calls **getrcc** to handle the cursor movement.

getrcc appears to the user like this: when the <ESC> key is typed to enter a relative cell reference, the reference [+0,+0] appears at the current entry position in the formula string. The CRT cursor is placed at the current cell on the sheet. Pressing any cursor-movement key moves the cursor on the screen, scrolling the window as necessary; the cell reference in the formula string is also adjusted accordingly. For example, assume the user is entering a formula for the cell at [23,10], presses <ESC> to enter cursor-movement mode, and then presses the "cursor up" key five times and the "cursor right" key twice. The cursor will then appear at cell [25,5] and the formula string will show the relative cell reference [+2,−5].

Once the cursor has been placed on the desired cell, the user presses <ESC> again. The relative cell reference is appended to the entered formula, and the sheet is redisplayed (if necessary) to return to its original window. The user may then continue entering and editing the formula as before, according to our normal rules. Here is **getrcc**:

```
procedure getrcc(crtcol, crtrow: integer);
{ Get relative cell coordinates from user's cursor-movement commands }

var
   ch: char;
   len, relcol, relrow, oldrow1, oldcol1, oldcrow, oldccol: integer;
   s: string;
   okchars: charset;
{-----------------------------}
{ Modules to be inserted here: }
{         ungetstr             }
{-----------------------------}
begin { getrcc }
   if crtcol > MAXCRTCOL - 10 then { no room }
      crt(BEEP)
   else begin
      okchars := cursorkeys + [chr(ESC)];
      oldrow1 := firstrow;
      oldcol1 := firstcol;
      oldcrow := cursrow;
      oldccol := curscol;
      len := 0;
      repeat
         relcol := curscol - oldccol;
         relrow := cursrow - oldcrow;
         ctos(relcol, relrow, TRUE, TRUE, s);
         posstr(s, crtcol, crtrow);
         if length(s) < len then
            write('_');
         len := length(s);
         gotoxy(XORG + colpos[curscol] - colpos[firstcol],
                                    YORG + cursrow - firstrow);
         if getkey(ch, okchars, FALSE) in cursorkeys then
            movecursor(ch)
      until ch = chr(ESC);
      if (firstrow <> oldrow1) or (firstcol <> oldcol1) then
         dispsheet(oldcol1, oldrow1);
      setcursor(oldccol, oldcrow);
      ungetstr(s);
      posstr('          ', crtcol, crtrow);
      gotoxy(crtcol, crtrow)
   end
end;
```

A relative cell reference may contain as many as ten characters, including the enclosing brackets. The first thing **getrcc** does is check to see if there is room in the formula string to store those ten characters; if not, it beeps at you and returns immediately to **getformstr**. (If you have modifed **getstring**, as suggested, to allow input of strings that overlap the screen boundaries, you may wish to make the analogous changes to **getformstr** and **getrcc** to allow input of longer formulas.)

getrcc uses **ungetstr** to put the relative cell reference string into the type-ahead buffer, from which it will be extracted by **getformstr**. This is slightly simpler than passing the string explicitly as a parameter.

The **ctos** procedure is used to convert a coordinate pair to a string:

```
procedure ctos(col, row: integer; relcol, relrow: boolean; var s: string);
{ Convert coordinate  pair to string }
var
    s1: string;

begin { ctos }
    s := '[';
    if relcol and (col >= 0) then
        addchar(s, '+', MAXSTR);
    itos(col, 0, s1);
    s := concat(s, s1, ',');
    if relrow and (row >= 0) then
        addchar(s, '+', MAXSTR);
    itos(row, 0, s1);
    s := concat(s, s1, ']')
end;
```

The two Boolean parameters **relcol** and **relrow** control whether the cell reference is relative or absolute. If **TRUE**, the corresponding coordinate is converted with a leading sign. (Note that in general *either* row or column coordinates may be relative or absolute.)

Recalculation

Now we come to the problem of *recalculation:* evaluating the formula at each cell and assigning the result to the cell's value. The first step is to design **recalc**, which recalculates all formula cells on the sheet:

```
procedure recalc;
{ Recalculate sheet }
var
    r, c: integer;
    cp: cellptr;
begin { recalc }
    center('Recalculating...', statline);
    if colcalc then
        for c := 1 to MAXCOLS do begin
            cp := colptr[c];
            while cp <> NIL do begin
                calccell(cp);
                cp := cp^.downptr
            end
        end
    else { recalc by row }
        for r := 1 to MAXROWS do begin
            cp := rowptr[r];
            while cp <> NIL do begin
                calccell(cp);
                cp := cp^.rightptr
            end
        end;
    eraseline(statline)
end;
```

The global Boolean parameter **colcalc** controls the order in which cells are recalculated. If **colcalc** is **TRUE**, recalculation is done by column, starting at cell [1,1], then [1,2], then [1,3], and so on, followed by [2,1], [2,2], and so on, then [3,1], and so on. If **colcalc** is **FALSE**, recalculation is done by row, proceeding left to right across row 1, then row 2, and so on.

Deciding which recalculation order is appropriate depends on the logical structure of the sheet; if Cell A depends on the value of Cell B, then Cell B should be recalculated before Cell A. If a given cell depends (directly or indirectly) on a cell (or cells) above it and to its right, then row calculation should be used. If a cell depends on a cell below and to its left, column calculation should be used.

recalc calls on **calccell** to evaluate a single cell's formula. Here is **calccell**:

```
procedure calccell(cp: cellptr);
{ Recalculate cell }

var
   i: integer;
{-------------------------------}
{ Modules to be inserted here: }
{        evalexpr              }
{-------------------------------}
begin { calccell }
   i := 1;
   if cp <> NIL then
      if cp^.fp <> NIL then
         with cp^.fp^ do
            if formula <> NIL then
               cellstat := evalexpr(formula^, i, cellval);
end;
```

The **evalexpr** routine called from **calccell** is the same routine used in Chapter Four's **calc**. In fact, this entire section of the program follows the same arrangement of modules as **calc**: routines nested within **evalexpr** are **xsub** and **evalterm**, both in **calc** and **pascalc**.

We can draw a "nesting diagram" showing how individual modules are nested within each other in this section of the program.

```
calccell
        evalexpr *
                xsub *
                evalterm *
                        xmul *
                        xdiv *
                        evalfact
                                stox *
                                findid *            (continued)
```

(*continued*)
```
                        getcoord
                        evalcell
                        evalid
                                findarg
                                evalsum
                                        summatrix
```

Here indentation is used to show how the routines are to be nested in the program's source text: **xsub** and **evalterm** are nested within **evalexpr**; **xmul**, **xdiv**, and **evalfact** are nested within **evalterm**, and so on.

An asterisk next to a routine's name in this diagram indicates that the routine is copied unchanged from **calc**. The others are either new routines or redesigned routines from **calc**. The first redesigned routine is **evalfact**, which must be modified to recognize cell references and functions. Here is **evalfact**:

```
function evalfact(var s: string; var i: integer; var x: xreal): xresult;
{ Evaluate factor }

var
   c: char;
   negfact: boolean;
   id: identifier;

{------------------------------}
{ Modules to be inserted here: }
{        getcoord              }
{        evalcell              }
{        stox                  }
{        findid                }
{        evalid                }
{------------------------------}

begin { evalfact }
   negfact := FALSE;
   if gnbchar(s, i, c) in ['+', '-'] then begin
      i := i + 1;
      negfact := (c = '-')
   end;
   if gnbchar(s, i, c) = '(' then begin
      i := i + 1;
      evalfact := evalexpr(s, i, x);
      if gnbchar(s, i, c) = ')' then
         i := i + 1
      else
         remark('Missing right parenthesis')
   end
   else if c = '[' then
      evalfact := evalcell(s, i, x)
   else if findid(s, i, id) then
      evalfact := evalid(s, i, id, x)
   else
      evalfact := stox(s, i, x);
   if negfact then
      x.frac := -x.frac
end;
```

The new portion of code

```
...
else if c = '[' then
   evalfact := evalcell(s, i, x)
...
```

checks for a left bracket indicating a cell reference; if it finds one, **evalcell** is called to extract the coordinates from the formula string and return the referenced cell's value.

```
function evalcell(var s: string; var i: integer; var x: xreal): xresult;
{ Evaluate cell reference }
var
   cp1: cellptr;
   col, row: integer;
begin { evalcell }
   x := zero;
   evalcell := OK;
   getcoord(s, i, col, row);
   cp1 := findcell(col, row);
   if cp1 <> NIL then
      if cp1^.fp <> NIL then
         with cp1^.fp^ do begin
            x := cellval;
            evalcell := cellstat
         end
end;
```

If the referenced cell is not on the sheet (signaled by a **NIL** pointer returned from **findcell**) or the cell contains a label instead of a formula (signaled by a **NIL** formula-information pointer), **evalcell** returns an **xreal** 0 as the cell's value. If the referenced cell has an error status (overflow, underflow, or division by 0), **evalcell** passes that information back to **evalfact**.

The **evalcell** function calls **getcoord** to extract the cell reference from the formula string and translate it into column and row coordinates. **getcoord** must deal with both absolute and relative references, which is slightly ticklish. Here is **getcoord**:

```
procedure getcoord(var s: string; var i, col, row: integer);
{ Get column and row numbers from cell reference }
{ NOTE - uses cell pointer cp declared in calccell procedure }
var
   relcol, relrow: boolean;
begin { getcoord }
   stoc(s, i, col, row, relcol, relrow);
   if relcol then
      col := col + cp^.cellcol;
   if relrow then
      row := row + cp^.cellrow
end;
```

The ticklish part is handling relative cell and row references. To calculate the coordinates for a relative reference properly, **getcoord** must know the coordinates of the cell being evaluated, the quantities **cp^.cellcol** and **cp^.cellrow**. The value of **cp** was passed to **calccell** as a parameter, and since **getcoord** is nested within **calccell**, it can (and does) access **cp**. Such a practice, while legal, is more than slightly unclear and dangerous.

The alternative, however, is passing **cp** as a parameter down through **evalexpr**, **evalterm**, **evalfact**, and **evalcell**, which is clumsy. The best procedure to follow when using such questionable programming techniques is to warn anyone reading the program of the practice with a prominent comment.

getcoord calls **stoc** to translate the cell reference in the formula string into a coordinate pair:

```
procedure stoc(var s: string; var i, col, row: integer;
                              var relcol, relrow: boolean);
{ Extract coordinate pair from string }
var
   c: char;
begin { stoc }
   if gnbchar(s, i, c) = '[' then
      i := i + 1;
   relcol := (gnbchar(s, i, c) in ['+', '-']);
   col := setparam(s, i, -MAXCOLS + 1, MAXCOLS - 1, 0);
   if gnbchar(s, i, c) = ',' then
      i := i + 1;
   relrow := (gnbchar(s, i, c) in ['+', '-']);
   row := setparam(s, i, -MAXROWS + 1, MAXROWS - 1, 0);
   if gnbchar(s, i, c) = ']' then
      i := i + 1
end;
```

stoc is called by other parts of the program besides **getcoord**, so it is a global routine instead of a routine nested within **getcoord**. It starts looking for the cell reference at the **i**th character of string **s**. It returns the two numbers seen as the integers **col** and **row**. The Boolean parameters **relcol** and **relrow** tell the calling routine whether or not the extracted column or row coordinates were relative.

The **setparam** routine is called by **stoc** to perform a common function: extract an integer parameter from a string and check to ensure it lies between minimum and maximum limits. If not, assign a default value.

```
function setparam(var s: string; var i: integer; min, max, default: integer):
                                                                     integer;
{ Extract integer from string, check against range }
var
   param: integer;
```

```
begin { setparam }
   if not stoi(s, i, param) then
      param := default
   else if (param < min) or (param > max) then
      param := default;
   setparam := param
end;
```

setparam is also called from a number of other routines in **pascalc**.

SUM Function

The **evalid** function from **calc** is drastically changed in **pascalc**. In **calc**, **evalid** was used to locate previously defined values in a binary tree. "Previously defined values" are cells in **pascalc**, and they have already been taken care of in **evalcell**. Thus, **evalid** has a totally different responsibility here: it evaluates whatever *functions* we decide to define.

As previously mentioned, **pascalc** has only one function: **SUM**. The syntax of the **SUM** function is as follows:

```
SUM(<arg1>, <arg2>, ... , <argN>)
```

SUM accepts an arbitrary number of arguments separated by commas; the result of the function is the sum of the values of all these arguments. Each one of these arguments can either be an expression or a *cell range*. If the argument is an expression, its value is the value of the expression. If the argument is a cell range, its value is the sum of all the cells within the range.

A cell range is constructed by separating two cell references with a colon.

```
[<col1>, <row1>]:[<col2>, <row2>]
```

This range defines (in general) a rectangular area of the sheet, with [<col1>,<row1>] in the upper-left corner and [<col2>,<row2>] in the lower-right corner. Sums over a single row can be obtained by setting <row1> = <row2>; sums over a single column are obtained by setting <col1> = <col2>. The cell references can be absolute or relative. If the second cell reference is absent, the range is considered to contain only the single cell [<col1>, <row1>].

To see how all this works, first consider **evalid**:

```
function evalid(var s: string; var i: integer; id: identifier; var x: xreal):
                                                                    xresult;
{ Evaluate identifier as function reference }
```

```
var
   c: char;
   arg: string;
{------------------------------}
{ Modules to be inserted here: }
{        findarg               }
{        evalsum               }
{------------------------------}
begin { evalid }
   if id = 'SUM' then
      evalid := evalsum(s, i, x)
   else begin
      remark('Undefined function');
      x := zero;
      evalid := OK;
      if gnbchar(s, i, c) = '(' then begin { skip argument list }
         while findarg(s, i, arg) do
            { nothing };
         if gnbchar(s, i, c) = ')' then
            i := i + 1
         else
            remark('Missing right parenthesis')
      end
   end
end;
```

evalid checks to be sure the function name extracted by **findid** was **SUM**. If it was not **SUM**, **evalid** considers this an attempt to use an undefined function; it displays a remark to that effect and skips over the undefined function's argument list if it has one.

If **SUM** was seen, **evalid** calls **evalsum** to evaluate the function:

```
function evalsum(var s: string; var i: integer; var x: xreal): xresult;
{ Evaluate sum function }
var
   status: xresult;
   c: char;
   x1: xreal;
   j: integer;
{------------------------------}
{ Modules to be inserted here }
{        summatrix            }
{------------------------------}
begin { evalsum }
   x := zero;
   status := OK;
   if gnbchar(s, i, c) = '(' then begin
      while (status = OK) and findarg(s, i, arg) do begin
         j := 1;
         if gnbchar(arg, j, c) = '[' then
            status := summatrix(arg, j, x1)
         else
            status := evalexpr(arg, j, x1);
         if status = OK then
            status := xadd(x, x1, x)
      end;
```

```
            if gnbchar(s, i, c) = ')' then
                i := i + 1
            else
                remark('Missing right parenthesis')
        end;
    evalsum := status
end;
```

evalsum calls **findarg** to extract successive arguments from the argument list (if present) and evaluates them one by one. If the argument begins with a left bracket <[>, **evalsum** evaluates it as a cell range by calling **summatrix**; otherwise it calls **evalexpr** to evaluate the argument as an expression.

The **findarg** function is called from both **evalid** and **evalsum**; it starts looking for a function argument at the (i+1)th character of the string s and returns it as the string **arg**. If no argument is seen at the specified position in s, **findarg** returns **FALSE** as its function result; otherwise it returns **TRUE**. It leaves i pointing at the character that delimited the argument, either a comma or a right parenthesis:

```
function findarg(var s: string; var i: integer; var arg: string): boolean;
{ Extract argument from string }

var
    nparen, nbrack: integer;
    done: boolean;
    c: char;

begin { findarg }
    arg := '';
    if gnbchar(s, i, c) in [')', chr(0)] then
        findarg := FALSE
    else begin
        nparen := 0;
        nbrack := 0;
        done := FALSE;
        repeat
            i := i + 1;
            c := gnbchar(s, i, c);
            if (c in [',', ')']) and (nparen <= 0) and (nbrack <= 0) then
                done := TRUE
            else if c = chr(0) then
                done := TRUE
            else begin
                addchar(arg, c, MAXSTR);
                if c = '(' then
                    nparen := nparen + 1
                else if c = ')' then
                    nparen := nparen - 1
                else if c = '[' then
                    nbrack := nbrack + 1
                else if c = ']' then
                    nbrack := nbrack - 1
            end
        until done;
        findarg := TRUE
    end
end;
```

Note that **findarg** is not as easy as we might have expected at first. It cannot simply scan down the string for a comma or right parenthesis to terminate the argument because an argument can itself contain a comma or right parenthesis. For example, in the formula

```
SUM([1,1]:[1,10], (1 + (1/3)), [43,38])
```

findarg must return the string "[1,1]:[1,10]" as the first argument, *not* "[1", as it would have if it simply scanned for the first comma. Similarly, the second argument has two right parentheses, but neither should be allowed to delimit the argument.

The solution **findarg** uses is to count the number of unbalanced left parentheses (**nparen**) and unbalanced left brackets (**nbrack**) seen so far in the argument. The argument only terminates when a comma or right parenthesis is seen *and* the counts **nparen** and **nbrack** are both less than or equal to zero. (How must **findarg** be changed to extract arguments from a Pascal procedure or function call?)

The only remaining matter is the **summatrix** procedure:

```
function summatrix(var s: string; var i: integer; var total: xreal): xresult;
{ Sum up matrix of cells }
var
   status: xresult;
   x1, x2, y1, y2, x: integer;
   cp: cellptr;
   c: char;
   done: boolean;
begin { summatrix }
   total := zero;
   status := OK;
   getcoord(s, i, x1, y1);
   if gnbchar(s, i, c) = ':' then begin
      i := i + 1;
      getcoord(s, i, x2, y2)
   end
   else begin
      x2 := x1;
      y2 := y1
   end;
   if (x1 >= 1) and (x1 <= MAXCOLS) and (y1 >= 1) and (y1 <= MAXROWS) and
      (x2 >= 1) and (x2 <= MAXCOLS) and (y2 >= 1) and (y2 <= MAXROWS)
                                                                    then begin
      x := x1;
      while (x <= x2) and (status = OK) do begin
         cp := colptr[x];
         done := FALSE;
         while (cp <> NIL) and (status = OK) and not done do begin
            if cp^.cellrow >= y1 then
               if cp^.cellrow <= y2 then begin
                  if cp^.fp <> NIL then
                     status := xadd(total, cp^.fp^.cellval, total)
               end
```

```
            else
                done := TRUE;
            cp := cp^.downptr
         end;
         x := x + 1
      end
   end;
   summatrix := status
end;
```

This procedure extracts the cell range coordinates from the argument string by calling **getcoord** twice (or only once, if no colon is seen after the first cell reference). Then, after checking that the entire range lies on the sheet, it adds up the cells within the range, accumulating the sum in the variable **total**.

Reformatting

After recalculation, the next step is reformatting. If a cell's value has been changed, its **display** field must be changed to the properly formatted string representation of the new value. Reformatting must also be done when a cell's format is changed.

Reformatting the sheet is logically similar to recalculating it, except that we do not have to worry about the order.

```
procedure reformat;
{ Reformat sheet }

var
    r: integer;
    cp: cellptr;
begin { reformat }
    center('Reformatting...', statline);
    for r := 1 to MAXROWS do begin
       cp := rowptr[r];
       while cp <> NIL do begin
          formatcell(cp);
          cp := cp^.rightptr
       end
    end;
    eraseline(statline)
end;
```

The real work is accomplished by **formatcell**, which formats an individual cell:

```
procedure formatcell(cp: cellptr);
{ Format numeric cell display }

var
    s: string;
```

```
        f: formatrec;
{-----------------------------}
{ Modules to be inserted here: }
{        xtos                  }
{        rightjust             }
{-----------------------------}
begin { formatcell }
    if cp <> NIL then
        with cp^ do
            if fp <> NIL then
                with fp^ do begin
                    if cellstat = OK then begin
                        if not usecolfmt then
                            f := cellfmt
                        else if not usesheetfmt[cellcol] then
                            f := colfmt[cellcol]
                        else
                            f := sheetfmt;
                        cellstat := xtos(cellval, f.fmt, f.ndigs, s);
                        rightjust(s, f.width)
                    end;
                    if cellstat <> OK then
                        s := 'Error';
                    erasestr(display);
                    if not storestr(s, display) then
                        memout
                end
end;
```

First, **formatcell** decides which set of formatting parameters to use, based on the precedence discussed previously. If the user has entered formatting parameters for the cell (**usecolfmt** is **FALSE**), those formatting parameters (contained in **cellfmt**) are used. Otherwise, if the user has not specified a format for the cell's column (**usesheetfmt[cellcol]** is **TRUE**), the default sheet formatting parameters (in **sheetfmt**) are used. Otherwise, the specified column format (**colfmt[cellcol]**) is used.

If the cell's status is not **OK**, the cell's display field is set to **Error**. (We could have displayed the type of error: "Overflow," "Underflow," or "Division by Zero.")

Both the **xtos** and **rightjust** routines used in **formatcell** were presented previously: **xtos** in Chapter Four and **rightjust** in Chapter Seven. As in Chapter Four, the routines **xtosci** and **xtofix** are nested within **xtos**.

This completes the code necessary for entering formulas and displaying their numeric results. Again, this is a natural place for compiling and testing what has been designed so far.

Commands

The last major design goal is to implement the commands listed in Table 8-1. The **docommand** routine is called from the main program:

```
procedure docommand(ch: char);
{ Do user command }

{------------------------------}
{ Modules to be inserted here: }
{         getacc               }
{         docopy               }
{         adjustcols           }
{         adjustrows           }
{         doerase              }
{         fmttos               }
{         stofmt               }
{         getformat            }
{         doformat             }
{         doinsert             }
{         doload               }
{         dodispmem            }
{         doprint              }
{         doquit               }
{         dosave               }
{         dotoggle             }
{------------------------------}

begin { docommand }
   if ch = '/' then begin
      eraseline(inpline);
      posstr('Command? (C/E/F/I/L/M/P/Q/S/T):', 0, inpline);
      ch := getkey(ch, cmdchars, TRUE);
      eraseline(inpline);
      case ch of
         'C': docopy;
         'E': doerase;
         'F': doformat;
         'I': doinsert;
         'L': doload;
         'M': dodispmem;
         'P': doprint;
         'Q': doquit;
         'S': dosave;
         'T': dotoggle
      end
   end
   else if ch = '!' then begin
      recalc;
      reformat;
      dispsheet(firstcol, firstrow)
   end
   else if ch = '>' then begin
      posstr('Go to', 0, inpline);
      getacc(6,inpline,1,MAXCOLS,curscol,1,MAXROWS,cursrow,curscol,cursrow);
      eraseline(inpline)
   end;
   setcursor(curscol, cursrow)
end;
```

docommand is called with the parameter **ch**; this is either an exclamation point <!>, a greater-than sign <>>, or a slash </>. An exclamation point signals recalculation, reformatting, and redisplay of the entire sheet; this is accomplished by calls to **recalc**, **reformat**, and **dispsheet**, all of which we have seen before.

The "greater-than" key is used to move to a specified cell. **pascalc** requests the user to enter column and row coordinates for the cell, resets the global variables **curscol** and **cursrow**, and then calls **setcursor** to move the cursor to that cell, resetting the window appropriately. (Actually, *all* commands wind up with a call to **setcursor** to be sure the cursor is left on the correct place on the screen.)

getacc (which stands for "get absolute cell coordinates") is called to obtain column and row coordinates from the user. Upper and lower bounds for the coordinates and defaults are passed to the routine; the coordinates are returned as the parameters **col** and **row**. Here is **getacc**:

```
procedure getacc(crtcol, crtrow, xmin, xmax, xdef, ymin, ymax, ydef: integer;
                                            var col, row: integer);
{ Get absolute cell coordinate from user }
begin { getacc }
   posstr('[..,...]', crtcol, crtrow);
   col := getint(crtcol + 1, crtrow, xmin, xmax, xdef, TRUE);
   row := getint(crtcol + 4, crtrow, ymin, ymax, ydef, TRUE)
end;
```

Now that we have taken care of the recalculation and go-to commands, we can take up the "slash" commands. If the user types the slash, **docommand** prompts for one of the ten valid slash commands, as follows:

```
Command?  (C/E/F/I/L/M/P/Q/S/T):
```

After the user types one of these keys, **docommand** calls the corresponding routine to execute the command.

Easy Commands

Whenever confronted with the need to design a large number of routines, all of seemingly equal importance, a good rule is *Do the easy ones first*. Following that rule, the first command routine to write is **doquit**:

```
procedure doquit;
{ Set up for exit }
begin { doquit }
   alldone := ask('Quit. Are you sure?(Y/N):', inpline, FALSE, TRUE);
   eraseline(inpline)
end;
```

Remember, **pascalc**'s main control loop exits when **alldone** is **TRUE**.

The **dodispmem** routine is almost as easy. It must scan through the free list, adding up the sizes of the free blocks, and then display the sum.

```
procedure dodispmem;
{ Display free memory }
var
    p: headerptr;
    sum: integer;
    s: string;
begin { dodispmem }
    sum := 0;
    p := freelist;
    repeat
        sum := sum + HDRSIZE * p^.size;
        p := p^.next
    until p = freelist;
    itos(sum, 0, s);
    remark(concat(s, ' bytes left'))
end;
```

Also relatively simple is **dotoggle**, which allows the user to display and optionally change 1) the order of recalculation, and 2) whether the recalculation is automatic (after every user entry that can change sheet values) or manual (whenever the user enters the <!> recalculation command). Here is **dotoggle**:

```
procedure dotoggle;
{ Display and (optionally) change recalculation parameters }
var
    ch: char;
    s: string;
begin { dotoggle }
    posstr('Recalculation: Order or Mode?(O/M):', 0, inpline);
    case getkey(ch, ['O', 'M'], TRUE) of
        'O': begin
            if colcalc then
                center('Recalculation is by column', statline)
            else
                center('Recalculation is by row', statline);
            if ask('Change it?(Y/N):', inpline, FALSE, TRUE) then
                colcalc := not colcalc
        end;
        'M': begin
            if autocalc then
                center('Recalculation is automatic', statline)
            else
                center('Recalculation is manual', statline);
            if ask('Change it?(Y/N):', inpline, FALSE, TRUE) then
                autocalc := not autocalc
        end
    end;
    eraseline(inpline);
    eraseline(statline)
end;
```

Displaying and Changing Formatting Parameters

The format command </F> is used to display and optionally change the formatting parameters for the sheet, the current column, or the current cell. After typing the command, the user is prompted

```
Format: Sheet, Column, or One cell?(S/C/O):
```

The user then presses <S> to look at the sheet format, <C> for the column format, and <O> for the cell format. The program displays the requested format and asks if the user wants to change it. If the user wants to change the format, the program asks for and accepts the new format.

All this is accomplished by the **doformat** routine:

```
procedure doformat;
{ Display and (optionally) change cell format }
var
   s: string;
   ch: char;
   f: formatrec;
begin { doformat }
   posstr('Format: Sheet, Column, or One cell?(S/C/O):', 0, inpline);
   ch := getkey(ch, ['S', 'C', 'O'], TRUE);
   eraseline(inpline);
   case ch of
      'S': begin
         fmttos(sheetfmt, s);
         center(concat('Current sheet format is ', s), statline);
         if ask('Change it?(Y/N):', inpline, FALSE, TRUE) then begin
            getformat(sheetfmt);
            setcolpos;
            labelcols(firstcol);
            reformat;
            dispsheet(firstcol, firstrow)
         end
      end;
      'C': begin
         if usesheetfmt[curscol] then
            f := sheetfmt
         else
            f := colfmt[curscol];
         fmttos(f, s);
         center(concat('Current column format is ', s), statline);
         if ask('Change it?(Y/N):', inpline, FALSE, TRUE) then begin
            getformat(f);
            colfmt[curscol] := f;
            usesheetfmt[curscol] := FALSE;
            setcolpos;
            labelcols(firstcol);
            reformat;
            dispsheet(firstcol, firstrow)
         end
      end;
```

```
            '0':
              if curcp <> NIL then
                with curcp^ do
                  if fp <> NIL then
                    with fp^ do begin
                      if not usecolfmt then
                        f := cellfmt
                      else if usesheetfmt[cellcol] then
                        f := sheetfmt
                      else
                        f := colfmt[cellcol];
                      fmttos(f, s);
                      center(concat('Current cell format is ', s), statline);
                      if ask('Change it?(Y/N):', inpline,FALSE,TRUE) then begin
                        getformat(f);
                        cellfmt := f;
                        usecolfmt := FALSE;
                        formatcell(curcp);
                        disprow(cellrow)
                      end
                    end
      end
end;
```

If the sheet format or a column format is changed, the sheet is reformatted and redisplayed; the **setcolpos** routine is also called in these cases to reset the **colpos** array.

New formatting parameters are obtained from the user with **getformat**:

```
procedure getformat(var fmtrec: formatrec);
{ Get new format }
var
   i: integer;
   s: string;
begin { getformat }
   fmttos(fmtrec, s);
   center('New format?:_____', inpline);
   getstring(s, 6, (MAXCRTCOL + 7) div 2, inpline, s,
             ['0'..'9', fmtchar[FIXEDPOINT], fmtchar[SCIENTIFIC], '.'],
                                                                 TRUE);
   eraseline(inpline);
   i := 1;
   stofmt(s, i, fmtrec)
end;
```

New formatting parameters are entered as strings, just as in other **get** routines; this means we need a way to represent the three formatting parameters as strings and to translate back and forth between strings and parameters.

We use a convention for representing formatting parameters similar to one used in FORTRAN; the first character is a letter signifying the formatting mode: <F> for **FIXEDPOINT**, <S> for **SCIENTIFIC**. Then follows the field width, a decimal point, then the number of digits after the decimal. For example, the **initpc** routine initializes the sheet format with the following code:

```
...
sheetfmt.fmt := FIXEDPOINT;
sheetfmt.width := 10;
sheetfmt.ndigs := 2;
...
```

These parameters would be represented by the string <**F10.2**>. As another example, the string <**S0.5**> represents scientific format with five digits after the decimal and a zero field width (which would left-justify the numeric string).

The **stofmt** procedure translates a string into a formatting parameter record:

```
procedure stofmt(var s: string; var i: integer; var fmtrec: formatrec);
{ Extract format paramters from string }
var
    c: char;
begin { stofmt }
    with fmtrec do begin
        if gchar(s, i, c) = fmtchar[FIXEDPOINT] then begin
            fmt := FIXEDPOINT;
            i := i + 1
            end
        else if c = fmtchar[SCIENTIFIC] then begin
            fmt := SCIENTIFIC;
            i := i + 1
            end;
        width := setparam(s, i, MINWIDTH, MAXWIDTH, width);
        if gnbchar(s, i, c) = '.' then begin
            i := i + 1;
            ndigs := setparam(s, i, MINDIGS, MAXDIGS, ndigs)
            end
        end
end;
```

The **fmttos** routine performs the inverse function, translating a set of formatting parameters into a string:

```
procedure fmttos(fmtrec: formatrec; var fmtstr: string);
{ Convert format paramters into Fortran-like format specification }
var
    s1: string;
begin { fmttos }
    fmtstr := '';
    with fmtrec do begin
        addchar(fmtstr, fmtchar[fmt], MAXSTR);
        itos(width, 0, s1);
        fmtstr := concat(fmtstr, s1, '.');
```

```
      itos(ndigs, 0, s1);
      fmtstr := concat(fmtstr, s1)
   end;
end;
```

Copy Command

Copying (also called *replicating* in some commercial programs) is probably *the* single most useful command in **pascalc**. Generally speaking, the command is used to make one or more copies of a user-specified range of cells into another user-specified range of cells. You can copy label cells, formula cells, or both. Our goal is to make this function as flexible as possible.

When the copy command is invoked, the program prompts

```
Copy from [..,...]:[..,...] to [..,...]:[..,...] step [..,...]
```

In words, the program asks the user to enter first a *source* range of cells to copy from, then a *destination* range of cells to copy to, and then column and row increments for the destination range, if necessary.

Ranges may specify *any* rectangular section of the sheet, as we saw in the discussion of the **SUM** function. Individual cells, single rows, and single columns are all special cases of such rectangular sections. In the following discussion, we will use the term "matrix" to denote a general rectangular section.

Since any range can specify a cell, a column, a row, or (in the most general case) a matrix, we have a total of 16 (4 times 4) different cases (cell copied to cell, cell copied to row, cell copied to column, and so on). We will consider the most useful cases here.

1. *Copying one cell to one cell* Here both the source and destination ranges are single cells. In this case the "step" values are not requested from the user. For example,

   ```
   Copy from [1,15]:[1,15] to [10,4]:[10,4] step [..,...]
   ```

   simply copies the cell at [1,15] to [10,4].

2. *Copying a column to a cell* Here the user specifies the source range as a column by entering the column's top and bottom coordinates. The destination range is entered as a *single* cell where the top of the column is to be copied; the remainder of the column is copied to cells below that point. Again, step parameters are not requested. For example,

```
Copy from [2,10]:[2,15] to [5,5]:[5,5] step [..,...]
```

copies the six cells [2,10] through [2,15] (some or all of which may be empty) into a column starting at [5,5] and extending down to [5,10].

3. *Copying a row to a cell* This is similar to case 2, except that we are copying a row instead of a column. The user specifies the left and right coordinates of the row to be copied. The destination range is the cell where the leftmost cell of the row is to be copied; the remainder of the row is copied to cells to the right of that cell. Again, step parameters are not requested.

4. *Copying a matrix to a cell* This is simply a generalization of the previous three cases. Instead of a single cell, a single column, or a single row, a *full range* of positions is given for the source range. Again, no step values are requested. Here is an example:

```
Copy from [1,1]:[10,10] to [21,21]:[21,21] step [..,...]
```

This copies the hundred cells in the 10×10 matrix with upper-left corner **[1,1]** and lower-right corner **[10,10]** (some, again, may be empty) into the same-sized matrix with upper-left corner **[21,21]**.

5. *Copying a cell to a column* Here the source range is, as in case 1, a single cell. The destination range is entered as the top and bottom coordinates of the column the user wants to copy the single cell into. Here a step size *is* requested since it is used to govern whether the cell is copied in every row, every other row, every third row, and so on. For example,

```
Copy from [5,10]:[5,10] to [10,1]:[10,10] step [..,1]
```

copies the cell at [5,10] into the ten cells [10,1], [10,2], ..., [10,10]. If the step size had been specified as 2 instead of 1, the cell would have been copied into every other row: [10,1], [10,3], ..., [10,9].

6. *Copying a cell to a row* This is analogous to case 5. The user specifies a single cell as a source and the left and right coordinates of the row to copy the cell into. A column step size is requested, governing the spacing of the copy.

7. *Copying a cell to a matrix* This is a generalization of cases 5 and 6. The source is a single cell and the user specifies a rectangular matrix as the

destination range. Both column and row step sizes are requested from the user.

8. *Copying a column to a row* Here a column is specified as the source range and a row as the destination. This is a generalization of case 2; instead of copying the specified source column to a single cell, resulting in one copy of the column, the user specifies a horizontal row of "starting positions" for the copied columns, resulting in more than one copy of the column. A step size for the destination row is requested and is used to specify different spacings for the copied columns.

9. *Copying a row to a column* This is analogous to case 8 and a generalization of case 3: a number of copies are made of the source row in a vertical column. The program requests a step size for the column spacing.

The remainder of the cases (column to column, column to matrix, row to row, row to matrix, matrix to column, matrix to row, and matrix to matrix) are generalizations of these nine cases. (Put another way, all the cases discussed previously are special cases of copying a matrix to a matrix.) Frankly, it is hard to see how some of these cases would be used in a practical application, but just possibly the *user* might find this flexibility good for something. It is a mistake to artificially restrict a program's features even if *we* cannot exactly figure out how the features will be used.

A pseudo-code version of **docopy** might look like this:

```
begin
   get source range
   get destination range
   get destination step sizes, if necessary
   for each cell in destination range
      copy source range
   if we ran out of memory
      inform the user
   if recalculation is automatic
      recalculate and reformat sheet
   redisplay sheet
end
```

Here is **docopy** in Pascal:

```
procedure docopy;
{ Do copy command }

var
```

```
      x1, x2, x3, x4, y1, y2, y3, y4, xstep, ystep, xdest, ydest: integer;
      success: boolean;

   {-------------------------------}
   { Modules to be inserted here: }
   {         copymatrix           }
   {-------------------------------}
   begin { docopy }
      posstr('Copy from [..,...]:[..,...] to [..,...]:[..,...] step [..,...]',
                                                                  0, inpline);
      getacc(10, inpline,  1, MAXCOLS, curscol,  1, MAXROWS, cursrow, x1, y1);
      getacc(19, inpline, x1, MAXCOLS,      x1, y1, MAXROWS,      y1, x2, y2);
      getacc(31, inpline,  1, MAXCOLS,      x1,  1, MAXROWS,      y1, x3, y3);
      getacc(40, inpline, x3, MAXCOLS,      x3, y3, MAXROWS,      y3, x4, y4);
      xstep := 1;
      ystep := 1;
      if x4 > x3 then
         xstep := getint(55, inpline, 1, MAXCOLS, xstep, TRUE);
      if y4 > y3 then
         ystep := getint(58, inpline, 1, MAXROWS, ystep, TRUE);
      center('Copying...', statline);
      success := TRUE;
      xdest := x3;
      while (xdest <= x4) and success do begin
         ydest := y3;
         while (ydest <= y4) and success do begin
            success := copymatrix(x1, y1, x2, y2, xdest, ydest);
            ydest := ydest + ystep
         end;
         xdest := xdest + xstep
      end;
      eraseline(statline);
      if not success then
         memout;
      if autocalc then begin
         recalc;
         reformat
      end;
      dispsheet(firstcol, firstrow);
      eraseline(inpline)
   end;
```

docopy calls **getacc** four times to get the source and destination ranges for the copy; the source range is **[x1,y1]:[x2,y2]** and the destination range is **[x3,y3]:[x4,y4]**.

docopy calls **copymatrix** to copy the source range to a cell within the destination range. **copymatrix** returns **FALSE** if the program runs out of memory while copying; this immediately terminates the copying process.

The **copymatrix** routine goes through the source range, copying each non-empty cell in the source range to the specified destination.

```
function copymatrix(x1, y1, x2, y2, xdest, ydest: integer): boolean;
{ Copy pascalc matrix to destination }
var
   x, y: integer;
   cp: cellptr;
   success, done: boolean;
```

```
{-----------------------------}
{ Modules to be inserted here: }
{        copycell              }
{-----------------------------}

begin { copymatrix }
   x := x1;
   success := TRUE;
   while (x <= x2) and success do begin
      cp := colptr[x];
      done := FALSE;
      while (cp <> NIL) and (not done) and success do begin
         y := cp^.cellrow;
         if y >= y1 then
            if y <= y2 then
               success := copycell(cp, xdest + (x - x1), ydest + (y - y1))
            else
               done := TRUE;
         cp := cp^.downptr
      end;
      x := x + 1
   end;
   copymatrix := success
end;
```

copymatrix copies the source range by column; this choice of order only matters if the user for some reason specifies copy parameters that cause two or more source elements to be copied to the same destination cell.

Each non-empty cell is copied to another position with **copycell**:

```
function copycell(cp: cellptr; col, row: integer): boolean;
{ Copy cell to specified position }

var
   newcp: cellptr;
   success: boolean;

begin { copycell }
   success := TRUE;
   if (col >= 1) and (col <= MAXCOLS) and
      (row >= 1) and (row <= MAXROWS) then begin
      newcp := findcell(col, row);
      if newcp <> NIL then
         erasecell(newcp);
      success := storecell(col, row, newcp);
      if success then
         with newcp^ do begin
            if cp^.display <> NIL then
               success := storestr(cp^.display^, display);
            if cp^.fp <> NIL then begin
               success := storeform(fp);
               if success then
                  with fp^ do begin
                     cellstat := cp^.fp^.cellstat;
                     cellval := cp^.fp^.cellval;
                     usecolfmt := cp^.fp^.usecolfmt;
                     cellfmt := cp^.fp^.cellfmt;
                     if cp^.fp^.formula <> NIL then
                        success := storestr(cp^.fp^.formula^, formula)
                  end
            end
         end
```

```
      end
  end;
  copycell := success
end;
```

This routine first checks to be sure the cell coordinates that are to be copied lie within the sheet limits. If a cell currently occupies the position to be copied to, it is erased. Then a new cell is created with **storecell**, and the contents of the source cell are copied to the destination cell using the appropriate memory-allocation procedures. Like **copymatrix**, **copycell** returns **TRUE** if the copy was successful; otherwise it returns **FALSE**.

Erase Command

Just as with a real worksheet, **pascalc**'s users will at times have to erase information from the electronic sheet. This is accomplished with the erase command, </E>. When the command is given, the program prompts

```
Erase: One cell, Columns, Rows, or Sheet?(O/C/R/S):
```

The user types <O> to erase the cell on which the cursor currently sits, <C> to erase a number of columns, <R> to erase a number of rows, and <S> to erase all information on the sheet. In all four cases, **pascalc** asks for confirmation that the user really wants to erase data. If a cell is to be erased, **pascalc** asks

```
Erase cell. Are you sure?(Y/N):
```

If the user answers <Y>, the cell is erased; otherwise it is left alone.

To erase columns, the user is asked

```
Erase how many columns?:
```

The user then types in the number of columns to be erased. Typing a value of 0 leaves the sheet as is. The columns erased are those including and to the right of the current cursor position. After erasure, all the columns to the right of the deleted columns are moved left by the number of columns deleted.

Row deletion is similar to column deletion. **pascalc** asks how many rows are to be deleted, and entering a value of 0 leaves the sheet unaffected. The rows erased are those including and below the current cursor position. Undeleted rows below the cursor are moved up by the number of rows deleted.

An alternative design for column and row deletion might ask the user for the range of column or row numbers to be deleted. This would be a slightly safer design than that used here but also somewhat more difficult to use. (You might try both methods to see which you like better.)

In the case of erasing the entire sheet, the user is asked twice to confirm. First the prompt

```
Erase sheet. Are you sure?(Y/N):
```

and then

```
Erase sheet. ARE YOU CERTAIN?(Y/N):
```

This kind of reconfirmation can be carried too far, but in this case it is probably justified. Accidentally erasing a sheet is a catastrophe.

The **doerase** routine handles cell and sheet erasure itself and delegates the more complex column and row erasures to **erasecols** and **eraserows**. Here is **doerase**:

```
procedure doerase;
{ Do erase command }
var
   ch: char;
   c: integer;

{------------------------------}
{ Modules to be inserted here: }
{        erasecols             }
{        eraserows             }
{------------------------------}
begin { doerase }
   posstr('Erase: One cell, Columns, Rows, or Sheet?(O/C/R/S):', 0, inpline);
   ch := getkey(ch, ['O', 'C', 'R', 'S'], TRUE);
   eraseline(inpline);
   case ch of
      'O': begin
            if ask('Erase cell. Are you sure?(Y/N):', inpline, FALSE, TRUE) then begin
               erasecell(curcp);
               if autocalc then begin
                  recalc;
                  reformat;
                  dispsheet(firstcol, firstrow)
               end
               else
                  disprow(cursrow)
            end;
            eraseline(inpline)
         end;
      'C':
         erasecols;
```

```
            'R':
               eraserows;
            'S': begin
               if ask('Erase sheet. Are you sure?(Y/N):', inpline, FALSE, TRUE) then
                  if ask('Erase sheet. ARE YOU CERTAIN?(Y/N):', inpline, FALSE, TRUE) then
                     center('Erasing...', inpline);
                     for c := 1 to MAXCOLS do
                        while colptr[c] <> NIL do
                           erasecell(colptr[c]);
                     dispsheet(firstcol, firstrow)
                  end;
               eraseline(inpline)
            end
      end
end;
```

Let's consider column erasure first.

```
procedure erasecols;
{ Delete columns from sheet }
var
   n, c: integer;
   cp: cellptr;

begin { erasecols }
   posstr('Erase how many columns?:', 0, inpline);
   n := getint(24, inpline, 0, MAXCOLS - curscol + 1, 0, TRUE);
   if n > 0 then begin
      center('Erasing...', statline);
      for c := curscol to curscol + n - 1 do
         while colptr[c] <> NIL do
            erasecell(colptr[c]);
      for c := curscol to MAXCOLS - n do begin
         colptr[c] := colptr[c + n];
         usesheetfmt[c] := usesheetfmt[c + n];
         colfmt[c] := colfmt[c + n];
         cp := colptr[c];
         while cp <> NIL do begin
            cp^.cellcol := c;
            cp := cp^.downptr
         end
      end;
      for c := MAXCOLS - n + 1 to MAXCOLS do begin
         colptr[c] := NIL;
         usesheetfmt[c] := TRUE
      end;
      setcolpos;
      adjustcols(n);
      eraseline(statline);
      if autocalc then begin
         recalc;
         reformat
      end;
      labelcols(firstcol);
      dispsheet(firstcol, firstrow)
   end;
   eraseline(inpline)
end;
```

For each column to be erased, **erasecols** repeatedly calls **erasecell** to delete the top cell in the column until the column is empty.

Then **erasecols** moves all the columns that are to the right of the deleted columns **n** columns to the left. This can be done rather simply by reassigning column pointers and the rest of the column information variables. We must also go down each column moved to readjust the cells' **cellcol** field. Erasing **n** columns leaves **n** empty columns at the right edge of the sheet, so those columns' pointers are set to **NIL**.

The one remaining task for **erasecols** is to "adjust" the cell references in all the cells' formulas to reflect the new column arrangement. This is managed by the **adjustcols** procedure; it goes through *all* formula cells on the sheet and changes their cell references, if necessary, to refer to the same cells as before.

The logic behind the adjustment is rather complicated. Assume, for example, that we have just deleted **n** columns from the sheet. Then consider a formula cell that contains a reference [col,row]; the column reference **col** can be absolute or relative.

We then have three distinct cases where we have to change the **col** reference:

1. The simplest case is where the column reference **col** is absolute and refers to a column that has been moved. Then we have to replace the reference [col,row] with [col−n,row].

2. If the column reference is relative, we only need to adjust it if the formula cell and the referenced cell have moved *relative to each other*, that is, if they are on opposite sides of the deleted columns. If the formula cell is on the left of the deleted rows and the referenced cell is on the right, the reference [col,row] should be replaced by [col−n,row], since the two cells have moved **n** columns closer and **col** is positive.

3. The other case is where **col** is relative, the formula cell is on the right of the deleted columns, and the referenced cell is on the left. In this case, **col** is negative and we have to make it *less negative* by **n** because the cells have moved **n** columns closer to each other. Thus, the reference [col,row] is replaced by [col+n,row]. (This last case is probably the hardest to understand; indeed, an early version of **pascalc** handled it incorrectly, resulting in a pesky bug.)

Here is **adjustcols**:

```
procedure adjustcols(n: integer);
{ Adjust column references in sheet formulas }

var
   c, col, row, i: integer;
```

```
              cp: cellptr;
              s, s1: string;
              change, relcol, relrow: boolean;
              ch: char;
         begin { adjustcols }
              for c := 1 to MAXCOLS do begin
                   cp := colptr[c];
                   while cp <> NIL do begin
                        with cp^ do
                             if fp <> NIL then
                                  with fp^ do
                                       if formula <> NIL then begin
                                            s := '';
                                            i := 1;
                                            change := FALSE;
                                            while gnbchar(formula^, i, ch) <> chr(0) do
                                                 if ch <> '[' then begin
                                                      addchar(s, ch, MAXSTR);
                                                      i := i + 1
                                                 end
                                                 else begin
                                                      stoc(formula^, i, col, row, relcol, relrow);
                                                      if relcol then begin
                                                           if (c >= curscol) and
                                                                (c + n + col < curscol) then begin { Case 3 }
                                                                change := TRUE;
                                                                col := col + n
                                                           end
                                                           else if (c < curscol) and
                                                                    (c + col >= curscol) then begin { Case 2 }
                                                                change := TRUE;
                                                                col := col - n
                                                           end
                                                      end
                                                      else if (col >= curscol) then begin { Case 1 }
                                                           col := col - n;
                                                           change := TRUE
                                                      end;
                                                      ctos(col, row, relcol, relrow, s1);
                                                      s := concat(s, s1)
                                                 end;
                                            if change then begin
                                                 erasestr(formula);
                                                 if not storestr(s, formula) then
                                                      memout
                                            end
                                       end;
                        cp := cp^.downptr
                   end
              end
         end;
```

adjustcols looks at all formulas on the sheet, changing column references as necessary. If a formula is changed, the old version is deleted with **erasestr** and the new version is stored with **storestr**.

The **eraserows** procedure is analogous to **erasecols**; it is slightly simpler because no "column formats" and the like have to be considered. Here is **eraserows**:

```
procedure eraserows;
{ Delete rows from sheet }
```

```
var
   n, r: integer;
   cp: cellptr;

begin { eraserows }
   posstr('Erase how many rows?:', 0, inpline);
   n := getint(21, inpline, 0, MAXROWS - cursrow + 1, 0, TRUE);
   if n > 0 then begin
      center('Erasing...', statline);
      for r := cursrow to cursrow + n - 1 do
         while rowptr[r] <> NIL do
            erasecell(rowptr[r]);
      for r := cursrow to MAXROWS - n do begin
         rowptr[r] := rowptr[r + n];
         cp := rowptr[r];
         while cp <> NIL do begin
            cp^.cellrow := r;
            cp := cp^.rightptr
         end
      end;
      for r := MAXROWS - n + 1 to MAXROWS do
         rowptr[r] := NIL;
      adjustrows(n);
      eraseline(statline);
      if autocalc then begin
         recalc;
         reformat
      end;
      dispsheet(firstcol, firstrow)
   end;
   eraseline(inpline)
end;
```

We also need an **adjustrows** procedure, exactly analogous to **adjustcols**:

```
procedure adjustrows(n: integer);
{ Adjust row references in sheet formulas }

var
   r, col, row, i: integer;
   cp: cellptr;
   s, s1: string;
   change, relcol, relrow: boolean;
   ch: char;

begin { adjustrows }
   for r := 1 to MAXROWS do begin
      cp := rowptr[r];
      while cp <> NIL do begin
         with cp^ do
            if fp <> NIL then
               with fp^ do
                  if formula <> NIL then begin
                     s := '';
                     i := 1;
                     change := FALSE;
                     while gnbchar(formula^, i, ch) <> chr(0) do
                        if ch <> '[' then begin
                           addchar(s, ch, MAXSTR);
                           i := i + 1
                        end
                        else begin
                           stoc(formula^, i, col, row, relcol, relrow);
                           if relrow then begin
```

```
                              if (r >= cursrow) and
                                 (r + n + row < cursrow) then begin { Case 3 }
                                 change := TRUE;
                                 row := row + n
                              end
                              else if (r < cursrow) and
                                      (r + row >= cursrow) then begin { Case 2 }
                                 change := TRUE;
                                 row := row - n
                              end
                           end
                           else if (row >= cursrow) then begin { Case 1 }
                              row := row - n;
                              change := TRUE
                           end;
                           ctos(col, row, relcol, relrow, s1);
                           s := concat(s, s1)
                        end;
                        if change then begin
                           erasestr(formula);
                           if not storestr(s, formula) then
                              memout
                        end
                     end;
                  cp := cp^.rightptr
               end
         end
end;
```

You may want to think about what happens in **adjustcols** and **adjustrows** when a cell formula refers to a just-deleted cell. Do the routines do the right thing? (What *is* the right thing?)

Insert Command

The insert command (</I>) is used to insert a number of blank rows or columns into the sheet. Existing rows or columns are moved to make room for the new ones. This is analogous to "cut and paste" editing on a paper worksheet, that is, making room for information you need to insert on the sheet without overwriting information you have already entered.

After the command is given, **pascalc** asks

```
Insert. Columns or Rows?(C/R):
```

The user types <C> to enter columns and <R> for rows. Here is **doinsert**:

```
procedure doinsert;
{ Insert empty rows or columns in sheet }
var
   ch: char;
```

```
{----------------------------}
{ Modules to be inserted here: }
{         insertcols           }
{         insertrows           }
{----------------------------}

begin { doinsert }
   posstr('Insert. Columns or Rows?(R/C):', 0, inpline);
   ch := getkey(ch, ['C', 'R'], TRUE);
   eraseline(inpline);
   case ch of
      'R':
         insertrows;
      'C':
         insertcols
   end
end;
```

doinsert calls **insertcols** to insert columns and **insertrows** to insert rows. Let's look at **insertcols** first:

```
procedure insertcols;
{ Insert columns }

var
   c, n: integer;
   cp: cellptr;
   ok: boolean;

begin { insertcols }
   posstr('Insert how many columns?:', 0, inpline);
   n := getint(25, inpline, 0, MAXCOLS - curscol + 1, 0, TRUE);
   if n > 0 then begin
      ok := TRUE;
      c := MAXCOLS;
      while (c >= MAXCOLS - n + 1) and ok do begin
         ok := (colptr[c] = NIL);
         c := c - 1
      end;
      if not ok then begin
         center('Warning: insertion will erase non-empty cells.', statline);
         ok := ask('Insert anyway?(Y/N):', inpline, FALSE, TRUE);
         eraseline(statline)
      end;
      if ok then begin
         center('Inserting...', statline);
         for c := MAXCOLS downto MAXCOLS - n + 1 do
            while colptr[c] <> NIL do
               erasecell(colptr[c]);
         for c := MAXCOLS downto curscol + n do begin
            colptr[c] := colptr[c - n];
            usesheetfmt[c] := usesheetfmt[c - n];
            colfmt[c] := colfmt[c - n];
            cp := colptr[c];
            while cp <> NIL do begin
               cp^.cellcol := c;
               cp := cp^.downptr
            end
         end;
         for c := curscol + n - 1 downto curscol do begin
            colptr[c] := NIL;
            usesheetfmt[c] := TRUE
```

```
            end;
         setcolpos;
         adjustcols(-n);
         eraseline(statline);
         if autocalc then begin
            recalc;
            reformat
         end;
         labelcols(firstcol);
         dispsheet(firstcol, firstrow)
      end
   end;
   eraseline(inpline)
end;
```

insertcols first asks the user for the number of blank columns to insert; a 0 entry causes no change to the sheet. Then it checks to see if inserting the columns would bump any non-empty cells in the rightmost **n** columns off the sheet; if so, it asks the user for confirmation before continuing.

Then **insertcols** deletes the **n** rightmost columns of the sheet to make room for the new columns. If there are any non-empty cells in these columns, the information in them is lost. Next, all the columns between the cursor position and the right edge of the sheet are moved **n** columns to the right by reassigning the column pointers and associated variables and resetting each cell's **cellcol** field, as in **erasecols**. Finally, the column pointers for the newly inserted columns are set to **NIL**.

After the **n** blank columns are inserted, **insertcols** calls **adjustcols** to adjust the column references in the formulas, again as in **erasecols**. In this case all the adjustments are the *reverse* of those required by column deletion; thus, the argument to **adjustcols** is −**n** instead of **n**.

insertrows is analogous to **insertcols**:

```
procedure insertrows;
{ Insert rows }

var
   r, n: integer;
   cp: cellptr;
   ok: boolean;

begin { insertrows }
   posstr('Insert how many rows?:', 0, inpline);
   n := getint(22, inpline, 0, MAXROWS - cursrow + 1, 0, TRUE);
   if n > 0 then begin
      ok := TRUE;
      r := MAXROWS;
      while (r >= MAXROWS - n + 1) and ok do begin
         ok := (rowptr[r] = NIL);
         r := r - 1
      end;
      if not ok then begin
         center('Warning: insertion will erase non-empty cells.', statline);
         ok := ask('Insert anyway?(Y/N):', inpline, FALSE, TRUE);
         eraseline(statline)
```

```
      end;
      if ok then begin
         center('Inserting...', statline);
         for r := MAXROWS downto MAXROWS - n + 1 do
            while rowptr[r] <> NIL do
               erasecell(rowptr[r]);
         for r := MAXROWS downto cursrow + n do begin
            rowptr[r] := rowptr[r - n];
            cp := rowptr[r];
            while cp <> NIL do begin
               cp^.cellrow := r;
               cp := cp^.rightptr
            end
         end;
         for r := cursrow + n - 1 downto cursrow do
            rowptr[r] := NIL;
         adjustrows(-n);
         eraseline(statline);
         if autocalc then begin
            recalc;
            reformat
         end;
         dispsheet(firstcol, firstrow)
      end
   end;
   eraseline(inpline)
end;
```

Loading and Saving

In order to be at all useful, **pascalc** must be able to save the sheet in memory to disk and load it back into memory at a later time. The save (</S>) and load (</L>) commands manage this; the save command writes enough information about the current sheet to a disk file so that when the sheet is retrieved with the load command, the sheet appears (at least outwardly) identical to the one that was saved. Thus, the disk file must somehow store all pertinent information about the sheet—not only the information contained in the cells but also information about the recalculation modes and formatting.

We choose to store the sheet as a text file on disk. This allows the file to be examined and changed with a normal text file editor, a utility presumably available in most systems. This decision also allows us to use the text file tools from Chapter 5 located in the separately compiled **textstuff** unit brought into **pascalc** with the **uses** statement in the main program.

The **dosave** procedure first asks for a file name to save the sheet under. Saving the sheet consists of three parts: (1) saving the sheet parameters, (2) saving the column formats, and (3) saving the information for each non-empty cell on the sheet. Each of these steps is carried out by a separate module: **writesp**, **writecols**, and **writecell**, respectively. All three of these routines pass any I/O error status back to **dosave** so that the user can be informed of anything that has gone wrong. Here is the **dosave** routine:

```
procedure dosave;
{ Save sheet to disk }

var
   f: tfile;
   tf: tfrec;
   status: iostatus;
   name: filename;
   c: integer;
   cp: cellptr;

{------------------------------}
{ Modules to be inserted here: }
{           writesp            }
{           writecols          }
{           writecell          }
{------------------------------}

begin { dosave }
   posstr('Save sheet. Filename?:', 0, inpline);
   gettfname(name, 22, inpline, '');
   if name <> '' then begin
      center(concat('Saving to ', name), statline);
      if tfcreate(f, tf, name, status) = GOODIO then begin
         if writesp(f, tf, status) = GOODIO then
            if writecols(f, tf, status) = GOODIO then begin
               c := 1;
               while (c <= MAXCOLS) and (status = GOODIO) do begin
                  cp := colptr[c];
                  while (cp <> NIL) and (status = GOODIO) do begin
                     status := writecell(f, tf, cp, status);
                     cp := cp^.downptr
                  end;
                  c := c + 1
               end;
               if status <> GOODIO then
                  remark('Error writing cell data')
            end
            else
               remark('Error writing column data')
         else
            remark('Error writing sheet parameters');
         if tfclose(f, tf, status) <> GOODIO then
            remark('Error closing file')
      end
      else
         remark(concat('Can''t create ', name));
      eraseline(statline)
   end;
   eraseline(inpline)
end;
```

The **doload** routine parallels **dosave**: the input file name is requested from the user; and then sheet parameters, column parameters, and cell data are read in by separate routines, **readsp**, **readcols**, and **readcell**:

```
procedure doload;
{ Load sheet from disk }

var
```

```
            f: tfile;
            tf: tfrec;
            status: iostatus;
            name: filename;
   {----------------------------}
   { Modules to be inserted here: }
   {       readsp                 }
   {       readcols               }
   {       readcell               }
   {----------------------------}
   begin { doload }
      posstr('Load sheet. Filename?:', 0, inpline);
      gettfname(name, 22, inpline, '');
      if name <> '' then begin
         center(concat('Loading ', name), statline);
         if tfopen(f, tf, name, status) = GOODIO then begin
            if readsp(f, tf, status) = GOODIO then
               if readcols(f, tf, status) = GOODIO then begin
                  while readcell(f, tf, status) = GOODIO do
                     { nothing };
                  if status <> ENDFILE then
                     remark('Error reading cell data')
                  end
               else
                  remark('Error reading column data')
            else
               remark('Error reading sheet parameters');
            if tfclose(f, tf, status) <> GOODIO then
               remark('Error closing file')
            end
         else
            remark(concat('Can''t open ', name));
         eraseline(statline);
         setcolpos;
         labelcols(firstcol);
         dispsheet(firstcol, firstrow)
         end;
      eraseline(inpline)
   end;
```

Writing and reading sheet parameters is the easiest part. First, consider **writesp**:

```
function writesp(var f: tfile; var tf: tfrec; var status:iostatus):iostatus;
{ Write sheet parameters to disk }
var
   s, s1: string;

begin { writesp }
   s := '';
   addchar(s, boochar[autocalc], MAXSTR);
   addchar(s, boochar[colcalc], MAXSTR);
   fmttos(sheetfmt, s1);
   s := concat(s, s1);
   addchar(s, chr(13), MAXSTR);
   writesp := tfwrite(f, tf, s, status)
end;
```

This translates the sheet parameters **autocalc**, **colcalc**, and **sheetfmt** into a string and writes the string as the first line of the text file: Boolean **TRUE** is converted into a <Y> character, Boolean **FALSE** into <N>. Thus, if **autocalc** is **TRUE**, **colcalc** is **FALSE**, and **sheetfmt** is <F10.2>, the first line of the text file becomes

YNF10.2

The **readsp** routine reads the first line of the file and translates it back into the sheet parameters **autocalc**, **colcalc**, and **sheetfmt**. Here is **readsp**:

```
function readsp(var f: tfile; var tf: tfrec; var status: iostatus): iostatus;
{ Read sheet paramters from file }
var
   s: string;
   i: integer;
   ch: char;
begin { readsp }
   if tfread(f, tf, s, MAXSTR, status) = GOODIO then begin
      autocalc := (gchar(s, 1, ch) = boochar[TRUE]);
      colcalc := (gchar(s, 2, ch) = boochar[TRUE]);
      i := 3;
      stofmt(s, i, sheetfmt)
   end;
   readsp := status
end;
```

Writing and reading the column formats to and from the file are only slightly less easy. We only need to store formats for the columns that have been assigned special formatting parameters by the user via the format command. But we also need to somehow save data that tells us which columns have the special formatting.

There are a number of ways we could accomplish this; our method will be first to write a 63-character string to the file showing which columns have special formats, with one character per sheet column. If the ith sheet column has special formatting, the ith character of the string will be <N>; otherwise it will be <Y>. Thus, if columns 1, 2, 5, 6, and 10 have specified formats, the string will be

NNYYNNYYYNYYYYYYYYYYYYYYYYYYYYYYYYYYYYYYYYYYYYYYYYYYYYYYYYYYYYY

After this string is written to the output file, we will write the string representation of each special format, one per line. In the preceding example, five lines would be written, each one corresponding to an <N> in the 63-character string.

Here is **writecols**.

```
function writecols(var f:tfile; var tf: tfrec; var status: iostatus): iostatus;
{ Write column data to file; assumes MAXCOLS < MAXSTR }

var
   i: integer;
   s: string;

begin { writecols }
   s := '';
   for i := 1 to MAXCOLS do
      addchar(s, boochar[usesheetfmt[i]], MAXSTR);
   addchar(s, chr(13), MAXSTR);
   if tfwrite(f, tf, s, status) = GOODIO then begin
      i := 1;
      while (i <= MAXCOLS) and (status = GOODIO) do begin
         if not usesheetfmt[i] then begin
            fmttos(colfmt[i], s);
            addchar(s, chr(13), MAXSTR);
            status := tfwrite(f, tf, s, status)
         end;
         i := i + 1
      end
   end;
   writecols := status
end;
```

The **readcols** routine first reads in the 63-character string showing which columns have special formats. Then, for each specially formatted column (each <N> in the string), **readcols** reads the line from the file containing the column's format string:

```
function readcols(var f: tfile; var tf: tfrec; var status: iostatus): iostatus;
{ Read column data }

var
   s: string;
   i, j: integer;
   ch: char;

begin { readcols }
   if tfread(f, tf, s, MAXSTR, status) = GOODIO then begin
      for i := 1 to MAXCOLS do
         usesheetfmt[i] := (gchar(s, i, ch) = boochar[TRUE]);
      i := 1;
      while (i <= MAXCOLS) and (status = GOODIO) do begin
         if not usesheetfmt[i] then
            if tfread(f, tf, s, MAXSTR, status) = GOODIO then begin
               j := 1;
               stofmt(s, j, colfmt[i])
            end;
         i := i + 1
      end;
   end;
   readcols := status
end;
```

Now let's consider writing and reading each non-empty cell's data to and from the file. For each cell we have to store the cell's coordinates, its display field, and some indication of whether the cell contains a formula or a label. If the cell contains a formula, we must store the **forminfo** data as well: the formula itself, the cell's value, calculational error status, and formatting information.

There are a lot of different ways we could go about this. We choose the following method: each non-empty cell on the sheet is represented by either two or three lines in the text file. Three lines are used only if the cell contains a formula; then the third line is the formula string itself.

The second line is the display field for the cell.

The first line contains everything else necessary for storing the cell information. The first item in the line is the location of the cell, expressed in [<column>,<row>] format. The character immediately following the coordinate pair indicates whether the cell contains a label or a formula: <L> if a label, <F> if a formula.

If the cell contains a label, no further information is stored on the first line. If the cell contains a formula, however, we press on. The next character after the <F> is for the **cellstat** field. It is a blank if **cellstat** is **OK**; otherwise it contains a letter indicating the error status: <O> for overflow, <U> for underflow, and <Z> for division by zero.

After that comes the cell-formatting information. If the **usecolfmt** field is **TRUE** (that is, the cell uses the default column format) a <Y> character is placed at the next position in the line. If **usecolfmt** is **FALSE** (the user has specified a format for the cell), an <N> character is placed at the next position, followed by the string representation of the formatting parameters and a comma to separate the format string from the following data. Finally, the value of the cell is appended to the string: first the value of **cellval.expo**, then a comma, then **cellval.frac**.

To see how this works, consider the following examples.

The simplest case is a cell containing a label. If the cell at [10,5] contains the label <Yearly Sales>, the lines stored in the file for the cell would be

```
[10,5]L
Yearly Sales
```

For a cell containing a formula things are slightly more complex. Assume the cell at [3,23] contains the formula **SUM([+0,−10]:[+0,−2])** and the value of the cell is 1223.45. Also assume the cell uses the default column format F10.2. Then the following three lines would be written to the text file for the cell:

```
[3,23]F Y68,122345000000
    1223.45
SUM([+0,-10]:[+0,-2])
```

The first line contains the coordinates [**3,23**], an <**F**> indicating that the cell contains a formula, a blank indicating a **calcstatus** field of **OK**, a <**Y**> indicating that the cell uses the default column format, and the numeric value of the cell shown as the **frac** and **expo** fields of the **xreal** value. (We assume **FIXSIZE** is 12 here.)

If, instead of the default column format, the cell had its own formatting parameters, they would be inserted in the first line. Suppose, for example, the cell format was specified by the user to be F8.2. Then the first line would become

[3,23]F NF8.2,68,122345000000

The display field on the second line would also change, reflecting the new format.

Translating and writing the data for a single cell to the output file are done with **writecell**:

```
function writecell(var f: tfile; var tf: tfrec; cp: cellptr;
                                  var status: iostatus): iostatus;
{ Write cell data to file }
var
    s1, s2, s3: string[81];      { MAXSTR + 1 -- allow room for CR at end }
    s: string;
begin { writecell }
   with cp^ do begin
      s2 := '';
      s3 := '';
      ctos(cellcol, cellrow, FALSE, FALSE, s1);
      if display <> NIL then
         s2 := display^;
      if fp = NIL then   { label }
         addchar(s1, 'L', MAXSTR)
      else { formula }
         with fp^ do begin
            addchar(s1, 'F', MAXSTR);
            addchar(s1, statchar[cellstat], MAXSTR);
            addchar(s1, boochar[usecolfmt], MAXSTR);
            if not usecolfmt then begin
               fmttos(cellfmt, s);
               s1 := concat(s1, s, ',')
            end;
            itos(cellval.expo, 0, s);
            s1 := concat(s1, s, ',');
            ftos(cellval.frac, 0, 0, s);
            s1 := concat(s1, s);
            if formula <> NIL then
               s3 := formula^
         end;
      addchar(s1, chr(13), MAXSTR);
      addchar(s2, chr(13), MAXSTR);
      addchar(s3, chr(13), MAXSTR);
      if tfwrite(f, tf, s1, status) = GOODIO then
         if tfwrite(f, tf, s2, status) = GOODIO then
```

```
            if fp <> NIL then
                status := tfwrite(f, tf, s3, status)
        end;
    writecell := status
end;
```

readcell reverses the process, reading the lines in from the text file, and then creating a new cell at the specified location with the specified values:

```
function readcell(var f: tfile; var tf: tfrec; var status: iostatus): iostatus;
{ Read cell data from file }
var
    s1, s2, s3: string[81];        { MAXSTR + 1 -- allow room for CR at end }
    i, col, row: integer;
    success, junk: boolean;
    c: char;
    cp: cellptr;
begin { readcell }
    if tfread(f, tf, s1, MAXSTR + 1, status) = GOODIO then begin
        i := 1;
        stoc(s1, i, col, row, junk, junk);
        if (col>=1) and (col<=MAXCOLS) and (row>=1) and (row<=MAXROWS) then begin
            cp := findcell(col, row);
            if cp <> NIL then
                erasecell(cp);
            success := storecell(col, row, cp);
            if success then
                with cp^ do
                    if tfread(f, tf, s2, MAXSTR + 1, status) = GOODIO then begin
                        chopchar(s2);
                        if s2 <> '' then
                            success := storestr(s2, display);
                        if success and (gchar(s1, i, c) = 'F') then begin { formula }
                            success := storeform(fp);
                            if success then
                                with fp^ do begin
                                    if gchar(s1, i + 1, c) = statchar[OK] then
                                        cellstat := OK
                                    else if c = statchar[OVERFLOW] then
                                        cellstat := OVERFLOW
                                    else if c = statchar[UNDERFLOW] then
                                        cellstat := UNDERFLOW
                                    else
                                        cellstat := ZERODIVIDE;
                                    usecolfmt := (gchar(s1, i + 2, c) = boochar[TRUE]);
                                    i := i + 3;
                                    if not usecolfmt then begin
                                        stofmt(s1, i, cellfmt);
                                        if gnbchar(s1, i, c) = ',' then
                                            i := i + 1
                                    end;
                                    cellval.expo := setparam(s1,i,MINEXP,MAXEXP,MINEXP);
                                    if gnbchar(s1, i, c) = ',' then
                                        i := i + 1;
                                    junk := stof(s1, i, 0, cellval.frac);
                                    if tfread(f,tf,s3,MAXSTR+1,status)=GOODIO then begin
                                        chopchar(s3);
                                        if s3 <> '' then
                                            success := storestr(s3, formula)
                                    end
                                end
```

```
                    end
                end;
            if not success then begin
                memout;
                status := ENDFILE
                end
            end
        end;
        readcell := status
end;
```

You may want to experiment with different methods of storing and retrieving sheet data. Decreasing the time needed to write and read the sheet to and from the disk would be an improvement, as would decreasing the amount of space a sheet data file uses on the disk.

Printing the Sheet

The last command to consider is the print command (</P>), which prints a user-specified section of the sheet on the printer. After the command is given, **pascalc** asks the user

```
Print sheet. Are you sure?(Y/N):
```

If the user answers <Y>, the program presents a "print parameter" screen, similar to the one in the **print** program in Chapter Five. The user may set the number of lines per printed page, initialization and termination strings to be sent to the printer, and left and right margins. In addition, the user also specifies the section of the sheet to be printed by entering the section's upper-left and lower-right corners.

After the parameters have been changed to reflect the user's desires, the section of the sheet is printed and the worksheet is redisplayed.

This section of the program reuses quite a bit of code from Chapter Five's **print** program. Here is the module-nesting arrangement for **doprint**:

```
doprint
        changepps
        printsheet
                    decode *
                            gesc *
                                    htoc*
                    initprinter *
                    termprinter *
                    lskip
                    printrow
                            lprint *
```

The only new routines to write are **doprint**, **changepps**, **printsheet**, **lskip**, and **printrow**; the remainder have previously been designed in Chapter Five. Here is **doprint**:

```
{$v-}
procedure doprint;
{ Print sheet }

const
   LSTRSIZE = 255;

type
   longstring = string[LSTRSIZE];

{-----------------------------}
{ Modules to be inserted here: }
{         changepps           }
{         printsheet          }
{-----------------------------}

begin { doprint }
   if ask('Print sheet. Are you sure?(Y/N):', inpline, FALSE, TRUE) then begin
      changepps;
      printsheet;
      drawsheet;
      labelcols(firstcol);
      labelrows(firstrow);
      dispsheet(firstcol, firstrow)
   end
end;
{$v+}
```

Here is **changepps**:

```
procedure changepps;
{ Change print parameters }

var
   margin: integer;
   s1, s2: string;

begin { changepps }
   crt(CLEAR);
   margin := (MAXCRTCOL - 39) div 2;
   center('Print Parameters', 2);
   itos(pagelen, 0, s1);
   posstr(concat('Page length (lines):', s1), margin, 4);
   itos(lmarg, 0, s1);
   posstr(concat('Left margin:', s1), margin, 6);
   itos(rmarg, 0, s1);
   posstr(concat('Right margin:', s1), margin + 17, 6);
   ctos(printx1, printy1, FALSE, FALSE, s1);
   posstr(concat('Upper left corner:', s1), margin, 8);
   ctos(printx2, printy2, FALSE, FALSE, s1);
   posstr(concat('Lower right corner:', s1), margin, 10);
   posstr(concat('Printer init. string:', pinit), margin, 12);
   posstr(concat('Printer term. string:', pterm), margin, 14);
   while ask('Any changes?(Y/N):', MAXCRTROW - 1, FALSE, TRUE) do begin
      pagelen := getint(margin + 20, 4, MTOP+MBOT+1, MAXPLEN, pagelen, TRUE);
      lmarg := getint(margin + 12, 6, 0, LSTRSIZE - 1, lmarg, TRUE);
      rmarg := getint(margin + 30, 6, lmarg + 1, LSTRSIZE, rmarg, TRUE);
      getacc(margin + 18, 8, 1, MAXCOLS, printx1, 1, MAXROWS, printy1, printx1,
                                                                      printy1);
```

```
            getacc(margin + 19, 10, printx1, MAXCOLS, printx2, printy1, MAXROWS,
                                              printy2, printx2, printy2);
            getstring(pinit, PCOMSIZE, margin + 21, 12, pinit, [' '..'~'], FALSE);
            getstring(pterm, PCOMSIZE, margin + 21, 14, pterm, [' '..'~'], FALSE)
      end
end;
```

After the parameters have been set, **doprint** calls **printsheet**:

```
procedure printsheet;
{ Print specified region of sheet }

const
   PRINTER = 6;              { Unit number of printer }

var
   status: iostatus;
   r, lineno: integer;

{---------------------------------}
{ Modules to be inserted here:    }
{       decode                    }
{       initprinter               }
{       termprinter               }
{       lskip                     }
{       printrow                  }
{---------------------------------}

begin { printsheet }
   if initprinter(pinit, status) = GOODIO then begin
      lineno := 1;
      r := printy1;
      while (status = GOODIO) and (r <= printy2) do begin
         if lineno <= 1 then begin
            status := lskip(MTOP, status);
            lineno := lineno + MTOP
         end;
         if status = GOODIO then begin
            status := printrow(r, status);
            lineno := lineno + 1;
            r := r + 1
         end;
         if (status = GOODIO) and (lineno >= pagelen - MBOT) then begin
            status := lskip(pagelen - lineno + 1, status);
            lineno := 1
         end
      end;
      if (lineno > 1) and (status = GOODIO) then
         status := lskip(pagelen - lineno + 1, status);
      status := termprinter(pterm, status)
   end
end;
```

There is nothing too complicated about **printsheet**. It initializes the printer and then calls **printrow** to print every row in the specified range. The remainder of the routine simply adds the page breaks at the right places. After the sheet is printed, **printsheet** calls **lskip** to advance the printer to the top of the next page and **termprinter** to send the termination string, if any.

The **lskip** routine is also easy:

```
function lskip(n: integer; var status: iostatus): iostatus;
{ Send n carriage returns to printer }
var
   ch: char;
begin { lskip }
   status := GOODIO;
   ch := chr(13);
   {$i-}
   while (n > 0) and (status = GOODIO) do begin
      unitwrite(PRINTER, ch, 1);
      status := ioresult;
      n := n - 1
   end;
   {$i+}
   lskip := status
end;
```

The real work is done in **printrow**. Instead of the CRT acting as a window onto the worksheet, in **printrow**, the printer takes that role. The logic we use is similar to that in **disprow**: for each cell in the row, calculate whether it appears between the specified left and right margins, and whether it is clipped on either end.

```
function printrow(r: integer; var status: iostatus): iostatus;
{ Print one row of sheet }
var
   s: longstring;
   cp: cellptr;
   done: boolean;
   c1, c2, ptrcol, ls: integer;
{-----------------------------------}
{ Modules to be inserted here: }
{          lprint                   }
{-----------------------------------}
begin { printrow }
   ls := 0;
   {$r-}
   fillchar(s[1], rmarg, ' ');
   cp := rowptr[r];
   done := FALSE;
   while (cp <> NIL) and not done do begin
      with cp^ do begin
         ptrcol := colpos[cellcol] - colpos[firstcol] + lmarg + 1;
         if (cellcol > printx2) or (ptrcol > rmarg) then
            done := TRUE
         else if display <> NIL then begin
            c1 := max(1, lmarg - ptrcol + 2);
            c2 := min(length(display^), rmarg - ptrcol + 1);
            if c2 > c1 then begin
               moveleft(display^[c1], s[ptrcol], c2 - c1 + 1);
               ls := max(ls, ptrcol + c2 - c1)
            end
         end
      end;
      cp := cp^.rightptr
   end;
```

```
      if ls > 0 then begin
         s[0] := chr(ls);
         status := lprint(s, status)
      end;
      {$r+}
      if status = GOODIO then
         status := lskip(1, status);
      printrow := status
end;
```

The line to be output to the printer is accumulated in the string s, and the string's current length is kept in the variable ls. After all the cells in the row have been examined (or we have gone off the right margin), s is printed by **lprint**.

Suggestions

pascalc is a large program, and the larger the program the more room there is for improvement. As with nearly all interactive programs, the faster you can make **pascalc** run, the better. If you made changes to **calc** to improve its efficiency, it is likely the same improvements will help **pascalc**. Your CRT may support advanced functions such as line insertion and deletion, which may be used to greatly improve the speed at which the sheet is scrolled.

Another area to investigate is a more efficient use of memory; this will allow **pascalc** to handle larger sheets in the same amount of memory as before.

Here is one specific suggestion: write a version of **pascalc** to "pre-interpret" formulas when they are first entered by the user. A good deal of the time **pascalc** spends is in recalculating the entered formulas, which involves a lot of time-consuming conversions in routines like **stox** and **stoc**. Pre-interpreting the formulas would involve doing these conversions once and then somehow storing the *actual numbers* in the formula instead of their string representations.

You may also want to investigate rearranging the formulas into *postfix* notation, which can then be easily evaluated with a single non-recursive routine. (See the recommended reading if you are not familiar with the term.)

There are many features (a square root function, trigonometric functions, logarithms, and an exponentiation operator, for example) that could be added to **pascalc** to increase its flexibility. Calendar arithmetic could also be added.

You might also find it useful to develop different versions of **pascalc** for different applications. For use in statistical work, built-in functions to calculate means, standard deviations, chi-squares, and so on would be worthwhile. An engineer might want a built-in matrix inversion routine. A manager might want functions for evaluating time series, such as moving averages, linear regression, and the like.

More flexible formatting would be useful: allow centering within a column, embedded commas in numbers, "floating" dollar signs, percent signs, and so on. You may find it useful to add a sorting command that would automatically arrange rows or columns in alphabetic or numeric order.

Other features could be added to increase **pascalc**'s ease of use. For example, the only way to alter a formula or label in this version of **pascalc** is to retype the whole thing, even if only minor changes are desired. A more sophisticated editing feature either added to **getstring** or implemented as a command within **pascalc** would be nice. Another idea is to allow cells to be named by using identifiers of mnemonic significance. For example, say the cell at **[5,1]** contains an interest rate. The user could then name the cell **INTRATE** and use the identifier in further formulas instead of the cell coordinates.

A very challenging project would be to implement an "undo" command, which would reverse the effects of the last command the user entered.

These suggestions only scratch the surface of possible improvements, of course. No doubt others have occurred to you already.

Recommended Reading

Different methods of dynamic memory management are analyzed in detail in the classic *Fundamental Algorithms* by D. Knuth (Addison-Wesley, 1973). The particular algorithms used here for **alloc** and **free** were adapted from ones presented in *The C Programming Language* by B. Kernighan and D. Ritchie (Prentice-Hall, 1978). Their versions of **alloc** and **free** are written in C, a language that does not require the tricky coding we used here.

Sparse matrices, FIFO lists, circular buffers, and postfix notation are discussed in books on data structures. In addition to Knuth's book, you may wish to consult *Data Structures Using Pascal* by A. Tenenbaum and M. Augenstein (Prentice-Hall, 1981) and *Data Structures and Their Implementation* by R. Baron and L. Shapiro (Van Nostrand Reinhold, 1980).

Information on the type-ahead buffer of Apple Pascal was obtained from *Attach-BIOS for Apple II Pascal 1.1* by B. Haynes (International Apple Core, P.O. Box 976, Daly City, California 94017). This document contains a wealth of information on how the Apple Pascal I/O system works.

A good discussion of program design philosophies and methods, including testing, may be found in *Techniques of Program Structure and Design* by E. Yourdon (Prentice-Hall, 1975).

Appendix A

Portability Problems And Solutions

Standard Pascal often makes it difficult to write portable programs that can be run on a large number of computers with little or no change. In designing the programs in this book, we decided to sacrifice a certain amount of program portability in order to improve the programs' clarity, efficiency, and usefulness. As a result, the programs are not entirely portable; they make use of a number of non-standard features of Apple Pascal version 1.1, features that may not be offered by your implementation of Pascal.

In this appendix we show how some of the non-standard Apple Pascal features we have used may be programmed in other versions of Pascal. Wherever possible, we designed portable solutions that may be used in any version of Pascal that supports Standard Pascal as a subset. In those cases where no portable solution is available, we have at least tried to provide some help.

Strings

Nearly all of our programs make use of the Apple/UCSD built-in **string** type. Unfortunately, Standard Pascal offers no general-purpose string-handling routines.

Portable Representation There are a number of methods we could use to define a string data type in a portable way. Of course, we need to represent the string characters themselves; we also need to somehow represent the *current number of characters* in the string since we want strings to hold different numbers of characters.

Our solution is to define the string data type as a record containing the length of the string and as an array containing the characters in the string.

```
<type>
   string = packed record
      length: 0..MAXSTR;
      c: packed array [1..MAXSTR] of char
   end;
```

In this representation, a string variable s has the length **s.length** (thus, our calls to the Apple/UCSD Pascal function **length(s)** can be replaced by the expression **s.length**). The **i**th character in the string is **s.c[i]**. The string may contain up to **MAXSTR** characters, where **MAXSTR** is a previously defined integer constant.

Output   In order to display a string, we can no longer use the built-in routine **write**; Standard Pascal's **write** (and **writeln**) can only handle reals, integers, characters, Booleans, and *fixed-length* packed arrays of characters. Thus, we need a special routine to output the string one character at a time.

```
procedure writestr(var s: string);
{ Write string }
var
   i: integer;
begin { writestr }
   with s do
      for i := 1 to length do
         write(c[i])
end;
```

Assignment   When strings are defined as record types, there is no portable way to specify a string constant in a program source text. We cannot make a direct assignment of a string constant to a string variable as we can in Apple and UCSD Pascal. For example, if **s** is a **string** variable as previously defined, we cannot simply write

```
s := 'Colette';
```

(This assignment would work in Standard Pascal if and only if s had been defined as

```
<var>
   s: packed array [1..7] of char;        { 7 = # of characters
                                              in 'Colette' }
```

but then s could not be used to hold strings longer or shorter than seven characters.)

Instead of using direct assignment, we must assign our strings character by character, as in the following:

```
...
with s do begin
   length := 7;
   c[1] := 'C';
   c[2] := 'o';
   c[3] := 'l';
   c[4] := 'e';
   c[5] := 't';
   c[6] := 't';
   c[7] := 'e'
end;
...
```

This "solution" for string assignment is bulky and becomes worse as strings get longer.

Comparisons Direct string comparison with the standard relational operators (<, >, =, and so on) also cannot be done portably under this arrangement. To compare two strings, we need to write another routine. **strcomp** accepts two strings as arguments and returns 0 if the two strings are equal, −1 if the first argument is less than the second, and +1 if the first argument is greater than the second:

```
function strcomp(var s1, s2: string): integer;
{ Compare strings; return -1,0,+1 if s1 <,=,> s2 }
var
   i: integer;
   c1, c2: char;
begin { strcomp }
   i := 0;
   repeat
      i := i + 1;
      c1 := gchar(s1, i, c1);
      c2 := gchar(s2, i, c2)
   until (c1 <> c2) or (c1 = chr(0));
   if c1 = c2 then { Strings are equal }
      strcomp := 0
   else if c1 < c2 then
      strcomp := -1
   else
      strcomp := 1
end;
```

To see how this works, consider the following program segment (extracted from **insertnode** in Chapter Four), which makes use of Apple Pascal's ability to compare strings directly:

```
...
if id < p^.name then
   insertnode(p^.left, id, x)
else if id > p^.name then
   insertnode(p^.right, id, x)
else
   p^.value := x
...
```

Using **strcomp** instead of the non-portable direct comparison would change the code into

```
...
case strcomp(id, p^.name) of
   -1:
       insertnode(p^.left, id, x);
    0:
       p^.value := x;
    1:
       insertnode(p^.right, id, x)
end
...
```

String-Manipulation Routines   We also need to rewrite any non-portable string-manipulation routines to manipulate the portable string representation instead. For example, here is a new version of **gchar**:

```
function gchar(var s: string; i: integer; var ch: char): char;
{ Extract character from string }
begin { gchar }
   with s do
      if (i < 1) or (i > length) then
         ch := chr(0)
      else
         ch := c[i];
   gchar := ch
end;
```

Our **addchar** routine, which appends a character to the end of a string, must also be modified, as follows:

```
procedure addchar(var s: string; ch: char; maxlen: integer);
{ Add character to end of string }
begin { addchar }
   with s do
```

```
            if length < maxlen then begin
               length := length + 1;
               c[length] := ch
            end
end;
```

A new version of **chopchar**, which chops off the character at the end of a string, is also easy to write:

```
procedure chopchar(var s: string);
{ Delete character from end of string }
begin { chopchar }
   with s do
      if length > 0 then
         length := length - 1
end;
```

In addition to rewriting our own string-manipulation routines, we must also design versions of the built-in Apple/UCSD Pascal string-manipulation routines. For example, a portable version of **concat**, which concatenates two strings, can be written as follows:

```
procedure concat(var s1, s2, s3: string);
{ Concatenate s1 and s2 into s3 }
var
   i: integer;
begin
   s3 := s1;
   with s2 do
      for i := 1 to length do
         addchar(s3, c[i], MAXSTR)
end;
```

Here the two strings **s1** and **s2** are combined into the string **s3**, which is returned to the calling routine as a **var** parameter; this is slightly less convenient than the Apple/UCSD version of **concat**, which accepts an arbitrary number of string arguments and returns the concatenation of the strings as its function result. Neither of these features can be accomplished in a portable Pascal routine.

We have also used the Apple/UCSD built-in routine **copy** to extract a substring from a string. Here is a portable version:

```
procedure copy(var s: string; i, n: integer; var substr: string);
{ Copy n characters starting at ith character of s into substr }
var
   last: integer;
begin { copy }
```

```
        substr.length := 0;
        i := max(1, i);
        last := min(i + n - 1, s.length);
        while i <= last do begin
            addchar(substr, s.c[i], MAXSTR);
            i := i + 1
        end
end;
```

This version of **copy** moves the **n** characters starting at the ith character of **s** into the string **substr**. Again, this is a little less convenient than the Apple/UCSD Pascal version of **copy**, which returns the substring as its function result.

A portable version of **pos**, which searches for a substring within a string, is also not too hard to write.

```
function pos(var pat, s: string; i: integer): integer;
{ Search for occurrance of pat in s starting at ith character of s }
var
    j, k: integer;
    found: boolean;
    c1, c2: char;
begin { pos }
    found := FALSE;
    while (gchar(s, i, c1) <> chr(0)) and not found do begin
        j := i;
        k := 1;
        c2 := gchar(pat, k, c2);
        while (c2 <> chr(0)) and (c1 = c2) do begin
            j := j + 1;
            k := k + 1;
            c1 := gchar(s, j, c1);
            c2 := gchar(pat, k, c2)
        end;
        if c2 = chr(0) then
            found := TRUE
        else
            i := i + 1
    end;
    if found then
        pos := i
    else
        pos := 0
end;
```

This version of **pos** searches for the string **pat** within the string **s**, starting the search at the ith character of **s**. (This calling sequence is slightly more useful than the Apple/UCSD version of **pos**, which can only search from the beginning of **s**.) If **pat** is found in **s**, **pos** returns the index in **s** at which **pat** was found. Otherwise, **pos** returns 0.

Summary Obviously, we can do just about anything with these "portable" strings that we could do with the built-in Apple/UCSD string type we have used throughout the book. There are a number of major disadvantages to this portable string representation, however. In addition to not being able to initialize strings concisely, we are not allowed to pass string constants portably to procedures and functions. For example, the following is legal in Apple/UCSD Pascal:

```
...
center('Press <RETURN> to continue.', MAXCRTROW)
...
```

Using the portable string representation, we must write

```
...
with tempstr do begin
   length := 27;
   c[1] := 'P';
   c[2] := 'r';
   c[3] := 'e';
   ...
   c[25] := 'u';
   c[26] := 'e';
   c[27] := '.'
end;
center(tempstr, MAXCRTROW)
...
```

and of course **tempstr** must be declared as a string variable.

Another major disadvantage of the portable approach is its inflexibility in storage requirements. By definition, the constant **MAXSTR** must be set to the number of characters in the *longest possible* string. If the strings in a given program have widely different lengths, much memory is wasted in storing the shorter strings. Apple and UCSD Pascal alleviate this problem somewhat by allowing the programmer to define different "flavors" of the string data type with different maximum lengths, as in the following:

```
<type>
   identifier = string[IDSIZE];
   word = string[MAXWORD];
   longstring = string[LSTRSIZE];
```

Apple and UCSD Pascal remember that all these different types are actually strings; all string-manipulation routines work with them. Standard Pascal does not allow even the most innocent intermixing of types, however.

One possible escape from this problem lies in the ISO Standard Pascal *conformant array*, an optional feature added to Wirth's original Pascal. (It is optional in the sense that a given Pascal may omit it and still claim to adhere to the ISO Standard.) Within limits, this feature provides the ability to write general-purpose routines to handle arrays of different sizes, including arrays of characters. The conformant array feature is not available in many Pascal implementations, but if your Pascal offers it, you may wish to explore its capabilities.

A final note. As previously stated, most Pascal implementations provide some sort of non-portable string-like data type as an extension to Standard Pascal. It is probably a better idea to adapt the programs in this book to your own Pascal's string type than to put up with the drawbacks of the portable implementation given here.

Long Integers

Another useful but non-standard data type provided by Apple and UCSD Pascal is the *long integer*. We have used long integers primarily in the **fixed** data type, defined as

```
<type>
   fixed = integer[FIXSIZE];
```

where **FIXSIZE** is a constant set to the maximum number of digits in the numbers. Again, our goal here is to show how the benefits of an extended-precision data type may be obtained in a portable way.

Portable Representation   There are a number of different methods we could use to represent a long integer. The method demonstrated here is to store the individual decimal digits of the number in an array, as follows:

```
<type>
   fixed = record
      sign: -1..1;
      digit: packed array [1..FIXSIZE] of 0..9
   end;
```

In this representation, a **fixed** variable **f** has a **sign** field of -1 if it is negative and 1 if it is 0 or positive. The number **f.digit[1]** is the units digit of the number, **f.digit[2]** is the tens digit, and so on. A clever compiler will pack these digits into a *binary-coded decimal* (BCD) representation, storing two digit fields per byte.

Assignment Just as with our portable strings, direct assignment is no longer possible to variables of the **fixed** data type. Where in Apple/UCSD Pascal we could write

```
f := 314159;
```

in the portable representation we have to assign the digits one by one, as follows:

```
with f do begin
   sign := 1;
   digit[1] := 9;
   digit[2] := 5;
   digit[3] := 1;
   digit[4] := 4;
   digit[5] := 1;
   digit[6] := 3;
   for i := 7 to FIXSIZE do
      digit [i] := 0
end;
```

(Here we are assuming **FIXSIZE** is at least 6.)

Conversions This arrangement calls for new versions of **ftos** (which converts a **fixed** number to a string) and **stof** (which converts a string to a **fixed** number). First, here is a new version of **ftos**; note that we retain the option of inserting a decimal point at a specified place in the number:

```
procedure ftos(var f: fixed; width, ndigs: integer; var s: string);
{ Convert fixed to string }
var
   nc, i, j: integer;
   ch: char;
begin { ftos }
   with s, f do begin
      length := 0;
      i := FIXSIZE;
      while (i > 1) and (digit[i] = 0) do
         i := i - 1;
      nc := 0;
      repeat
         nc := nc + 1;
         addchar(s, chr(digit[nc] + 48), MAXSTR);
         if nc = ndigs then
            addchar(s, '.', MAXSTR)
      until (nc >= i) and (nc > ndigs);
      if sign < 0 then
         addchar(s, '-', MAXSTR);
      while length < width do
         addchar(s, ' ', MAXSTR);
      i := 1;
```

```
            j := length;
            while i < j do begin
               ch := c[i];
               c[i] := c[j];
               c[j] := ch;
               i := i + 1;
               j := j - 1
            end
      end
end;
```

This version of **ftos** assumes that strings are implemented portably as before; adapting **ftos** to other string representations should be relatively easy.

The following **stof** function also requires only minor modifications to its previous version:

```
function stof(var s: string; var i: integer; ndigs: integer; var f: fixed):
                                                                      boolean;
{ Convert string to fixed }
var
   j, nsig, nafter: integer;
   c: char;
begin { stof }
   with f do begin
      for j := 1 to FIXSIZE do
         digit[j] := 0;
      sign := 1;
      nsig := 0;
      nafter := 0;
      j := 1;
      if gnbchar(s, i, c) in ['+', '-'] then begin
         if c = '-' then
            sign := -1;
         i := i + 1
      end;
      while gnbchar(s, i, c) = '0' do
         i := i + 1;
      while gnbchar(s, i, c) in ['0'..'9'] do begin
         if nsig < FIXSIZE then
            digit[FIXSIZE - nsig] := ord(c) - 48;
         nsig := nsig + 1;
         i := i + 1
      end;
      if c = '.' then begin
         i := i + 1;
         if nsig = 0 then
            while gnbchar(s, i, c) = '0' do begin
               nafter := nafter + 1;
               i := i + 1
            end;
         while gnbchar(s, i, c) in ['0'..'9'] do begin
            if (nsig < FIXSIZE) and (nafter < ndigs) then
               digit[FIXSIZE - nsig] := ord(c) - 48;
            nsig := nsig + 1;
            nafter := nafter + 1;
            i := i + 1
         end
      end;
```

```
              if (nafter < ndigs) and (nsig > 0) then
                while (nsig < FIXSIZE) and (nafter < ndigs) do begin
                  nsig := nsig + 1;
                  nafter := nafter + 1
                  end;
              if (nsig < FIXSIZE + nafter - ndigs) and (nsig > 0) then begin
                for j := 1 to nsig - nafter + ndigs do
                  digit[j] := digit[j + FIXSIZE - nsig + nafter - ndigs];
                for j := nsig - nafter + ndigs + 1 to FIXSIZE do
                  digit[j] := 0
                end
            end;
        stof := (nsig - nafter) <= (FIXSIZE - ndigs)
        end;
```

As an exercise, write other conversion routines: fixed to integer, integer to fixed, fixed to real, and so on; none is particularly difficult.

Comparisons Apple and UCSD Pascal allow direct comparison of long integers via the relational operators; as with strings, we have to write a separate routine to do the job portably:

```
function fixcomp(var f1, f2: fixed): integer;
{ Compare fixed numbers, return -1,0,-1 if f1 <,=,> f2 }

var
   i: integer;
   done: boolean;

begin { fixcomp }
   if f1.sign <> f2.sign then
      fixcomp := f1.sign
   else begin
      i := FIXSIZE;
      repeat
         done := (f1.digit[i] <> f2.digit[i]);
         if not done then begin
            i := i - 1;
            done := (i = 0)
            end
         until done;
      if i = 0 then
         fixcomp := 0
      else if f1.digit[i] > f2.digit[i] then
         fixcomp := f1.sign
      else
         fixcomp := -f1.sign
      end
end;
```

Addition More importantly, Apple and UCSD Pascal allow direct *arithmetic* on long integers with the standard arithmetic operators; in this portable representation we have no such luxury. First, consider the following routine to add two **fixed** numbers:

```
function fadd(f1, f2: fixed; var f: fixed; var status: xresult): xresult;
{ Add two fixed numbers, f := f1 + f2 }

var
   dig, carry, i: integer;
```

```
begin { fadd }
   if f1.sign <> f2.sign then begin
      f2.sign := -f2.sign;
      fadd := fsub(f1, f2, f, status)
   end
   else begin
      f.sign := f1.sign;
      carry := 0;
      for i := 1 to FIXSIZE do begin
         dig := f1.digit[i] + f2.digit[i] + carry;
         f.digit[i] := dig mod 10;
         carry := dig div 10
      end;
      if carry <> 0 then
         status := OVERFLOW
      else
         status := OK;
      fadd := status
   end
end;
```

If the two numbers to be added are of opposite signs, **fadd** switches the sign of the second and calls **fsub** (shown next) to subtract them. Otherwise, **fadd** adds up the two numbers digit by digit (just as you learned to do in grade-school arithmetic), keeping track of carries into the next digit position. If the variable **carry** is non-zero after all **FIXSIZE** digits have been added, we have an overflow.

fadd reports any error status back to the calling routine as a variable of type **xresult** as defined in Chapter Four; it will return either **OK** or **OVERFLOW** both as the **var** parameter **status** and its function result.

Subtraction   The **fsub** routine is slightly more advanced than grade-school arithmetic, but not by much.

```
function fsub(f1, f2: fixed; var f: fixed; var status: xresult): xresult;
{ Subtract two fixed numbers, f := f1 - f2 }
var
   i, dig, carry: integer;
begin { fsub }
   if f1.sign <> f2.sign then begin
      f2.sign := -f2.sign;
      fsub := fadd(f1, f2, f, status)
   end
   else if f1.sign * fixcomp(f1, f2) < 0 then begin { abs(f1) < abs(f2) }
      fsub := fsub(f2, f1, f, status);
      f.sign := -f.sign
   end
   else begin
      carry := 1;
      f.sign := f1.sign;
      for i := 1 to FIXSIZE do begin
         dig := f1.digit[i] - f2.digit[i] + carry + 9;
         f.digit[i] := dig mod 10;
         carry := dig div 10
      end;
```

```
            status := OK;
            fsub := status
      end
end;
```

If **f1** and **f2** have opposite signs, **fsub** inverts the sign of **f2** and then calls **fadd** to add **f1** and **f2**. Otherwise it checks whether the absolute value of **f1** is less than **f2** by calling **fixcomp**; if **f1** is less than **f2**, **fsub** calls itself recursively to calculate f2 − f1 and switches the sign of the result **f**.

If neither one of these cases holds, the subtraction takes place normally. In this case, there can be no overflow (why not?) and the sign of the result will be unchanged from the sign of **f1** and **f2**. Like addition, the subtraction is carried out digit by digit starting from the units digit; the only non-grade-school feature is the variable **carry**. **carry** acts as an "inverse borrow," that is, **carry** is 1 if there was no borrow in the previous digit position and 0 if there was a borrow. (If you are skeptical, work one or two examples by hand.)

Note that **fadd** and **fsub** call each other; this means that one must be declared as a **forward** function in an actual program.

Multiplication When two n-digit numbers are multiplied together, the result is either a $2n$-digit number or a $(2n-1)$-digit number. When we multiply two **fixed** numbers together (each with up to **FIXSIZE** digits), we may get a number with as many as 2 ∗ **FIXSIZE** digits. We could either return the product as a **FIXED** number, signaling **OVERFLOW** if the answer exceeds **FIXSIZE** digits, or return the product as a "longer" integer, a new data type big enough to contain the digits in the product (and thereby postpone the overflow problem).

Here we choose the latter course. If you recall the **calc** program in Chapter Four, we defined the **register** data type to hold intermediate results of our calculations, as follows:

```
<type>
   register = integer[REGSIZE];      { REGSIZE = 2 * FIXSIZE + 2 }
```

In our portable representation, we make the following analogous definition:

```
<type>
   register = record
      sign: -1..1;
      digit: packed array [1..REGSIZE] of 0..9
      end;
```

where, again, **REGSIZE** has been chosen as 2 ∗ **FIXSIZE** + 2. The value is slightly larger than necessary, but it helps us convert our **xreal** arithmetic routines from Chapter Four to this portable representation.

Given the **register** type, writing the multiplication routine is rather easy.

```
function fmul(var f1, f2: fixed; var reg: register; var status: xresult):
                                                                  xresult;
{ Multiply two fixed numbers, reg := f1 * f2 }
var
   n1, n2, i, j, carry, dig: integer;
begin { fmul }
   reg.sign := f1.sign * f2.sign;
   for i := 1 to REGSIZE do
      reg.digit[i] := 0;
   n1 := FIXSIZE;
   while (n1 > 1) and (f1.digit[n1] = 0) do
      n1 := n1 - 1;
   n2 := FIXSIZE;
   while (n2 > 1) and (f2.digit[n2] = 0) do
      n2 := n2 - 1;
   for j := 1 to n2 do
      if f2.digit[j] <> 0 then begin
         carry := 0;
         for i := 1 to n1 do begin
            dig := reg.digit[i + j - 1] + f1.digit[i] * f2.digit[j] + carry;
            reg.digit[i + j - 1] := dig mod 10;
            carry := dig div 10
         end;
         reg.digit[j + n1] := carry
      end;
   status := OK;
   fmul := status
end;
```

Here **n1** and **n2** hold the number of significant digits in **f1** and **f2**, respectively. (We only have to multiply significant digits, of course.) Instead of calculating "partial products" and summing them together to arrive at the final answer (the grade-school method), we accumulate the answer directly in **reg**, carrying out the multiplication and addition at the same time.

Division Building **fdiv**, our division routine, is more difficult than the other arithmetic routines. Again, the ideas behind the algorithm are based in grade-school arithmetic (long division in this case). The quotient is calculated one digit at a time. After a quotient digit is calculated, the divisor is multiplied by the digit and the result is subtracted from the dividend, giving a new dividend for the next quotient digit to be calculated. After all quotient digits have been calculated, the leftover dividend is the remainder.

Our design for the division routine is the following: the input is a dividend of the **register** type and a divisor of the **fixed** type. The output is a **register** quotient and a **fixed** remainder. Any error status is returned to the calling routine as both the function result and a **var** parameter, as usual. The only error that can occur is division by zero; our choice for the sizes of the input and output numbers ensures that all other cases will be properly handled.

Some of the logic behind **fdiv** involves chopping off "special cases" that require less work than normal. Those special cases are

1. *Division by 0.* In this case, we just return the error status.
2. *Divisor has more digits than the dividend.* In this case, the quotient is 0 and the remainder is equal to the dividend.
3. *Divisor is a single digit.* In this case, the division can be carried out by a simple algorithm that involves much less work than the more general case.

The following initial pseudo-code for **fdiv** reflects this case structure:

```
begin
   assign signs to quotient and remainder
      (after this we can behave as if dividend and divisor
                                                  are positive)
   zero quotient and remainder digits
   count significant digits in dividend (n1) and divisor (n2)
   if divisor is zero
      return ZERODIVIDE error status
   else if n1 < n2 then
      quotient is zero
      remainder := dividend
   else if divisor is single digit (n2 = 1)
      do division directly
   else
      do normal case
end
```

Assuming the three special cases are properly handled, we consider the "normal" case where the divisor and dividend both have two or more digits. Aside from the expected bookkeeping complexity (making sure digits line up properly and correctly handling carries and borrows), the main problem is efficiently and accurately "guessing" each quotient digit. (You may wish to work some long divisions by hand at this point to remind yourself of how time-consuming this guessing process was in pre-calculator days.)

A reasonably good guess for each quotient digit may be obtained by dividing the leading two digits of the divisor into the leading two or three digits of the current dividend. (Admittedly, this is vague; see the **fdiv** routine for the precise method.) Figure A-1 shows how this works under conventional long division.

```
                865143
        3142 ) 2718281828     guess:= 271 div 31 = 8
               25136
               -----
                20468         guess:= 204 div 31 = 6
                18852
                -----
                 16161        guess:= 161 div 31 = 5
                 15710
                 -----
                  4518        guess:= 45 div 31 = 1
                  3142
                  ----
                  13762       guess:= 137 div 31 = 4
                  12568
                  -----
                   11948      guess:= 119 div 31 = 3
                    9426
                    ----
                    2522      − remainder
```

Figure A-1. Long division example

This guessing method will always give us either the correct quotient digit or a digit that is 1 greater than the correct digit. (The proof of this assertion, while not too difficult, is beyond the scope of this book.)

Given the guessing method, we can write the following pseudo-code for the "normal case" part of the division routine:

```
{ normal case }
begin
    calculate number of digits in quotient (nq := n1 - n2 + 1)
        (leading digit of quotient may be zero)
    set v := first two digits of divisor
    for each quotient digit
        set u := (leading two or three digits of dividend)
        calculate guess for quotient digit := u div v
            (if u div v > 9, then guess := 9)
        multiply divisor by guess, subtract from dividend
        if resulting dividend < 0, guess was too big
            guess := guess - 1
            correct dividend by adding back divisor
        set quotient digit to guess
    end-for
    remainder := leftover dividend
end
```

Finally, we put everything together into **fdiv**:

```
function fdiv(dividend: register; divisor: fixed; var quotient: register;
              var remainder:fixed; var status: xresult): xresult;
{ Divide dividend by divisor, yielding quotient and remainder }
var
   n1, n2, nq, i, j, dig, carry, borrow, guess, u, v: integer;
begin { fdiv }
   quotient.sign := dividend.sign * divisor.sign;
   remainder.sign := dividend.sign;
   for i := 1 to REGSIZE do
      quotient.digit[i] := 0;
   for i := 1 to FIXSIZE do
      remainder.digit[i] := 0;
   n1 := REGSIZE;
   while (dividend.digit[n1] = 0) and (n1 > 1) do
      n1 := n1 - 1;
   n2 := FIXSIZE;
   while (divisor.digit[n2] = 0) and (n2 > 1) do
      n2 := n2 - 1;
   status := OK;
   if (n2 = 1) and (divisor.digit[1] = 0) then { divisor is zero }
      status := ZERODIVIDE
   else if n1 < n2 then { quotient := 0, remainder := dividend }
      for i := 1 to n1 do
         remainder.digit[i] := dividend.digit[i]
   else if n2 = 1 then { Division by single digit }
      while n1 > 0 do begin
         dig := dividend.digit[n1] + 10 * remainder.digit[1];
         quotient.digit[n1] := dig div divisor.digit[1];
         remainder.digit[1] := dig mod divisor.digit[1];
         n1 := n1 - 1
      end
   else begin { Normal case }
      nq := n1 - n2 + 1;
      v := 10 * divisor.digit[n2] + divisor.digit[n2 - 1];
      while nq > 0 do begin
         with dividend do
            if n1 < REGSIZE then
               u := 100 * digit[n1 + 1] + 10 * digit[n1] + digit[n1 - 1]
            else
               u := 10 * digit[n1] + digit[n1 - 1];
         guess := min(u div v, 9);
         borrow := 1;
         carry := 0;
         j := nq;
         for i := 1 to n2 do begin
            dig := guess * divisor.digit[i] + carry;
            carry := dig div 10;
            dig := dividend.digit[j] - (dig mod 10) + 9 + borrow;
            dividend.digit[j] := dig mod 10;
            borrow := dig div 10;
            j := j + 1
         end;
         if u div 100 <= carry - borrow then begin { guess too big }
            guess := guess - 1;
            carry := 0;
            j := nq;
            for i := 1 to n2 do begin
               dig := dividend.digit[j] + divisor.digit[i] + carry;
               dividend.digit[j] := dig mod 10;
               carry := dig div 10;
```

```
                    j := j + 1
                end
        end;
        quotient.digit[nq] := guess;
        nq := nq - 1;
        n1 := n1 - 1
    end;
    for i := 1 to n1 + 1 do
        remainder.digit[i] := dividend.digit[i];
        status := OK
    end;
    fdiv := status
end;
```

Summary   As with strings, the primary drawbacks to using this portable representation for the **fixed** data type are the inability to use **fixed** constants in expressions, greatly reduced speed, and storage inflexibility. For these reasons, it may be a good idea to use a non-portable extended-precision type provided by your version of Pascal in preference to the portable representation developed here.

On the other hand, this portable representation may be more flexible than your Pascal's extended-precision data type. If you want hundred-digit precision, for example, it may be obtained simply by setting **FIXSIZE** to 100.

Sets

Throughout this book, our primary use of sets has been to hold sets of characters. For example, **getkey** uses a set of "legal" characters, accepting only typed characters present in the set and rejecting others. We have also freely used code like

```
...
while gnbchar(s, i, ch) in ['0'..'9'] do begin
    ...
    i := i + 1
end;
...
```

and

```
...
if ch in ['A'..'F'] then
    ...
```

as a means to test concisely whether a character lies within a certain range.

Both these uses depend on the legality of the type **set of char**. But Standard Pascal does *not* guarantee that sets of characters are legal; they will only be available when the number of characters in the underlying character set is less than or equal to the maximum number of elements that a set can hold. Both these numbers are implementation-dependent.

If your Pascal implementation does not allow sets of characters, what can you do? You may be able to switch to a version of Pascal that *does* allow sets of characters. Other things being equal, this may be your best strategy. If, on the other hand, you are stuck with a Pascal that prohibits sets of characters, you have two main strategies: avoiding them or inventing them.

Avoiding Sets   In many cases, you can easily replace set-based code with equivalent non-set-based code. For example, the previous **while**-loop could be written as

```
...
ch := gnbchar(s, i, ch)
while (ch >= '0') and (ch <= '9') do begin
   ...
   i := i + 1;
   ch := gnbchar(s, i, ch)
end;
...
```

and the **if**-test could be written as

```
...
if (ch >= 'A') and (ch <= 'F') then
   ...
```

This approach is not always convenient or concise, however.

Inventing Sets   Sets are often implemented as bit arrays with each bit representing the absence or the presence of a set element. This implies we can replace the declaration

```
<type>
   charset = set of char;
```

with

```
<type>
   charset = packed array [char] of boolean;
```

Many compilers will implement a packed array of Boolean as a bit array, resulting in very efficient storage. Now instead of writing code like

```
...
if not(ch in valid) then
   ...
```

(assuming **valid** is a variable of type **charset**) we can write

```
...
if not valid[ch] then
   ...
```

All other set operations can be easily converted over to this Boolean array representation. The drawbacks are the usual ones: there is no way to represent Boolean array constants in a program's source code, and therefore there is no concise way to initialize the arrays.

Miscellany

Apple and UCSD Pascal provide a number of additional non-portable features occasionally used in the programs in this book.

Record Comparisons   Apple and UCSD Pascal allow record variables to be compared for equality or non-equality as a whole; Standard Pascal demands that each field of the records be compared individually. For example, assume the following declarations:

```
<type>
   cardrec = record
      suit: (SPADE, HEART, DIAMOND, CLUB);
      rank: (ACE, KING, QUEEN, JACK, TEN, NINE, EIGHT,
         SEVEN, SIX, FIVE, FOUR, THREE, TWO)
   end;
<var>
   card1, card2: cardrec;
```

In Apple/UCSD Pascal, we can test cards directly for equality, as in the following:

```
...
if card1 = card2 then
   ...
```

In Standard Pascal, we must instead write

```
...
if (card1.suit = card2.suit) and (card1.rank = card2.rank) then
...
```

Powers of Ten   Apple and UCSD Pascal provide a built-in function called **pwroften** that returns (non-negative) powers of ten. The following routine duplicates the function of **pwroften**:

```
function pwroften(n: integer): real;
{ Return 10 to the nth power }
begin { pwroften }
   if n <= 0 then
      pwroften := 1.0
   else if odd(n) then
      pwroften := 10.0 * sqr(pwroften(n div 2))
   else
      pwroften := sqr(pwroften(n div 2))
end;
```

This version of **pwroften** does not check for values of **n** that result in overflow, although it could be modified to do so. As an exercise you can modify it to correctly handle negative values of **n**.

Random Numbers   Apple Pascal provides a random number generator in the **applestuff** unit in the System Library, which was used in the **theseus** program from Chapter Two. The **random** function returns an integer in the range 0 to 32767.

There are a number of different methods that can be used to generate random numbers. (See the recommended reading.) The following Pascal routine uses the same algorithm as the Apple-supplied routine:

```
function random: integer;
{ Return random integer in the range 0..32767 }

var
   i, j, carry, t: integer;
begin { random }
   for i := 1 to 7 do begin
      carry := 0;
      for j := 1 to 4 do begin
         t := 2 * seed[j] + carry;
         carry := t div 256;
         seed[j] := t mod 256
      end;
      if (seed[1] div 128) <> (seed[4] div 128) then
         seed[1] := (seed[1] + 1) mod 256
   end;
   random := 256 * (seed[1] div 2) + seed[3]
end;
```

Here **seed** is an array of four bytes:

```
<var>
    seed: array [1..4] of 0..255;
```

This array must be global in order to keep its values intact between calls to **random**. The array should also be initialized before any call to **random**; for example:

```
...
seed[1] := 90;
seed[2] := 178;
seed[3] := 246;
seed[4] := 147;
...
```

If we "wire in" the initial values of the **seed** array like this, however, we will get the same random sequence every time (which is desirable under many circumstances). To avoid this, Apple Pascal provides the **randomize** procedure, which causes different random sequences to be generated. The same effect can be obtained by changing the elements of the **seed** array to some other values before any calls to **random** are made; just how this is done is up to you. For example, you could time the interval between two keystrokes in machine cycles.

Remaining Problems

All the remaining portability problems are thorny ones. They are problems that cannot be solved by designing portable representations of Apple Pascal built-in data types or by writing portable routines to replace built-in Apple Pascal functions. Instead, they deal with matters that the authors of Standard Pascal chose to ignore or leave unspecified—usually, it should be pointed out, with good reason. As a result, it is impossible to specify general "solutions" to these portability problems that will work under all versions of Pascal.

I/O Functions   Apple and UCSD Pascal, like most real-world versions of Pascal, allow a program to access the following I/O functions provided by the underlying operating system:

- Accessing files by name
- Non-echoed keyboard input

- I/O error detection
- Reading/writing files a "page" at a time
- Sending text to the system's printer (without declaring it as a file).

Apple Pascal (but not UCSD Pascal) also provides the **keypress** function, which allows a program to discover whether the user has typed a key not yet read by the program.

Since Standard Pascal provides no way to accomplish any of these functions, we cannot offer any portable solutions as we did for strings and long integers. We have tried wherever possible to isolate such non-portable code into a limited number of "primitive" routines (**getkey**, **tfopen**, **lprint**, and so on); converting the programs to other versions of Pascal will involve minor or major changes to these primitives. Fortunately, since many if not most versions of Pascal provide equivalent services, this job will often involve only simple translations from the Apple dialect.

Even if your Pascal does not provide these features directly, they may still be obtained if you can make direct calls on the operating system. This may be done either through an assembly language subroutine or a (non-portable) built-in **call** procedure that allows machine language routines to be called by address. For example, if you are working under the CP/M operating system, all these functions can be carried out by calling the CP/M's BDOS.

Byte-oriented Built-ins   Apple and UCSD Pascal provide the non-portable "byte-oriented" routines **moveleft**, **moveright**, and **fillchar**, which we have used in a number of places in our programs. In those cases where we simply used these routines for their speed, they may be easily replaced with the equivalent portable **for**-loops. The more important characteristic of these routines, however, is that they may be used with variables of *nearly any* type, bypassing Pascal's normal type checking. And there is no general, portable way to accomplish this function.

There are three possible ways around this. Many versions of Pascal provide built-in routines equivalent to **moveleft**, **moveright**, and **fillchar**, often under the same names. If your version of Pascal has a decent assembly language interface, the routines are simple enough to be programmed easily in assembly language. Finally, some variant of the free type-union trick (shown in Chapter Eight in the discussion of **peek** and **poke**) can often be used to bypass type checking.

Memory Management   In designing the dynamic memory allocation and deallocation routines in the **pascalc** program from Chapter Eight, we made extensive use of our knowledge of the way memory was used by the Apple

Pascal operating system and the built-in routines **mark**, **release**, and **memavail**. Standard Pascal provides no way to do this portably.

Often a version of Pascal will provide routines that obviate the need to design your own general-purpose memory management routines. As noted in Chapter Eight, this is the case in UCSD Pascal versions IV.0 and later, where **varnew** and **vardispose** routines are offered.

Some versions of Pascal provide a memory management scheme more or less similar to that used by Apple Pascal: a stack and heap organization and **mark**, **release**, and **memavail** procedures. In this case, the routines shown in Chapter Eight may be used with little or no modification.

If neither option applies in your case, you may have to roll up your sleeves and do some serious programming. Controlling how memory is used by a Pascal program is usually done by some combination of your local operating system and run-time routines provided by the Pascal implementation. In general, you will have to examine the documentation for both software systems in order to figure out where your "free memory list" may be set up.

Special Language Features   In addition to non-standard data types and routines, the Apple Pascal system provides the following extra features that make the programmer's job easier:

- Separately compiled units
- Segment procedures
- Assembly language interface
- Compiler options.

Many Pascal implementations provide similar if not identical features to those we have used in this book in one form or another. Often, however, use of these features is optional. For example, instead of modularizing code in separately compiled units, you may compile programs all at once at the cost of larger source code files, decreased modularity, and increased compile time. You may avoid segment procedures at the cost of a less efficient use of memory. You may code all routines in Pascal and avoid assembly language completely at the cost of slower programs.

What about the cases where we have used non-portable compiler options ({$r-}, {$s+}, and so on)? Generally, a usable version of Pascal will provide *some* method to accomplish the functions achieved via compiler options in Apple Pascal. If your Pascal does not provide equivalent options, the offending code will have to be rewritten.

Hardware   The least portable aspect of the book's programs has been where we have assumed certain hardware capabilities to be present in the target computer system. *All* the programs have assumed a CRT-based system and interactive user keyboard input. Many programs have assumed a mass storage system like a disk. Translating these programs to systems with other than this assumed "lowest common denominator" hardware will be difficult and the results will probably be less than satisfactory.

We have also presented programs that used the Apple II's graphics and (in one instance) sound generation capabilities. If your computer has equivalent hardware capabilities and your Pascal can access them, it should be relatively easy to translate these hardware-dependent routines into ones that work on your system.

Recommended Reading

For another method of portably defining a string-like data type in Pascal, see *Software Tools in Pascal* by B. Kernighan and P. J. Plauger (Addison-Wesley, 1981).

Most of the routines designed in this appendix are excellent candidates for translation into assembly language. If you use a 6502- or Z-80-based microcomputer system, good sources for assembly language programming techniques are *6502 Assembly Language Subroutines* and *Z-80 Assembly Language Subroutines*, both by L. Leventhal and W. Saville (Osborne/McGraw-Hill, 1982 and 1983). These books contain both string-manipulation and BCD arithmetic routines.

The **fixed** arithmetic routines given here were based on algorithms extracted from *Seminumerical Algorithms* by D. Knuth (Addison-Wesley, 1981). This classic work contains information on both random number generators and arithmetic.

Index

Acceleration, 228-29, 236-38
addchar procedure, 38, 345-46
addmove procedure, 172
adjustcols procedure, 322-23
adjustrows procedure, 324-25
Algorithms
  minimax, 175-78
  Shell sort, 185-86
alloc function, 282
Alpha-beta pruning, 176-78
  measuring efficiency of, 186-89
Animation, 202-45. *See also* **bouncer**
  program; *see also* **isaac** program
  of bouncing balls, 208-32
  defined, 204
  of gravitational pull on objects, 232-45
ANSI standard, 11
Apple Pascal
  applestuff unit in, 17, 225
  and assembly language routines, 120-21
  comparing strings with, 102
  compiler directives in, 63
  disk files in, 58
  I/O routines in, 139
  long integer data type in, 46, 53
  maximum length of file names in, 109
  maximum number of elements in sets in, 33
  memory management in, 285-88
  mod operator in, 115-16
  packed records in, 46
  real data type in, 215
  rewriting routines for portability, 342-66
  scalar types in, 189
  segment routines in, 263-64
  string data type in, 33-34
  text file format of, 107
  transcend unit in, 233
  turtlegraphics in, 190-92
  type-ahead buffer in, 274-75
  vs. Standard and UCSD Pascal, *x-xiii*
Apple II 80-column board, 194-95
applestuff unit, 17
  keypress function in, 225
  note routine in, 230
  random routine in, 17, 227, 362
  randomize routine in, 17
Arithmetic
  operations, routines for, 91-95
  operators, 70
Arithmetic calculator program. *See* **calc**
  program
Array data types
  cell, 250
  maze, 16
  ndiscs, 158
  page, 108
  picture, 192

Array data types *(continued)*
  r, 240
  relpos, 240
  rsq, 240
  sq, 158
  trixrec, 276
  twobytes, 276
  vector, 206
Arrays
  in **bouncer**, 224
  in **calc**, 79-80
  in **crt**, 16
  in **isaac**, 240
  in **reversi**, 156-58, 161-62
  in **theseus**, 17-18
ASCII character set, 33
ask function, 48
Assembly language
  execution time of routines, 127-29
  reversi execution in, 187-88
  routines and Apple Pascal, 120-21
  text file routines in, 122-25
assign procedure, 100
Assignment, 83-84
  of long integers, 350
  of strings, 343-44

blockread built-in function, 109-10
blockwrite built-in routine, 107-08
Boolean
  functions, 169
  input, 48-50
bouncer program, 208-32
  main routine of, 209-11
  moveballs procedure in, 228-31
  routines for input to, 212-21
  runbouncer procedure in, 224-26
  suggestions for modifying, 231-32
buildpath procedure, 24-25

calc program, 69-104
  arithmetic routines in, 91-95
  converting between strings and **xreals**
    in, 95-99
  formatting directives in, 71, 82
  main routine of, 77-79
  statement syntax in, 83-85
  suggestions for modifying, 102-04
  use of, 69-72
  variable storage in, 75-77, 100-02
  xreal data type in, 72-75
calccell procedure, 298
Cartesian coordinate system, 204-05, 237
Cathode ray tube. *See* CRT
center procedure, 49
changeparams procedure, 135
changepps procedure, 337-38
checkfoot procedure, 67

checkhead procedure, 66-67
chopchar procedure, 39, 346
Compiler, Pascal
  and **applestuff** unit, 17
  directives, 39, 46, 60, 130-31
  portability of directives, 365
concat built-in routine, 48
concat procedure, 346
Concatenation, 48
Consistency of programs, 3
copy built-in routine, 346
copy procedure, 346-47
copy program, 127-29
copycell function, 318-19
copymatrix function, 317-18
createmaze procedure, 20-22
CRT, 10-28. *See also* **theseus** program
  defined, 10
  display of electronic worksheet on, 246-47
  display of game board on, 162
  procedure to scroll the screen of, 80
  program to create and solve mazes on, 16-20
  screen for graphics, Apple II, 190-91
  size of, 14
  special features of, 12-16
  specific routines for, 21-28
crt procedure, 12-13
crtscroll procedure, 80
crtstuff unit, 126-27
crunch procedure, 116-17
  in assembly language, 124-25
ctos procedure, 296-97

Data structures. *See also* Data types
  for CRT screen manipulation, 16, 17-18
  free memory list, 280-84
  for game programs, 155-58
  for interactive input, 46-48
  for simulation, 204-07, 239-41
  sparse matrix, 250-53
  for text files, 107-09
Data types. *See also* by name
  array, 156-58
  long integer, 46-47
  ordinal, 166-67, 189
  pointer, 251-53
  real, 72, 208-09
  record, 40
  set, 359-61
  string, *x-xi*, 33-34, 342-49
datecomp function, 63
datestuff unit, 126-27
Debugging, 271
declarewinner procedure, 173, 198
decode procedure, 140-41, 336

367

Default answer, 35
delmove procedure, 172-73
Disk files, 58
dispgasform procedure, 61
dispgrid procedure, 162, 194
dispose built-in function, 279
disprow procedure, 267-68
dispscore procedure, 167, 198
dispsheet procedure, 266-67
dispsquare procedure, 22, 166, 196
disptitle procedure, 80-81
docommand procedure, 308
docopy procedure, 316-17
dodispmem procedure, 310
doerase procedure, 320-21
doformat procedure, 311-12
doinsert procedure, 325-26
doload procedure, 329-30
doprint procedure, 337
doquit procedure, 309
dosave procedure, 329
dotoggle procedure, 310
drawsheet procedure, 264
dropline procedure, 117
  in assembly language, 123-24
dtos procedure, 57

Efficiency of programs, 3-4
Electronic worksheet. See **pascalc** program
eof function, 31
eoln function, 31
erasecell procedure, 291
erasecols procedure, 321-24
eraseform procedure, 292
eraseline procedure, 49
erasemove procedure, 28
erasestr procedure, 289
Error recovery
  in **calc**, 71-72, 103
Escape sequences, 131-32
  decoding, 140-42
eval function, 184-85
evalcell function, 300
evalexpr function, 87-88
evalfact function, 90-91, 299-300
evalid function, 101, 302-03
evalstmt function, 85
evalsum function, 303-04
evalterm function, 88-89
exit built-in procedure, *xii*
Expressions, 83-84
  routine for evaluation of, 87-88
Extended real. See **xreal** data type

Factors, 88-91
fadd function, 352-53
fdiv function, 358-59
Files. See Disk files; see Text files
fillchar built-in routine, 111
findarg function, 304-05
findcell function, 252-53
findcomment function, 148-49
findfile function, 60
findformat procedure, 82
findid function, 86
findincdir procedure, 147-48
findmax function, 179-80
findmin function, 181

fixcomp function, 352
Fixed-point numbers, 47
  formatting of, 98-99
  interactive input of, 50-55
  use in **calc** program, 71
fixstuff unit, 127
flanking function, 169-70
  in assembly language, 187-89
fmttos procedure, 313-14
fmul function, 355
formatcell procedure, 306-07
fprint function, 142-44
frame procedure, 191
free procedure, 283-84
fsub function, 353-54
ftor function, 63
ftos procedure, 51-52, 350-51

Games. See also **reversi** program
  example of, 158-73
  example with graphics, 192-99
  interactive input for, 153-54
  strategy for one kind of, 158-73
gaslog program, 39-68
  data entry routines in, 61-64
  data file initialization for, 58-61
  data structures in, 46-48
  input routines of, 48-58
  interactive input in, 39-43
  main routine of, 44-46
  report generation routines in, 64-67
  suggestions for modifying, 67-68
gasreport procedure, 64-65
gcenter procedure, 196
gchar function, 345
gdisptitle procedure, 196
geraseline procedure, 195
gesc function, 141, 336
getacc procedure, 309, 317
getboolean function, 49-50
getbparams procedure, 211-12
getcomputer function, 171, 178-79
getcoord procedure, 300-01
getdate procedure, 56
getfixed procedure, 50-51
getformat procedure, 312
getformstr procedure, 294-95
getformula procedure, 293-94
getgasrec procedure, 62
gethuman function, 170-71
getkey function, 31-33, 272-74
getint function, 212-13
getiparams procedure, 235-36
getlabel procedure, 271-72
getmove function, 170
getnames procedure, 136
getrcc procedure, 295-96
getreal function, 216
getstmt function, 81-82
getstring procedure, 33-38
  listing of, 36-38
  use of, 33-36
gettfname procedure, 118
Global variables
  initializing for **bouncer**, 211
  initializing for **calc**, 79-80
  initializing for **pascalc**, 262-64
  initializing for **print**, 134
  initializing for **reversi**, 159-62

gotoxy procedure, 14-16
gposstr procedure, 195
grabline procedure, 114-16
  in assembly language, 122-23
Graphics, Apple II, 189-92
Gravity, 236-38

Hardware
  needed to run these programs, 365-66
Heap, 285-88
htoc function, 142, 336

Identifiers
  length of in **calc**, 70
  mnemonic, 7
  routine to recognize, 85-87
initalloc procedure, 287-88
initbrun procedure, 226-227
initcalc procedure, 79-80
initgame procedure, 164-65, 196-98
initgasfile procedure, 58-59
initgraphics procedure, 194
initoutput function, 138
initprint procedure, 134
initprinter procedure, 66
initrev procedure, 160-62
initrev2 procedure, 160-62, 193
initirun procedure, 241
initisaac procedure, 235
initpc segment procedure, 262-64
initprinter function, 138-39, 336
Input
  Boolean, 48-50
  date, 56-57
  integer, 212-14
  keyboard, 31-33
  real, 214-21
  string, 33-38
  text, 30-31
Input/Output routines, *xi*
  in Apple and UCSD Pascal, 139
  portability of, 363-64
  in Standard Pascal, 105-06
insertcols procedure, 326-27
insertnode procedure, 100
insertrows procedure, 327-28
Integer data types
  iostatus, 108
Integers. See also long integers.
  action of **trunc** function on, 53
  routine for input of, 212-14
Interactive input, 30-58, 61-64. See also g
  program
  Boolean, 48-50
  data entry routines for, 61-64
  of dates, 56-57
  of fixed-point numbers, 50-55
  in **gaslog** program, 39-46
  in **pascalc** program, 319-20
  in **reversi** program, 153-54
  types of, 30-38
ioresult built-in routine, 60, 137
isaac program, 232-45
  calculation of position and acceleration in, 236-38
  main routine of, 232-34
  moveobjs procedure in, 242-44
  suggestions for modifying, 244-45

Index

ISO Standard Pascal, *xiii*, 348-49. *See also* Standard Pascal
itos procedure, 167-68

Keyboard
   input from, 31-33
keypress built-in function, 225

labelcols procedure, 265
labelrows procedure, 264-65
legalmove function, 169
legalpath function, 23-24
length built-in function, 37-38
Libraries of routines, 125-27
line procedure, 231
long integer data types
   fixed, 46-47, 73, 349
   register, 76, 354-55
Long integers, *xi*, 46-47
   arithmetic operations on, 352-59
   assignment of, 350
   comparisons of, 352
   maximum length of, 76
lprint function, 145, 336
lskip function, 339

Macro definitions, 120-22
magnitude function, 207
makelist function, 168
makemove procedure, 171-72
mark built-in procedure, 287
Matrices. *See* Arrays
max function, 268
memavail built-in procedure, 287
Memory allocation, dynamic, 278-80
Memory management, 280-88
   in Apple Pascal, 285-88
   data structures for, 280-84
memout procedure, 272
Menu-driven programs, 3
min function, 268
Modularity of programs, 7-8
moveballs procedure, 228-31
movecursor procedure, 270
moveleft built-in function, 117, 284
moveobjs procedure, 242-44
moveright built-in routine, 220-21

new built-in routine, 278-79
note built-in routine, 230
Numbers
   extended real, 72-75
   fixed-point, 47
   integer, 212-14
   long integer, 46-47
   random, 227, 362-63
   real, 214-21
   in scientific notation, 71, 74

ord built-in function, 283
Ordinal data types
   byte, 276
   contents, 156
   coordinate, 206-07, 232
   crtcommand, 12, 15
   direction, 158
   format, 77, 255
   player, 156
   squarenum, 156-57

Ordinal data types *(continued)*
   xresult, 76
other function, 166

Parameters
   changing print, 135-36
   checking for, 14-15
   print, 130
pascalc program, 246-341
   copy command of, 314-19
   data structures of, 250-57
   erase command of, 319-25
   format command of, 311-14
   formulas in, 292-97
   insert command of, 325-28
   load and save commands of, 328-36
   main routine of, 257-62
   memory management in, 280-88
   print command of, 336-40
   recalculation routines for, 297-302
   suggestions for modifying, 340-41
   sum function in, 302-06
   "un-input" routines for, 272-78
   use of, 247-50
   worksheet display routines for, 264-68
peek function, 277
playagame procedure, 163-64
plotball procedure, 227
Pointer data types
   cellptr, 252
   formptr, 256
   headerptr, 259, 281
   nodeptr, 76
   stringptr, 254
Pointers
   use in calc, 76, 80
   use in free list data structures, 280-84
   use in pascalc commands, 322, 327
   use in sparse matrices, 251-53
   variable, 275-78
poke procedure, 277
Portability of programs, *viii-ix*, 342-66
   other problems with, 361-66
   using long integer data types, 342-49
   using set data types, 359-61
   using string data types, 342-49
pos function, 347
posstr procedure, 38
print program, 129-50
   formatting printouts with, 146-47
   fprint function of, 142-44
   main routine of, 129-34
   printfiles procedure of, 137-40
   suggestions for modifying, 149-50
Printers
   changing parameters for, 135-36
   initializing, 65-66
   parameters for, 130
   program for printing files on, 129-34
printfiles procedure, 137-38
printfoot function, 147
printhead function, 146
printrow function, 339-40
printsheet procedure, 338
Programs
   ease of use of, 2-3
   efficiency of, 3-4
   flexibility of, 4

Programs *(continued)*
   incremental testing of, 270-71
   modularity of, 7-8
   portability of, 6, 342-66
Programs, quality of, 1-9
   programmers' criteria for, 5-9
   users' criteria for, 2-5
Programming languages, 8-9
Pseudo-code, 20-21
pwroften built-in routine, 218, 362
pwroften function, 362

randdir function, 23
random built-in function, 17, 362
random function, 362-63
randomize built-in routine, 17
randreal function, 227
Ranges, source and destination, 302, 314
read built-in routine, 30-31
readcell function, 335-36
readcols function, 332
readgasrec procedure, 61
readln built-in routine, 30-31
readsp function, 331
Real numbers
   function to produce random, 227
   routines for input of, 214-21
   use in simulation programs, 208-09
recalc procedure, 297
Record data types
   ballrec, 224
   board, 158
   cellrec, 250, 252
   date, 46
   formatrec, 255
   forminfo, 257
   gasrec, 47-48
   header, 259, 281
   node, 75
   objectrec, 234
   tfrec, 108-09
   xreal, 72-75, 95-99
Records, 40
   in bouncer program, 224
   in calc program, 75
   comparisons of, 361-62
   file types in, 109
   in gaslog program, 46-48
   in pascalc program, 253-57
   in reversi program, 157-58
Recursion, 24
   routines that use, 100-01
reformat procedure, 306
release built-in procedure, 287
remark procedure, 64
reset built-in function, 60
Reversi game, 152-53
   strategy for, 174-78
reversi program, 153-89, 192-201
   data structures in, 155-58
   main routine of, 158-59
   modifying for graphics, 192-99
   playagame procedure in, 163-64
   routines for computers moves in, 178-82
   routines for legal user's moves in, 168-73
   running, 153-55

reversi program *(continued)*
  simple routines in, 165-68
  strategy for, 182-84
  suggestions for modifying, 199-201
  theory for, 174-78
rewrite built-in routine, 111
rightjust procedure, 220
rnd function, 22-23
rtofix procedure, 217-19
rtos procedure, 217
rtosci procedure, 220
runbouncer procedure, 224-26
runisaac procedure, 236

Scientific notation
  formatting numbers into, 99
  use in **calc**, 71, 74
Screen-oriented programs, 10-11
  procedures needed to write, 12-16
Segment procedures, *xi-xii*, 263-64
Set data types
  charset, 32-33
Sets, 359-61
setcolpos procedure, 266
setcursor procedure, 269-70
setparam function, 301-02
setsquare procedure, 22, 166
showmove procedure, 28
Simulation, 202-45. *See also* **bouncer**
  program; *see also* **isaac** program
  of bouncing balls, 208-32
  defined, 202-04
  of gravitational pull on objects, 232-45
sizeof built-in function, 291
skip function, 145
solvemaze function, 25-26
sortlist procedure, 186
Sparse matrix, 250-53
Stack, 285-88
Standard Pascal
  and buffered output, 13
  comparing strings with, 102
  file types allowed in records in, 109
  I/O procedures in, 105-06
  memory allocation in, 278-80
  rewriting Apple Pascal routines in, 342-66
  text input in, 30-31
  vs. Apple and UCSD Pascal, *x-xiii*
Statements
  defined, 69
  as factors, 89-90
  syntax of in **calc**, 83-85
stoc procedure, 301

stod procedure, 56-57
stof function, 53-55, 351-52
stofmt procedure, 313
stoi function, 213-14
stor function, 221-24
storecell function, 289-91
storeform function, 292
storestr function, 288-89
stox function, 96-97
strcomp function, 344-45
String data types
  filename, 108
  identifier, 76
  longstring, 348
  pcommand, 133
  word, 348
Strings
  accessing characters of, 55
  comparison of, 344-45
  concatenation of, 48
  converting between xreals and, 95-99
  defined, 33
  interactive input with, 33-38
  routines for manipulation of, 38-39, 345-47
  sending to a printer, 145-46
sum function in **pascalc**, 249, 302-06
summatrix function, 305-06
Syntax diagrams, 83

termgraphics procedure, 195
termoutput function, 140
termprinter function, 140, 336
Terms, 88-89
Text files, 105-50
  assembly language routines for, 119-25
  data structures of, 107-09
  print program for printing, 129-34
  procedures in **print**, 134-49
  routines for, 109-19
  units and libraries of, 125-27
textstuff unit, 126-27, 328
tfclose function, 111-12
tfcreate function, 110-11
tfopen function, 109-10
tfread function, 112-13
tfwrite function, 116
theseus program, 16-29
  createmaze procedure in, 20-25
  main routine of, 16-20
  solvemaze function in, 25-28
  suggestions for modifying, 28-29
Transcend unit, 233
Transcendental functions, 208, 233

Tree
  binary, 75, 100
  game, 175-78
trunc function, 52-53
try function, 27
trymove procedure, 181-82
turtlegraphics, 190-92

UCSD Pascal
  applestuff unit in, 17
  comparing strings with, 102
  disk files in, 58
  I/O routines in, 139
  long integer data type in, 46, 53
  segment routines in, 263-64
  string data type in, 33-34
  vs. Apple and Standard Pascal, *x-xiii*
ungetkey procedure, 273, 277-78
Units, 125-27
Untyped files, 60, 108

Variables. *See also* Global variables
  dynamic, *xi*
  initializing game, 164-65
  in **pascalc** program, 261
  routines for storing and retrieving, 100-02
  storage of in **calc** program, 75-77
  xreal, 74-75
Vectors, 205-07, 237
Video display. *See* CRT

wait procedure, 64
wchars function, 146
Wirth, Nicklaus, *vii*, 30-31, 349
writecell function, 334-35
writecols function, 332
writesp function, 330
writegasrec procedure, 61
wrstr function, 145
writestr procedure, 343

xadd function, 91-92
xdiv function, 94-95
xmul function, 94
xnorm function, 92-94
Xreal data type, 72-75
  converting a string to, 95-97
  converting to a string, 97-99
  normalizing a variable of, 92-94
xsub function, 94
xtofix function, 98-99
xtos function, 97-98
xtosci function, 99